With appreciat[ion]
& congratulat[ions]
for the Public[...]

[signature]

23/5/93

ROBERT LAWS

SERVANT OF AFRICA

Hamish McIntosh

The Handsel Press Ltd
The Stables, Carberry, EH21 8PY, Scotland

Central Africana Ltd
Box 631 Blantyre, Malawi

ISBN 1 871828 15 5

British Library Cataloguing in Publication Data:
A catalogue record for this publication is available from the British Library

Typeset in 10.5 pt. Garamond at the Stables, Carberry
Printed in Scotland by McQueen Ltd, Galashiels TD1 2UH

CONTENTS

PART IV

There are two photographs, of Robert Laws and of Margaret Laws, courtesy of Edinburgh University Library.

Maps 1 and 2 were drawn by Lynne Campbell from material in the possession of the Church of Scotland Dept. of World Mission and Unity; Map 3, reproduced with acknowledgement to 'Life and Work', was originally published in the Record of the United Free Church.

The jacket design, by John McWilliam, shows the *Ilala*, and the flag which flew at her masthead (the dove with the olive leaf in its beak was the symbol of the United Presbyterian Church - see p.160).

FOREWORD

I have few memories from my childhood outside the family circle. One exception has stayed with me - an occasion when, as a small boy invited to tea in the Heriot Row Manse of St Andrew's Parish in Edinburgh, I was told to shake hands with an elderly gentleman whose name, Dr Laws, meant nothing to me but whose presence was such that I felt certain that this was someone of great importance. The impression of that meeting never faded, and reading this book I begin to understand why this should have been.

Three years ago, during a Moderatorial visit to Malawi, my wife and I were welcomed to Livingstonia, took part in an unforgettable service in the great church there, and knew again the impact that Dr Laws had made upon so many people. We visited the technical college that he built (some of his equipment still in use); and the secondary school, so remarkably ahead of its time in its use of space and light; and had the privilege of sleeping in the 'Stone House', large, cool, dark, high-roofed, bow-windowed. I was generously presented with a carved stone from the house itself, which I asked should be retained in the museum which contains so many memorials to his own creativity, so much to link the past with the present. The presentation was made by the Revd S.M.Nyirenda whom it was a pleasure to meet again a few weeks before writing these lines during his visit to Scotland as Moderator of the Synod of Livingstonia when his essential pilgrimage was to the grave of Dr Laws, the father of his church.

I was therefore particularly grateful when my colleague and friend Hamish McIntosh invited me to write a few words by way of Foreword to his work on one of the greatest of Scottish missionary pioneers and statesmen. This book has been needed. The name, 'Laws of Livingstonia' is one of the phrases that trip off the tongue. But beyond that too few in his native country or in the world church know about his life and work. He was a giant:

there is no doubt about that. His influence was immense, and his versatility was remarkable even in an age when people turned their hands to many things. It may be that his stature was such that a fair assessment could not easily be made within his own generation. This quite admirable study, so well researched and documented, will introduce a new generation to one of the great figures that Scottish church life has produced, and one of the key figures in the development of Central Africa.

Mayfield Manse   W.J.G. McDonald
Edinburgh   July 1992

The help of the following bodies is gratefully acknowledged:

The Carnegie Trust for the Universities of Scotland
The Drummond Trust, 3 Pitt Terrace, Stirling
The Hope Trust, Edinburgh

PREFACE

The name of Robert Laws is much less well known today than it deserves to be. In some ways this is strange for he was a man comparable in stature to David Livingstone and many would consider him a better missionary. It is now 70 years since *Laws of Livingstonia* was eagerly read by a great many people in Scotland and beyond, and W.P.Livingstone's book, although it tends to be uncritical, is still a thrilling account of an outstanding man. Its author had the great advantage of having known Laws personally and of having seen him at work in Central Africa.

Laws died almost 60 years ago, and the time has come for a new appraisal of him, based on original sources, and these are plentiful almost to the point of embarrassment. At the same time, the story of the early years of the Livingstonia missionary enterprise constitutes a tale of adventure which may appeal to many more than those who have a specific interest in missionary activity or the development of a part of Central Africa into an independent state.

The people of Malawi have not forgotten Laws and it is hoped will welcome an account not only of the setting up of the mission station at Kondowe but of the rapid transformation brought about in their country last century by a number of agencies of which the Livingstonia Mission was one. I have tried to do justice in this account to the many Africans who very soon became themselves the best exponents of the new faith which had come to them from overseas. It is almost 70 years since the Church of Central Africa Presbyterian (CCAP) became an independent church, and the northern part of it recognises Laws as the one who was the most outstanding among the many devoted men and women whose labours brought it into being.

Thirty years passed after the death of Laws before Malawi became a nation in its own right, but to that also Laws had made a contribution through his vision of the need to offer to the Africans an advanced education, accompanied by character training, which would fit them for positions of high responsibility.

Malawians may also be glad to have made available to them, in the opening chapters, an account of the early life of Robert Laws and of Margaret Gray who became his wife. Between them they gave 94 years of service to Central Africa. Many of the letters which Margaret Gray wrote to Laws while she was gaining experience as a teacher, and he was studying in Aberdeen, Edinburgh and Glasgow, have become available since the death of their daughter Amelia Nyassa Laws in 1978.

vii

In the preparation of this book I have found great encouragement from conversations with many people who are much more knowledgeable about Malawi than I am, including Professor John McCracken, of Stirling University, Dr Andrew Ross of New College, Edinburgh, Emeritus Professor George Shepperson of Edinburgh, and above all from Professor Andrew Walls, Director of the Centre for the Study of Christianity in the Non-Western World, now situated at New College. He has at all times made his time and helpful advice available to me. Emeritus Professor Alex Cheyne was kind enough to read the opening chapters at an early stage and to offer helpful comments. Shortly before he died the Revd Neil Bernard, with his wide knowledge of Africa, read the whole book and gave me much wise counsel, and Dr Fergus Macpherson, who was the last European head of the Overtoun Institution at Livingstonia, and who has many years of experience of Malawi and of Zambia, has taken pains to correct my mis-spellings of many African words and has offered invaluable comments on a wide variety of issues.

Thanks are due also to Dr Gavin White, of Trinity College, Glasgow, who was good enough to read through the entire typescript and to advise on how it might be reduced to more manageable size.

At the Church of Scotland Offices, the Revd James Weatherhead, Principal Clerk of Assembly, gave me ready access to the *Proceedings of the General Assembly* of past years; his secretary, Miss Chris Brown MBE, at all times found me accommodation where I could consult them; and Miss K.Ramsay DCS, who formerly acted as archivist to the Board of World Mission and Unity, allowed me to read several volumes of Foreign Mission Minutes, which are now in the National Library.

My thanks are also due to Dr Henry Sefton, Principal of Christ's College, Aberdeen; and to the Revd Jim Wilkie, secretary for sub-Saharan Africa and the Caribbean in the Dept of World Mission and Unity, who has at all times been most helpful. It has been of great value also to have on hand the books on Central Africa received from the Revd Duncan Campbell, whose time of service at Livingstonia was so sadly cut short by illness, and who died recently.

To none do I owe more than to Dr Kings Phiri, of Chancellor College, Zomba, whose house-guest I was for almost a month in 1985, while researching in the Malawi National Archives. It was invaluable to be able to discuss with him so many points about African culture. From the start I was made welcome in Malawi by Africans and Europeans alike, beginning with John and Sheila Phillips whose home in Lilongwe is a haven of rest for the travel weary. I cannot mention all those to whom I was indebted, but would like to thank especially Miss Anne

Dawson, formerly head of Robert Laws Secondary school at Embangweni, and now again head of Ekwendeni Girls' Secondary School, Sister Elizabeth Mantell of Ekwendeni Hospital, and Miss Alice Jones, formerly stationed at Kondowe. At Ekwendeni I also had the privilege of meeting Levi Silu, believed at the time to be over 100, and Inkosana Jere, both of whom had known Robert Laws, and, at Kondowe, Chiswakata Mkandawire MBE, who had been educated at Livingstonia, receiving some of his early training from Mrs Laws, and rising to become Head of Station there. He spoke with affection of Dr and Mrs Laws.

Thanks are due also to the Keeper of the National Archives at Zomba, and his staff; to Mr I.C.Cunningham, Keeper of MSS at the National Library, Edinburgh and members of staff there; to Mr J.V. Howard of the Special Collections Department, Edinburgh University Library, and his assistants; to Mr Colin McLaren, head of Special Collections, and Dr Dorothy Johnston, Archivist, Aberdeen University Library; to the Archivist and staff of the School of Oriental and African Studies, London University; to Mrs Marianne Hay, Local Studies Librarian, The Mitchell Library, Glasgow; to W.J.McDowall, Superintendent of the Glasgow City Mission; to the staff of the SRO, Edinburgh; to Dr Norman Reid, archivist, Heriot-Watt University; to Mrs Brenda Cluer, archivist, Grampian Region; to Donald Gordon, Director of Education, and Mrs Dorothy M.Sieber, archivist, Borders Region; to Dr Sheila Brock, of the Royal Scottish Museum, for allowing me to see her unpublished paper on Miss Jane Waterston; and to the Revd Fergus Macdonald, General Secretary of the NBSS for so readily giving me access to the Records of the Society. Dr William Petrie kindly allowed me to read the Diary kept for some months in the First World War by Mrs Charles Stuart, and Mrs M.E.Sinclair was good enough to show me some of the letters written by her father, Jack Martin, from Bandawe and Ekwendeni, in the 1920s. I am indebted also to the late Archie MacLean for information about army customs in the 1870s, as referred to in chapter 7.

The Revd Alex Caseby, who worked on the Livingstonia Staff in the 1920s before Laws' retirement, and died in the summer of 1991, Mrs Caseby, and their daughter Mrs Hansford, have given me much valuable information, and Mrs Hansford has allowed me to read about 100 letters, written by Dr and Mrs Laws to their daughter Amy, while she was a child living with her aunt in Edinburgh. A number of others, whose parents knew Laws, kindly agreed to be interviewed. The Laws papers and the Caseby papers, formerly at King's College, Aberdeen, in what was known as 'The Laws Room', (now unfortunately no longer in existence) are now in the Special Collections Dept. of Aberdeen University Library. The documents which were formerly known as 'The Shepperson Collection' are now in the NLS, as Acc.9220, and the Diary of the Revd James W.C.Dougall, who later became General Secretary of the Church of Scotland Foreign Mission Committee, and other papers relating to education in Nyasaland in the 1920s, formerly in Edinburgh House, London, are now at the School of Oriental and African studies, the University of London. Mrs Helen Neil, daughter of Mr and Mrs Alex Chalmers, has kindly let me see the articles her mother wrote for the Nyasaland Times in 1952, and Mr John Sleeman, formerly of the Dept. of Economics in the University of Glasgow, has advised me about the difficulties of estimating the purchasing power today of salaries earned over a century ago.

I appreciate very much the readiness with which my own minister, the Very Revd W.J.G.McDonald DD, has supplied a Foreword, and mentioned briefly his own impressions of Malawi and of what it owes to Robert Laws.

I am grateful to Mrs Lynne Campbell of Edinburgh for the maps reproduced at the start of chapter 5 and chapter 9; and to the editor of Life and Work for permission to reproduce the T.Cullen Young map showing the Livingstonia area superimposed on Britain and Ireland, at the start of chapter 20. The photographs of Robert and Margaret Laws are reproduced by permission of Edinburgh University Library.

The Revd George Martin, lately chaplain at Kamuzu Academy, prepared the index as a labour of love at short notice.

Consistency and accuracy in spelling have been hard to achieve; the missionaries themselves did not always get names correctly, and in any case changes have been made over the years, e.g. Nyassa is nowadays spelt Nyasa, and the Nsessi River is now Nsesi. The great Angoni chief Mombera is nowadays M'mbelwa. Robert Laws referred to the high plateau where Livingstonia is as Kondowi; Margaret called it Kondowe, and linguists now recommend Khondowe. Where Hebrew names are transliterated, eg Yuraia, these may be spelt with or without a final h.

All those mentioned have been most helpful but I accept full responsibility for the views expressed in the following pages.

Hamish McIntosh

ABBREVIATIONS

ALC	African Lakes Company
AUC	Aberdeen University Calendar
AUL	Aberdeen University Library
BFBS	British and Foreign Bible Society
BMJ	British Medical Journal
BSA	British South Africa Company
CCA	Church of Central Africa
CCAP	Church of Central Africa Presbyterian
CLAIM	Christian Literature Association of Malawi
CMS	Church Missionary Society
CofS	Church of Scotland
CUP	Cambridge University Press
DCS	Deaconess of the Church of Scotland
DRC	Dutch Reformed Church
EUL	Edinburgh University Library
FCS	Free Church of Scotland
FMC	Foreign Mission Committee
FO	Foreign Office
GA	General Assembly
KAR	King's African Rifles
LMS	London Missionary Society
MNA	Malawi National Archives
NBSS	National Bible Society of Scotland
NLS	National Library of Scotland
OUP	Oxford University Press
RGS	Royal Geographical Society
SCHS	Scottish Church History Society
SOAS	School of Oriental and African Studies (London)
SRO	Scottish Records Office
UF	United Free (Church)
UMCA	Universities' Mission to Central Africa
UP	United Presbyterian (Church)
YMCA	Young Men's Christian Association

Note: most dates are given in full (e.g. 2/5/1877), but a few have been shortened (2/5/77) to save space in typesetting

To Elizabeth,
wife, friend, and companion
for so many years,
and to the members of my family
for their patient support

PART I

1 THE POLISHING OF A SHAFT

Something of the excitement generated by the landing on the moon of Neil Armstrong and Edwin Aldred in 1969, and by the subsequent prospect of interplanetary travel, was occasioned in the 19th century by David Livingstone crossing the continent of Africa from coast to coast between 1853 and 1856. This journey and his other forays into the interior of Africa revealed to the wondering gaze of the western world the conditions of life prevailing in what had for so many centuries been 'a dark continent'. Harbours around the coast had been used by mariners for generations, but in the centre all was a blank. Suddenly, all this was changed. Livingstone was not the only explorer but he was the one who penetrated furthest, and his discoveries brought to the notice of Europeans the existence of millions of the human race, most of whom had had no opportunity of hearing the Christian Gospel.

In the steps of Livingstone others followed, and among the greatest of them was Robert Laws of Aberdeen. To him it was given, in a way that happens to very few, to see in his own lifetime, and to a large extent as a result of his own varied talents and dedicated life, the transformation of a vast area of Central Africa from the bondage of superstition and fear to the freedom and fellowship of the Christian Church.

Not many men in any age have served an apprenticeship in cabinetmaking and then gone on to qualify in both medicine and in divinity. Fewer still have, in addition, shown themselves skilled in the fields of civil and electrical engineering, displayed considerable expertise in brickmaking and navigation, and become conversant with more than one African language. Yet such was the versatility of Robert Laws, who became known, while still a young man, as 'Laws of Livingstonia' that he possessed a wide variety of practical skills and could use them to advantage, along with his more academic gifts, in the work to which he devoted his life.

Laws was born in Aberdeen in 1851, and went out to Central Africa, originally for two years, to help to set up the Livingstonia Mission of the Free Church of Scotland. When he finally returned home he had given 52 years of his life to Central Africa and its people.

Laws went out at a time when it could take ten months to receive a reply to letters home. He went out when the true source of malaria was unidentified, and when the debilitating effects of fever were almost unavoidable. He found thousands living behind stockades, or high up on mountain ledges, some in fear of raids by the fierce Angoni warriors, or of attacks by wild beasts, and some in fear of slave traders. We can understand why the Africans were slow to believe that in coming among them the white strangers were motivated by altruism and love.

Certainly the picture was not all negative. Dr Fergus Macpherson has drawn my attention to the descriptions of 'peaceful villages, fruitful fields, and bustling markets' which can be found in the writings of Joseph Thomson, the Dumfriesshire explorer, alongside accounts of grimmer things.

When Laws left Africa for the last time in 1927, slave trading was a thing of the past; trial by poison ordeal was no longer practised; many of the languages spoken around Lake Malawi had been reduced to writing and copies of the Scriptures made available in at least eight tribal tongues. Thousands of pupils were attending village schools; higher education of different kinds was being provided for hundreds; and there was a large Christian community.

The Livingstonia Mission may be said to have begun with the death of Livingstone at Ilala, on 1st May 1873, and the action of Jacob Wainwright, Chuma, and Susi in bringing their master's body home to Britain. That action caught the public imagination and kindled fresh interest in Central Africa. When Livingstone's body was laid to rest in Westminster Abbey, in April 1874, one of those present was the Revd James Stewart, who had spent some time in Central Africa in association with Livingstone in the early 1860s, and who had been serving at Lovedale, in South Africa, since 1867. Stewart had long cherished the idea of continuing the work of Livingstone by the establishment of a mission in Central Africa, but not till the death and burial of Livingstone did he find ears attuned to the suggestion. A month after Livingstone's interment at Westminster, Stewart urged the General Assembly of the Free Church of Scotland to honour his name and to continue his work in Afrca by setting up a mission station in Central Africa.[1]

A report of this speech by Dr Stewart was read by Robert Laws, then a young man of 23, who had felt a year or two earlier that he was being called to serve as a missionary in Africa, and who had been equipping himself since then to undertake that responsibility. Dr Stewart's speech seemed to provide him with the opportunity he was seeking.

There were many strands in Robert Laws' call to be a missionary and not least, whether Robert was aware of it or not, was the fact that his father, Robert senior, had wanted to serve overseas but had felt that his educational qualifications were insufficient. Inwardly he longed for his son to become a missionary. He did not speak of this to young Robert but the home atmosphere was such that from his earliest years the boy learned what it meant to live with a real trust in God and with a real concern to serve people. The Laws family were regular attenders at St Nicholas Lane United Presbyterian Church in Aberdeen, which took a keen interest in what were then known as 'Foreign Missions'. Mr Laws was an elder in that congregation and was greatly respected for his integrity, for the honesty of his business dealings and for the sincerity of his faith.

In 1846 he married Christian Cruickshank of Kidshill in Buchan, and on 28th May 1851 their son Robert was born. At this time his parents lived at 6 Little Chapel Street, in the Mannofield district; Mr Laws described himself in the census of that year as 'a house carpenter, cartwright and ploughwright' - employing three journeymen and three apprentices.[2] Robert's grandfather, William Laws, also had these skills, having been apprenticed in 1810 to John Milne, Cartwright and Ploughwright in Middlemuir of Belhelvie 'for the space of four full and complete years.' Clearly, Robert's skill in working with wood was an inherited as well as an acquired characteristic.[3]

Sadly, when the child was just over two years old his mother died at the early age of 24.[4] For a year or two the boy was cared for by his mother's people at Kidshill, the birthplace of Alexander

Cruickshank, a younger cousin, who was later to give many years of service to the UP Mission at Calabar.

After a lapse of three years Robert's father married again, his second wife being Isabella Cormack of Aberdeen. Young Robert returned to his father's home, now at 48 Summer Street, but found his stepmother rather strict in her ways. Many years later Dr Laws' daughter, Miss Amelia Nyassa Laws, wrote in these terms of her father's relationship with his stepmother:

> The child's stepmother was upright in character, kind at heart, but stern in manner, ordering him to sit still until she gave him permission to do otherwise. To this discipline he ascribed his capacity to listen, to refrain from comment, and in later years to assess the value of statements made in ignorance before discussing or correcting them.[5]

Laws was known as a man of few words and one may trace the beginnng of this reticence to these early years when the death of his own mother was followed by his upbringing by a stepmother who did not readily enter into the thoughts and feelings of a child. He was also an only child.

A contrast to the rather austere home in which Robert grew up was provided by another home, not far away, in South Constitution Street, Aberdeen, where a girl was growing up who was to play a big part in the life of Robert Laws and who was, in fact, to become his wife. Her name was Margaret Gray and she was two years older than Robert. While Robert experienced the loneliness of an only child, Margaret's position could hardly have been more different for she was the middle child in a family of nine. She had four brothers and sisters older than herself and four younger. Her father, Charles Gray, who had been born at Fetteresso, Kincardineshire, worked for a firm of coopers, first as manager and later as book-keeper.[6]

In this home the children were allowed to talk freely at table, unless visitors were present, and a dictionary and an atlas lay beside Mr Gray's place at table so that questions which arose in the course of family discussion could be quickly answered. Grammar and the correct use of language were highly valued. Miss Laws, from whom this information comes, tells us that these things greatly helped her mother when she came to reduce the Chinyanja language to writing.[7]

Robert Laws and Margaret Gray both attended Sunday School at St Nicholas Lane UP Church, where for some part of their training, they had Miss Janet Melville as their teacher. No fewer than five pupils, who passed through the hands of this remarkable lady, afterwards gave outstanding service to the missionary cause of the church. The five were James Shepherd (of Rajputana), Alex Cruickshank (of Calabar), James Webster (of Manchuria) and Dr and Mrs Laws of Livingstonia. In particular Miss Melville encouraged Robert Laws and seemed to discern in him gifts not noticed at the Free East Church School which he attended on weekdays.[8]

Robert left day-school at the age of twelve to become an apprentice in the firm of cabinet-makers in which his father was foreman. His wage was 2/6d (12p) per week.[9] Like other apprentices he would have to kindle the fire to heat the gluepot and perform other unskilled tasks while he learned his trade. He was a member of the Young Men's Mutual Improvement Association and at the age of 12, when asked to read a paper at it, chose as his subject 'David Livingstone'.[10]

Three years later, his desire to serve in the mission field ceased to be an aspiration and became a definite 'call'. It happened at a meeting in Aberdeen which was addressed by a representative of the London Missionary Society.[11] Robert was waiting shyly after the meeting when a congregational minister, Mr Arthur, noticed him and introduced him to Mr Fairbrother of the LMS. When Robert told his father next day of his resolve to become a missionary the news must have aroused conflicting emotions in the older man - pride that Robert was now aiming to do what he himself had been unable to achieve, and sadness at the realisation of what this would mean in terms of separation for many years at a time from his only son.

For a youth of fifteen, whose formal schooling had ceased at the age of 12, and for whom money was in short supply, the way ahead must have seemed daunting. Yet Laws was not content with the minimum qualifications that would enable him to serve as a missionary. He was determined to qualify both as a doctor and as a minister. The first thing to be done was to gain the passes that would entitle him to University entrance, and to this he now addressed himself. In Miss Melville he had a keen supporter. She told his father that she had a small fund set apart for Christ's work, and asked permission to pay for a tutor for Robert out of it, if his father could arrange for him to be off work for an hour or two each day.[12]

W.P.Livingstone, whose book *Laws of Livingstonia* was published in 1921, tells us that when young Robert was in his teens both he and his father experienced a period of unemployment, when the firm which employed them failed. Certainly, in the 1861 Census, Mr Laws (who had described himself as 'cartwright and ploughwright' in 1851) makes no mention of the employees referred to in the earlier census. Ten years later, however, he again sets himself down as the employer of three men, one woman and three boys.[13] Better times had returned.

The period of unemployment must have reduced the financial resources of the household when Robert was beginning his studies in 1866, yet W.P.Livingstone tells us that he saw the spell of unemployment as a 'blessing in disguise' since it enabled him to devote more of his time to study. He even returned to school for a time but still required the help which a tutor could give.[14]

In those days, long before student grants were thought of, and before Andrew Carnegie had provided the funds which subsidised so many Scottish students of later generations, the best an aspiring student could hope for was to win a bursary which would take him to University. Laws worked hard to prepare himself for the bursary exam but although seventy students were successful, Laws was not one of them.[15] He was bitterly disappointed, but it was no discredit to him. He had been trying to overtake something like five years study in two years, studying only part time at that.

In the autumn of 1868, and again the following year, he was in correspondence with the Revd Hamilton MacGill, Secretary of the UP Foreign Mission Committee about the possibility of a bursary. Other applicants had stronger claims, being further on in their course, but in December 1869 he was awarded a grant of £10 for the year ending 31 October 1870, 'to aid you in your studies'.[16]

Money came in small amounts from various sources,[17] and when he had completed his 'Bajan' Session and entered what was called in Aberdeen his 'Semi' Session, which began in October 1869, he was nominated for the Braco Bursary of £17 *per annum*, tenable for four years. This was a Presentation Bursary and not open to competition.[18] The total fees for the four year course in the Faculty of Arts, including matriculation and exam fees, added up to £36.11s, or an average of £9/2s/9d (£9.14p) per year.[19] With his grant and his bursary, and with what he earned by tutoring and by doing part time work for his father, Robert would manage - without any 'extras'.

He planned, as well as doing an MA, to take the degree of MB, CM (Bachelor of Medicine, Master of Surgery) and at the same time to qualify as a minister. When he first went up to the University he was just over seventeen. His grounding in school subjects would be much less than that of many of the 86 'Bajans' of 1868,[20] but his experience of life would be much greater.

With Mr Laws again established in business on his own account,[21] the financial situation would be eased. Even so Robert gave private tuition early in the morning, and after a day's work and several hours of study, would sit up to do his father's books late at night. Somehow or other he also found time to learn shorthand! The bookkeeping was not work that he liked but, like everything else that came his way, it was turned to good account. Even before the expedition sailed, for example, Laws was nominated as Mission Treasurer.[22]

In the MA course of that time an Aberdeen student was required to take two years of Latin, Greek, and Mathematics, and one year of English, Physics ('Natural Philosophy'), Natural History, Logic, and Moral Philosophy.[23] During his four years Laws was one of a small number of students who was not absent from any class on even a single occasion. That he found his studies hard going, along with the many other things he was doing simultaneously, can be seen from the fact that in his first two years he 'just passed' in five out of the six subjects. Only in Junior Maths did he do what the University records call 'pass respectably'.[24]

In his 'Tertian Session' his placings improved; as a 'Magistrand' or final year student, he won the 10th Prize in Botany.[25] At Aberdeen Natural Science then included Zoology, Chemistry and Botany, so that by adding Practical Anatomy, Laws had covered the subjects required in first year medicine by the time he completed his MA course.

The excessively heavy work load which Laws had set himself took its toll on his health and on 31st May 1872, just three days after his twenty-first birthday, he succumbed to the smallpox epidemic which was current at the time. He was admitted to hospital next day and was ordered two pints of claret per day - presumably to build up his strength, indicating that he was physically run down. One wonders what effect some eight to ten glasses of wine per day was likely to have on a youth whose upbringing was quite unlikely to have included even the smallest indulgence in alcohol! At all events the prescription was stopped after two days, but whether on medical grounds or because Robert had a conscientious objection to receiving alcohol is not clear. His body was badly covered with boils and by 15th June his temperature had risen to 101.2° with a pulse rate of 124. However, he had youth and a good constitution on his side and by 26th June his body was free of scales and he was ready to be discharged.[26]

These four weeks must have been painful and distressing, but like so much else that happened to the youthful Robert Laws, they proved to be part of the preparation for his life work. No minister visited the fever hospital at Mounthooly, and Laws, following up a suggestion from his stepmother,[27] realised that he had in front of him an opportunity for Christian service. Rather diffidently he asked his fellow patients if they would agree to him reading aloud a chapter from the Bible. He found the suggestion welcomed, and so had a foretaste of the work he was shortly to undertake in the fever hospitals of Glasgow, which in turn helped to prepare him for the caring ministry he exercised for so many years once he reached Africa.

While he was in hospital, his application to become a candidate for the ministry was accepted by the UP Presbytery of Aberdeen.[28] A month later, hearing that, because of illness, he had been unable to sit the entrance exam in Hebrew, the Presbytery resolved that he could be admitted to the Hall without it, on condition that he passed the following year. Robert Laws was present at this meeting. He was 'examined in regard to personal piety, character and motives; and it was unanimously agreed to certify him to the Hall'.[29]

What made it easier for Laws to take his Divinity course and his Medical course at the same time, was the fact that until 1876, the UP Church College met for only two months, in the autumn of each year, the classes being conducted by men who for the rest of the year discharged the duties of parish ministers.[30] The Revd Dr John Cairns of Berwick and the Rev Dr John Eadie of Lansdowne Church, Glasgow, were the UP College professors with whom Laws had most to do at that time,[31] and they would also set the students exercises to be done at other times of the year.

On 8th October 1872, the Presbytery of Aberdeen heard that Robert Laws, among others, had attended the Divinity hall (presumably during August and September) and instructed him to prepare a homily on 1 Timothy 1.15 for presentation at a later date.[32] Robert Laws had come a long way, but the polishing of the shaft was to continue.

2 GROWTH OF A PARTNERSHIP

AT THE SHIPROW MISSION - IN 'DIGS' IN EDINBURGH - GLASGOW CITY
MISSION - MARGARET GRAY TEACHES AT CRIMOND - FINANCIAL SUPPORT
FOR 'LIVINGSTONIA' - LAWS OFFERS HIMSELF - MARGARET MOVES TO
GALASHIELS - LAWS APPOINTED M.O. WITH AGREEMENT OF UP & FREE
CHURCHES - LICENSING & ORDINATION - PASSES MEDICAL FINALS - LEAVES
FOR LONDON

In the winter of 1872-73 Robert Laws MA was occupied not only
with the work prescribed by the Presbytery but with his medical
studies, and acquiring practical experience. He often began study at
5am, and then gave an hour or more of tuition, before going on to
spend his forenoons in Hospitals and his afternoons at Marischal
College.[1]

Being very strong in mind and body, Laws still found time to
help at the Shiprow Mission in Aberdeen . In January 1873 he had
prepared a special New Year message, and urged his hearers to go
forward into the New Year 'Humbly; Trustfully; Faithfully;
Hopefully; in Reliance upon the power of God Almighty; and
Prayerfully'.[2] All the more effective coming from a young man who
was practising what he preached.

Margaret Gray, who shared what she called 'the work and
pleasures of the Shiprow' with him[3] was herself training to become
a teacher, and Robert and Margaret kept up a frequent exchange of
letters while he was at the UP College in Edinburgh, and later when
he moved to Glasgow. Margaret is concerned about Robert working
too hard, and tells him to write less if it will give him time for a walk.[4]
At the same time she is always hoping for a letter from him:

On Friday, (the day your last came and was expected), again and
again I left my geography on table-land while I ascended Mount
Pleasure to view from its summit the sunny South, where, in
bold relief, stood 'Edinburgh toon' in all its magnificence,
beauty and attraction.[5]

Robert was in 'digs' in Tarvit Street. Today the King's Theatre stands
at the corner, but then the theatre site was occupied by Drumdryan

Brewery. One route from there to the UP College at 5 Queen Street would take Robert through the Grassmarket, past the end of the Cowgate; and Margaret, responding to his description of these places, expresses concern at 'such dreadful localities', where 'It would need a regiment of Christ's soldiers to combat with the enemy's legions.'[6]

Correspondence resumes the following autumn when Robert returns to Edinburgh for his second Session at the Divinity Hall. He had duly passed his entrance Hebrew, and the various exercises required of him by the Presbytery had been sustained.[7] Margaret, for her part, had qualified as a Primary Teacher with a third class certificate; on 23rd August 1873 she was appointed as Assistant at Crimond, some 35 miles north of Aberdeen, at £40 per annum.[8]

During that second Session in Edinburgh, Robert's thoughts began to turn to the possibility of a job with the City Mission in Glasgow. This would provide him with a small income and would, at the same time, give him an opportunity of developing his pastoral gifts. The Glasgow City Mission had been formed in 1826 by David Nasmith, who wanted to go out to Africa as a missionary, but, in his own words, 'fell back on missionary effort nearer home'. In that crowded city, the Mission also had a number of more specialized activities, such as its Mission to Cabmen, and to the Night Men of the Police Force.[9]

The Directors had now decided to appoint a visitor to the Smallpox and Fever Hospitals, dreaded places from which so many failed to return. In one month at this time, forty-one died from smallpox alone. The decision of the Directors was intended to remove the reproach that no Protestant clergyman visited these hospitals. With his own severe dose of smallpox behind him and with his knowledge of what it was like to be a patient in a fever hospital, Laws was well suited for such an appointment. He applied for the job and passed the strict scrutiny to which all applicants for a post with the City Mission were subject. To encourage him in what they called 'onerous and self-denying work' the Directors gave him twenty pounds more salary than was paid to their other missionaries.[10] It is a measure of the risks involved that none of the others on the staff of the Mission, forty in all, had been willing to accept the post before Laws came on the scene.[11]

The appointment dated from the autumn of 1873, at the close of the two month session in the Divinity Hall - and the Annual

Report of the City Mission, issued in March 1874, shows by the amount of space devoted to the work Laws was doing, how important the Directors considered this aspect of their work to be. Laws tells us that there were 250 to 280 patients in the two hospitals, at Belvidere and in Parliamentary Road, and reports as follows:

> My proceedings consist of holding meetings with the convales-
> cents and conversing with those who are recovering but who
> are confined to bed... I endeavour by kindness shown to make
> them feel that I am a friend and then seek to lead them to that
> Friend that sticketh closer than a brother. Those dying of fever
> I can seldom converse with, as they are generally unconscious;
> but in the majority of cases of smallpox, there is an interval of
> consciousness between the period of delirium and the time of
> death. Often during that season the real state of the individual
> God-ward is revealed.[12]

There were occasions when he was able to write home on behalf of patients from a distance, and more than once he was instrumental in reconciling 'prodigal sons' with their parents.[13] In his work in the hospitals for infectious diseases, we see a glimpse already, at the age of 22, of that combination of evangelical zeal and practical concern which were to mark his 52 years of service to Central Africa.

Robert moved from Edinburgh to Glasgow in October 1873, and when he left two winters later, the City Mission Annual Report read:

> The Missionary to the hospitals has heartily devoted himself to
> his arduous and self-denying work, and not without tokens of
> God's blessings upon his labours.[14]

Almost everything that Robert Laws did in those early years proved to be of use to him later on in Africa. During his time at the Mission, he not only gained experience in visiting and comforting those who were gravely ill, but would pause on his way to Belvidere Hospital to watch carefully men who were at work in a brickworks, and a ropeworks which he passed. When asked why he wasted his time in this way, Robert explained that so far from wasting time, he was trying to learn how to make bricks and how to make ropes, as he thought that the knowledge could be useful to him when he got to Africa.[15] How right he was!

In the same month that Robert began his period of service with the Glasgow City Mission, Margaret took up her appointment at

Crimond. At the census taken two years earlier, Crimond had a population of 883 adults, and 152 children between the ages of 5 and 13 years of age were receiving instruction.[16]

Margaret got a room with two maiden ladies who lived in a small cottage at what was called Roadside No 1.[17] They were Episcopalians and one Sunday afternoon she accompanied them to their service at Lonmay some miles away. It was very different from what she was accustomed to and Margaret was highly critical of worship conducted in that way.[18] There was no UP Church in Crimond and she normally worshipped in the Parish Church.

Today Crimond has a fine new school but the school of Margaret Gray's day is still standing and is used as a leisure centre. The lovely school-house continues to be occupied by the head teacher at the present time.

During Margaret's time at Crimond, the school roll seems to have varied between 80 and 130. Margaret was responsible for 22 pupils at first but was shortly asked to look after 32.[19] Mr Robertson, the headmaster, expected Margaret to use a cane to maintain discipline while she was resolved to do without it.[20] She seems largely to have succeeded but not entirely; a reference, in a later letter to Robert, to 'nippy palmies' would suggest that her idealism had to give way to the realities of the situation.[21]

For her room Margaret paid 3/9d (19p) per week, including 1/3d (6p) for coal. She had her breakfast porridge provided but otherwise seems to have been responsible for her own food, and to have supplied her own candles which she preferred to the dirtiness of an oil lamp.[22] Mr Robertson thought she was paying too much for her room, and in January 1874, he and his wife offered her a room in the ten-roomed schoolhouse at 8/6d (42.5p) per week, including food but not washing. Margaret had offered to pay 10/- (50p) so that the dominie and his wife were giving her fair terms. She tells Robert that she now often has meat, and perhaps egg or fish for breakfast.

'Here I have every comfort,' she says, 'but that of writing when I feel inclined.' The schoolhouse children were liable to interrupt her writing, and if she retired to her own room she felt that it looked as if she was being 'huffy'. Margaret Gray was not a lady to be easily put off, however, and one way or another the flow of letters continued.[23]

Christmas was not a school holiday but the New Year of 1874 enabled Margaret to spend a few days at home. Robert also had managed to have a few days in Aberdeen before returning to what Margaret called his 'labour of love' in the fever hospitals.[24]

In Glasgow Robert combined his work at the hospitals with attendance at medical classes at Glasgow University and at the Anderson College, and in May he heard that his second year's work in divinity had been sustained.[25] Since he had moved from Aberdeen, he now came under the UP Presbytery of Glasgow and at its meeting in July they certified him ready for admission to his third Session at the Divinity Hall.[26]

It was on 26th May of that year that Dr James Stewart made his speech to the General Assembly of the Free Church in Edinburgh urging the desirability of setting up in Central Africa a mission station to be known as LIVINGSTONIA, in memory of David Livingstone. This was the first public use of the name LIVINGSTONIA.[27]

Dr Stewart's speech was delivered at a thinly attended evening session of the Assembly but, nevertheless, bore rich fruit. A group of Glasgow businessmen, with whom Stewart had already discussed the project, were willing to find the money for it.[28] They included James Stevenson of Largs, to whom over the years the Mission was to be greatly indebted, and John Stephen of Shieldhall, a brother-in-law of Dr Stewart.[29] And the speech led also to the recruitment of Robert Laws, who was to become the Mission's longest serving member and most outstanding leader.

The businessmen were not long in pursuing the matter. At a meeting held in the Queen's Hotel, Glasgow on 3rd November 1874, and attended by Dr Stewart himself as well as by Dr Duff and Dr Mitchell of the Free Church FMC, it was resolved to found the Livingstonia Mission in Central Africa as an 'industrial and educational settlement'. It was clearly realised that such an enterprise would require 'Money, Effort, Time and Great Determination.'[30] The Committee set about raising £10,000 to launch the Mission and a similar sum to provide support in its early years. That provided the money. The other three requirements were to be forthcoming from Robert Laws.

Mr James Young of Kelly, a small estate near Wemyss Bay, who had been a friend of Livingstone - known locally as 'Paraffin Young' since he was a major supplier of that commodity - offered £1,000; Mr James Stevenson, who was a member of the Reformed

Presbyterian Church which had agreed to support the venture, promised the same amount. Messrs William and Peter Mackinnon contributed a further £1,000 between them, and Mr James White of Overtoun and Mr George Martin of Auchendennan on Loch Lomondside each gave £500. With 11 other donations of £100 the sum of £5,100 had come from only 17 contributors. Many smaller contributions were also forthcoming, including the cost of a boat from Mr John Stephen. Auxiliary Committees were set up in Edinburgh, Aberdeen and Dundee.[31]

When a Statement of Accounts was published some 18 months later, it showed that the initial target of £10,000 had been surpassed by £474. £5,587 had been raised by subscriptions in Glasgow and the West of Scotland, £3,705 in Edinburgh, £542 in Aberdeen and £640 in Dundee.[32] On all four Auxiliary Committees the number of lay people greatly exceeded the number of ministers.

While the businessmen were raising funds, Robert Laws was wondering, praying about whether he should offer as a candidate for service with the Mission. His difficulty was that this was a Free Church project. How would the UP FMC feel about one of their candidates offering to serve the Free Church? It was not so long since negotiations to bring about a union of the two churches had broken down![33] In June he tells Margaret what is in his mind and she replies:

> Livingstonia! Ay, I thought when reading the article contain-
> ing that best of suggestions that such a field would, at times,
> present itself before you.[34]

The Laws of later years is such a dominant figure, triumphing with such apparent ease over difficulties, that we forget how great were the barriers he had to surmount as a young man, and how uncertain he must have been about what was the right field of service for him to embark on. To himself, failure in his exams was a real possibility and out of her own strong faith Margaret gave him every support. About this time, she sent him an acrostic to encourage him:

> Rejoice! for now the Lord
> On thee a rich reward
> Bestows; the sweet trust of
> Early days His great love
> Reinforces hourly
> That trust strengthens surely.

> Long hath He been thy stay!
> And shall He turn away
> When fresh requests are made?
> Seek still His powerful aid.[35]

Margaret's faith in God and her confidence in Robert were justified. He passed his exams, and returned to Aberdeen for a brief holiday at the end of July before going to Edinburgh for the autumn session at the Divinity Hall. Presumably the Directors of the Glasgow City Mission were willing to give him two months' leave of absence to enable him to do this, recognising his excellence as their Hospital Visitor and the strength of his call to the Foreign Mission Field.

At Crimond, relations between Margaret and the schoolhouse folk were uneasy. In the school itself she worked hard to gain the confidence of the children, but the dominie seems constantly to have expected more of her. The report he submitted to the School Board must have been unfavourable for on 28th August its Minute runs,

> The Board, taking into consideration that Miss Gray's teaching in several respects was not giving that satisfaction which could be wished, especially in arithmetic and sewing and in the maintaining of due discipline, reluctantly resolved not to require her services as Assistant Teacher any longer and that the Clerk be instructed to send a remit to her to this effect.[36]

The decision seems to have taken Margaret by surprise but she applied at once for a post in Galashiels for which there was one other applicant. Margaret was unanimously appointed at a salary of £60 a year, and within a fortnight started work at Bridge Place school.[37]

The School met in the Masonic Hall. Conditions were crowded and the staff were looking forward to having a new building.[38] With the companionship of other lady teachers, the whole atmosphere was more congenial to Margaret than at Crimond, and she quickly settled in. There were times when her charges were noisy: once, when they had been left on their own for a short time, she declared that they sounded 'like Aberdeen fishmarket'.[39] She persevered, mixing firmness with a genuine concern for the children's welfare, and was pleasantly surprised when Christmas came, to receive a workbox, complete with 'scissors, reels, thimbles and needles. There was also a lady's ring knife... fancy writing paper and envelopes.' One of the girls read out a message, which ran:

> We, the girls of Bridge Place School, present this work box as
> a token of our respect and affection.[40]

Although a presentation was customary at Christmas, it showed the
relationship Margaret had developed with her pupils.

Meantime, after his second session at the UP College in Edinburgh,
Robert returned to Glasgow to resume work at the fever hospitals,
medical studies and the theological exercises that his Presbytery
required of him. He also associated himself with the Glasgow
Medical Mission and 'attended 10 cases of practical midwifery'.[41]

Early in October 1874 he heard from the Revd H.A.MacGill
of the UP FMC that the Archer Bursary, for which he had applied
without success in 1869, had become vacant and had been awarded
to him.[42] Margaret was delighted and wrote, 'Surely such fresh
provision from the Lord calls for praise and gratitude.'[43]

After a few days at home at the New year of 1875, Robert
returned to Glasgow on 5th January and on the 17th he wrote from
his rooms at 114 Blythswood Terrace with news which must have
been a source of great satisfaction,

> I was last night asked to go out to Livingstonia in March as
> doctor for two years. The company to be a sailor as leader, a
> missionary (ordained), a doctor, a blacksmith and a joiner.[44]

He went to see Dr Stewart, told him that he had had a letter from his
father giving his approval to what was proposed, and said that if Dr
Stewart and Dr Duff (Secretary of the Free Church FMC) got the UP
Mission Board to say to him, 'Go with the expectation of two years,
or altogether,' then his answer to the call would be, 'I go'.[45]

In February, Dr MacGill, of the United Presbyterian Mission
Board, wrote to say that he had had a talk with Dr Duff and suggested
that if the UP Church were to 'lend' Laws to the Free Church for two
years he could be a link between the two Foreign Mission Committees
and this would give the UP Church time to decide about a mission
of its own in Central Africa. He adds that they would prefer to pay
Laws themselves, and writes,

> I could not resist the strong sense of duty under which you wish
> to give yourself to this mission, secondly, I would not wish to
> give you up at present as one of our men.[46]

Shortly after this, on 23rd February 1875, the UP FMC agreed to the
request of the Nyassa Mission Committee to give them Laws'
services for two years,

... it being understood that this Board shall be entitled to reclaim his services at the end of that period .... and that Mr Laws' salary to the extent of £300 has been provided by the Trustees of the George Laing Bequest.

This kept the financial support for Laws within the UP Church for the late George Laing had been a member of Bristo UP congregation.[47]

The Committee then resolved to 'ask the Presbytery of Aberdeen to take him on trials for Licence and Ordination without delay.'[48] This was his home presbytery, even though Laws was actually under the supervision of the UP Presbytery of Glasgow. Curiously, there is no mention in the latter's minutes of his ordination in Aberdeen or of his departure for Livingstonia.[49] Normally, on completion of his Divinity Course, a candidate for the Ministry would be examined by the Presbytery and on giving a satisfactory performance would be 'licensed to preach'. He would then serve as a probationer for some time before being ordained; he might conduct public worship, but was not yet authorised to celebrate the sacraments. Ordination normally followed when a man was called to a charge of his own, or was to be set apart for the Mission Field.

In Laws' case the Aberdeen Presbytery decided that one set of Trials should stand for both Licence and Ordination.[50] What was required of Laws was that he should deliver a Sermon, a Lecture and a Homily on prescribed passages of Scripture, give a detailed exposition of a New Testament verse and present an exercise dealing with a theological topic set by Presbytery. The passages to be dealt with were fixed by the Presbytery on 23rd March and it met again on 13th April to take Laws on his Trials so that the intervening three weeks must have been busy ones, even by Laws' standards.[51]

Twelve ministers and five elders heard Laws preach on the text set for him which was from John 4.35:

Say not ye, There are yet four months and then cometh the Harvest? Behold I say unto you, Lift up your eyes and look on the fields; for they are white already to harvest.

Whoever chose that text for Laws was surely aware how appropriate it was, and the 'Lecture', which was on the parable of the Sower, was no less so.[52] The Homily required of him was on Psalm 1.1, and it is a thoughtful exposition, not just of verse 1, but of the whole Psalm.[53]

Sermon, Lecture and Homily, Exposition and Theological Exercise were duly delivered, and in the dry words of the minute, 'after remarks, were sustained'. One might have thought that the business was concluded, but not so: Laws was then examined in Hebrew, Greek, Church History and Theology! He was then licensed as a Preacher of the Gospel, and given the right hand of fellowship by the Presbytery.[54]

Less than a fortnight later, on Monday, 26th April 1875, the Presbytery met, as planned, for Laws' Ordination in St Nicholas Lane UP Church, his own minister the Revd John Rutherford having been appointed Moderator for the occasion. Representatives of the Free Church Presbytery of Aberdeen were present by invitation, and both the Revd Hamilton MacGill, Secretary of the UP FMC and the Revd Dr Alexander Duff of the Free Church FMC, were present also.[55] The Revd D.K.Auchterlonie preached on the words of the Prophet Amos:

Seek him that maketh the seven stars and Orion, and turneth the shadow of death into the morning, and maketh the day dark with night; that calleth for the waters of the sea, and poureth them out upon the face of the earth; The Lord is his name.[56]

It was a text to lift mind and imagination beyond the narrow bounds of any one congregation or denomination, and was in harmony with the attitude with which Robert Laws approached his life's work.

Speaking of the reason for their gathering together that evening, the Moderator said, 'The peculiarity of the case was the charm of it', referring to the fact that a UP missionary was going out with a Free Church Mission. The Mission was to be 'a memorial to our great countryman, David Livingstone... the grand object... the introduction of the Gospel into the dark regions of Central Africa.'

When Laws had been ordained, Dr Hamilton MacGill of the UP Church addressed the new ordinand, and Dr Alexander Duff, the veteran Free Church missionary, addressed the congregation.[57]

Dr MacGill's address made a deep impression on Laws, and in one of his first letters home, written from the mouth of the Zambezi in the month of August to report arrival at that point, he asked Dr MacGill for a copy of what he calls 'that excellent address delivered at my ordination.'[58]

Dr Duff, who was then in his 70th year, addressed the congregation 'in a voice that was low and tremulous' and said that he would not have been present but for his profound interest in missions.

In the weeks prior to his ordination, Laws had been busy, not only with the subjects on which he was to be examined by the Presbytery, but also with Practical and Clinical Medicine, Midwifery and Jurisprudence - the final subjects of his medical course. He passed his exams and graduated MB CM. A Bachelor of Medicine was entitled to graduate 'Doctor of Medicine' on attaining the age of twenty-four, provided that he was already Master of Arts, and had, since graduating in Medicine, spent two years in Medical or Surgical practice.[59] Laws' post-graduate experience was not gained through attachment to a hospital, but Aberdeen University wisely accepted that in Central Africa his medical and surgical experience would be of a kind to entitle him to the higher degree, and he became an MD two years after first graduating in medicine.

Less than a fortnight after his ordination, Laws travelled to Edinburgh, where he preached in Bristo UP Church on the afternoon of Sunday, 9th May. That evening there was a Farewell Meeting for Laws and two other missionaries, one of whom was going to Japan and one to Kafraria in South Africa.[60] In Edinburgh he was the guest of Mr James Thin, one of the Laing trustees, and a member of Bristo UP Church. By this time, Robert and Margaret Gray were engaged to be married, and Margaret also was at the Thins that weekend along with Robert's father and stepmother.[61]

On 13th May, Dr MacGill introduced him to the UP Synod as one about to proceed to the Livingstonia Mission Field of the Free Church, and the Moderator addressed him suitably with words of congratulation and encouragement.[62]

Laws travelled that night to London and put up at the Bedford Hotel, Covent Garden.[63] He was not to see Scotland again for ~~eight~~ nine years.

3 A COMPANY OF GOD'S SERVANTS

A STEAMER BUILT IN SECTIONS - E.D. YOUNG AS LEADER - THE OTHERS
ON THE STAFF - HENRY HENDERSON - SALARIES & OUTFIT ALLOWANCES
- LAWS IN LONDON - THE *ILALA* IN THE ILLUSTRATED LONDON NEWS -
THE SEND-OFF ON SS WALMER CASTLE - DR DUFF'S BLESSING

While the Auxiliary Committees were gathering in subscriptions
and Laws himself was steadily surmounting one by one the hurdles
that stood between him and the high qualifications he had set himself
to acquire, Dr James Stewart and his closest supporters had been
assembling other members of the mission party, and arranging for
the construction of a steamer which could carry them from place to
place on the huge inland sea known then as Lake Nyasa. When what
was formerly known as 'Nyasaland' became independent in 1964 it
took the name 'Malawi', or 'Marawi' from the name of the people
who had entered the area some centuries ago, and at the same time
the Lake also became known by this name.

　　　　A steamer would enable the mission party to establish contact
with a great number of places and tribes along the lake shore, but it
was necessary to get the steamer on to the Lake first. Dr Stewart's
experience in Central Africa led him to urge the route from
Quilimane up the Zambezi for about 120 miles, and then via the
Shire river to the Lake.* The great difficulty about this route was the
presence of the Murchison cataracts (named by Livingstone after Sir
Roderick Murchison, Chairman of the Royal Geographical Society),
which for a distance of 60 to 70 miles made navigation on the Shire
impossible. It was therefore necessary to have a steamer built in
sections, and capable of being transported overland and then rebuilt
at the top of the rapids. After that it would be an easy matter for the
vessel to complete the journey to the Lake under its own steam.

* According to H.H. Johnstone the name 'Quilimane' is derived from 'Kaliman', coast
Arabic for 'Interpreter', referring to an individual who formerly lived at a village 12 miles
from the river mouth and acted as interpreter between the Portuguese and the Africans
(British Central Africa p.55). The River Shire is pronounced Sheer-eh.

The firm of Yarrows was commissioned to build the steamer at their yard on the Isle of Dogs. It was to be wholly of steel, was to be called the *Ilala* after the place where Livingstone died, and was to draw only three feet of water. The cost, plus that of two teak boats, came to £1724.[1]

Dr James Stewart had in the meantime become more and more involved in mission work at Lovedale. He was very willing to maintain contact with the Nyasa Mission but could not himself undertake the permanent leadership of it. He put forward as ideally suited to be leader in the initial stages of the enterprise the name of Edward Daniel Young RN, who had been in charge of the expedition sent out in 1867 to investigate a report that David Livingstone had died. The Admiralty had given him leave to do this, and in seven months he had accomplished his task and proved the rumours to be false. In *The Search for Livingstone*, published in 1868, Young gave an account of his travels in the course of which he had sailed on the Zambezi and Shire rivers, and had reached and spent some time on Lake Nyasa. Six years later he was one of those present at the burial of Livingstone's body in Westminster Abbey.[2]

Dr Stewart described him as 'a man of thoroughly Christian character, of great nautical skill, of enterprising spirit, and of pity for down-trodden Africa, amounting to a vehement passion.' His home town was at Lydd, in Kent, and he was serving as a Divisional Officer in the Coastguard Service at Dungeness only a few miles away. E.D.Young was now forty and, as a married man with a family, might well have been excused for declining further ventures into unknown Africa.[3]

Dr Stewart and Dr Murray Mitchell were authorised by the Committee to travel to the south of England to ask him if he would undertake to lead the expedition for a period of two years. Mr Young agreed to what was proposed and submitted an application for leave. This was supported by a memorial to the Lords of the Admiralty from the Glasgow Committee.[4]

The Admiralty consented to release Mr Young to undertake what they called 'the guidance of an Educational Mission in Central Africa', while the Missionary Society met his salary during his two years of secondment. Mr Young's time with the Mission would count towards his pension but their Lordships would give no guarantee of his reinstatement at the level of Divisional Officer at the end of the period. The furthest they would go was to say that they would treat his case with every consideration when he returned.[5]

The other Englishman in what was otherwise an all-Scottish expedition was another navy man, William Baker. It is not known how he was recruited but as his home was at Winchelsea in Sussex, just across the Kent/Sussex border from Lydd, it may be that he was already known to Mr Young.[6]

Of the others, George Johnston, a carpenter, came from Aberdeen; his brother and Laws' father were certainly in touch with each other after the expedition had set out, whether or not they had been known to each other previously.[7] John McFadyen, engineer and blacksmith, came from Govan; Alan Simpson, the second engineer, from Cupar, Fife, and Alexander Riddel, described as an 'agriculturist', came from Leochel-Cushnie, near Alford, on Donside. These four were unmarried.[8]

E.D. Young was to be in command for the first two years, and at the end of that time Dr James Stewart, should he be able to be present at Livingstonia, would be in charge. Robert Laws was appointed Second in command and Medical Officer. The Free Church party was to be accompanied by Mr Henry Henderson of the Established Church of Scotland, who was to report on possible sites for the establishment of a Church of Scotland Mission.[9]

Of the mission party Dr Laws alone was an ordained minister, the other six being laymen with various practical skills. This is in marked contrast to the Universities Mission to Central Africa whose personnel in its early days had three ordained men out of seven.[10]

There was a wide variation in the amounts paid by the Livingstonia Mission Committee to its different members of staff. Mr Young, as Leader, received £350 per annum,[11] Dr Laws, as Doctor, Minister and Second in command received £300, provided by the Laing Trustees.[12] He had known what it was to be very short of money during his years of study but his new salary was considerably more than the average stipend of a UP Church minister at that time.

The artisans were paid at the rate of £100 per annum, except that Riddel the agriculturist was to receive £80 in his first year, rising to £100 in his second. They arranged in one way or another for their salaries to be paid in whole or in part to relatives at home.[13] William Baker received £80 per year because he expected to receive a naval pension, but his salary was to be made up to £100 should the pension not be forthcoming.[14]

Each expedition member was paid an outfit allowance, and was to receive free rations for the first year of service. When the second group of volunteers was being selected in 1876, some confusion arose about rations in subsequent years. By 1879 artisans were given £25 of credit, as well as their salaries, and were expected to make their own arrangements about provisions with the Trading Company, which was by that time in being.[15]

Laws had hoped to meet Dr Stewart in London but something prevented the meeting taking place and one senses the young man's eagerness as he made his own way to the Isle of Dogs to see what he could of the *Ilala*. 'It is now nearly all to pieces' he wrote, 'and getting packed up. The boilers are the only uncomfortably large portions, and will be so. They can be divided into three pieces but that is all.'[16] Laws is clearly wondering how things will turn out when they reach the Murchison cataracts and these heavy pieces of metal have to be transported overland across many miles of difficult ground.

That the expedition was of interest well beyond the circle of those engaged in the affairs of church and mission is shown by the fact that the Illustrated London News of 12th June 1875 carried a picture of the *Ilala*, showing her with two masts and two funnels, giving her length as 50 feet, and her beam as 10 feet. There was also a portrait of E.D.Young revealing a face of strong character, with a large nose, a firm mouth, and lips with a slight cupid's bow; there was no moustache nor any hair on his chin, but he did sport luxuriant side-whiskers.[17]

The few days Laws spent in London were full of activity. He very much wanted to visit Livingstone's grave in Westminster Abbey, but, although he passed the Abbey on one occasion he had not time to go in.[18] His daughter tells us that in later years, when home on furlough, her father 'never failed to rededicate himself at Livingstone's memorial in Westminster Abbey'.[19] He did manage while in London in 1875 to hear Spurgeon the famous preacher, and he called on Dr Robert Moffat, the pioneer missionary to South Africa, then living in retirement.[20]

The party were given a good send off. Dr James Stewart had already sailed, to make preparations for their arrival at Cape Town, but Dr Duff of the Free Church FMC and Dr Goold, representing the Reformed Presbyterian Church, were present when the SS Walmer Castle left London.[21]

Forty-six years earlier Alexander Duff had been the first missionary to be sent out by the General Assembly of the Church of Scotland and he had given 34 years of service in India. He was now in his seventieth year (he had 'come out' to support the Free Church at the Disruption of 1843), and Laws wrote of this occasion,

> It was a solemn moment.... to have the venerable old missionary leading our devotions and commending us to the care of our Divine Lord and Master.[22]

The Revd Horace Waller, who had served with the UMCA, and who had edited *Livingstone's Last Journals*, published in 1874, always maintained a lively interest in the Free Church Mission, and was also present at the send off.[23] The journey down channel to Dartmouth was not without incident. The Walmer Castle only just missed a collision with another vessel in the dark.[24]

Robert was now a fully qualified doctor and minister, and second-in-command of an expedition that was to have tremendous consequences for Central Africa, and for the whole future of what is now Malawi, but he was still a young man. His twenty-fourth birthday lay a week ahead of him at the date of sailing.

4 THE JOURNEY TO THE LAKE

EXTENT OF THE SLAVE TRADE - INSTRUCTIONS ABOUT IT FROM THE FREE
CHURCH - AFRICANS RECRUITED AT CAPE TOWN -ENTRY ONTO ZAMBEZI
- ACCIDENT TO *SPHINX* - THE CATARACTS - HELP FROM THE *MAKOLOLO* -
CONTACT WITH M'PONDA - ENTRY ONTO THE LAKE - CAPE MACLEAR
CHOSEN - 'LIVINGSTONIA IS BEGUN'

An interesting fact comes to light in a letter written by Robert's
father the year after Robert had set out for Africa. By then he had
seen the slave trade at first hand and must have written about it in
strong terms to his father. The latter writes to Mr Young of the
FMC:

> I do not wonder at his blood rising at seeing the two slaves in
> fetters. I had an uncle who trespassed into slavery from
> Aberdeen long ago, which was said to be the cause of my
> Mother's death, a very pious woman, when I was about fifteen
> months old.[1]

Mr Laws goes on to hope that his son will be able to break the yoke
of slavery not of the body only but of the souls of many, and it was
certainly to this two-fold task that Robert felt himself drawn.

Before the expedition sailed, many meetings had been addressed
by E.D.Young RN, the Revd Horace Waller or Captain Wilson RN
who had worked with Livingstone, all of them drawing attention to
the horrors of the slave trade.[2] Mr Young reported one slaver's
estimate that some 10,000 slaves were carried across Lake Nyasa
from east to west each year on their way to the east coast.[3] These
figures have been challenged, but Roland Oliver has shown that the
custom-house records, at the single port of Kilwa alone, record as
many as 22,000 slaves in 1866; he estimates that more than three
times that number reached the coast every year from some part of
the interior.[4]

Young's hatred of the slave trade led him to be over optimistic
in his reckoning of the force needed to suppress it. He thought that
a six month campaign, carried out by twenty men, along with the

expenditure of £10,000 would have been sufficient to eliminate it.[5] In the event it took very much longer, and required the combined efforts of the missionaries, the development of what was called at that time 'legitimate trade', and finally the intervention of Government in the form of the establishment of a Protectorate.

The Free Church FMC had clearly given some considerable thought to the question of how to deal with the slave traders. Possibly because it had James Stewart to advise it, it avoided rhetoric and issued a clear sighted directive which recognised that the elimination of the slave trade in the long term was more important than achieving the immediate release of any particular group of captives, however heart-rending it might be to leave such a group in their misery.

Article IX of 'Instructions to Lake Nyassa Mission Party from the Foreign Mission Committee of the Free Church' is headed, 'Active Interference with the Slave Trade', and reads:

On this difficult question no rule can be laid down, except this, which is *absolute, and to be observed by all members of the party, that active interference by force initiated on your side is in no case, and on no account whatever, to be resorted to.* By showing the people in kindly, loving, conciliatory ways, that they are acting against their own interests, and destroying themselves in carrying on this trade, more will be gained in the long run, than by any armed interference with Arab caravans.

It should never be forgotten that the first shot which is fired in any hostilities against Arab or native slave-dealers will do more to paralyse the varied efforts of the members of the expedition than any temporary success in the liberation of slaves can possibly counterbalance.

Fire arms were to be used only in self-defence.[6]

This may seem hard but it was surely right, for if the small number in the mission party had forcibly liberated each group of captives they came in contact with, they would soon have found themselves ambushed or killed by the slavers; no progress would have been made. A basic difficulty, and one which the Committee at home may not have realised, was that to set a man or woman free at a spot many hundreds of miles from home and tribe was in itself of little help. It was merely a first step, but one which required to be followed up by many others if a freed slave was really to be rehabilitated.

Archdeacon W.P.Johnson, who served for fifty years with
UMCA, asks the important question how it is possible truly to free
a slave 2,000 miles from home and points out that when he sought
to find a Yao word meaning 'freeman' the best he could do was to
render it by a phrase which means 'of the family.'[7] A man living with
his family, as part of his own tribe, was 'free', but an African several
thousand miles from home, separated from family and tribe, could
not truly be described as 'free' even although he had no slave stick
on his neck, no fetters on his feet, and no tyrant standing over him
with a whip. Roland Oliver even goes so far as to say that for
Africans separation from their tribe was 'a worse disaster than
slavery.'[8]

Some missionary bodies tried to establish 'colonies' of ex-
slaves near the coast, but this was not an ideal solution; and if slaves
were freed by purchase from slave dealers, this in itself could act as
a stimulus to the very trade it was designed to prevent.[9] The Nyasa
Mission approached their task on a broad front, instructed:

> To lose no time in making known to the natives the *grand
> leading object* of your mission, which is the enlightenment of
> their minds, the salvation of their souls, and [so] the elevation
> of their character and the improvement of their general condi-
> tion.[10]

While recognising that the proclamation of the Gospel would be
central to its message, and would for a long time be most effectively
presented through what the Commitee called 'the holy character and
consistent lives' of the missionaries,[11] those who supported the
Mission were aiming from the start at a mission which should be
'Evangelistic, Educational, and Industrial'. As well as preaching the
Gospel, the Mission would aim at training the young at least to read
and write, and would also give training in practical skills, helping
to introduce the arts of civilised life and so develop that legitimate
trade of which Livingstone often spoke as one of the most powerful
means of repressing the abominable traffic in human flesh and
blood.[12]

Nowadays the journey from London to Malawi takes less than
twelve hours aboard a plane. In 1875, Robert Laws and his companions
took five months. Leaving London on 21st May they arrived at Cape
Town on 17th June and were enthusiastically welcomed at a public
meeting arranged by the Kirk Session of the Scots Kirk.[13]

At Cape Town they made contact with a number of ex-slaves, freed by David Livingstone and Bishop Mackenzie of UMCA, and chose some of them to accompany the expedition. Lorenzo Johnston was engaged as seaman and cook at £4 per month; Samuel Sambani, Thomas Boquito and Frederick Sorokuti were taken on as interpreters at £2.10/-; their wives were to receive a monthy allowance.[14]

Dr James Stewart who met the party at Cape Town had chartered a schooner to take them to the mouth of the Zambezi, a German vessel of 135 tons, named the *Harah*. The cost, £350, was borne by Mr James Stevenson of the Glasgow Committee.[15]

They reached the Kongone mouth of the Zambezi in just under four weeks. The *Harah* after a three day delay due to rain and fog, crossed the bar at the river mouth on a rising tide, and a wooden shelter was erected where the *Ilala* could be rebuilt.[16] Many of the nuts and bolts required to secure her plates had rusted and there was strong criticism of the shipbuilders. Messrs Yarrow & Co. replied more in sorrow than in anger that they had sent out a completely new set of bolts and had simply put in those which had already been used in England as extras.[17] Eventually the rusty parts were cleaned and the vessel was put together in eight days and launched on 3rd August.[18]

Meantime African labour had been engaged at the rate of a yard of cloth per day.[19] A yard of cloth was highly valued by the Africans and any payment in money would have been irrelevant up country. The Home Committee had given instructions about wages for it was greatly concerned lest, by setting too high a level at the start, it might find itself committed to making higher payments later than it could afford. Even so its attitude was less than generous, and we find it saying, under the heading of 'Wages to Native Porters and Labourers':

> This rate should be fixed at first at the very lowest amount for which porterage can be obtained. This direction should especially be borne in mind in reference to the porterage over the Murchison cataracts, inasmuch as the first rate will continue for all time to come to be the fixed rate... Taking the price of native labour in India and China and other such countries into account, about sixpence a day ought to be amply sufficient.[20]

Sixpence a day it was, for the Portuguese official Snr Azaveido told Laws that the Africans counted one yard of calico as the equivalent of sixpence.[21]

On Sunday evening, 25th July, a service was held at which, Laws tells us in his Journal, almost all the men were present, and 'most of them understood to some extent what was read and said.'[22] As early as 29th July, Laws records that he finds the Africans 'good workers, intelligent, and honest.'[23] From a man who had such high standards both for himself and others this is high praise. It is just as well that the Africans were 'good workers', for in this first expedition an astonishing amount of goods had to be transported by human labour.

The list runs to several pages and includes such things as calico, beads and pocket knives for barter, £91 worth of provisions, bedding for eight, cooking apparatus, tools, guns and ammunition, writing materials, lamps and binoculars. Laws himself had a small medical list of 153 items, and these included two cases of brandy, two of sherry, and one of champagne.* In addition he took what he called his 'amputation case', purchased from W.B.Hillard of Glasgow for £11.8/6d - a charge on the Mission Committee;[24] in all over 200 packages to be transported apart from the sections of the steamer and its fitments.

The party also had with them two teak boats ,the *Ethiop* and the *Sphinx* useful for ferrying goods ashore and for taking them on the first part of their journey where the river was shallow and it was necessary to lighten the *Ilala* as much as possible. There was an unhappy incident early in the journey when the *Sphinx* was caught in a sudden squall and Lorenzo Johnston was unable to get her sail down before she turned over. Captain Young reported that 'one if not two of the native crew was drowned.' He himself lost all his goods and resolved that he would have to make himself a suit out of a blanket, while several others in the party lost many of their belongings.[25]

Laws' account of the episode is more sensitive to the loss of life; he writes in his Diary, 'Our personal luggage we might dispense with, but the loss of one life makes the mishap a sad one.'[26]

Four canoes and their crews were hired to provide further help with transport, and 268 yards of calico were paid out, the bow men and stern men in each canoe receiving four fathoms (eight yards)

---

* Champagne was believed to quiet the stomach of those with malaria, making it possible for them to take some food [M & E King, *Story of Medicine and Disease in Malawi*, Blantyre 1992 p19].

each, other members of crew three.[27] The sheer toil of getting the *Ilala* up the Zambezi and the Shire rivers was considerable and was made the harder by the presence of sandbanks, not easily detectable until the keel struck them. On 25th August Laws writes:

> There was no help for it but to get out all the cargo and land it... lay out anchors and cables, heave at the windlass, turn astern with steam, set the negroes jumping first at the bow and then at the stern, set them overboard to push first one side and then the other.....

until at length the steamer was clear of the sandbank and the voyage could be resumed.[28] At other times they had to cut their way through reeds or 'sudd'; once at least they collided with a hippopotamus![29]

After travelling for over 100 miles up the Zambezi, passing the grave of Mary Livingstone at Shupanga, they turned northwards into the Shire river. At the confluence of the Shire and the Ruo, they paused again at the grave of Bishop Mackenzie who had died in 1862.

A further 100 miles or so on the Shire brought the party to the foot of the Murchison Cataracts where the most laborious part of the whole journey began. A distance of between 60 and 70 miles had now to be traversed on foot, and all the items already detailed, including the *Ilala* itself in its component parts, had to be carried on men's heads or backs along a narrow path which constantly ascended or descended, and ran along the edge of the river gorge.

A shed was built for the purpose of storing the goods which could be left to be collected later on, and Alexander Riddel supervised the preparation of all that was to be transported, into loads of roughly 50 lbs. each, and carefully numbered the plates and sections of the steamer.[30] The sheer bulk of the boilers presented a problem; only one was taken at this time, being carried on an axle and two wheels.[31]

By now they had made contact with the Makololo chiefs who had known Livingstone, and had asked them to find some 600 men to help with the porterage.[32] With a wage rate of a yard of calico a day, two fathoms were paid in advance and a third fathom was promised on arrival at the top of the rapids.[33]

September 12th was a Sunday and the party rested in the morning; later, 100 men were sent on ahead with the boiler and its fitments.[34] Messrs Henderson, Johnston, McFadyen, and Simpson, set out the following day with orders to start rebuilding the *Ilala* at the top of the cataracts when the necessary parts had arrived.[35] A day

or two later, Captain Young and Dr Laws set out on their journey
leaving Alexander Riddel and William Baker to wait for the canoes.[36]

The march through wild country is described in Laws'
Journal. With no road, and a path sometimes as little as 8 to 10 inches
wide, they

> had to scramble up and down the sides of rocky gullies making
> use of 'all fours' on many occasions. When we reached the top
> of the pass, we could not help admiring more than ever the poor
> black fellows who had dragged wheels (a kind of cart on which
> the boiler was mounted) over a place where there was only a
> foot or two more than the breadth of the wheels and axle and
> then a precipice going down 300 feet to the river roaring
> below.[37]

It was a Sunday on which Laws recorded this and that evening he
spoke to the Africans, encamped on the same spot as himself, and
'taught them a parable about a Chief who loved his rebellious
tribe.'[38]

Two days later they overtook the boiler party, finding them
worn out and short of food. They gave them some food and cloth to
renew their supply, and learned that the boiler had been upset only
once.[39]

A very large number of Africans helped with the porterage.
E.D. Young spoke of 800 men taking part.[40] Laws spoke of 650 when
he wrote home from above the cataracts on 22nd September,[41] but
in a pamphlet *Woman's Work in Livingstonia* (1886) he stated that
more than 1,000 men had been employed.[42] Certainly, the expedition
would never have reached the top of the rapids with all the goods and
stores but for the willing and able-bodied help of many hundreds of
Africans.

When Young and Laws caught up with the advance party they
found McFadyen and Simpson down with fever, Henderson ill, and
Johnston looking pale, and when Baker and Riddel arrived a few days
later the former was suffering from fever too.[43] The *Ilala* was tried
out with a single boiler and, after a stop to make some adjustments
the engine raised sufficient steam for satisfactory travel.[44] The
distance from the top of the cataracts to the lake was about 80 miles,
including the passage through Lake Pamalombe. With difficulty
they identified the spot at which the Shire river, having flowed out
of Lake Nyasa, entered Lake Pamalombe, and on October 11th
Captain Young and Dr Laws sought out Chief M'ponda, who was

overlord of the land around Cape Maclear, to ask his permission to settle in that vicinity.[45]

They were well received by M'ponda and given cushions to sit on, while *pombe* (native beer) was offered them; two of the younger wives of the chief began to massage Captain Young's stomach as they would do for the chief himself while he drank his beer, but Mr Young would not allow it. They told M'ponda that they wished to be friends, spoke of the kindness he had shown to Livingstone years before, and explained that they wanted to teach his people about God and the arts of civilisation. When they asked for land on which to settle, M'ponda told them to choose for themselves.[46]

The following day, October 12th, they arrived at Lake Nyasa and this is how Laws tells the story in his Journal:

> At 6.30a.m. we entered Lake Nyassa, as the sun rose o'er the eastern hills, a fitting symbol of what we hoped and prayed the coming of the *Ilala* might be to the inhabitants around the Lake carrying, we trust, some rays from the sun of Righteousness to lessen the gloomy darkness by which their souls are sur-rounded. Never perhaps did any member of the party with so full a heart join in singing the 100th Psalm as we did that morning while skimming across the waters of the Lake.[47]

Their feelings of thankfulness and expectancy were mingled with sadness as they observed that villages which had been in the area on Captain Young's previous visit were no longer to be seen, their inhabitants having either fled before the slaver or been captured.[48]

It was no small feat in the year 1875 to have carried a portable steamer, over 200 packages, and eight Europeans, from Britain and got them all safely to a point in the interior of the largely unknown continent of Africa, almost 400 miles from the sea as the crow flies, and up more than 350 miles of river, 60-70 miles of it cataract. Young rightly pays tribute to the African porters:

> Let this ever stand to the African's credit, that 800 of these men worked and worked desperately for us, free as air to come and go as they pleased, over a road which furnished at almost every yard an excuse for an accident, or a hiding place for thief or deserter, *but yet at the end of the sixty miles we had everything delivered up to us unmolested, untampered with and unhurt, and every man merry and content with his well-earned wages.*[49]
> (Young's italics)

One wonders what the Africans thought of it all!

After a few days exploring, the Mission party returned to the west side of Cape Maclear and fixed on a spot for their first settlement. Captain Young liked the site. There was an excellent bay which offered good anchorage for the ship; Chief M'ponda was willing for them to settle; there were no mosquitoes; it was breezy; and it was cool at night. In addition, fish were plentiful, he judged the soil to be suitable for growing rice and maize, and he saw no reason why Europeans should not live well there.[50] Young's assessment proved over-optimistic, although to be fair it was the Home Committee who, on the advice of Dr Stewart, had suggested Cape Maclear as the most suitable site for the Mission.

It was certainly necessary to fix on a site quickly, in order to erect a dwelling house before the rains came. Laws was aware of this but realized that one of the main drawbacks of the site was the distance from the nearest village. The trouble was that they had not yet seen a village which was not beside a marsh and this had to be avoided because of the increased danger of fever.[51]

So the choice was made, and while Captain Young went back on the *Ilala* with some of the party to bring up the remainder of their goods, Laws, Henderson, Riddel, and Johnston, with the help of three Africans, began to build their first house. It was to be 50 feet long, by 25 feet wide, with a door and two windows at each end, and a door and four windows front and back.[52]

A week after their arrival at the Lake, Laws wrote a letter, which was published in Edinburgh early in 1876 along with other letters and an account of the origin of the Mission in a small book entitled *East Central Africa, Livingstonia*. The opening sentence reads:

> Another stage of our journey has been reached, and, for the time being, I suppose I may say that Livingstonia is begun, though at present a piece of canvas stretched between two trees, forming a sort of tent, is all that stands for the future city of that name.[53]

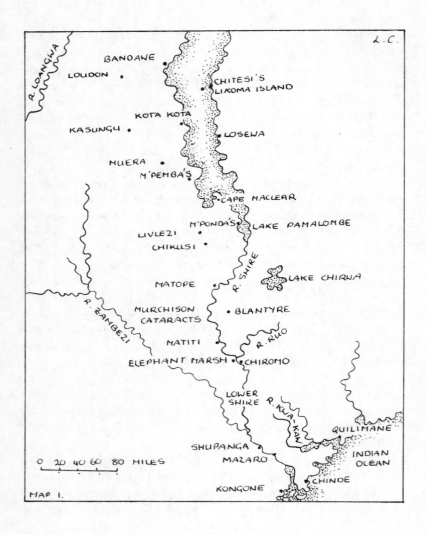

L.C.

R. LOANGWA

BANDAWE
LOUDON
CHITESI'S
LIKOMA ISLAND
KOTA KOTA
KASUNGU
LOSEWA
MUERA
M'PEMBA'S
CAPE MACLEAR
M'PONDA'S
LAKE PAMALOMBE
LIVLEZI
CHIKUSI
MATOPE
R. SHIRE
LAKE CHIRWA
MURCHISON
CATARACTS
BLANTYRE
MATITI
R. RUO
ELEPHANT MARSH
CHIROMO
R. ZAMBEZI
LOWER
SHIRE
R. KWA-KWA
QUILIMANE
SHUPANGA
MAZARO
INDIAN
OCEAN

0 20 40 60 80 MILES

KONGONE
CHINDE

MAP 1.

PART II

5 NEW BEGINNINGS

JOURNAL KEPT - HARD LABOUR - ACTS OF WORSHIP - EXPLORATION OF
LAKE - SIGNS OF SLAVERY - MAIL FROM HOME - MAKANJIRA & CHIMLOLO
- FIRST OPERATION UNDER CHLOROFORM - EDUCATIONAL WORK BEGINS
- *MVAVI* ORDEAL - PROBLEMS OF DISCIPLINE - DR STEWART TAKES OVER -
E.D. YOUNG AT HOME - UNSUITABILITY OF CAPE MACLEAR - ARRIVAL OF
JAS. STEWART CE - SECOND VOYAGE ROUND LAKE -AFRICAN EVANGELISTS
- CELEBRATION OF COMMUNION - REINFORCEMENTS - BETTER HEALTH -
LAWS STRUCK BY FEVER

The Home Committee was particularly concerned to know about
conditions which might affect the life of its agents in Central Africa,
and issued this instruction:

> For some considerable time - perhaps for two or three years -
> a Daily Journal should be kept, recording all matters of general
> interest, and especially records of daily temperature (three
> observations if possible), atmospheric changes, the setting in of
> rains, the direction of winds, the kind of daily employment
> engaged in by the staff, and immediately following on this, a
> statement of the health of the party... This work is committed
> to Dr Laws as part of his duty as Medical Officer, and as second
> in charge, at present. If the form of entry is to be tabulated and
> abbreviated, the record can easily be made in a few minutes.[1]

The book was to be submitted to Mr Young's inspection once or
twice a week, and communicated from time to time to the Committee
at home. No more meticulous recorder of facts and observations
could have been found than Laws. From 23rd July 1875, when the
party crossed the bar at the Kongone mouth of the Zambezi, Laws
kept for a year what is headed 'Diary, Weather Reports and Journal
of Events'.[2] This is his personal record and he continued to keep his
own diary for many years, although there are gaps from time to time.
As well as this, there is a Livingstonia Mission Journal for 1875. This
is largely a copy of Laws' diary, but when he was absent - exploring,
or making contact with one of the chiefs at some site round the Lake,

or travelling to the Zambezi mouth to pick up mail - the Journal was kept by another of the mission party. The record was continued in the Cape Maclear Journal.[3]

From the 'Diary' and 'Journals' the picture that emerges from the early days is of men heavily and almost continuously engaged in manual work. At the beginning there are trees to be cut down in order to build houses; there are provisions to be brought up river from the store constructed to hold them; there are journeys to be made to buy food of different kinds from local residents and there is the need to chop wood to keep the *Ilala* in fuel. The steamer functioned well enough on its one boiler but its firebox was voracious and required constant stoking with wood, a task in which Laws took his share. Not all the wood available was suitable, as much of it was too soft.

The first Sunday after arrival at the Lake was a working day but a week later the party worked only until midday, and thereafter it was usual to keep Sundays as days of rest and worship.[4] This, in itself, would be a 'witness'; it would lead to questions, and much could then be said about the importance of the Lord's Day as a celebration of Christ's resurrection, or about the gift of the 'Sabbath' through Moses. It would not be long before the value of a day of rest one day in seven became apparent, although at a later stage in the history of Livingstonia Dr Donald Fraser was concerned about the danger of the more positive aspects of the Christian Faith being overshadowed by a kind of legalism which thought that if one avoided pounding meal on a Sunday then that in itself meant that the person concerned was free of sin and a true Christian.[5]

As early as 14th November the entry in Laws' Diary reads, 'A day of rest enjoyed by us all'. Bible pictures were shown and explained and the mission party held their own service in the evening when 'all our own black boys were present dressed in clean shirts.'[6]

It was usual to hold at least two services on a Sunday, one in English and the other in the local native language once some knowledge of it had been acquired. Laws applied himself from the start to learning Mang'anja (as Chinyanja was then called) and Alexander Riddel also engaged in linguistic studies. When Riddel returned to Scotland in 1879 the Glasgow Committee agreed to publish 200 copies of a Dictionary and Grammar of the Chinyanja language prepared by him. In the event, 500 copies were printed and a gift of 15 guineas was made to Riddel in recognition of his work.[7]

Riddel the agriculturist showed bimself a useful man in the schoolroom, and it was usually Riddel who took the service for the Africans when Laws was absent, and sometimes even when he was present. When both Laws and Riddel were absent there were times when one of the others would read a Bible passage from a translation made by Riddel.[8]

Meanwhile, just over a month after entering the Lake, E.D.Young and Robert Laws set out on a voyage of exploration which lasted for between three and four weeks. Messrs Henderson, McFadyen and Baker accompanied them on the *Ilala* along with Sam Boquito the interpreter, and Joe.[9] The use of the term 'Lake' may raise up a false picture in our imagination. It does not refer to a stretch of water akin to Lake Windermere in England or Loch Lomond in Scotland, but to a vast inland sea, the length of which, from its most northerly point to the place where the Shire River runs out at the southern end exceeds the distance between London and Berwick-upon-Tweed.

Livingstone had first set eyes on the lake on 16th September 1859 -and gave it the name Lake Nyasa. The word 'Nyasa' simply means 'a stretch of water' and it looks as if the explorer misunderstood the word and took it to be the actual name of the Lake.

When E.D.Young and Robert Laws set out on their first major voyage of exploration, they had no certain knowledge of how far the Lake extended and very little information about how its shores were inhabited. Livingstone had estimated its length as 200 miles, being misled by the configuration of the hills at the furthest point he reached, into thinking that he was looking at its northern extremity. Young and Laws now revealed its true extent to be over 350 miles, and the Malawi Department of Surveys (1979) gives its length as 367 miles, with its breadth varying from 10 to 50 miles.

The mission party reached the north end of the Lake and Young named the steep range of mountains on the east side of it at its northern end 'The Livingstone Mountains', and gave Horace Waller's name to the steep peak on the west side near which the Livingstonia Institution was to be built many years later.[10]

Several severe storms, one of which lasted for 48 hours, tested the seaworthiness of the *Ilala* and led her captain to speak of 'her wonderful qualities as a seaboat'.[11] But sheltered anchorages around the Lake were not easy to find and the base remained at Cape Maclear.

They made contact with a number of local chiefs, not all of whom were willing to receive them. Again and again they saw traces of slavery and of the slave trade. In one of his earliest letters home, written from the mouth of the Zambezi on 9th August 1875, Laws had spoken of seeing a Portuguese attended by two or three slaves,

A miserable, bare-footed creature, he appeared, but ready to bully his slaves, as if they were not human beings as well as himself.[12]

That same day, looking for a suitable place to build the *Ilala*, they had come on a human skull and other bones on the shore, and Laws wrote:

This, and the sight of several moving skeletons, made one sigh that better days may soon come for benighted Africa.[13]

He could not forget, either, the sight of a man with no hands whom they had met at the foot of the cataracts. He had been punished by the Chief Rama Ku Kan for adultery with his wife. The man was told to meet the mission party at the top of the rapids, clear of the chief's territory, but the unhappy man was never seen again.[14]

Further evidence of the extent to which life was dominated by fear of the slavers was to be found in many places round the shores of the Lake. Young and Laws met women going to plant cassava up in the hills although there was plenty of fertile ground near at hand; they saw villages in ruins after slave raiding; they found island settlements built on piles 300 yards from the shore to make access from the land difficult; in one place they found tribesmen who had their houses on an island, but their cultivated fields and poultry on the mainland.[15]

One of the main ports on the west coast of the Lake used by the slave traders was Kota-Kota, from which they crossed to Losewa on the eastern shore. At Kota-Kota the chief was known as the Jumbe. In conversation with him, Young and Laws condemned slaving and spoke in favour of what in those days was called 'legitimate trade'.[16]

At the time the Jumbe was suffering from what was diagnosed as syphilis, and Laws gave him some medicine to relieve the pain.[17] The village people at Kota-Kota were willing to have Europeans settle nearby to teach them about God and the civilised arts. This was the only village so far discovered without a marsh nearby, so they expected it to be healthy.[18] Unfortunately the coast was exposed towards the north and north-east and was unsuitable for an anchorage.

When the exploring party returned to Cape Maclear, they found that Johnston, Simpson and Riddel had all suffered from fever or diarrhoea and were looking distinctly pale.[19] A few days later, Young and Laws took fever and Henderson fell ill too. By this time the rains had started and a marsh had developed close to the camp.[20]

Christmas Day was a Saturday and was treated as a working day as it would have been at that time in Scotland. No service is mentioned. All that Laws says in his diary is,

> Rather strange like to have the flowers growing when most likely snow and frost... at home.

The following day, being Sunday, a service was held, and eight Africans, who had remained to work in the following week, were instructed in the Christian faith and 'gazed in wonder as the resurrection and judgement were spoken about'.[21]

As a Scot of his own time, Robert seems to have been much more aware of his isolation when New Year's Day arrived, for he records,

> To most of us it seemed a rather strange New Year's Day, and thoughts of home would come stealing over our hearts'.[22]

February 14th was a red letter day, for it brought the first mail from home - after more than 8 months. Even so, the most recent letter was dated 2nd September, which only increased their sense of isolation.[23]

An important contact was made with Chief Makanjira, on the east side of the Lake. Two boys acted as guides and were rewarded with cloth and with a spoonful of sugar, which they at once shared with each other. At the Chief's village they waited for forty minutes for him to appear - this was regarded as a good sign, which indicated that the Chief would presently see them. When he did appear they found his demeanour 'quiet and impressive... and a contrast to the blustering M'ponda'.[24]

The Chief did not object to a doctor or a teacher coming to live in his village, or to his people supplying the mission party with food. This was a promising opening. Meantime, another chief, Chimlolo, had been talking of settling beside the mission. This led to a larger meeting than usual on the following Sunday evening, for the men from Shupanga, Chimlolo and his people, and others from the nearest village, 'all sat together listening to the story of the Redeeming love.'[25]

An opportunity pregnant with good or ill for the whole future of the Mission arose when one of M'ponda's wives was ill and

the help of Laws was sought for her, for other two men who were
ill, and for a third man, Koomeponjeera, who had a cystic tumour
above his left eye. On this man Laws decided to carry out an
operation under chloroform. Three of the man's friends who were
present were astonished at the effect of the chloroform and at the
successful removal of the tumour. At the same time, M'ponda's wife,
and the two other men, were brought under treatment.[26] It can be
imagined how important it was that this first operation should be
successful and how relieved Laws must have been when the man was
able to return to his own village twelve days later.[27]

In March the *Ilala* was hauled up on the slip and shored up so
that her hull could be painted. To the satisfaction of all concerned,
and to the astonishment of E.D.Young, her bottom was found free
of rust.[28]

The following month, all seven members of the Free Church
party - Mr Henderson of the Established Church having set out in
search of a suitable site for a Church of Scotland Mission - were ill,
mostly with fever, within the space of eight days, although the
passing of another week saw them all fit again.[29]

The Africans were in the habit of making fishing nets out of
the inner bark of a shrub, and they undertook, with the help of a
rope-jack which the mission party constructed, to make some of this
fibre into twine.[30] The pauses Laws had made outside the ropeworks
in Glasgow were already proving their value.

One of the boys who had been taught the alphabet one day
returned a few weeks later with some friends bringing with them
'batatas' or 'sweet potatoes' for sale. Laws was pleased to find that
the boy remembered a good deal of what he had been taught, and a
class of four boys anxious to learn the alphabet now began. This may
be regarded as the beginning of educational work at Livingstonia.[31]

It was not only slave raiding that aroused fear in the villages
at that time. One of the prevalent evils was the custom of trying to
establish the guilt or innocence of a person accused of witchcraft, or
some other crime, by forcing them to drink the *mwavi* (poison)
made from the bark of a certain tree. If an accused person vomited
up the poison, this was taken as proof of innocence, but if he died,
as was much more likely to happen, then guilt was held to be
established. Laws spoke at one of the Sunday Services of the sin of
giving *mwavi*, 'treating it as an omniscient God, able to kill the guilty
and to spare the innocent.'[32]

Awareness that the slave trade was being pursued in close proximity to the Mission was heightened when several of those who had been working at the Mission were carried off as slaves, and when it was learned that a chief called Kasanga, and another chief, had started from M'ponda's village for the coast, with ivory carried by slaves from their own villages, including some of Kasanga's own wives.[33]

Gradually people began to come in search of medical treatment or a place of safety from the slaver. One woman was captured by *Maviti*, a name used for armed bands of Angoni raiders, and later bore twins. Her husband was compelled to bury one of the twins alive to save the woman from being killed. She made her way to Cape Maclear and was given the kitchen to sleep in until a more permanant arrangement could be made.[34]

Later 22 people from the island of Melene sought refuge at the station, including four men, seven women and eleven children. They were carefully listed. A man's name was recorded first, followed by that of his first wife, the names of her children, then the second wife's name was set down and the names of her children.[35]

The number of those who settled at the mission station steadily grew. This meant the growth of a community of Africans who were in close touch with the Mission and who were therefore well placed to learn the truths it was teaching about the love of God. At the same time the growth of a 'colony' of this kind was not without its problems, apart from the fact that such people were cut off from their own background and culture.

To provide a place of refuge for an ill-treated slave was something the Mission could hardly refuse, but to encourage a wife to desert her husband was quite another matter, and it was not easy for Europeans to discover where the truth lay when it was presented from two angles.[36]

Another problem, as numbers grew, was that of exercising discipline. Those who came to live at Cape Maclear had turned away from the authority of their own tribal chief, and yet neither the leader of the Mission party nor any other member of it, was entitled to exercise civil jurisdiction over them. The rules prevailing at the station were carefully explained at the start to anyone who sought to reside at it,[37] but even so, serious difficulties could arise, as we shall see.

One of the things that troubled W.P. (later Archdeacon) Johnson of the UMCA, who worked in the area to the east of the Lake, was the small amount of food the Africans had for themselves. He was reluctant to deplete their meagre resources by buying from them and on one occasion he even sent a man on the long journey to the Lake to obtain goods on credit from Dr Laws.[38]

The Livingstonia party do not seem to have encountered the same difficulty. Not only had they taken with them a good supply of provisions but additional stores were sent out from home from time to time. For example, in April 1876 the Army and Navy Stores sent out 50 lbs of coffee, 20 lbs of sugar, 20 lbs of soap, and three large cheddar cheeses, while in May of the following year, as many as four tons of stores were brought up to the Lake by steamer.[39]

They quickly began to grow at least some of what was required and as early as January 1876 we find Laws recording that 'we had our first taste of our garden in the shape of a dish of French beans.'[40] They had also purchased two nannie goats and one billy goat and for a time enjoyed a supply of fresh milk.[41]

The Africans seem to have been very willing to sell food in exchange for calico. In March 1877, 620 lbs of potatoes were bought by the Mission for just under 10 yards of cloth, and 23 water melons for one yard. Other purchases at this time included three fowls for a yard of calico and one fowl for two strings of beads. Two strings of beads were given for half a dozen eggs, and three strings for 16 fish.[42]

Dr James Stewart had arrived from Lovedale on 21st October 1876 to take charge at Livingstonia when Captain Young left for home. This he did on 2nd November, 'his mission accomplished'. Young wrote:

> To myself had been assigned the task purely of pioneering ... To the Rev Dr Stewart of Lovedale ... it was deputed to appear ... as soon as I had done my part.[43]

Young was over-optimistic about the site at Camp Maclear, but he was entitled to claim that he had seen Livingstonia 'fairly established on Lake Nyassa' and he was wise enough to realise that the civilising and Christianising of the tribes would take years to complete.[44]

On his return, E.D. Young addressed meetings in Edinburgh, Glasgow and twenty-three other places in Scotland,[45] giving information and stirring up interest, and, with some help from the

Revd Horace Waller, published his *Mission to Lake Nyassa (A Journal of Adventures)*. What Young had done clearly aroused public interest at home for what was in those days called a 'Testimonial' was raised for him and the sum of £700 was contributed.[46] The established Church of Scotland, recognising the help given to Mr Henderson, expressed its thanks to Mr Young, as also did the Free Church of Scotland.

The Admiralty, after allowing him three months in which to address the meetings referred to, attached him to HMS Excellent at Portsmouth and not long after, transferred him to his old job at Dungeness where he was reinstated as Divisional Officer of the Coastguard.[47]

Mrs Young, who had been anxious about her husband's welfare, must have been delighted. Young himself was pleased, too, but shows just a tinge of regret at leaving Africa behind. In a letter to the Revd Robert Young of the Foreign Mission Committee, he writes:

> I am fully installed in my former position, but it is rather tame work compared with African exploration.[48]

Meantime, Dr James Stewart was in charge at Livingstonia. It owed its origins largely to his initiative but by now he was head of Lovedale, where his wife was in residence, and he was anxious to return there. On Stewart, at this point in his life, Professor McCracken writes,

> Aged over forty when he arrived at Cape Maclear, he believed himself to be too old to respond to the challenge of his own creation. Impatient to get back to Lovedale, he was consumed by 'a slow burning anger... that I should be kept toiling away at rough work which suited me twenty years ago but does not suit me now.'[49]

It was becoming increasingly clear that when he left the mantle of leadership was likely to fall on the shoulders of Robert Laws. He was still in his mid twenties, but both E.D. Young and Dr James Stewart spoke of him in the highest terms. Young wrote:

> Dr Laws was indefatigable in his many occupations - doctoring the sick who came to him, planning houses, teaching, and picking up the Mang'anja language as fast as he could.[50]

In a long report sent home towards the end of December 1876, Dr Stewart gave his view:

I sincerely hope that all idea has been given up of recalling Dr Laws merely because his period of engagement is nearly expired .... if the Committee is really desirous that the Livingstonia Mission should succeed, *they will retain Dr Laws till* he himself wishes to go - which he does not at present.[51] (Dr Stewart's italics)

Dr Stewart remained in charge at Livingstonia for fifteen months,[52] longer than he had at first intended. On 6th August 1877 his is the first signature on a memorial submitted to the Home Committee regarding the unsuitability of the site at Cape Maclear. Its only recommendation, the memorial claims, is its possession of a good harbour. It is unsuitable through the smallness of its area, its isolated position, and the poverty of the soil. The memorial is also signed by Robert Laws, George Johnston, Alexander Riddel, Allan Simpson and John McFadyen of the original party and by Robert Ross, John Gunn and Archibald Miller, who had gone out in 1876.[53]

Riddel and Gunn were both agriculturists and added letters of their own, testifying to the unsuitability of the soil near the station for the production of ordinary crops. Riddel added that there was a lack of water for irrigation and that the tsetse fly was prevalent.[54]

Concurrence with the petition for a new site was expressed by Mr James Stewart, who had made his appearance at Lake Nyasa in February of that year. Stewart was a highly skilled civil engineer, who in more ways than one, made a big contribution to the Mission. He was a cousin of Dr James Stewart of Lovedale, and they were boyhood friends. Mr Stewart belonged to the village of Kirkmichael in Perthshire where his father, Charles Stewart, had been minister at the time of the Disruption in 1843, and had 'come out' to join the Free Church.*

Mr Stewart had been engaged on work on the Sirkind Canal in India and had decided to visit the Nyasa Mission during his furlough. He offered a year's help and Dr Stewart urged the home Committee to authorise his cousin to construct a much-needed road over the 60 miles of the Murchison cataracts, and then to go on to build at the north end of Lake Nyasa a road which would link it up with Lake Tanganyika.[55]

---

* To avoid confusion, the Revd James Stewart of Lovedale will be referred to as Dr Stewart, and his cousin the engineer as Mr Stewart.

In the autumn of 1877 Dr Stewart and Dr Laws set out on what Stewart, in his address to the Royal Geographical Society in March 1879, called 'The Second Circumnavigation of Lake Nyassa' - the first being that carried out by E.D. Young.[56] The object was to examine the north end of the lake with a view to an extension of mission work, and at the same time, to transport Captain Elton, H.M. Consul at Mozambique, and party, who were on an exploring and hunting expedition. There were 28 aboard the *Ilala* when she set out. The presence of the hunting party put something of a strain on good relations and we find Laws writing in his Diary on Sunday 7th October:

> A day of rest but little of the quiet, peaceful enjoyment I had anticipated. Our friends do not pull in harmony on religious matters.[57]

Elton, and Herbert Rhodes, brother of Cecil Rhodes, went elephant shooting, and Rhodes was hurt when a gun exploded. Laws travelled five miles to render help, but decided that Elton had bandaged the wound adequately. Some weeks later, on his way to the east coast, Elton took ill and died.

Contact was made with chiefs on both sides of the lake. The party landed on the Island of Dikomo, about a third of the way up the Lake, but decided that it was not suitable for settlement. However the UMCA established a site here a few years later, calling the island 'Likoma', the name by which it is still known.[58] Many of the chiefs spoke of the threat of war from neighbouring tribes but were willing to listen when the mission party told how the Bible brought a message from God the Father of Peace to all. They were invited to put questions to William Koyi, who would answer them in their own language. Many heard them with interest and said they would bring others to hear the good message.[59]

It is to the credit of Robert Laws that early on he saw the need for African evangelists and wrote of it to Dr Stewart at Lovedale. The latter had shortly before received letters from Glasgow offering to provide financial support for two African assistants at Livingstonia. Accordingly, he made an appeal to the young men at Lovedale and of 14 who volunteered, 4 were sent to Livingstonia in 1877, William Koyi being outstanding among them.[60] He was a Xhosa, one of the breakaway groups from Shaka's Zulu empire, and was therefore able to communicate with the Angoni in some form of Zulu. We shall hear more of him.

Meantime, Dr Stewart and Dr Laws continued their voyage, and named a bay on the west side of the Lake, under the high plateau on which the Livingstonia Institution was to be built years later, 'Florence Bay' after Dr Stewart's daughter. When they reached the end of the Lake they established that no river flowed out of it at the north end.

About half way up the west coast of the lake, on the west side, was the village of Chief Mankambira, who showed himself friendly. From here, Dr Stewart, seeking a better site, travelled overland for about a hundred miles in a southerly direction to Kota Kota, where the *Ilala* picked him up again.[61] Everywhere there was evidence of the fear in which so many lived, Marenga's village being protected by a triple stockade and Katonga's by a double one, which ran out into the Lake.[62] Dr Stewart told the Royal Geographical Society:

Central Africa has no worse enemy than the Arab traders. Their footsteps may generally be traced in blood and fire and in the tears and misery of the unhappy natives.[63]

The party returned to Cape Maclear in mid-November having found at least two places which seemed to offer safe anchorage for the steamer. As Dr Stewart pointed out it was now possible to sail all the way from London to the north end of Lake Nyasa, except for 60-70 miles at the Murchison cataracts.[64]

What is claimed as the first celebration of the Sacrament of the Lord's Supper at Lake Nyasa took place on 26th November 1877, with 12 communicants. Shortly after this, Dr Stewart handed over the leadership of the Mission to Dr Laws and returned to Lovedale.[65]

Meantime, a reinforcing party for Livingstonia had left Britain towards the end of 1876, and travelled out, in the manner of the day, in two classes of accommodation on the SS *Windsor Castle*. The Revd William Black MB CM travelled first class, at a cost to the Home Committee of £34.13s. Three third class berths cost £23.2s. each and were presumably occupied by the three 'artisans' - John Gunn, agriculturist, Robert Ross, engineer, and Archibald Miller, weaver.[66]

From Dr Black we learn that his colleagues had taken the initiative in starting up a daily prayer meeting among themselves. He goes on to say that he had then got one started in the First Class cabin, conducted in turn by the clergymen aboard.[67] On arrival at Cape Maclear, Dr Black found its situation 'charming' but with the disadvantage of being five miles from the nearest village, and with the quality of the soil poor.[68] Dr Black's sojourn at the Mission was sadly brief for he contracted malaria and died on 7th May, 1877.[69]

In his report on the second year spent in Central Africa, Dr Laws observed that the members of the original party who were still there had all had fewer attacks of fever than in their first year, and that those who had joined them, except for the unfortunate Dr Black, had experienced better health than could have been expected. Good health during the second year, he wrote, had been helped by the larger supplies of provisions from home, and he went on to say,

> The arrival of a large mailing is in itself an excellent medicine from the exhilaration produced by news from the outer world.[70]

Of the three deaths which occurred at Cape Maclear in 1877 - Dr Black, Shadrach Ngunana, one of the men from Lovedale, and John Mackay from the established Church Mission at Blantyre - Dr Laws reckoned that only that of Dr Black was directly due to the climate and malaria.[71]

The medical work among the Africans, Laws recognised was still in its infancy:

> I can present no glowing report of a series of brilliant operations and crowds of people daily receiving medicine. As yet, ours is more sombre [his word] work such as prescribing Epsom salts, rhubarb pills and extracting teeth. Yet, even in this, the confidence of the natives has greatly increased.[72]

Laws mentions that the Africans have several times shown their gratitude 'by bringing a present of a fowl, or some native flour to the mission station', and says, 'This is pleasing - not so much for its value as for the spirit it evinces.'[73]

He is aware that it is impossible to separate out the various strands of missionary work. The gospel cannot be preached in a vacuum. People must be cared for wholly, both in body and soul - an incarnational religion with Christ at the heart of it. A missionary does not heal bodies as a bribe to allow him to heal their souls. The gospel is one, to be proclaimed in word and in deed. The liberation of the body from disease, and of the soul from sin, go closely together. Yet, what Laws says was undoubtedly true:

> The good we do to people's bodies they can appreciate and so are more ready to listen to the great truths we proclaim, and on returning to their villages they carry a good report of our

transactions with them and so open up a way for our reception among them when we are itinerating.[74]

Laws had made no mention in this report of his own health but he was no more immune to fever than the others. Soon after he met Mr James Stewart for the first time he had a particularly severe attack. The two men were travelling up the Zambezi in separate boats towards a place where a Goanese lady lived, whose daughter Laws had treated medically on his first voyage up the Zambezi on the *Ilala*. Presently a severe squall blew up and the boats became separated; Mr Stewart's boat, with the provisions on board, got well ahead. The absence of food did not worry Laws, for he could not eat, owing to the fever. That evening, his men made the boat fast by the river bank and went off - presumably to seek for food. Laws was left on his own. He passed a miserable night of fever, but it was alleviated by an act of kindness on the part of one of the Africans. In Laws' own words,

I heard the patter of running feet coming towards the boat, then a man jumped in at the bow and crawled aft, bringing me three hot, roasted sweet potatoes. He knew I had no food and wished to share his with me. I was unable to eat it, but never forgot his kindness.

The episode happened in 1877. The account given above comes from Laws' *Reminiscences*, written 57 years later.[75]

Dysentery followed the fever, but the next day Laws' men got his boat to the rendezvous where Mr Stewart was waiting. Laws was so weak that Stewart could hardly hear him when he spoke. They were made welcome in the house of the Goanese lady by her daughter. The lady herself was away at the time, and Laws was carried in on a stretcher. He was very ill for for more than a week; at times his temperature was so high that he became delirious.[76] Mr Stewart nursed him with great care and attention - the beginning of a close association between the two men.

6 JOURNEYINGS BY WATER AND LAND

SOS FROM BLANTYRE - EXPLORATION OF WEST SIDE OF LAKE - GOD'S
LOVE FOR ALL - REJECTION OF PACIFISM - AT CHIPATULA'S - DISCUSSION
WITH THE *JUMBE* - BACK TO CAPE MACLEAR - THE WEST SIDE AGAIN -
MARENGA AND MANKAMBIRA - CHIPATULA & BROTHERS - STEWART AT
BANDAWE; RIDDEL & KOYI AT KANING'INA - REPORT ON 1878 - ALC
ESTABLISHED - LAWS NOW IN CHARGE - JAS.STEWART JOINS OFFICIALLY -
MARGARET GRAY TRAVELS OUT - MARRIAGE AT BLANTYRE - BEGINS
TEACHING

Mr Henry Henderson, of the Established Church of Scotland, had
travelled out with the Free Church party. Soon he journeyed south
from Cape Maclear, with Tom Boquito to act as interpreter, and
chose for the Church of Scotland Mission a site in the Shire
Highlands, which was given the name Blantyre after Livingstone's
birthplace. It was a beautiful site and a healthy one.

But having settled on a site, Henderson was at a loss what to
do next, and the coming of reinforcements in summer 1876 seems to
have added to his burdens rather than lessened them. He knew that
Laws' commitment to the Free Church Mission was for two years,
and that Dr Black had now reached Livingstonia; so he hoped that
Laws might be willing to take charge, for a time, at Blantyre,[1] and
sent an urgent request for help. This happened while Dr Stewart was
still with Dr Laws, and the two men felt that they could not ignore
the 'flag of distress' and proceeded to Blantyre. When they reached
it they found that Dr Macklin, because of his health, felt he could not
undertake some of the work needing to be done, while some of the
artisans, who had come out with the second party were discontented,
partly because they were not doing what they considered their own
proper work. 'I want to work my tred', the smith said in his broad
accent, 'I dinna like felling trees and building houses.'[2]

The Livingstonia party were dismayed to find at Blantyre
neither church nor school, neither Bibles nor books. There were five
habitable huts and three which were uninhabitable.[3]

Mr Henderson, Dr Macklin, Dr Stewart and Dr Laws had a conference to discuss the situation. Laws felt that 'one Mission would not be justified in holding aloof from the other', while Dr Stewart also took the view that the success or failure of the two Missions hung together. So it was agreed that Dr Stewart should take charge for a period. After that Dr Laws would serve for some months followed by Dr Black with William Koyi the Xhosa evangelist, as teacher, and Thomas Boquito as manual worker and interpreter. The Established Church of Scotland would pay the salaries of the men from the Free Church Mission for the period during which they served at Blantyre.[4]

Presently Dr Macklin gained enough confidence to take over the leadership, and was in charge at Blantyre until the Revd Duff MacDonald arrived in July 1878.[5]

Back at Livingstonia, Dr Laws and Mr Stewart set out in August 1878, accompanied by William Koyi and Fred Zarakuti to explore the territory on the west side of the Lake. With them were 45 Africans, presumably to act as carriers, and the object was 'to seek a better site'.

On reaching Kota-Kota, they were warned by the Jumbe of war further north between the Tonga chief, Mankambira, and the Angoni chief, Chipatula, but this did not prevent them from spending some time with each of these chiefs.[6]

In Mankambira's territory they noticed that the villages were protected by stockades, many of them being on spits of sand running out into the Lake. In this area they found that cassava was a more popular crop than maize or mapira because, being a root crop, it was harder for the enemy raiders to carry off.[7]

At Chipatula's village they explained further that they were teachers come with a message from God, telling that He loved all his children, black as well as white. Chipatula's people 'listened patiently, said our words were good and expressed themselves as being very glad that we had come to visit them.'[8] In speaking with the Angoni, William Koyi's knowledge of the language was invaluable.

Although they came as messengers of peace they were by no means pacifists, and they believed in the right of self-defence. Mr Stewart thought it wise on this occasion to demonstrate the power and accuracy of his revolver by setting up a target at a distance and firing at it. This made a powerful impression and Laws wrote in his *Reminiscences* many years later, that this show of strength had prevented them from being attacked by a group of Angoni, who were highly suspicious of them, and hostile to them.[9]

The paramount chief M'mbelwa, successor to the Zulu king Zwangendaba, and his brother Mtwaro sent word that they were coming to visit the missionaries but no meeting took place at this time.

Shortly after this they shot and killed two elephants; men, women and children set about cutting them up with great enthusiasm for they welcomed the unusual supply of meat and prepared to dry much of it.[10]

After spending four days at Chipatula's the party made the steep descent to the coast at Bande. They came on a possible anchorage for the *Ilala* at Nkata Bay and as the ground nearby was fertile and there was a good supply of timber they considered it a possible site for the Mission. It was, however, too near the level of the Lake, and, in Laws' words, 'there was no room for a city.'[11]

About this time too they were made sharply aware of the danger from crocodiles for a young girl, sitting on the side of a canoe beside the Lake, was suddenly seized by a crocodile and could not be recovered.[12] They were in this area when 12th October came, the third anniversary of their arrival at the Lake, but Laws makes no mention of the occasion in his diary. His thoughts were on the possibilities of a new site.[13]

On returning to Kota-Kota they heard that all was well at Cape Maclear. They were well received by the Jumbe and had a long talk with him. They told him that before there could be any thought of their settling in his territory he must understand that they would not interfere in any way in quarrels with his neighbours; they were thoroughly opposed to the slave trade, and it was their purpose to teach about God and the arts of civilisation. The Jumbe replied that he understood the first point; that he had given up slaving and that, so far as teaching was concerned, he could not force children to attend school but he had no objection to them doing so.[14]

From Kota-Kota they travelled south on land to M'pemba's, a distance of about 50 miles, and were then picked up by the *Ilala*, Laws having sent word to Gunn at Cape Maclear to send the steamer for them.[15]

They had covered 700 miles on their three month trip, and on their return, Laws told 'the industrial members of staff' about the journey and Mr Stewart showed them a sketch map in illustration.[16]

Only two weeks after returning to the station in November 1878, Dr Laws and Mr Stewart set out again for the west coast of the Lake, taking Alexander Riddel and William Koyi and 40 carriers.[17] They were well received by the local chiefs. Chief Marenga agreed to Mr Stewart remaining near his village, and Stewart immediately began to have a house built for himself. It was completed by 6th December and 37 men and women received 74 yards of calico in payment for their work.[18] Although regarded as an 'observation post' at the time, it was in fact the beginning of Bandawe, three years later the Mission headquarters.

While Stewart developed relationships at Marenga's and at Mankambira's, about three hours' journey away on foot, Laws, Riddel and Koyi sailed north to Nkata Bay in the *Ilala* and then travelled inland and upwards until they came to Kaning'ina, some 2,000 feet up on a high plateau to the west of the Lake. They were not far from the village of the Angoni chief, Chipatula, who had shown himself friendly on the previous visit some three months earlier, and they now met his brothers, Njomani and Magoda. These chiefs made Laws welcome, but urged him to see M'mbelwa, the paramount chief of the Angoni in that area. Laws explained that he could not visit M'mbelwa then, but promised to return two months later. Meantime, William Koyi, with his knowledge of the language, would visit the chief.[19] So it was that Laws returned to Cape Maclear on 13th December, leaving James Stewart at Bandawe, Alexander Riddel and William Koyi at Kaning'ina. Foundations of missionary work among both Atonga and Angoni were now being laid.[20]

On the day on which Laws arrived back at Cape Maclear two boys, Chiko and Kambona, boarded the steamer and found a revolver belonging to Crooks in his hammock. While Kambona was playing with it it went off and damaged Chiko's left hand, wrist and arm. Dr Laws dressed the wounds and considered that the outlook was not serious.

'Though very sorry that such an accident should have happened', he wrote to the Revd Thomas Main, 'I confess liking the youngsters all the better that they should have so much mischief in them.'[21]

When he sent home his report for 1878, Laws classified the work under six heads - Evangelistic; Educational; Medical; Carpentry Work; Agriculture; and Journies (*sic*).

1 Evangelistic Under this head it is noted that on Sundays two Services are normally held for the Africans, the second being a kind of adult Sunday School, and an English service in the evening. The average attendance on Sunday mornings had been 120, but sometimes rose to 300. In the dry season services were also held at three villages to the south-west of the station, and these were well attended.

2 Educational The school roll had risen over the past year from 29 boys to 65. The latter figure must have included girls, since girls are mentioned as being among the prize-winners in August. The day began with a half hour Bible lesson. Writing and arithmetic, including multiplication in the advanced classes, was taught. In addition, two hours a day were spent on manual labour, chiefly work in the fields or in clearing the roads and grounds of the station.

3 Medical Among the Europeans health had been much better and there had been less fever. Among the Africans medical work had increased and several operations had been performed. Confidence had grown considerably.

4 Carpentry Work This had included repairs to houses, boats and tools. A school building, also used as a church, had been built and benches made for it. The woodwork had all been sawn by Africans.

5 Agriculture There had been a severe drought the previous year but since then 13 acres of fairly good soil had been reclaimed. Details are given of crops in each field, showing 20 acres under cultivation, including ground nuts, sesame, water melon and sugar cane. The wheat failed because of the drought but some of the ground was replanted with castor oil beans. Produce of the vegetable garden included cabbages, shallots, chillies, tomatoes, cape gooseberries, and Indian sorrel. Bananas were abundant, and there were pineapples, custard apples, orange plants, lemon plants and date palms. In addition 34 cocoa nut palms were doing well, and 600 blue gums. The walks in front of the station were planted with palms, and those in the rear with mangos.

6 Journies Many had been undertaken and greater confidence was being shown by Africans. In 1875, at Mankambira's near Nkata Bay

Dr Laws had been kept as hostage while the head man went with Mr Young aboard the *Ilala* and in 1877 Dr Stewart had difficulty in persuading two men to show him where Mankambira lived. Attitudes had changed by November 1878; when the *Ilala* arrived unexpectedly, 40 men, women, and children were willing to start for the hills as carriers the next morning.

The report concludes by saying that the number of Africans resident at Cape Maclear had increased from 127 in September 1877 to 327 at the end of December 1878.[22]

An important development which affected the immediate running of the Mission and was to be a continuing influence on the trade and commerce in the country as a whole, was the setting up of what was known at first as the Livingstonia Central Africa Company, which was incorporated in June 1878. Later it was known as the African Lakes Corporation and as the African Lakes Company. Its purpose was to 'encourage legitimate and beneficial trade amongst the natives', to 'promote civilisation' and to 'assist to a great extent in the suppression of the slave trade.' It was thus following the lines recommended by David Livingstone to replace the slave trade with legitimate commerce, but from the beginning there were 'interim arrangements with the Livingstonia and Blantyre missions to manage the purchase of their supplies.'[23]

The capital for the venture was provided to a large extent by the same group of men in the west of Scotland who had financed the Livingstonia Mission and they were fortunate in securing as their first managers two Edinburgh brothers John and Frederick Moir. The two storey building occupied by the Moirs, part house and part store, not far from the Blantyre Mission, has been made a National Monument in Malawi, and vans marked 'Mandala' can be seen standing near it.*

The African Lakes Company is generally thought to have suffered from lack of capital but it provided a much needed source of supply and soon it had 12 trading stations and a staff of 25 Europeans.[24]

*The name 'Mandala', in the local language, originally referred to the sunlight glinting off John Moir's spectacles. It was transferred in popular use to the trading station at Blantyre, and then came to be used of any store or trading post.[25]

Close relations were maintained, with some disagreements from time to time, between the Livingstonia Mission and its trading partner. Sometimes staff were transferred from the one body to the other, and presently the Company became responsible for running the *Ilala*.

In March of 1879, the Glasgow Committee heard that Mr Stewart had had permission from the Government of India to receive remuneration during his furlough. It was fixed at £300 p.a., the same as Laws was paid. At Mr Stewart's request, payment was to date only from 1st January 1878 though he had in fact been working for the Mission since early 1877.[26]

The minutes record the satisfaction of the Committee at learning that in the course of the journeys undertaken by Dr Laws and Mr Stewart 'a tentative station had been selected' - i.e. as an alternative to Cape Maclear.[27]

The position of Dr Laws was under consideration at this meeting. He could have become a minister in the Free Church under what was called 'The Mutual Eligibility Act' and this was the course recommended by Dr Stewart. Laws, however, seems to have felt that loyalty to the UP Church prevented him from seeking a transfer to the Free Church, and the Committee decided not to press the matter 'having regard to his valuable services.' The UP Church was still willing to maintain him for a term of years and it was resolved that he should be considered the official head of the Mission, unless Dr Stewart were present.[28] As Dr Stewart had plenty to occupy him at Lovedale this meant that in practice Laws was now the head of the Livingstonia Mission. He held the position for the next 48 years.

By February 1879 Mr Stewart had been on furlough from India for two years. He now had permission to remain other two years i.e. until September 1880. He offered to resign and give full time 'to the cause of Christ in Africa'. The drop in income he would suffer did not bulk large in his mind.

Laws wrote from Lovedale in May, and Dr Stewart in July, urging the Committee to accept Mr Stewart's offer. 'We have wrought together in perfect harmony', wrote Laws. These letters were before the Committee when it met in Glasgow on 3rd September 1879, and it was unanimously agreed to appoint Mr Stewart as a full member of Mission staff.[29]

The presence of Laws at Lovedale in May of that year arose from the fact that, after four years of waiting, Margaret Gray was on her way out to marry him, and he had been given six months' leave of absence from Livingstonia to meet her at the Cape.[30] Margaret Gray's employment by Galashiels School Board had lasted only one session because the opening of the new school in Galashiels had led to a reorganisation of pupils, and to a redeployment of staff. Miss Gray, and two other teachers, accordingly had their employment terminated on 1st July 1875.[31] It is not known what Margaret did between that date and setting out for Central Africa in April 1879.

Robert and those with him sent mail home as opportunity offered, sometimes, in the early days, sending men to the coast for the specific purpose of carrying mail. A package of letters cost £10 to send home and despatches were normally limited to one package every two months, although, in 1880, the Home Committee authorized Laws to send mail oftener if something of importance should have arisen.[32]

The one glimpse we have of Margaret during this period comes from Miss Jane E. Waterston, a woman of remarkable gifts whose brief connection with the Livingstonia Mission will be mentioned later. She was a friend of Dr and Mrs James Stewart, and travelled out to Lovedale with them in 1867. Later she took a medical course and offered for service at Livingstonia. In a letter to Dr Stewart, written from Scotland in January 1879 she referred to Margaret Gray with some impatience as one who 'couldn't seem to make up her mind to go... Laws is not settled or something is wrong', she wrote.[33]

As Robert's original appointment was for two years, Margaret may have harboured the hope that he would return for furlough at the end of that period and that they would then be married in Scotland. As it was, Laws' time at Livingstonia simply stretched out and out. It seems unlikely that Margaret had any doubts about marrying Robert but she may easily have been uncertain whether it was better to go out to him, or to wait until he came home on furlough to be married.

In the end she travelled out via Naples, where her eldest brother, James Gordon Gray, was now the Free Church minister. Robert had expected her to travel via Cape Town, rather than by the East Coast route via Zanzibar, and left Livingstonia in February 1879 to visit Lovedale before going on to meet her. He wanted to see the methods used at Lovedale. Margaret did not receive his letter asking her to come via Cape Town, and the result was that when he reached East London, after being at Lovedale, he learned that she had come after all by the East Coast route. At Quilimane he heard that she had proceeded up the Zambezi in the company of Dr Macklin and two ladies who were bound for Blantyre.[34] Laws followed and the two met at Blantyre in the third week Marriages of August. Their Banns of Marriage were called on Sunday 24th August, in accordance with Scottish custom, and on August 28th they were married in the school room at Blantyre by the Revd Duff MacDonald. Mr James Stewart sent out the invitations to the wedding, and he and Dr Macklin signed the marriage schedule as witnesses.[35]

Laws' own mention of this important event in his life to the Secretary of the Free Church FMC is, characteristically, surrounded by comment on the affairs of the Mission:

> On the 28th [August] Miss Gray and I were married and the mission accounts with Nunes (the Portuguese Consul) being separated and balance sheets sent on to Quilimane, we started for Livingstonia on the 2nd September, arriving on the fore-noon of the 5th and receiving a hearty welcome from our companions and the natives at the station.[36]

Mrs Laws became the first white woman to reside on the shores of Lake Malawi, and W.P.Livingstone tells us that she quickly began to help in the schoolroom, giving special attention to teaching women and girls to sew.[37] She must also have taken up the study of the local language at an early date. A small booklet including Hymns in the native language, dated 1879-82, and with the initials 'ML' attached can be seen in Edinburgh University Library, which also has a copy of an 'Early Reader' in Mrs Laws' handwriting.[38]

A month later Laws set off from Cape Maclear to visit what had been called 'the observation post' on the west coast, but before we give our attention to this we must try to understand the problems that faced the missionaries once a considerable number of Africans began to reside in proximity to the mission station.

7 A COLONY OR A MISSION?

CAN THE GOSPEL BE PROCLAIMED IN ISOLATION? - SHOULD THOSE
ATTRACTED LEAVE THEIR OLD ENVIRONMENT? - PROBLEMS OF DISCIPLINE
WHEN THEY DO - FLOGGINGS RESORTED TO - A CONSULAR APPOINTMENT
SOUGHT - HOME COMMITTEE AWAITS ADVICE FROM DRS STEWART &
LAWS - LAWS ABSENT A LOT IN 1878 - JANE WATERSTON, WELCOMED BUT
NOT FULLY USED - SHE RESIGNS - FOREIGN OFFICE WARNS AGAINST
RECEIVING FUGITIVE SLAVES

Once the Mission station at Cape Maclear had become established
and several hundred Africans, largely because of the protection the
Mission afforded against enslavement, had settled beside it, the
question of how order was to be maintained, and discipline
administered, was bound to arise, although this does not seem to
have been foreseen by the Committee at home. The way this
problem was answered was likely to vary according to one's
philosophy of mission.

All who went out as missionaries to Central Africa went to
proclaim the Good News of the Christian Faith to those who did not
know it - to bring light into a dark world. But, is it possible to do
this, so to speak, in isolation? Can one simply proclaim the Gospel
and leave it at that? What will be the effect upon those who hear the
message? Will they continue to reside in their own villages, and, in
the midst of a non-Christian environment, do their best to live the
Christian way? Or will they leave their village behind and come to
live beside those who have brought them the Good News?

The latter course has certain advantages. It enables those who
are attracted by the Christian message to learn more of it by close
contact with those who proclaim it, and, inasmuch as they are living
in an environment that may be called Christian over against an
environment that may be called pagan, they will find it easier to
practise the Christian faith and grow in an understanding of it.

In addition, the Mission station has certain practical benefits
to offer, such as medical help, which can achieve things which the

tribal medicine man cannot, and the opportunity of learning to read and write. And since the missionaries are known to be opposed to the slave trade, a fugitive can expect to be sympathetically received.

But there are also considerable disadvantages. When Africans seek to live in close association with a Mission settlement they cut themselves off from their own environment and from the chief who is the natural head of the group. The chief for his part may well resent the influence of the Mission settlement which may seem to be working against his interests in encouraging his people to leave him.

An instance of the clash of opposing points of view occurred when an African called Sogoli, speaking on behalf of M'ponda as well as himself, complained that although M'ponda had readily given permission to the missionaries to settle on his land, they were in fact making his people leave him. Those who sought refuge at the Mission station, claiming that they were liable to be sold, were not speaking the truth. Why, argued Sogoli, should they be allowed to run away and not be brought back?[1]

Apart from this kind of difficulty the growth of large numbers of settlers at Cape Maclear raised problems of law and order for those in charge of the Mission. The normal arbiter of disputes for an African at that time would be his tribal chief - but when a person or group had left to settle at the Mission, what was to happen then? Disagreements were bound to occur. Thefts did occur. Physical attacks on individuals and sexual assaults on young girls did take place. Moral persuasion was not enough.

This may lessen our surprise that a set of stocks was built at Cape Maclear to confine offenders. On 6th September 1878 while Dr Stewart and Dr Laws were absent on a voyage of exploration a man called Golingo was found guilty of deserting an expedition in which he was acting as a porter. The Journal reads:

Acting on Dr Laws' orders relative to deserters, Golingo was placed in the stocks... his case being aggravated by the fact that he was one in whom special confidence had reposed.

Three days later work was begun on a prison and on 21st September Golingo was 'remanded to it from the stocks.' At the end of the month Golingo was liberated after 24 days in confinement. The punishment was a severe one, and without the sanction of Laws.[2]

Laws was also absent from the Mission when a woman called Ntitaji, apparently an employee at the Mission, was convicted of stealing ground nut oil from the store. She was imprisoned for 3 days, made to forfeit a month's calico and told not to return until sent for.[3]

To withhold some quantity of calico, of which the Mission was the provider and the source, seems justifiable when the guilty party was actually employed by the Mission, and had stolen Mission property, but what authority had the Mission on another occasion to punish an African who was not on the staff but was guilty of an offence against a third party?

In November 1878, an African named Kaondo, who had gone to purchase food was seized and sold. The guilty party was discovered in Nun Rumba's village. The chief and his councillors asserted that such an offence should be punished, and the guilty man was given eight lashes.[4] This would seem to have been done under the authority of the chief concerned, but there occurred another case at Cape Maclear which caused Robert Laws considerable concern both then and later.

A man had taken advantage of a young girl and forced her to live with him. A kind of court consisting of local headmen was set up at Laws' request in order to try him. When he was found guilty Laws left it to the headman to decide his punishment; they sentenced him to 30 lashes. Laws was there as Doctor when the punishment was administered but intervened to stop it after 13 lashes. He applied ointment to the man's back and discharged him from the station the next day.[5]

Away from Cape Maclear and the moderating influence of Robert Laws, floggings were more frequent. On the west side of the Lake, where 'observation posts' had been established at Bandawe and Kaning'ina, flogging took place on seven occasions in the first six months of 1879, and there were four other occasions when it was threatened. Mr Stewart was responsible in one case, Mr Miller in one, and Mr Simpson in five, of the cases where men were flogged. Early in the following year Simpson excelled himself, having no fewer than 31 flogged, one of them for swearing. He wrote in the Journal of 'the need to flog evil out of the Atonga', and added 'It has always done good.... it has a better effect than all the moral lectures that could have been coined for them'.[6] He seems quite unaware of the damage such punishments might do to the Christian cause.

It should be said in partial extenuation that many of the offences punished by flogging involved the stealing or attempted stealing of women or of children; it is also true that soldiers in the British Army could still be punished in this barbarous way. Flogging in the Services had been restricted from 1859 onwards, but proposals for its total abolition were rejected by the House of Commons in 1876, 1877 and 1879, and it was not finally abolished until the Army Discipline Act of 1881.[7] To say this is not to defend the practice in Central Africa, but to try to see it against a wider background.

By the summer of 1879 there were some 360 Africans resident around the station at Cape Maclear, with 1,000 at Kaning'ina, and the Glasgow Committee resolved to ask the Government to establish consular authority over the area.[8]

The Government replied that flogging was generally illegal, and that the missionaries had no authority whatever over Africans. Appointment of a consul would not improve matters, for a consul could only deal legally with British Subjects. The Mission was advised to have lay magistrates chosen by the people themselves.[9]

The Committee resolved to take no final decision before it heard from Dr Stewart and from Dr Laws,[10] and a long Memorandum from Dr Stewart was in the hands of the Committee at their November meeting, written at Lovedale on 23rd September. Dr Stewart comes out strongly against the Mission taking into its hands the power of life and death, and recommends deportation for those guilty of murder. On flogging he says, 'I am utterly and without qualification of any kind opposed to flogging... at a mission station.'[11]

The Committee gave general approval to Dr Stewart's recommendations but decided still to await a report from Dr Laws. However, the next letter they received from Laws was concerned mainly with equipment. He asked for a new dinghy, a turning lathe, a seine net and a papyrograph (for stencilling) and these requests were all approved.[12]

The problem of discipline was dealt with by Laws in a later letter, which the Glasgow Committee had before it in June. Laws feels that if he has to exercise civil power he is 'apt to be hindered somewhat in Evangelical work'[13] and a month later he writes again, making the point that deportation, which was regarded by Dr Stewart as the most suitable action to take, was no punishment at all to some, but was too severe on others as it was tantamount to handing them over to the slave trader. As to flogging, he writes, 'Personally, I feel it to be a sickening thing to have to take part in the infliction of such a punishment and shall be glad to have nothing more to do with it, if such is the wish of the Committee.'[14]

To keep things in perspective he adds that in a community grown to 500 the prison has been unoccupied for eight or nine months and observes that this compares favourably with the situation at home.[15]

For more than six of these months - since he brought his bride to Cape Maclear in September 1879 - Laws himself had been almost continually present. In the two previous years this had not been so. Professor McCracken has pointed out that during 1878, which he calls 'a typical year', the artisans were in charge at Cape Maclear for over 200 days.[16] The following year Laws was away from the station in the early months paying a brief visit to Blantyre in January.[17] Later that month he spent some three weeks at the 'observations posts' on the west side, at Bandawe and Kaning'ina;[18] then on 21st February[19] he left for the Cape with a view to meeting his fiancée and did not return with her until 5th September,[20] so that he was almost entirely absent from Cape Maclear from January to early September 1879.

The artisans were men of considerable ability, as their later careers were to show, but even as a young man - and he was still under 30 - Laws would seem to have had a personal authority that was recognised both by the Mission staff and by many of the Africans.

One member of staff who was deeply horrified by the reports of floggings was Miss Jane E. Waterston who was referred to in Chapter 6. She was the first woman missionary at Livingstonia apart from Margaret Laws who was there as a missionary's wife. Jane Waterston was born in Inverness, then after training as a nurse in Glasgow accompanied Dr James Stewart and his wife Mina (sister of John Stephen the shipbuilder) to Lovedale in 1867. There she was in charge of a girls' seminary; the number of boarders increased from 10 to 66 in five years; Miss Waterston won the affection and respect of her charges who called her 'Mother of Activity.' She was forthright and not afraid to speak her mind or even, on occasion, to criticise Dr Stewart himself. She held strong views on women's rights and abilities. Her job at Lovedale gave her satisfaction, but she responded to the plea of her parents that she pay a visit to Scotland, and did so in 1873. While in South Africa on her journey home, she took a refresher course in nursing at Cape Town, and when she was at home studied in Elizabeth Garret Anderson's hospital in 1874. Later she went to Dublin where she took classes in midwifery and opthalmic surgery at the Rotunda Hospital, and was duly licensed in 1877 as a

LKQCPI (Licentiate of the King's and Queen's College of Physicians of Ireland).[21] She was well qualified medically, although the regulations of the time did not permit a woman actually to graduate in medicine.

From W.P.Livingstone we learn that some time in 1875 Robert Laws met Miss Waterston along with others in the home of Miss Janet Melville in Aberdeen. She was studying medicine at that time with a view to offering herself for service with the Livingstonia Mission. Laws was impressed by her 'buoyant spirits' and her 'good sense', and said, 'If God spares her she will be useful to the Mission.'[22]

Her appointment was made in February 1879.[23] It had already been agreed that she should be female assistant at the Mission, her duties to 'include the management of a boarding school for native girls and assisting the medical men.' Her salary was to begin at £150 and rise over five years to £200 pa.[24] Laws wished her to receive a 'liberal supply of surgical instruments' as he himself had only brought the minimum. 'In this way', he adds, 'the confidence placed in us now with regard to medical work will be much increased.'[25]

Miss Waterston herself wrote enthusiastically on 11th November, 1879, of the warm welcome she had received at Livingstonia, and was pleased with her 'two decker-house decorated with 100,000 Welcomes in Gaelic.'[26] Within three months she had resigned. What had gone wrong with so promising a beginning?

It is not easy to understand fully but certain factors emerge. For one thing we know that she had protested to Dr Laws and Mr Gunn about the use of an 'utterly dark cell' at Cape Maclear as a prison and in particular about incarcerating a woman in it.[27] She resented having to teach sewing and primary subjects when (as she understood it) she had come out to be a doctor,[28] and one suspects that Dr Laws was not treating her as an equal when it came to medical matters. Yet at that time, there was surely a great deal of medical care which could have been given to African women and children in their own huts where the presence of a male doctor would have been less acceptable, if permitted at all. Whatever the reason, by 29th December Miss Waterston declared that she was 'already ashamed of being a missionary', and in February 1880, she resigned.[29] In his own diary Laws writes on 20th March about a number of men whose time with the Mission was over, and then says:

Miss J.E.Waterston goes some four months after arrival. And what of her work? No one who has been in the Mission said more about what he was to do before leaving home and I do not think any member of the Mission has done less. Honest, good, hard, self-denying work is what is required here, and in these respects compared with her engagement her work has been found wanting. It is true we might have had worse, but certainly there have been many better.[30]

This is very damning and shows no awareness that as head of the Mission Laws himself should have assessed her talents more accurately and realised how greatly she was frustrated. It looks as if Laws kept the medical work too much in his own hands and in doing so not only lost a well qualified woman missionary but missed a great opportunity for developing, as early as 1880, medical work among African women. Certainly Jane Waterston gave satisfactory service at Lovedale for the next three years and thereafter practised as a doctor in Cape Town for 49 years, being awarded an honorary doctorate by the Cape of Good Hope College in 1889, and given an LLD by Cape Town University in 1929.[31]

Since she was technically in breach of contract Miss Waterston was liable to forfeit her passage money, but in the end Mr R. Young, the Secretary, returned to her the £20 she had repaid, along with £27 for articles taken over from her by Dr Laws.[32] It is good to be able to record that when Malcolm Moffat offered himself in South Africa for service with the Livingstonia Mission in 1894 it was to Dr Waterston that Laws recommended him to go for his medical examination.[33]

Towards the end of 1880 Laws wrote to tell the Committee that he had been told by Consul O'Neill that the Mission had 'no legal right to receive fugitive slaves.' Accordingly he seeks instructions from the Committee and pleads to be allowed to retain the right of giving sanctuary to fugitives to lessen the number of trials by poison ordeal.[34] The Committee again instructed Dr Smith to communicate with the Foreign Office; this led to a quite unequivocal statement from Lord Granville that 'the only rights enjoyed by the Mission are those conceded by the local chiefs.' At the same time he warned the Mission authorities to take great care in dealing with refugees.[35]

The frequency with which the question of discipline crops up helps us to understand why the Mission was presently to be found among the strongest advocates of the establishment of a Protectorate by the British Government, a step not taken until 1891 and taken then with great reluctance.

8 MISSION EXPANSION AND TRIBAL RIVALRY

RIDDEL & KOYI VISIT M'MBELWA - SCHOOL AT KANING'INA - LAWS & M'MBELWA MEET-JAS.STEWART IN CHARGE-KOYI MAINTAINS CONTACTS WITH ANGONI - LAWS REVISITS THE 'OBSERVATION STATIONS' - WARNS AGAINST INVOLVEMENT IN AFRICAN DISPUTES - MARRIES THREE COUPLES - MILLER FEELS HURT - ST MARK'S GOSPEL IN CHINYANJA - WORK AT BANDAWE DEVELOPS - LAWS FIVE YEARS ORDAINED - HIS CAUTIOUS APPROACH - FIRST REQUEST FOR BAPTISM - ALBERT NAMALAMBE'S WORK; BAPTISED; RECEIVES COMMUNION

After Laws had left the west coast of the Lake in December 1878, Alexander Riddel and William Koyi visited M'mbelwa the Angoni chief as promised. The chief had an ox killed to welcome them, and an intimidating array of 38 councillors and 94 village headmen was assembled to meet them. They explained that they had come with a message from God, and showed M'mbelwa a Bible. Riddel claimed, in words that were certainly open to misunderstanding, that the Bible was what had 'made our nation rich and powerful.' Koyi addressed the company in Zulu and when he had spoken M'mbelwa invited them to come and live with the Angoni, instead of favouring the Atonga with their presence. The possibility that they were spies was not ruled out and a rumour was current that presently the steamer would bring up an army against the Angoni.[1]

M'mbelwa and his counsellors offered Riddel and Koyi 20 head of cattle and goats if they would come and live in the hills with them. 'Why do you try to milk fish?', they asked.[2]

When New Year's day 1879 dawned Alexander Riddel, Scot that he was, observed it as a holiday, although he was the only European present.[3] Three days later a school was started at Kaning'ina with 10 pupils, though Riddel thought it unlikely they would continue once the supply of elephant meat, which had been purchased from both Atonga and Angoni, ran out. In fact 4 to 15 people kept coming over the next few weeks.[4] Sunday services were held with 15 on 5th January, but over 300 attended two weeks later, and numbers continued high. Koyi addressed them in their own tongue.[5]

January 15th saw Laws back at Cape Maclear from Blantyre; before leaving the area to go to meet his bride, he had set out to visit the 'observation stations.'[6] Mr Fred Moir had joined the mission party at Blantyre and now accompanied Laws.[7] Mr Miller was left at Bandawe to replace Mr Stewart, and Laws, Stewart and Moir sailed north to Nkata Bay, en route for Kaning'ina.[8] From there they went on to M'mbelwa's to fulfil the promise Laws had made to return. The historic meeting between M'mbelwa, paramount chief of the Angoni, and Robert Laws, head of the Livingstonia Mission, took place on 22nd January 1879.[9]

In a little booklet entitled *Lonely Warrior*, in which he pays tribute to William Koyi, George Campbell describes M'mbelwa:

He was a short stout man, unlike many of his lithe warriors. The carelessness of the calico thrown round him showed clearly that his main dress was the heavy ivory rings on his arms and the brass wire circling his legs. Under his partly-shaven head, crowned with the Zulu ring of plaited hair, twinkled a pair of quick intelligent eyes. A great cry of 'Bayete' arose as he entered the royal kraal: a great open circle formed by a fence which was sprouting into young trees. He and Laws eyed one another shrewdly, they appeared to like what they saw and became friends at once.[10]

Laws explained that they had come 'to be friends; to teach about God and what he had done... to teach the children so that they might read God's word for themselves.'[11]

M'mbelwa again asked why the missionaries should stay down at the Lake, repeating the question, 'Can you milk fish?' He asked for a teacher, but no one could be spared. Koyi offered to remain, and to eat with the Angoni to make him independent of supplies from the Mission, but Laws felt that he could not allow this, as he would be in considerable danger should there be any change of feeling among the Angoni. He undertook to seek further African volunteers from Lovedale and meantime told Koyi to return to Kaning'ina.[12] The important thing was that Laws and M'mbelwa had met, and had begun to think of each other with respect.

Alexander Riddel's health was poor and Laws now advised him to return to Scotland. At Kaning'ina he was replaced first by John McFadyen and then, after two months, by Archibald Miller.[13]

As described in chapter 6, Laws left Livingstonia in February 1879 for Lovedale, expecting to go on from there to Cape Town to meet his fiancée.[14] James Stewart was in charge at Cape Maclear for the seven months Laws was away, with Miller (later Simpson) at Bandawe.[15] There was normally only one European at either Bandawe or Kaning'ina at this time.

William Koyi remained at Kaning'ina and from there maintained contacts with the Angoni further north. Chipatula was particularly friendly[16] and M'mbelwa gave Koyi and Miller five head of cattle, and wanted them to establish a mission station in one of his villages. During this period, William Koyi accompanied Mr Moir on a six week excursion in which trading and preaching were to be combined. They were well received wherever they went.[17]

In October, a month after returning to Cape Maclear with his bride,[18] Laws set out to visit the 'observation stations' on the west coast of the Lake. He put a note in the Bandawe Journal at this time saying that in the preceding months there had clearly been 'too marked a tendency to decide native disputes', and reminded Mission staff that they must not initiate interference with the slave traders. Refugees might be received if no crime were proved against them within a month, provided that they were willing to work to earn the price of their ransom, this to be either the price paid for the slave in question, or the price current at the time.[19]

There is no doubt that with Atonga and Angoni each eager to have the missionaries as allies it was essential to avoid taking sides. This left them free to proclaim the Gospel to both parties and to urge upon them both the advantages of settling disputes in a peaceful way instead of waging war. Three couples at Bandawe, all of whom were permanent servants of the Mission, were married by Laws at this time. He left to return to Cape Maclear early on the following day, and Simpson, who was in charge in Laws' absence, gave the people a holiday to celebrate the weddings. This was done with singing and dancing.[20]

Laws did not, on this visit to the western shore of the Lake, make the steep uphill journey to Kaning'ina but sent letters to Miller from Bandawe and Nkata Bay, saying that he did not wish the station at Kaning'ina kept open throughout another wet season, and telling Miller to move to Bandawe.[21] Miller was deeply disappointed and writes in the Journal with great indignation:

Dr Laws arranged to meet me on the 21st at Nkata. He arrived
six days before the appointed time and would not even wait for
my letters. I just draw from the treatment that the heads of the
Mission here at Livingstonia just don't care for my interest so
long as their own ends are served. And as I have been treated
in the same way once or twice I will not submit to such neglect
any longer.[22]

The loneliness of being the only resident European during a period
of seven months no doubt magnified Miller's sense of grievance.

William Koyi, for his part, had now completed three years at
Livingstonia and wanted to return to Lovedale to get married.[23] He
might come back to the Mission after marriage, but meantime his
services as an interpreter would be badly missed. Mapas Ntintili had
gone to Kaning'ina to replace Koyi but his health was not good[24] and
Laws' hopes of securing further help from Lovedale came to nothing.
In the circumstances Laws had little choice but to close down the
station in the hills, but it was a pity that he did not explain his reasons
to Miller. In fact Miller had already arranged with Mr Moir his own
transfer to the African Lakes Company,[25] and Laws had agreed.

In August of that year John Moir and William Koyi finished
a translation of St Mark's Gospel. The station Journal does not say
into which language the translation was made but we learn from Dr
Laws, writing many years later in his *Reminiscences*, that:

To Mr John Moir assisted by William Koyi belongs the credit
of having been the first to complete the translation of Mark into
Nyanja.[26]

But if the station at Kaning'ina, on the hills to the west of Nkata Bay,
near Angoniland, was abandoned at that time, the work at Bandawe
among the Atonga was developing rapidly. In the year ending 30th
November 1879, we are told that the station there had cost £68,
excluding the cost of the resident European; 4,550 people had been
at meetings since April, with attendances varying from 50 to 300.[27]

A start was made with a children's school, and Marenga
himself brought 14 boys to this school in February of 1879. 50 were
present the following day but attendances were erratic, and in the
first year averaged out at only 10 per day. In that year also 41 medical
cases, presumably of a non-serious nature since Laws was largely
absent, were dealt with.[28] In March Archibald Miller and Allan
Simpson left for home and Robert Ross took charge at Bandawe.[29]

1880

The Bandawe Journal came to an end on 23rd April 1880, and was not resumed until 1st April the next year; by then preparations were in hand to transfer the headquarters of the Mission from Cape Maclear to Bandawe, which was considered to have a better climate. It was not markedly more healthy, but its soil was good, it had a large population round about, and the Atonga were friendly.

In 1880 the 26th April brought the fifth anniversary of Laws' ordination and he made a special entry in his diary:

Five years show little work done. Yet God has blessed and encouraged me in the past. To his name be the glory and the praise. Of those who took part in my ordination services Dr Duff and Mr Bell have both been called away, perhaps more - five graves at Livingstonia and I am spared. O God, grant me new zeal, enthusiasm and plodding earnestness and perseverance.[30]

His prayer was certainly answered for zeal, enthusiasm and plodding perseverance are characteristic marks of Robert Laws.

Of the original seven members of the party who settled at Cape Maclear it is a remarkable fact that not one lost his life in the early days of the Mission, although all suffered from time to time quite severe bouts of fever. The reinforcing party of four who went out in 1876 were less fortunate, for Dr Black died about six months after arrival and John Gunn within four years. The five graves at Cape Maclear to which Laws refers may still be seen each marked with a cross: those of Dr Black (died 1877), John Mackay of Blantyre (died 1877), Shadrach Ngunana, from Lovedale (died 1878), along with those of George Benzie, Master of the *Ilala* for a brief two years, and of the agriculturist John Gunn, both of whom died in 1880.

Up to this time not a single African had become a Christian, partly at least because Laws was very careful not to lead anyone to take such a big decision without fully understanding what was involved. He has been criticised by those who feel that the preparation period was too long, and for keeping in his own hands the decision whether or not a particular individual should be baptized.[31] Later on, when scores of people were seeking baptism, a bottle-neck would have been created if it were insisted that either Laws himself or one of the other European ministers should examine each candidate individually, but in the early days it was surely right to be cautious. Had he been too ready to admit Africans, he might well have been accused of trying to swell the numbers at the Mission by adding the names of people who would have been called elsewhere 'rice Christians' or, in words more appropriate to the African scene, 'calico Christians.' Laws' practice of consulting the elders in a person's own village about the quality of life of those attending the catechumens' class meant that responsibility was shared with Africans who knew those concerned much more intimately than Laws often did.

However, the days of rapid church growth lay in the future. In the meantime the first request for baptism came from Albert Namalambe. He had come to Cape Maclear as the servant of one of the Makololo princes who were sent there to learn to read and write,[32] and had himself done so well at school that he was awarded a prize in the highest class in June 1879. That prize-giving took place during the period of Laws' absence, and Mr Stewart addressed the scholars. The prizes were not of the kind associated with such occasions in Scotland, but included a variety of things such as handkerchiefs, pocket knives, Jews harps, whistles, neckties, brooches and earrings.[33]

Albert Namalambe often travelled to one of the outlying villages on a Sunday to speak to the people there about Christ; he took an increasing share of work in the school, and worked closely with Laws on his translation of St Matthew' Gospel.[34]

When Albert told Laws in February 1881 of his desire to be baptized as a Christian, his only doubt was whether or not he was fit to take the step. 'His daily life is the answer', writes Laws in his diary.[35]

Sunday 27th March was fixed for Albert's baptism, a red-letter day for the Mission giving evidence of the first fruits of the harvest so long awaited, and of no less significance for the peoples of Central Africa as one of their own number, without coercion of any kind and without any hope of reward beyond the joy of committal to Christ, made his profession of faith.

On the previous Sunday, Dr Laws had intimated that Albert Namalambe would be baptized that day, and a large number of people assembled in the school since there was no church building. Dr Laws gave an address on the fundamentals of Christianity and its two signs, Baptism and the Lord's Supper, and then, before administering the sacrament of Baptism, asked Albert to address those present. This Namalambe did, telling them the reasons for his faith and urging them to follow his example. 'His address,' writes Laws, 'was manly, outspoken, yet respectful in the manner he spoke to the older people present.'[36]

Five months later the Mission Journal recorded that on 28th August, 'Albert Namalambe sat down at the Lord's Table for the first time', seven people in all taking Communion on that occasion.[37]

MAP 2.

9 THE MOVE TO BANDAWE

WEST COAST DESCRIBED - BANDAWE BEST SITE - TRANSFER OF HQ -
SERVICES HELD; SCHOOL BEGUN - CHRISTMAS DAY - *ILALA* TRANSFERRED
TO ALC - NEUTRALITY IN TRIBAL QUARRELS - THREATS OF ATTACK -
ANGONI & ATONGA WORSHIP TOGETHER - LAND FOR THE MISSION - VISIT
TO ANGONILAND - M'MBELWA SENDS FOR MISSIONARIES - KOYI REMAINS
ON HIS OWN - MVULA BAPTISED - HANNINGTON INVALIDED -
W.P.JOHNSON SEEKS MEDICAL CARE - WORK AT CAPE MACLEAR -
BAPTISMS & CHRISTIAN MARRIAGES - MEDICAL WORK - *MWAVI* ORDEAL
AGAIN - ATONGA & TUMBUKA BUILD ROAD - SCHOOL BUILDING BEGUN
- CHRISTIAN OUTREACH

Once the Home Committee agreed that the Mission headquarters
should be moved from Cape Maclear, it was left to Laws to make the
final decision as to place and date. Considerations which influenced
him are likely to have been very much those described by James
Stewart in The Record for August 1880. There Mr Stewart carefully
described the land right along the west coast, from M'pemba's in the
south to the north end of the Lake, taking account of the soil, the
density of the population, the availability of good anchorages, and
the likelihood of the area being healthy or not. He concluded that the
choice lay between Bandawe and the Rukuru valley much further
north, and for the present favoured Bandawe. The construction of
a short breakwater would make it a rival to Kota-Kota as a port from
which to cross to the east side of the Lake, and this might strike a
blow against the slave trade which flourished from Kota-Kota.[1]

It is doubtful whether Bandawe was really more healthy than
Cape Maclear. In the six years from 1875 until the move to Bandawe
in 1881, out of 31 Europeans and Africans employed by the Livingstonia
Mission, four (plus Mr Mackay of the Blantyre Mission) had died at
Cape Maclear by 1881, and three had been invalided home. By
comparison, in the six years after the move to Bandawe, out of 30
Europeans and Africans serving the Mission - some in Bandawe,
some in Angoniland - nine (including Mrs Kerr Cross) died in the
field and four were invalided home).[2]

On 29th March, the Tuesday after Albert had been baptized, Laws left Cape Maclear for Bandawe after breakfast;[3] by 9th April enough ground had been cleared at the new site for the line of the station to be laid out.[4] On Sunday 10th the practice was begun of hoisting a flag to indicate that it was the Lord's Day, and as an invitation to those nearby to come to worship. Many did attend morning worship that day. An English service was held in the evening.[5]

Dr Laws spent three weeks at Bandawe. When he and Mrs Laws returned to Cape Maclear, he left James Sutherland the agriculturalist engaged on road-making, and Robert Reid the carpenter putting a roof on a shop. On Sundays both conducted services.[6]

The actual transfer of Mission headquarters to Bandawe took place on 27th October 1881, when Robert and Margaret Laws arrived there accompanied by a number of boys from the Bandawe area who had been at school at Cape Maclear.[7] The name 'Livingstonia' was now applied to the station at Bandawe.

Dr Laws recorded in his diary that 'Sutherland and McCallum had made great progress in building and must have been working hard.' (Peter McCallum, a recent arrival, was a carpenter).[8] Robert Reid was ill and Dr Laws thought it best that he should return home. The engineer, Mr J.A.Paterson, also went home at this time. Both had served for three years.[9]

On Sunday 30th October some 6-700 were present at the service at Bandawe. Later in the day Peter McCallum and Albert Namalambe conducted a meeting at one of the neighbouring villages while Dr Laws held another among a number of refugees.[10] School was opened next day with over 40 present at half an hour's notice; other 60 came in the next few days. Each day started with a Bible lesson; after that the alphabet was taught in small groups with the help of 7 Africans.[11]

As the rains were expected very soon, Dr Laws began to help the artisans with the bricklaying:

> They deserve encouragement after the effort they have made. I am keen to get the young teachers also in a regular course of instruction in manual labour of some kind. I therefore took Albert, Dan, Marengo and Iodi on the work of bricklaying along with me, telling them my reasons for doing so, that they might be strong in body and fitted to give manual instruction as well as in reading and the like.[12]

Bandawe was on a promontory jutting out into the Lake about 100 feet up, and by the time the steamer brought Dr and Mrs Hannington, new arrivals, and William Koyi, returning from Lovedale with his wife, a few days before Christmas, three buildings had been completed and one was in course of erection, namely a workshop, a house for Dr Laws, a store which was the temporary home of the artisans, and a manse.[13]

Christmas Day was a Sunday and over 1,000 were present at an open air service conducted by Dr Laws and addressed also by William Koyi. In the afternoon eight services were held nearby. Dr Hannington accompanied Dr Laws to three successive villages while Sutherland went with Koyi, and McCallum with Namalambe, to others. At the English service in the evening Dr Laws spoke on the text 'Glory to God in the highest, on earth peace, goodwill to men.'[14]

Some time after this, the *Ilala* was transferred from the Livingstonia Mission to the African Lakes Company on terms agreed at the General Assembly; the ship was to be available for the transmission of letters and stores on behalf of the Mission at stated intervals.[15]

One of the most difficult things was to convince the Atonga chiefs like Marenga, whose village was nearest to Bandawe, Mankambira whose village lay about 3 hours journey to the north, and Fuka, who lived a little to the south, that the friendship of the missionaries did not mean that they would take their side in quarrels with other tribes, or fight with them against the marauding Angoni. Laws emphasised that they must settle their own quarrels 'as if there were no English there', urging them to send messengers to confer with representatives of the Angoni.[16] Rumours of impending attacks persisted. In November Laws had set out to see the Angoni chiefs, with Albert Namalambe and Mvula, unarmed. Laws felt that he could not order them to go with him into a situation which might be one of considerable danger but they declared that if it was in his heart to go they would go with him: 'As well die with you as at home when the Angoni come.'[17]

In fact no contact was made with the Angoni on this occasion, and when Laws asked his two supporters if they understood why the missionaries would not fight the Angoni, Mvula answered that it was because, when Christ was put to death he had power to destroy those who killed him but did not do so because he loved them.[18]

The chiefs however had not reached the same understanding. In their anger at the missionaries' refusal to support them by force of arms they ordered their men and women who had been working for the Mission to stop doing so: threatening to burn down the men's houses and to beat the women if they disobeyed. For a time the situation was so tense that Laws set a watch to guard against surprise attack.[19]

On Sunday 12th February 1882, there was a large attendance at worship. Chipatula and Njomani, Angoni chiefs, and Marenga and Katonga, Atonga chiefs, were among those present that day and Laws noted in his diary: 'Enemies met at peace in the House of God.'[20]

On the following Wednesday a long *mrandu*, or discussion about a point of disagreement, took place, many of those present being heavily armed. They met on the verandah of Dr Laws' house, with Angoni headsmen occupying the area to the right of the door and 14 Atonga chiefs occupying the area to the left. Dr Laws, Mr Stewart, Dr Hannington and Mr Koyi were in the centre. A chair was placed for Chipatula, who spoke for the Angoni. When he had finished speaking the chair was transferred to the opposite side for Chinyenta, and, in Laws' words, 'By this means, confusion was avoided.'[21]

The Atonga agreed to send cattle to the Mission, for Dr Laws to hand over to the Angoni, promising that there would be peace. Both sides seem to have been satisfied for the time being.[22]

Meantime the Mission continued to acquire land from the local chiefs. From Fuka, at Konde, Laws records that they 'Bought the hills on the north side of the stream and its foundations and tributaries,' agreeing to pay '12 yards of white calico, 4 yards blue serampore and 4 yards handkerchiefs.' Laws adds, 'This gives us all the wood on the hills.'[23] It was a very good bargain for the Mission, but Laws would not have seen anything unfair in it, as nothing was done for the personal gain of anyone connected with the Mission; their whole aim was to further the well being of those living in the area. Next day they bought '30 gardens (or fields) costing 61 yards white calico, and 3 yards blue,' and another 22 gardens the following day.[24]

In April, Dr Laws set out for Angoniland accompanied by Mr Koyi and Dr Hannington, and found it 'very cold up in the hills'.[25] Chipatula was friendly. His wife was undergoing a difficult labour, and Laws seems to have given help. This was not easy - by Angoni custom, even a husband does not enter a woman's house during her confinement. Laws must have found a way, for William Koyi reported that the women were 'speaking loudly in our praise', and on the next Sunday, 30th April, Chipatula called all his people together for a service of worship.[26]

But a week later M'mbelwa sent for the missionaries, and they found themselves seated for a long time in the heat before being brought into the coolness of a hut. Mtwaro and Mahalule were seated inside along with 30 headmen of varying rank. A guard was set so that no one should approach. It quickly became very close inside. They were told that M'mbelwa was ill and had sent his brother Mtwaro to hear the missionaries. The latter explained that they had come with the Word of God, but that the Bible was not to be regarded as a charm but had to be received into the heart before it could help a man, just as maize had to be eaten before it could give a man strength.[27]

The Diary tells us little more until we come to 18th June, when we learn that 150 people at Chipatula's village attended Sunday service and listened with close attention to the exposition of John 3. A start was made with a school, and Chipatula himself and Ntsikane learned fast. Suddenly there came a message from M'mbelwa that he did not wish a school to operate until he himself had received the News. He was unwilling to have his own children taught and he forbade preaching in the villages.[28] Fortunately William Koyi was willing to be left on his own in Angoniland. As Laws wrote in his diary:

William Koyi is full of the true missionary spirit, and... thinks he would have more freedom of speech in answering M'mbelwa than at present when he might in any way implicate me or those here. In this his prudence and discretion are shown.[29]

The Record of November 1882 mentions the baptism at Bandawe on 16th July of James Brown Mvula, who, although he could not read, regularly went with Mr McCallum to help conduct village services on Sundays.[30] Albert Namalambe was delighted to have an African companion to share with him in the membership of the Church in Central Africa. Professor Henry Drummond, for whom Mvula acted as guide the following year spoke years later of his reliability and added: 'I have never heard anything more touching than the prayers of James Mvula.'[31]

In July, Dr Hannington had to leave for home owing to continuing ill health. Laws accompanied him and his wife as far as Mandala and would have gone on with them to Quilimane if necessary.[32] He returned to Bandawe in August, and moved with Mrs Laws into their new house there.[33]

The following month the Revd W.P.Johnson of the UMCA, who served for nearly as long as Laws himself, came across from the east side in the *Ilala* for medical care. On a previous occasion he had suffered greatly from a very restricted diet and had developed severe ulcers on his hands. On that occasion he managed, with a struggle, to make the long journey from Mwembe to Monkey Bay and from there sent a message to Cape Maclear telling of his plight. Dr Laws at once sent the steamer to bring him to the Mission station, and in Johnson's own words, 'Then my troubles were at an end.'[34] Now, some 18 months later, he was ill again and on arrival at Bandawe was so weak that he had to be carried up from the beach in a *machila*. Proper feeding and medical care greatly improved his health. Three weeks later he was able to leave for Chitesi on the east coast.[35]

Now that Bandawe had become the centre of the Mission's work, Cape Maclear was regarded as an outstation but the work was not neglected. There Chimlolo was headman, Andrew Mwana Njobu conducted the Sunday services, Sunday School and the Wednesday Prayer Meeting, and Komani ran the Day School under the supervision of Chimlolo. Harry Zamatonga was in charge of the store, and the *Ilala* called from time to time.[36]

At Bandawe, five months after the baptism of Mvula, three more of the Mission helpers asked to be baptized; the ceremony took place on Sunday 17th December. On this day, Charles Nkonde, Andrew Mwana Njobu and John Kurukuru having spoken briefly of their past life and of coming to know the truth in Jesus Christ, made their profession of faith and were baptized by Dr Laws.[37]

Early in the New Year, Albert Namalambe went to Cape Maclear on the *Ilala* to bring back Jessie to be his wife. She was not yet baptized, but that followed a year later. Albert was accompanied by one or two friends, and when the steamer returned to Bandawe on 29th January, there were five brides among its passengers. Laws' diary records that on 8th February he married Albert to Jessie, Andrew Njobu to Maraia, George Fairly to Mbafumira, John to Janie and Lijunja to Ann.[38]

Medical work continued and from time to time Dr Laws had some severe surgical cases to deal with. Many made a good recovery but not all were willing to accept surgical treatment. One man who required amputation at the knee refused to allow it. The doctor's comment was 'How shall I walk seemed... of more importance than "Shall I live?"' The best Laws could do for him was to put on a long splint.[39] He himself was suffering from fever and also developed opthalmia, having apparently caught the infection from one of those he was treating.[40]

News came in about this time that two people had been forced to undergo the *mwavi* ordeal. One died while the other vomited up the poison. This led to a quarrel in which Mwanda's village was attacked and burned; Mwanda in turn was preparing to fight Chimbano when Laws persuaded him to agree to join Chimbano and himself to discuss the problem.[41]

The following day Laws showed chiefs Chikoko and Fuka how the *mwavi* ordeal could be manipulated. The Doctor urged them to put down the practice of 'trial by ordeal' which was by no means infallible, but the chiefs maintained that the Atonga people insisted on it. Probably Dr Laws felt that he had taken the matter as far as it was possible to go at that point.[42]

If Laws felt disappointment over that issue, his heart must have been uplifted at the end of the same week when, on Sunday 6th May, James Brown Mvula and Andrew Mwana Njobu sat at the Lord's Table for the first time and received Communion.[43]

There was encouragement too in the response Laws achieved to his pleas for help in the construction of a road in the Bandawe area and with the building of schools in the neighbouring villages. He had many conversations with the Atonga chiefs, such as Marenga, Katonga, and Fuka, and with the Tumbuka chief Mbiwi about these matters, and, on 4th June, 122 workers began on the road and 'wrought most heartily'. They had agreed to give three days' work free. The Mission was to pay them for the remaining working days of the fortnight which they had undertaken to work on the road and by the end of the month it had been completed as far as Kande.[44]

Dr Laws persuaded Marenga's people to help in building the school, for the sake of their children, and after considerable talk, 25 to 30 men began to bring in trees. By 18th July 'Progress was visible' and at the end of that month, Fuka undertook to build a school in his village.[45]

On the first Tuesday of each month, when the Livingstonia Mission was particularly remembered in prayer by people in the Church at home, Laws started holding a Missionary Meeting at Bandawe at which he or one of his colleagues would speak about missionary work in other places, particularly other places in Africa.

On 5th June, it was of David Livingstone that Laws spoke. Messrs Smith and Sutherland also gave addresses and Albert Namalambe gave an account of the work he had been doing. The collections taken during the past three months amounted to 10/7d (about 53p) and Laws proposed that they should use the money to support Charles Nkonde in the work he was engaged in at Cape Maclear. It was agreed that he should receive 2/- per month (10p) if he conducted the services at Cape Maclear on Sundays and took the Wednesday meeting, and 3/- per month if in addition he went on other three days of the week to conduct meetings in other villages roundabout. Each month he was to send an account of his work by the steamer. This arrangement would leave Charles free on the remaining days of the week to cultivate his own ground, which would be his main means of subsistence.[46]

Dr Laws was well aware of the significance of the decision taken. This is shown by the comment made in the Bandawe Station Journal which reads, 'Thus the native Church on Lake Nyassa has taken its first decided step towards self-support and self-extension.'[47]

10 MEN OF THE BOOK

All this time, while carrying on the day to day work of the Mission, using his medical and surgical skill, pleading with the chiefs to abandon the use of *mwavi*, trying to persuade Atonga and Angoni to settle their disputes by discussion rather than by fighting, endeavouring to obtain labour for the making of roads and the building of schools, and taking his share in the conduct of daily prayers and Sunday services, Dr Laws was engaged in reducing to writing what had hitherto been a spoken language only, and then beginning to translate the New Testament into it.

In his *Reminiscences*, written more than half a century later, Laws gives us some insights into the difficulties involved.[1] 'Nyanja was spoken,' he writes, 'in the Shire Highlands and at some of the villages at Cape Maclear, whereas Yao was the predominating language at Mponda's, the chief village at the south end of the Lake.'

Laws considered that Nyanja was easier for English speaking people to pick up, and as many Africans were bilingual he thought that Nyanja would be the best *lingua franca* for the whole Lake District.[2] On going out to Africa the party had been supplied with short vocabularies and grammatical notes, prepared by two members of the UMCA, and a dictionary published by a Mr Rebman of Mombasa. These were the only helps available in Chinyanja.[3]

Laws had been unfortunate, when travelling out, not to meet Dr Bleek at Cape Town Library, for the latter was an authority on

African language and Laws reckoned that half an hour with Dr Bleek
would have saved him two years of labour.[4] He had assumed, for
example, that the plural of a noun would be formed by some
alteration to its ending, as in English, Latin or Greek, but the Bantu
group of languages operates on a quite different principle, which it
took Laws many weeks to understand.

As early as he could Laws began to translate the Lord's Prayer,
and the Ten Commandments, and to make a summary of the
parables and miracles of the New Testament. This paved the way for
the translation of Mark, 'being the shortest and simplest of the
Gospels'. Laws was very aware of his own shortcomings as a linguist
and made several fresh starts.[5] John Moir and William Koyi's
translation of Mark into Chinyanja was ready for printing by the
end of January 1881. Laws himself completed Matthew's Gospel by
March 17th of that year, and began work on Luke the following day.[6]

A thousand copies of Mark were printed by the Lovedale
press but when the edition was on its way back to Livingstonia all
but 10 copies were lost as a result of a tribal raid on a Shire River
Portuguese station. Replacements were printed in Scotland by the
National Bible Society, the cost being met by a special gift, and 1050
copies were sent out some time in 1884, or early 1885.[7] The fourth
Gospel had already been printed by the NBSS the previous year.[8]

Laws was aiming at the production of the whole New
Testament in Chinyanja, and much of his translation work was done
with the help of the more advanced pupils at school from whom he
would receive guidance as to the use of particular words or phrases.
The translations made were tested by being used at public worship
daily and those attending were encouraged to draw attention to
anything that appeared to them to be a mistake.[9]

Some extracts from Laws' Diary for 1883 will give an idea of
how steadily he pursued this work:

March 1st	Translation work getting on.
5th	Finished copying St John's Gospel. Began at Romans 10,16; Acts 9,1. None done. By translating 25 columns a week (R.V.) (D.V.) and no hindrances - N.T. in 4 months.
April 13th	Finished 1 Corinth. and began 2 Corinth.
21st	Finished 2 Corinthians.
23rd	Began Galatians.
24th	Finished Galatians and began Ephesians.[10]

In the Bandawe Station Journal the entry of May 11th has the words 'First draft of N.T. in Chinyanja completed. To God be all the praise.'[11]

Up to this time the Annual Reports of the National Bible Society of Scotland had spoken a great deal about the work being done by the Society in places like Egypt, India, and China, but had said almost nothing about any work in Africa, which was represented by only four and a half lines in the 1879 report.[12] It was some years before Africa featured more adequately in the Annual Reports of the NBSS, and when it did so it was in no small measure due to the work of Laws and the Livingstonia Mission.

At the Annual Meeting of the NBSS in March 1879, Dr Stewart drew attention to a phrase he had used the previous year to distinguish himself and other missionaries from traders, hunters, or Europeans who were in Africa for some other reason. He had described himself and his colleagues then as 'Men of the Book.' The expression delighted Laws who exclaimed, 'I am glad of that phrase for it will really be descriptive of us.'[13]

The phrase drew attention to the importance placed by the Scottish missionaries on church members being able to read, and of there being copies of the Scriptures available for them in their own tongue. At a later stage in the Mission's history Dr Laws was reluctant to admit new communicants unless they could read. When younger people sought to become members of the church, Laws was apt to insist on a degree of literacy, but he did not press it with those who were older.[14]

The Africans themselves were eager to acquire a copy of a Gospel, or a portion of Scripture, in the vernacular, and were willing to pay for them out of their very limited wages.[15]

In the earliest days of the Mission Laws had been frequently on the move. Now, with headquarters at Bandawe, although his days of what he called 'itinerating' were not over, he had a much more settled spell. Certainly, in the first seven months of 1883 Laws himself preached on a Sunday evening at the English service at Bandawe on 27 out of the 30 Sundays involved. Copies of these addresses survive,[16] taken down perhaps by Mrs Laws, at the time of their delivery. They would last for about 30 minutes, and it is noted on one of the sermons that the speaking rate was 87 words per minute,[17] which indicates a slow, deliberate form of delivery.

These sermons* were delivered to a congregation of five or six white people, and perhaps a handful of Africans, but, for all that, the addresses are most carefully prepared. As an example, take the sermon Laws preached on the text, 'Come unto me all ye that labour and are heavy laden, and I will give you rest', in which he dealt in turn with what he called 'The Burden, The Promise, and The Invitation'. In the middle section, dealing with the Promise, he says that rest and labour are counterparts of each other, and goes on to make this very revealing statement, characteristic of one who was never detected in idleness even for the briefest of periods: 'A person who has nothing to do is to be pitied. Rest becomes his burden.'[18]

In this sermon he urges that for those weary of their failures the first step is back to God. That is why the Invitation comes first in the text. Laws ends on a note of gentle pleading: 'Come to me, weary wanderer, that you may receive a Father's Blessing, and share a brother's smile.'[19]

On another occasion Laws spoke of the number of people in different lands who think of God as one whose anger must be appeased, and contrasted this with the Christian God, declaring, 'Salvation is beyond ourselves, rooted in God's love and in the finished work of Christ.'[20]

By October 1883 Dr Laws had been in Central Africa for eight years, and Margaret had been there to share the last four of them with him. The Home Committee was well aware that his furlough was overdue and had agreed two years previously that Mrs Laws' passage home should be paid for as well as his.[21] The difficulty was that there was no one to take his place. By this time 27 Europeans had been on the staff of the Mission for longer or shorter periods, but only three were still in the field. The longest serving of them, James Sutherland, an agriculturist from Wick, had come out in 1880, while Peter McCallum, carpenter, and Donald Munro, builder had joined the staff in 1881.[22] The breakdown in health of Dr Hannington, who had to return home in 1882 after only seven months,[23] removed one who might have taken Laws's place as head of the Mission during his furlough.

The Committee did not find it easy to recruit someone qualified both as doctor and as minister and so sought to find doctor and minister separately. George Johnston had been carpenter with

* For further study of Laws' sermons, see the author's article, "Robert Laws as Preacher" in the Bulletin of the Scottish Institute of Missionary Studies (New Series no.3-4, 1985-87)

the first party, and on return had engaged in medical studies; he was well on in his course and the Committee agreed, in August 1882, to approach him. He was not due to qualify, however, until the spring of the following year, and accordingly, without abandoning the idea of recruiting Johnston, the Committee decided to seek another doctor as well.[24]

Johnston was very willing to return to Livingstonia to enable Laws to have his furlough, and was quite prepared to serve under Laws when the latter returned to the field. He had, however, some criticisms to make of the Mission and sought assurance that, if a minister without previous experience of Central Africa were to be sent out, he himself would not be regarded as subordinate to the new appointee simply because the latter was an ordained man.[25]

In March 1883 the Committee resolved to appoint Johnston for five years with a possible break after three. He was to be in charge during Laws' absence but would otherwise be under Dr Laws.[26] This last provision was acceptable to Johnston but he was disappointed that the Committee gave no answers to the questions he had raised. He had travelled to Glasgow at Christmas, 1882, in the hope of discussing the situation but the Committee refused to see him.[27] In the end, Johnston's health broke down - he suffered digestive disorders - and he was unable to go to Africa.[28]

That George Johnston and Robert Laws were on good personal terms and that Laws thought highly of his former colleague, is shown by a letter Johnston wrote to Laws in March 1883, thanking Laws for sending him £40 to help with his medical course. He expresses appreciation of Laws' generosity but explains that he does not require the money and will put it on deposit receipt until Laws' return.[29] Johnston's health improved later and he became a doctor in Liverpool.[30]

By June 1883 both a doctor and a minister had been found - Dr William Scott, and the Revd J.A.Bain. Both are in the list of staff included in the minutes of the Glasgow Committee for 26th June, and the same list gives the salaries being paid at this time:[31]

Dr Laws and Dr Scott	£300, married
Revd J.A. Bain	£225, unmarried
Mr C.F. Smith, Teacher, and	
Mr Sutherland, Agriculturist	£135, incl. rations
Mr Koyi	£105, incl. rations
Carpenter (Peter McCallum)	£115, incl. rations

In terms of purchasing power, £1 in the 1880s would be the equivalent of at least £50 in 1990. If that is so, and it may well be an underestimate, then Dr Laws and Dr Scott were receiving, in today's terms, £15,000, while the highest paid among those who were neither ministers or doctors, received the equivalent of £6,750. The difference lay not only in the salaries received but in terms of the contracts under which they served, and the different ways in which different members of the staff were regarded.*

The Revd J.A.Bain, and Dr and Mrs William Scott arrived at Bandawe on the *Ilala* on 20th September 1883.[32] They were accompanied by the Revd Henry Drummond, Lecturer in Natural History at the Free Church College, Glasgow, who was inducted as Professor there the following year. In his book *Tropical Africa*, published in 1889, Professor Drummond wrote vividly but misleadingly of the situation at Cape Maclear, giving the impression that the station there had been entirely abandoned.[33] Certainly, the headquarters of the Mission had been moved to Bandawe but, as we saw in the last chapter, work at Cape Maclear continued.[34] On another occasion, after work had been going on for some time at M'mbelwa's village in Angoniland, the Home Committee learned that a new station was to be opened at Mweniwanda's, a good many miles further north. When the Secretary enquired if this meant that the new station would supersede that at M'mbelwa's, Laws emphatically replied, 'Certainly not... "Forward" must be understood to mean "Hold all behind as well as simply advance"'[35] It was the same at Cape Maclear; Mission headquarters had moved to Bandawe but the work at the Cape had not been abandoned.

Two days after Mr Bain and Dr Scott reached Bandawe, the *Ilala* returned from a trip to Nkata Bay with her ensign at half mast. High seas prevented anyone from coming ashore immediately but Mr Harkness, the engineer, wrote on a board the news that Mr James Stewart, the civil engineer, had died.[36] He had been at work on the Stevenson Road, north of Lake Malawi and between it and Lake Tanganyika. Donald Munro who had been working with him sent Dr Laws an account of his death after six days illness, and of his burial beside Captain Gowans at Karonga.[37] This was news which must

*For a detailed study of *Contracts of Employment in the first Thirty Years of the Livingstonia Mission*, see article by the author in 'Records of the Scottish Church History Society', vol xxiii pt 1, 1987-88

have caused Robert Laws a great deal of sorrow, for James Stewart and he had established an excellent relationship with each other.

The way was now open for Dr and Mrs Laws to take their furlough, and the entry in the Bandawe Journal for 1st December 1883 reads: 'Dr Laws handed over the Journal to Dr Scott.'[38]

At the morning service on the Sunday before he left Dr Laws baptized Dan, the teacher, and his own cook, Kifanjanja, and also Jessie, wife of Albert Namalambe, and Maria, who was married to Andrew. The two young men were both aged 20, and in the face of the congregation they gave their reasons for seeking baptism. Their desire was to obey and serve God now that they had learned of him and of his true nature.[39] In the afternoon the Lord's Supper was celebrated and communion was received by 11 Europeans and 7 Africans, including the 4 who had been baptized in the morning.[40]

There were now nine African Christians after eight years of hard work. It may seem a small return but it was the first-fruits of a much greater harvest to come. Laws must have sensed this and he was certainly entitled to set out on his first furlough with a feeling of quiet satisfaction at what had been accomplished.

Chiefs Chimbano, Fuka, and Marenga came to say 'Goodbye' to Dr and Mrs Laws and they did so with much sorrow. It was a pleasant testimony to his work, and still more to their regard for him as a person, that his temporary absence was so much felt.[41] At last, at 3pm on Tuesday 4th December, the steamer left Bandawe for Cape Maclear taking Dr and Mrs Laws on the first stage of their journey home.

The first furlough lasted for close on three years but it was far from being a time of inactivity. That would have been entirely out of character for Robert Laws, and his time at home was, in one way or another, almost entirely devoted to the affairs of the Mission. A considerable portion of that time was given to seeing the Nyanja version of the New Testament through the press on behalf of the NBSS. Laws was certainly entitled to consider himself one of the 'Men of the Book.'

11 FURLOUGH, AND PERIL ON RETURN

ROME - GLASGOW & EDINBURGH - VARIED ENGAGEMENTS - PROOFS OF
CHINYANJA NT - BERLIN CONGRESS - IDEALS NOT ATTAINED - KERR
CROSS, WALTER EMSLIE & FIANCÉES - *WOMEN'S WORK IN HEATHEN
LANDS* - *LIVINGSTONIA* - PRICE OF SLAVES - DUEL WITH MISS RAINY -
FINANCIAL APPEAL - ENGLISH AUXILIARY - CORRESPONDENCE & USE OF
MONEY - RETURN TO AFRICA - AMELIA NYASA BORN - KERR CROSS &
ELMSLIE MARRY - WELCOME BACK TO BANDAWE - SCHOOL PRIZES -
MISSION COUNCIL - BAIN & MACINTOSH TO MWENIWANDA - LAWS &
GOSSIP VISIT CHIKUSI - MRS LAWS & BABY REACH BANDAWE - KOYI'S
DEATH - ANGONI CHIEFS BAN WAR; PERMIT SCHOOLS & WORSHIP - LAWS
& M'MBELWA - GEORGE WILLIAMS & ELMSLIE DISAGREE - DEATHS OF
MRS KERR CROSS & MACINTOSH - LAWS AS ARBITER - MCCURRIE'S
OFFENCE - AMELIA BAPTISED - HENRY & MCINTYRE TO LIVLEZI VALLEY
- DANGER AT BANDAWE - PEACE

Dr and Mrs Laws had travelled home, not by the Cape Route, but
via Cairo, Naples and Rome where Mrs Laws' eldest brother, the
Revd Gordon Gray, had been minister of the Scots Kirk since 1881.
He was a bachelor and for many years Isabella, the oldest daughter
in the Gray family kept house for him while Amy, the youngest
daughter, often made her home with them. From Rome the Laws
went to Florence, arriving in Edinburgh near the end of April, 1884.[1]

An old friend, George Milne of Aberdeen, had written as far
back as the previous September urging that the Laws' first public
engagement at home should be in Aberdeen under the auspices of the
UP Young Men's Missionary Association.[2] No doubt Laws would
have been happy to accept this, but he was plunged at once into a
series of meetings in Glasgow and Edinburgh. He went to the
Livingstonia Sub-Committee in Glasgow on May 2nd,[3] preached in
Bristo UP Church on Sunday 4th,[4] was at the UP Synod on May 5th[5],
and the FMC of the Free Church on May 6th.[6]

Mr James Thin had asked Laws to be his guest at 22 Lauder
Road.[7] They did not avail themselves of this kind offer for, after the

death of Margaret's father, Mrs Gray had moved to Edinburgh and taken up house at 14 Upper Gray Street, along with her daughter Mary. Robert and Margaret spent a good deal of their furlough there.

Laws, at 33 not yet a legend, but with a considerable reputation, was in demand as a speaker. His friend George Johnston warned him not to accept all the invitations that came to him,[8] but he still undertook a heavy programme of engagements.

When visiting small communities with several churches he preferred to speak twice rather than once, and three times was better still! He seems to have declined an invitation to Lanark because an evening service could not be guaranteed.[9]

He regularly attended the Livingstonia Committee in Glasgow, and was equally ready to address the Juvenile Missionary Association of Free St George's,[10] the Foundry Boys' Religious Society,[11] the General Assembly of the Free Church,[12] a meeting of the NBSS,[13] or to travel to Belfast for a meeting of the Pan-Presbyterial Council,[14] or London to address the people of Highbury Park Church,[15] who provided the salary of William Koyi.[16] Laws could be speaking in Broughton Place UP Church, Edinburgh,[17] or addressing a conference in the Presbytery of Strathbogie.[18] In August Dr and Mrs Laws established themselves at Auchattie, Banchory, and Laws devoted six hours daily to correcting proofs of the Chinyanja New Testament, which Morrison and Gibb were printing for the NBSS.[19]

Towards the end of 1884 the Congress of Powers (a dozen European nations, plus the USA and Turkey) was convening at Berlin; the Livingstonia Committee and the ALC thought it would be desirable to make representations about the continuing evils of the slave trade in Central Africa, and the need to consider the well-being of the native population. Accordingly Dr Laws, along with Mr Ewing and Mr Fred Moir of the ALC, went to Berlin to give the Congress

> the fullest information regarding the eastern commercial territory and to guard the interests of our missions, as well as to maintain the system which has hitherto kept destructive liquors out of the Nyassa region.[20]

The powers present pledged themselves 'to seek the well-being of the native peoples' and committed themselves to the following statement:

> Each power binds itself to employ all the means at its disposal for putting an end to this [slave] trade and for punishing those who engage in it.[21]

The idea of seeking the well-being of the native peoples was splendid but what followed in Central Africa was a tragic negation of this resolution. Cecil Rhodes' regime, says Dr Fergus MacPherson:

> was ruthless, shattered the social and economic structures of the Rhodesias, relentlessly taxed people who did not have a money economy, and drove thousands down to South Africa by 'forced labour'.[22]

One of those who volunteered to serve in Livingstonia at this time was the Revd Kerr Cross who, like Laws, was qualified both in medicine and divinity. He was anxious that his fiancée, Miss Gibson of Glasgow, should accompany him when he sailed, but Laws was strongly against this and the outcome was that Dr Kerr Cross went out on his own, and Miss Gibson, along with Miss Grant of Wick, who was engaged to another recent recruit, Dr Walter Elmslie, travelled out with Dr and Mrs Laws the following year.[23]

A small booklet *Women's Work in Heathen Lands - Livingstonia* was published in January 1886 by Parlane of Paisley, price 1d.[24] After mentioning that in all types of work African women and girls got more than their fair share to do, Laws said that direct educational work among women began in the Nyasa area in 1876 when a group of women asked E.D.Young to take them to Cape Maclear. There they were taught to sew by Mr Gunn, Mapas Ntintili, William Koyi and others, and after 1879, by Mrs Laws, and, briefly, by Miss Jane Waterston.[25] When the garments made were for the Mission a small payment was made to the women, and between April and December of 1880 they had made 360 garments in all.[26]

In this booklet Laws gives the current price of slaves in 1880:[27]

A strong young man	40 yards of calico
Young unmarried schoolgirl	56
Young mother	36
plus child	4
Elderly man or woman	4
Toothless old man	2

It was in connection with this pamphlet that Laws suffered one of the few diplomatic defeats of his life, and that at the hands of a lady. His eagerness to raise funds for Livingstonia led him to arrange with Messrs J.& R.Parlane to print an appeal for £20,000 for Livingstonia on the front cover. This led to the strongest possible objections being raised by Miss Rainy, sister of Principal Rainy of New College, who was Convener of the Women's Committee which published the booklet. She made it plain to Laws, with courtesy but complete firmness, that no such appeal must appear on any subsequent issue. The Booklet was one of a series dealing with 'Female Education in all our Stations' and if the author of each booklet were to make an appeal for his own particular field that would be thoroughly confusing. Miss Rainy added that there was goodwill towards the Livingstonia Mission, and that a grant had been made by her Committee towards the work among the women there.[28]

There were nine Europeans on the staff at this time plus two Africans, and an appeal for £22,500 was made to cover the next five years.[29] The appeal was not confined to Scotland, and The Record of May 1886 records that £8,000 had been raised, mainly from the west of Scotland, and that 'large hearted Scots in London, Liverpool and Manchester had suggested the formation of an English auxiliary' to continue support for the Mission.[30]

In a speech in support of the appeal Laws said 'Every hour 720 of our fellow men die in Africa and of these only two have ever had the opportunity of hearing about Jesus'.[31]

From Central Africa many colleagues and others wrote to Laws to keep him in touch with the situation there. Dr William Scott, who had taken his place at Bandawe, wrote to him, and Dr Kerr Cross and Dr Walter Elmslie, who left Scotland while Laws was at home both expressed appreciation for the help and advice he had given them. Of the two Africans from Lovedale, George Williams, who had come to Livingstonia in 1882, and William Koyi, who had been with the Mission since 1877, both wrote to Laws in Scotland, the former an occasional letter but the latter about once a month.[32] Almost all the letters are marked 'Answd.' along with the date on which the reply was written - usually soon after receipt.

So very little is known of the more personal side of the life of Robert Laws that it is interesting to notice that he was human enough to indulge - very occasionally - in the expenditure of money not strictly necessary. In June 1884 we find him arranging with Alex Gill, jeweller, 59 Union Street, Aberdeen, for setting four round brooches and a scarf pin,[33] possibly for Margaret, her mother Mrs Gray, her sister Mary who lived with her mother in Edinburgh, and for Isabella and Amy in Rome.

Laws was comfortably off financially by this time but he did not forget the needs of those who might experience hardship in their

University years. His cousin Alex Cruickshank wrote to thank him for £17.10s which Laws had sent to help him through his course, but as he had not needed the money, he returned it - without interest, since he felt that this would be in line with Laws' wishes.[34] Nor did Laws forget the needs of St Nicholas Lane UP Church in which he had grown up. With £5 he sent to the minister, the Rev Dr Robson purchased a new Bible, Psalter and Hymn Book for pulpit use. A few years later, when a new church was being built, Laws sent a further £20 which Dr Robson gratefully acknowledged. In a post-script to the same letter Dr Robson told Laws in what way he had used some money which the latter had left him to assist divinity students intending the mission field.[35] Nor did Laws forget the workers at Morrison and Gibb who had printed the Nyanja New Testament. To them he sent a number of African spears which were divided among the compositors, the reader, and the foreman in charge.[36]

Laws' colleagues in central Africa were men of character but they missed the leadership which Laws provided and were eager to have him back. Once the General Assembly of 1886 was over Dr and Mrs Laws set out again for Africa. Their party sailed from London on the *Garth Castle* on June 9th.[37] The furlough lasted for two years and nine months, but just over two years of that time had been spent at home, months of almost ceaseless activity in the cause of Livingstonia.

Personal happiness came to Robert and Margaret Laws when, on their way north up the Shire River, a baby girl was born on 10th August 1886,[38] not far from what was known as 'elephant marsh'. Mrs Laws had suffered at least one miscarriage while in Scotland so that the delight of herself and her husband would be all the greater. The child was called Amelia Nyasa - Amelia after her mother's youngest sister. The name Nyasa did not please its owner when she grew up and in later life she asked a friend how her father would have liked to be known all his life as 'Robert Aberdeen Laws'?[39]

Mrs Laws and the baby remained for almost three months in the neighbourhood of Blantyre so that they were not with Dr Laws when he returned to Bandawe on 28th September.[40] Dr Elmslie and Jane Grant, who had been married at Blantyre, arrived with Laws on the *Ilala*, while Dr and Mrs Kerr Cross, also recently married, reached Bandawe later the same day on the *Charles Janson* belonging to the UMCA. The African chiefs were pleased at the doctor's return and came to Bandawe to welcome him.[41]

The school holidays were due and a prize-giving ceremony was held at which Dr Laws distributed thirty one shirts and dresses as prizes. 180 pupils had attended school regularly and all present were given a tablespoonful of salt. On the Sunday after Laws' return it was estimated that as many as 3000 Africans attended worship either at Bandawe itself or in one of the villages nearby.[42]

On the following day, Monday 4th October, the first meeting of the Livingstonia Mission Council was held, in accordance with the authorisation given by the Free Church FMC,[43] Membership of the Council was, at this time, confined to ordained men and doctors. Neither teachers nor artisan missionaries were considered eligible until 1894, when limited representation was permitted to them, and no African ever had a seat on the Mission Council as such at any time.

The sederunt at the first meeting consisted of the Revd Dr Laws, the Revd J.A.Bain, the Revd Dr Kerr Cross, and Dr W.A.Elmslie.[44] After the Council Mr Bain travelled north on the *Ilala*, returning to his pioneering work at Mweniwanda's, some miles northwest of Karonga after an absence of some months. Mr Hugh MacIntosh, a carpenter who had been appointed somewhat hurriedly to the staff shortly before Dr Laws and party left Scotland, went north with him to erect a house for Dr and Mrs Cross.[45]

Chikusi, chief of what were sometimes called 'the southern Angoni' in the Livlezi Valley, had invited the missionaries some years earlier to send teachers to his village. Laws now wanted to respond, but with the rainy season due, felt he could not immediately open a station at Chikusi's. He decided to go in person to explain this and took with him Mr R.Gossip, who had recently joined the staff as bookkeeper. While Laws was absent Dr and Mrs Kerr Cross remained at Bandawe, and on his return they set out for the north.[46]

Shortly before this Mrs Laws and the baby had arrived at Bandawe. They were soon to find themselves in considerable danger.

Two pieces of news had reached Laws when he arrived at Quilimane on his return journey. One was the sad news of the death of Mr William Koyi on 4th June. This left a big gap in the missionary staff in Angoniland. For nine years Koyi had served the Mission, living for the greater part of that time among the Angoni, speaking a language which they understood and witnessing by his own life to the Christian ideals of service and humility.[47]

Dr Elmslie devoted a well deserved chapter to William Koyi when he brought out his book *Among the Wild Ngoni* in 1899,[48] and

Laws on learning of his death wrote home from Quilimane that
when Dr James Stewart had asked at Lovedale for volunteers to go
to Nyasaland in 1876 William Koyi offered himself with considerable
hesitation. He felt he had not sufficient education but was willing to
go as 'a hewer of wood and drawer of water.' Later, he wrote of
himself as having 'only half a talent' but that he was willing to use
it for Christ. 'This spirit of humility', wrote Laws, 'so alien to the
tribe to which he belonged, has been honoured of God.'[49]

Dr Kerr Cross, who had known William Koyi for less than a
year, wrote 'I believe his death will do more for these proud Angoni
than ever his life did. The Memory of "Umtesani" ("the interpreter"
or "the go-between") will now be sacred.'[50]

The other piece of news which Laws received at Quilimane
was in a letter from Dr Elmslie written on 10th May, with
understandable excitement, saying that the Angoni were to go to war
no more, and that a union between M'mbelwa and his brothers had
been agreed on. 'Best of all,' he wrote, 'the Councillors were sent to
inform us that the children were ours to teach and that they desire
us to do so, and to preach throughout the length and breadth of the
land.' He added that the chiefs had attached no stipulations at all.[51]

For Laws himself M'mbelwa continued to have great respect.
They were very different: M'mbelwa given to overindulgence in
native beer, with considerable personal vanity, and Laws a man of
austere personal habits whose whole being was devoted to furthering
the work of the Mission without thought of himself. There must
have been in each man a perception of greatness in the other - a
perception which formed a bond between them in spite of so much
in the character of each that was different. M'mbelwa had promised
Laws before the latter went on furlough that he would not attack the
Atonga without first letting them know, and he not only kept his
word but held in check some of the younger warriors who were eager
to 'blood their spears'. From time to time messengers between
Bandawe and Angoniland were attacked and, at one point, even
when the rate of pay was doubled, men could hardly be found to take
the risk of carrying letters for the Mission on that route.[52] However,
full scale war between the two tribes was kept in check although
there were many anxious moments.

After Koyi's death the only African from Lovedale now
serving with the Livingstonia Mission was George Williams who had
joined the staff in 1882. He showed special ability teaching at the

outstation at Chinyera. When some Angoni were showing hostility to Dr Elmslie in February 1886 Williams was also threatened.[53] Later, sadly, relations between Dr Elmslie and Mr Williams became strained. Basically the two men approached their work with the Angoni in totally different ways. Elmslie tended to hold rather inflexibly to what he believed to be fixed standards of conduct, while George Williams was much more ready to try to come alongside the Angoni by sharing in their tribal celebrations. Elmslie complained that Williams 'associated with the natives at beer drinking and at girls' coming of age occasions when there were native dances'.[54]

Towards the end of 1886 the spirits of the Mission staff had been greatly cast down by the news from Karonga that Mrs Cross had died after only three months in Africa.[55] She had been giving able support to her husband but her health had been poor from the start. Dr and Mrs Cross had been married for just two months. Hugh Macintosh the carpenter died shortly after this - described by Alex Bain as 'a true and faithful friend', and as 'a great favourite with all the natives who liked his kindly ways'. Macintosh had been allowed to leave Scotland without a medical certificate because a carpenter was urgently needed.[56] He left behind him in Perthshire a wife and three children, and the Committee made some endeavour to provide for the children's education by giving the sum of £50 to the Kirk Session of Aberuthven to be used for the children's schooling over a period of five years.[57] To provide for them at all was more than strict legality demanded but it was not over-generous and compared ill with the provision made two years later for the widowed mother of the Revd J.A.Bain for whom £50 per annum was provided.[58]

The Livingstonia Committee resolved that for the future a satisfactory medical certificate must be obtained before a candidate would be accepted.[59]

The Mission faced other problems too and these had to be dealt with by Robert Laws, the recognised 'leader in charge.' Two examples may be given. One situation arose when a young African closely associated with the Mission was accused by Chimbano of adultery with his wife, to whom he had previously given some beads. The young man admitted having given the beads but denied the charge of adultery completely. There was a great deal of talk and discussion in which Laws himself and a number of local chiefs took part. In the end the charge of adultery was dismissed but Laws censured the man for having given beads to another man's wife, and ordered him to give his *tumba*, or bag - which contained six yards of cloth - to Chimbano as a fine.[60]

Some months later Laws had to pass judgement on a member of staff, Mr McCurrie, who had joined the Mission the previous year. McCurrie had grown impatient at what he regarded as laziness on the part of some of the men working under him, and foolishly discharged his shotgun in their direction. He meant only to frighten them but in fact some of them were wounded. No-one was seriously hurt but, in compensation, payments in cloth were made in proportion to the seriousness of the injury. That evening Dr Laws ruled that McCurrie had broken an order that offenders of any kind were to be brought before the head of the Mission. Although Mr McCurrie had acted under provocation Laws felt he had no option but to dismiss him, especially as relations were strained at that time between Angoni and Atonga, and an outbreak of trouble could have ruined the Mission.[61]

In August the Revd George Henry MB CM arrived at Bandawe and on 28th August he baptized Amelia Nyasa Laws at the English service, a number of Africans being present.[62] In October Dr Henry set out for Chikusi's and along with Mr McIntyre began missionary work among the southern Angoni of the Livlezi Valley, fulfilling the promise which Dr Laws had made to Chikusi several years before.[63]

Further north, uneasy relations continued to prevail between Atonga and Angoni and Dr Elmslie even thought it possible that if the Mission had to withdraw from Angoniland it might have to leave Bandawe also.[64] Dr Laws advised the Atonga chiefs to send their wives and children to places of safety. They were inclined to look to the Mission for protection but Laws warned them that the Mission would neither fight with them against the Angoni, nor with the Angoni against them. Laws undertook to visit M'mbelwa to try to avert the war but he was not hopeful of success.[65]

There were considerable differences between the two tribes. The Atonga, who lived mainly along the lake-shore, were a loosely knit group of largely independent villages, while the Angoni formed a much more centralised 'state' and recognised the authority of a paramount chief. They frequently raided neighbouring tribes and young men who were captured were enrolled in the Angoni *impis* along with the young warriors of Angoni birth. In this way many who belonged to other tribes were assimilated into the Angonis.

As a precaution against an Angoni raid on Bandawe, Mr and Mrs Smith and their goods were sent to Cape Maclear along with goods belonging to Mr McCallum, and cases of surgical instruments belonging to Dr Elmslie, boxes containing the Encyclopaedia Brittannica, and Communion vessels were all put aboard the *Ilala*. Mr and Mrs McCallum chose to remain at Bandawe.[66]

Later a further 18 boxes were loaded on to the steamer but this time Chimbano intervened to stop the evacuation of the station.[67] Presently, several chiefs, including Fuka, Chikuru, Marenga, and Chikoko, all came to see Laws who asked them why Chimbano was acting as he was. Dr Laws had himself advised them to send their wives and children to safety and claimed that members of the Mission staff should be free to do the same. When the chiefs spoke to Chimbano he said that he had no quarrel with the missionaries but that he would not open the beach until the men returned from Mandala[68] - apparently a reference to twenty-five Atonga who had gone to Mandala to work some months previously for the ALC.

The real problem of course was the fear that if the missionaries left Bandawe the Atonga in that neighbourhood would be exposed to attack by the Angoni. Laws and his colleagues made it clear that they intended to remain but asserted they had a perfect right to leave if they wished. It was plain that great suspicion would be aroused if they continued to evacuate a lot of their goods. Even so, they managed to convey a further forty loads of beads, medicines and calico to the steamer.[69]

A week later two quantities of mail got through from the hills bringing the news that Mrs Elmslie, whose baby had been still-born about three weeks before, was keeping well and that Dr Elmslie was of the opinion that war between Angoni and Atonga was imminent. He urged Dr Laws to come up soon to Angoniland; perhaps he would be able to save the station there even if Bandawe had to be abandoned.[70]

It is testimony to the courage of both Robert and Margaret Laws that Robert did as Dr Elmslie suggested and went up to Angoniland leaving Margaret and their fourteen month old baby in the highly tense situation at Bandawe.

In a letter home, written on 11th October 1887, Mrs Laws said: 'In fact we have been prisoners whether we care to believe it or not. Dr Elmslie begged us to clear out.' She expresses some concern about the effect on Amy if the local population should cause an

uproar, perhaps smashing the windows of the Mission house in an
endeavour to gain shelter for wives and children. She mentioned the
threats which had been used against the carrying of goods to the *Ilala*,
and said that the steamer was guarded by men carrying guns 'lest we
should escape by night and so leave them at the mercy of the
Angoni... We were thoroughly in their power, but Robert calmly
yet resolutely demanded the freedom of giving out the principle he
had striven always to work upon amongst them.'[71] This we may take
to refer to the principle of neutrality which Margaret calls their
'social password.' She goes on to say:

> Regret exceedingly that Robert left for the hills yesterday... it
> was deemed imperative that he should go *now.*

Margaret herself thought that it was a trap to ensure that the head of
the Mission would reside with the Angoni and was afraid that Robert
would be detained in Angoniland while an attack was launched on
the Atonga in the Bandawe area.[72]

On November 1st the Bandawe Journal runs: 'Dr Laws came
in from Njuyu at 7 p.m.'[73] It is not clear whether he had been absent
from Bandawe all the time from 10th October to 1st November, but
it is certain that in the intervening period Dr Laws and Dr Elmslie
had had long talks with M'mbelwa and the other Angoni chiefs
which at length bore fruit.

The whole affair was of considerable interest to people in Scotland
well beyond the ranks of the Livingstonia Mission supporters, and
The Scottish Leader of January 19th 1888 carried half a column of
news from Livingstonia, including an account of how the situation
had developed up to the 12th of October 1887. The report mentioned
that Dr Laws had gone to meet the Angoni chiefs, leaving Mrs Laws
at Bandawe, 'the Atonga being unwilling that she should depart.'
Analysing how much depended on Laws' influence with the chiefs,
the article said that the work of diplomacy could not be in better
hands. Eight days later, after a further despatch from Dr Laws, dated
8th November, the Leader gave its readers reassuring news.[74]

M'mbelwa had insisted that Laws should settle in the hills,
among the Angoni, and Dr Elmslie expressed his willingness to
change places with Laws and go to Bandawe if this would satisfy
M'mbelwa. In some ways it seemed a step forward, for up till then
the chief had been urging that all the missionaries should leave the
Atonga and settle among the Angoni.

A long meeting with Angoni chiefs and councillors began at 8am on October 27th. Laws was accused of unfaithfulness to M'mbelwa who had killed an ox and given him cattle, still in the Kraal, yet Laws, it was said, had left a lawful husband (M'mbelwa and the Angoni) to go to live with another (the Atonga). What made it worse was that the latter were not the equal of Laws but simply slaves of the Angoni.

The conference lasted for many hours, and at one point M'mbelwa withdrew into the shade, leaving Laws, Elmslie and George Williams in the broiling sun. The missionaries explained why they could not abandon Bandawe. They needed a port and spoke of how much calico they had already brought in and how much the Angoni would benefit from the development of trade. Some of the chiefs explained that they had no quarrel with the Atonga at Bandawe. Their quarrel was with the Atonga at Chinteche, about a dozen miles to the north of Bandawe, and if those at Bandawe would refrain from helping the people at Chinteche then they would not find themselves attacked. In reply Dr Laws and his colleagues said that they could make no agreement on behalf of the Atonga but would pass on what had been said.[75]

Chief M'mbelwa was throughout an influence for peace and adhered to his promise of many years before, even though he lost popularity with his younger tribespeople.[76] If complete peace had not been achieved at least a large scale war had been avoided, and the way prepared for a gradual improvement of relations between Atonga and Angoni.

To Mrs Laws it must have been a great relief to see her husband safely back in Bandawe on 1st November. Throughout this anxious period Dr George Smith had written regularly to Laws about the concern felt by all at home, expressing confidence in Laws' 'wide experience, calm judgement and courage born of a lively faith.'[77] George Smith not only wrote regularly to Laws on behalf of the FMC but often sent personal letters in which his own affection for Laws, and genuine concern for his welfare, are abundantly plain.

When Dr Laws' Annual Report for 1887 arrived home in the course of the following year, the very real dangers of these autumn weeks had been reduced by Laws to the dry statement, 'The trials have been averted but time was lost removing mission property to Cape Maclear.'[78] Of the danger that had threatened Mrs Laws and Amy there is not a word.

12 WAR IN THE NORTH, AND RESPONSE TO THE GOSPEL

ARAB SLAVERS - ALC SUPPORT WAKONDE - BAIN SENT FOR - CONSUL
O'NEILL & LAURENCE SCOTT - DR CROSS AS M.O. - CONCERN AT HOME
- LUGARD ON THE SCENE - SULTAN OF ZANZIBAR'S INTERVENTION -
MOUNTAIN GUN IN USE - BAIN'S DEATH - TREATY OF PEACE - MOTIVES OF
BRITISH GOVT. & THE MISSION - DEFEAT OF MLOZI - CHURCH GROWTH
AT BANDAWE; AMONG NORTHERN ANGONI; IN LIVLEZI VALLEY; AT CAPE
MACLEAR; AT KARONGA & CHIRENJI - BAPTISMS AT BANDAWE - FIRST
ANGONI BAPTISMS - CONTRIBUTION OF KOYI, WILLIAMS & SUTHERLAND
- DEATH OF M'MBELWA - EKWENDENI - PRINTING BEGUN - AFRICAN
INTEREST IN THE BIBLE - LAWS ILL, SUMMONED HOME - CHARLES
DOMINGO & YURAIAH CHIRWA TO LOVEDALE - HIGHBURY
CONGREGATIONAL CHURCH

The threat to members of the Mission staff as a result of hostilities
between Atonga and Angoni might be at an end but at the north end
of the lake there was an increasing threat from Arab slave-traders in
the vicinity of the ALC trading post at Karonga, and in the area lying
to the north and west of it between Lake Nyasa and Lake Tanganyika.
For a time the Arabs were content to deal in ivory with the ALC, but
some of them decided that it would be more profitable to capture
Africans and sell them as slaves on the east coast of the continent after
they had acted as carriers for the ivory.

The trouble began in July 1887 with a quarrel between some
members of the Wakonde tribe and an Arab in the course of which
an African was shot. The intervention of L.Monteith Fotheringham,
the African Lake Company's agent, led to a settlement, as the Arab
leader at the time, Salim Bin Najim, was willing to pay compensation.
This avoided a conflict in which Africans with spears would have
been opposed by Arabs with guns.[1] Later, a further quarrel developed.
Fotheringham, the only European on the spot, realised how isolated
he was and sent two runners to the Mission station at Mweniwanda
to ask the Revd Alex Bain to come down and join him with all
possible speed.[2]

Bain and Dr Kerr Cross had a consultation and it was agreed that Bain should make his way to Karonga at once. He left at 10pm after a busy day but marched steadily, arriving at Mpata shortly after sunset the next day. As the moon was up he soon resumed his journey and reached Karonga before dawn on the following day.[3] Work was begun at once to fortify the station but when Mlozi, who had become leader on the Arab side, demanded that work on the fortifications should cease Fotheringham decided to acquiesce to avoid a confrontation.[4] The Arabs, however, were not seeking an accommodation with the white men and the Wakonde; having driven many of the latter to take shelter in the reeds by the lake shore, they set fire to the reeds. Dozens of unfortunate Wakonde were caught between the lake with its crocodiles and the burning reeds, or were shot while trying to escape.[5]

Fotheringham and Bain were in very considerable danger until reinforcements arrived early in November in the person of Consul O'Neill of Mozambique and other three Europeans.[6] One of these was O'Neill's brother-in-law the Revd Laurence Scott, a brother of C.P.Scott of The Manchester Guardian. Unsuccessful attempts were made to establish peace, but presently Karonga had to be abandoned in the face of Arab pressure in favour of a situation on the Nsessi River further north where the Konde had their encampment.[7] Here Dr Cross joined the party. An attack on Mlozi's stockaded village some 12 miles away proved unsuccessful. The onset of the rainy season brought operations to an end for the time being and Mr Bain and Dr Cross withdrew to Mweniwanda's.[8]

In the spring of 1888 a second expedition was launched, this time with Mr Fred Moir in charge, and with Dr Cross as a non-combatant present to attend to the wounded. The Arabs had strengthened all their defences and the Europeans were driven off with severe casualties, Fred Moir being wounded.[9]

Reports of the struggle appeared in the British press. There was a feeling among representatives of the ALC that the British Government was not giving as much support as it should. In February The Scotsman quoted a Manchester Guardian report that the news from Karonga was serious, referring to the siting of Arab camps at commanding points on the slave routes, and to their influence over African chiefs.[10]

In April the Livingstonia Sub-Committee agreed to put *Office* pressure on the Foreign Ofice by seeking, along with representatives of the established Church of Scotland and the UP Church, joint conference with the Government about British interests in Central Africa. In particular they wanted them to make it clear to the Arabs that the British Government was as opposed to slavery as ever.[11]

A meeting with MPs and with the Prime Minister was held on 24th April 1888, and Lord Salisbury made three negative and three positive statements:

1 The Government would not send an expedition to Central Africa.
2 The Government would not interfere in the German sphere of influence.
3 The Government would not annexe Nyasaland or declare it to be British.

On the other hand, the Government would insist on the free navigation of the Zambezi; it would resist any claim to Portuguese sovereignty over the Nyasa region; and, although it would not send armed assistance to the ALC or to the Mission, it recognised that they had the right to defend themselves, and arms and ammunition could be freely imported with this in view.[12]

In May and June a third expedition against Mlozi was being planned this time with help from Captain Frederick Lugard (later Lord Lugard) of the Norfolk Regiment who happened to be on furlough in Africa at the time. There were 20 white men in the party, including John Moir of the ALC, and 190 Atonga under Mr Sharpe. At the request of Lugard and Moir, and with the consent of Dr Laws, Dr Kerr Cross again went with the expedition as a surgeon and non-combatant.[13]

The Mission authorities were anxious to maintain their position of neutrality when it came to quarrels between one tribe and another, and also to adhere to their rule that fire-arms should not be used at all except in self-defence. At the same time they were fully in favour of the ALC standing up to the Arabs.

Laws saw the whole business as 'a preconcerted movement by Arabs and coastmen to seize Lake Nyasa', and was glad that the ALC had withstood them. He longed for peace, but not a peace based on wickedness.[14]

The Government had not been entirely idle for it had brought pressure to bear upon the Sultan of Zanzibar who sent special envoys to express his displeasure with the Arabs who had attacked Karonga, and with instructions not to continue with hostilities against the Mission and the ALC.[15]

The expedition which had been launched in June under Lugard and Sharpe was driven off, the fortifications proving much stronger than anticipated and Lugard himself was shot through both arms and received a bullet wound in his chest.[16] John Moir set off for Quilimane to bring up a gun to enable the attackers to make a breach in the Arab stockade. He and Captain Lugard returned in October but it was not until January 1889, that 'an Armstrong M.L.R., jointed 7lb. mountain gun' was brought up.[17]

Captain Lugard was again in command in February when hostilities were renewed, with Mr Crawshay of the ALC operating the mountain gun. The shells from the latter passed clean through the woodwork of the stockade leaving a small hole, but not exploding until they hit the ground beyond. They were therefore a serious danger to personnel within the stockade but ineffective in making a breach in it. Lugard had finally to leave the area in March, presumably because his army leave was at an end, but the gun continued to be used against the stockade.[18]

Meantime Alex Bain was living in isolation at Malindu on the Ukukwe plateau where a start had been made in setting up a new mission station.[19] The Arabs destroyed some villages in this area and got to within 7 miles of Ukukwe. Mr Fotheringham accordingly sent a party of 20 men to escort Mr Bain to Karonga. Bain did not leave immediately but delayed for some time to see that his people were safe from Arab attack. When he did arrive at Karonga, on 22nd April, it was clear that his health was far from good, and that he had had a severe bout of fever.[20] Two days later he sailed for the south but died of nephritis at Bandawe on 16th May 1889.[21]

Hostilities continued on and off for the next few months until the arrival of Sir H.H.Johnston, who had been Consul in Portuguese East Africa and had now been sent by the Foreign Office to bring about a settlement. After some preliminary negotiations a treaty was signed on 22nd October 1889, which was described by Fotheringham as a 'red letter day in the history of Nkondé, and, for that matter, of Nyasaland.'[22]

The Wakonde were to be allowed to return to their villages and not thereafter to be molested by the Arabs. The ALC undertook to be responsible for the behaviour of their allies while any act of hostility on the part of the Arabs against the Africans was to be regarded as an act of hostility against the ALC. The treaty was celebrated with considerable rejoicing on both sides. J.W.Jack claims that the Arabs were almost starving and were thankful to agree to terms.[23]

Hugh Macmillan claims that the greatest significance of the Arab war lay in the propaganda value which was extracted from it by the ALC and the Mission's supporters in Britain, and says,

> There can be little doubt that the war played an important part in arousing the interest of the British public in the area ,and in bringing pressure to bear on Lord Salisbury's Government to declare a protectorate over the region which now comprises Malawi and Zambia.[24]

The British Government was not deliberately seeking to extend her Empire but was forced by the continuance of slave dealing, and by the pressure of public opinion at home, to take such action as would eliminate slaving and provide protection for British nationals who were serving the missions or developing trade. The latter was still seen as the best antidote to the continuance of the slave trade.

Nor were the Scottish Churches acting from imperialist motives in pressing for the establishment of a Protectorate. They looked forward to such a step not because they wished to deprive the people of Central Africa of their freedom but for precisely the opposite reason.

British Colonial rule, when it came, was not always appreciated by the Africans, and its administrators did not always understand the problems posed, and the resentment roused, in a subsistence economy when the Africans were asked to pay 'hut tax' or to give so many hours of labour in lieu. In origin, however, colonial rule had the well-being of the African in mind with their delivery from the slave trade as its main concern. In 1891 the British Protectorate over the countries adjoining Lake Nyasa was proclaimed.[25] Sir H.H. Johnston was appointed as the first Commissioner and established his headquarters at Zomba.

In the north the Treaty of 1889 had brought a cessation of hostilities which was welcome both to the ALC and to the Mission, but it did not bring real peace. Uneasy relations continued between the ALC and the Wakonde on the one hand and the Arab traders on the other, and the terms of the treaty were frequently broken by Mlozi, with slave trading and raiding continuing.

As Bandawe was fully 150 miles from Karonga, Dr Laws had not been personally involved in the struggle at the north end, and was not nearly so closely affected by it personally as he and his family had been by the struggle between the Atonga and the Angoni. Apart from Mr Bain's journeying from Mweniwanda's to Karonga to give support to Mr Fotheringham in 1887, the Mission, as distinct from the ALC, had taken no active part in the fighting. Dr Cross, however, had been involved almost throughout the struggle as a doctor and non-combatant.

The attitude of the Mission to the Arab war was ambivalent. It was anxious to maintain its neutrality and to stick to its rule of not using arms except in self-defence, but in no sense could the missionaries be considered 'neutral'. In their sympathies and their hopes they were whole heartedly behind the ALC and the various Europeans who volunteered to fight against the Arabs. Fred Moir claimed that the Arab war had been 'undertaken, or at least, carried out by consent of the Mission' and he not unreasonably claimed that the war had cost the Company thousands of pounds and that the Mission should share the cost.[26]

It was fortunate for the Mission that men like the Moir brothers and Monteith Fotheringham of the ALC, an army officer on leave like Lugard, and a big game hunter like Alfred Sharpe, should have been willing to carry on the fight against the Arabs, and to do so at very real risk to themselves. The concern felt at home for the threat to British lives, and the fortuitous circumstance that the Revd L.Scott was the brother of C.P.Scott, editor of The Manchester Guardian, helped to overcome Government reluctance to declare a Protectorate.

When the time came for Laws' second furlough, passing the southern end of the Lake on his way to the coast, he found H.H.Johnston engaged in his war against slaving and forcing Mponda to release a body of slaves.[27] Johnston then meant to turn his atttention to Mlozi, although four more years were to pass before he finally brought the struggle with the Arabs to an end.

For convenience we may anticipate a little and record here the final events of the struggle. In July 1895 Johnston visited Karonga to negotiate. Mlozi refused to see him, and wrote saying:

The British have closed my route to the coast: very well, I will close their road to Tanganyika.[28]

Johnston accordingly assembled a strong force of 100 Sikhs and 300 Africans. Neither the *Ilala* nor the *Domira* nor the UMCA's steamer the *Charles Janson* was large enough to allow him to transport his troops in one movement, which he was anxious to do to prevent the Arabs being forewarned and calling up reinforcements. He therefore asked the German commander on the Lake to allow him the use of the German steamer the *Wissman* and this was at once granted.[29]

On arrival at Karonga there was a march of 11 or 12 miles to Mlozi's stockade. After heavy shelling an assault was launched on the walls, the ramparts were scaled, and the stockade captured. The day was won but Mlozi himself had disappeared. Later he was found in hiding by an Atonga, Sergeant Major Bandawe. Some of the runaway slaves reported that a good many of the Africans held as hostages by Mlozi had been put to death on his orders, and Mlozi was charged with their murder before a council of Wakonde chiefs under the superintendence of Johnston. He was sentenced to death, and hanged the next day.[30] This put an end to slave trading in that area.

Meantime, in the years between Laws' first furlough and his second spell at home there were signs of growth throughout the whole area covered by the activities of the Mission. There was a slow but definite increase in the number of Africans seeking baptism, and an increasing number were attending school and doing so now with something approaching regularity. The medical work was now being undertaken by four doctors. Laws himself was at Bandawe, Dr Elmslie was with the northern Angoni, and Dr Henry with the southern Angoni, while Dr Kerr Cross had been labouring in the country between Lake Nyasa and Lake Tanganyika since 1885, often on his own.[31]

In this period, 22 men and four wives (not counting Mrs Laws who had come out in 1879) had joined the mission staff. Of that number Mr W.McEwan (civil engineer), Mrs Kerr Cross, Mr George Rollo (teacher), Mr Hugh MacIntosh (carpenter), the Revd J.A.Bain, and Mr M.McIntyre (teacher) had died, and Dr and Mrs William Scott had been invalided home.[32] The others were scattered throughout a wide area of what is now Malawi, from Mweniwanda in the North, on the Stevenson Road from Lake Nyasa to Lake Tanganyika, to Chikusi in the south. Dr Laws was described as 'senior missionary in principal charge',[33] and at this period he was mainly stationed at Bandawe once the trouble with the Angoni had been settled. Work was proceeding at this time at five different places.

At Bandawe itself, apart from Dr and Mrs Laws, the station was staffed by Mr and Mrs Peter McCallum and by the bookkeeper

Mr Robert Gossip. 1300 children were attending school in 1888 with a further 100 at schools in villages nearby, and the numbers were growing. An hour of school was normally held before breakfast which was taken at 8am. For the 300 girls at the school a sewing class was run by Mrs Laws and Mrs McCallum and attendance at this class was treated as a prize for those who did best with their general work. Each afternoon Dr Laws would take the seniors and the lesson he taught them was passed on by them to the younger children the following morning.[34] Instruction was also given in the afternoon in carpentry and printing, and native industries such as mat and basket making were encouraged to keep the pupils from looking down on manual work.[35]

After dinner, which was taken at noon, Mr Gossip and some of the Africans would go to a village about two miles away and hold school there for some 200 pupils. In addition there was another school at Marenga, also two miles from Bandawe, run by Albert and Dan, products of the Mission themselves, with 150 in attendance. This school had been built by the local people and was already being enlarged. At Fuka's village, a mile or two further still, over 100 trees had been brought in for the construction of a school.[36] Clearly 'education' had caught on among the Atonga.

Among the northern Angoni Dr Elmslie was building on their slowly growing confidence, now that M'mbelwa had given permission for the opening of schools.[37] In 1888 school attendances over the year increased from 8 to 22. In evangelistic work there was 'both encouragement and discouragement' for the Gospel message was 'offensive to the proud Angoni'.[38]

After six years of useful work George Williams would have liked to bring his wife out from Lovedale to join him, but his contract was not renewed. As we saw in the last chapter Dr Elmslie did not always approve of his endeavours to identify himself with the Angoni.[39]

At Chikusi, in the Livlezi valley, Dr Henry had been joined by Mrs Henry. There were then three classes in the school there, Dr and Mrs Henry taking one each and Maurice McIntyre, the teacher, taking the third. The girls' class, for which Mrs Henry was responsible, met separately from the rest. It was said of the 25 pupils attending the school at this time that they needed to learn 'regularity'. Books were scarce and a larger building for the school was needed. Medical work was growing also with Dr Henry seeing about 70 patients a week.[40]

Mr McIntyre died in 1890 and when the Henrys had to return home for a period because of Dr Henry's health the work of the Mission was carried on by Africans, no European being available.[41] The Revd A.C.Murray of the Dutch Reformed Church came out to work for a time with the Livingstonia Mission with a view to establishing a station of the DRC, and in 1888 Mr Murray and Mr Vlok, also of the DRC, began work at Mvera, in Chiwera's territory, west of the lake and about 100 miles south of Bandawe. In four and a half months Mr Murray had 200 'patients', and urged the need for a doctor being sent to that area.[42]

At Livlezi Mrs Henry died in May 1892 and her husband in July of the following year, only six years after beginning the work there. As we shall see in Chapter 13, by 1895 Livlezi had been transferred to the DRC.[43]

At the original Mission site at Cape Maclear educational and evangelistic work was still going on, Albert Namalambe the first convert being largely responsible for it. Here Dr Laws baptized four men, three women and 10 children in the year 1888, and 14 Africans, including the first couple to be married there according to Christian usage, received communion. One of those who became a Christian at this time had been employed on the *Ilala*, getting most of his instruction from the engineers Harkness, Morrison, and Howat.[44]

At the north end of the Lake, 40 miles north west of Karonga was Chirenji, or Mweniwanda's. Here, despite the interruptions caused by the Arab wars, missionary work was carried on among the Wakonde, and other tribes in that area.

Progress continued generally and the General Assembly of 1891 was told that throughout the Livingstonia Mission there were now 53 African Christians, with numerous enquirers of both sexes. It was noted that the organisation of native congregations with their own office-bearers would soon be necessary. 125 Africans, including six women, were teaching in the mission schools, in which enrolments numbered 4200.[45]

At Bandawe, on 21st April and 20th October of 1889, Dr Laws baptized a total of 37 adults and four children,[46] one of the children being Isaac, the son of Albert Namalambe. More significant still were the baptisms of two brothers among those whom Dr Elmslie had called 'The Wild Ngoni.' Even before the opening of schools had been allowed by M'mbelwa among this proud and warlike people, three young men, whose father was described as a witch doctor called Kalengo, had been receiving teaching secretly each evening - first from William Koyi, to whom one of them had been a servant boy and by whom he had been greatly influenced, and later from George Williams. These men not only wanted to learn to read but used to join in prayer with the missionaries in the days when the future of missionary work among the Angoni was still uncertain.[47]

Dr Elmslie writes of the pleasure it gave him, before going on furlough in 1890, to see the two younger of the three brothers baptized. As he himself was not at this time ordained, Dr Laws must have gone up to Ngoniland to perform the baptismal ceremony at Njuyu. Mawalera and Makara Tembo were the names of the men baptized, and Tengo Tembo, Mawalera's infant son was baptized at the same time - 13th April 1890. Laws entered this in his notebook: 'The first fruits of the Ngoni tribe to Christ.'[48]

Chitezi, the oldest of the Tembo brothers had attended the teaching classes with them and was himself eager to profess his faith in Christ. He was, however, married, and had three wives, and the missionaries told him that before he could be baptized he must put away two of his wives. We read that 'He made offer to provide for two at their parents' villages but they refused to be sent away. He cannot force them.'[49] Accordingly the husband remained outwith the Christian church.

The missionaries were no doubt right to insist that any man who was already a Christian must marry only one wife, but it must at least be asked whether the conduct of the oldest of the three brothers, who refused to divorce two of his wives against their will,[50] was not closer to the mind of Christ than the course urged by the missionaries? The social conditions of African tribal society at that time required a woman to be under the protection of either her father, her husband, or a brother, and regarded it as disgraceful for a wife to be sent back to her father by her husband for any reason whatever.

It was a notable thing that the parent of these three men was what was referred to as a 'smelling out doctor', but that he nevertheless readily acknowledged the difference the coming of the missionaries had made to the Angoni.[51]

If 1878 is taken as the year in which more than casual contacts were first made with the Angoni, with the establishment of a sub-station of the Mission at Kaning'ina, manned for a time by William

Koyi and one European, then it will be seen that it had taken 12 years for the first Ngoni convert to the Christian faith to be won.[52] It had not been easy and was due to the work of many. William Koyi and George Williams, both men with a knowledge of the Zulu language, had played their part, as had several Scottish members of the Mission. At one time when it looked as if the Europeans were going to have to leave the area altogether James Sutherland the agriculturist was prepared to become a household slave in an Angoni household - and had even chosen his 'owner' - to make it possible for him to remain and carry on the work.[53] In 1885 Dr Walter Elmslie arrived, and the same year Sutherland died of fever causing great sadness among the Africans.

Chief M'mbelwa himself, although he never became a Christian, made it possible for progress to be made by the Mission. M'mbelwa died in August 1891, and the Foreign Mission Report of the following year speaks of him as 'the instrument in God's hand for admitting the Gospel to his tribe.'[54] It was notable that when M'mbelwa's death occurred we read nothing of either wives or slaves being slaughtered, and that when his brother Mtwaro died some ten months previously his request to M'mbelwa not to attack his people as custom would have dictated, was respected. In contrast to this, when Chikusi died in the same year as M'mbelwa, thirty people at least lost their lives through the poison ordeal, which was administered to find out whether or not they had brought about his death by witchcraft.[55]

The winning of so proud and independent a people as the Angoni was no mean achievement, although the baptism of the Tembo brothers was indeed only the 'first fruits' of the harvest. A new station, which was to become increasingly important, had been opened at Ekwendeni, Mtwaro's village, in 1889. It lay 15 miles to the northeast of Njuyu. A station at Hora, southwest of Njuyu, followed in 1893.[56]

At Bandawe printing started on the Mission's own press in September 1888, and Mr William Thomson, aged 21, a young printer from Aberdeen, was recruited to the Mission staff the following year. By the end of 1890 the press at Bandawe had printed 250 copies of 'The Sermon on the Mount and the Parables', 250 copies of 'Harry's Catechism' (the work of Miss Rainy) translated into Chingoni, 750 Hymns with Sol-fa, 500 copies of St Mark's Gospel in Chitonga, translated by Dr Laws, and 500 copies of St Mark in Chingoni, translated by Dr Elmslie. The latter had reduced to writing both Chingoni and Chitumbuka, and grammars and dictionaries in both these languages were published as well as a Chingoni Hymn Book. Mrs Laws helped to reduce Chinyanja to writing, did some of the proof reading of St Mark, and also translated the Chinyanja version of Harry's catechism.[57]

Mr Bain was an accomplished linguist and acquainted himself with the languages used by the Awanda, the Akonde and the Amwamba peoples at the north end of the Lake, and arrangements had already been made at the time of his death for printing his translation of St. Mark's Gospel in Chimwamba.[58] Sometimes the NBSS undertook to see to the printing, while at other times the printing was done at Bandawe with the NBSS making a grant towards the cost.[59]

Although the cost of producing the Scriptures was subsidised by the Bible Society, it is still remarkable that the Africans, earning as little as they did, should have been so ready to buy their own copies, and beyond that, willing to subscribe to the work of translation. In the Quarterly Record of the NBSS in December 1889 Laws describes Sabbath morning services as 'attended by young and old, book in hand, ready to turn up the chapter' - with 1251 children and 50 native teachers using the Chinyanja version of the New Testament. He also mentions that £25.8/4d had been subscribed 'from the heart of the dark continent in return for the Lamp of Life.'[60]

Similarly, in his report for the year 1890 Laws says of the native evangelists that although they are not highly advanced yet 'all have received much Bible instruction and all are able to read their New Testaments with more or less fluency.'[61]

Dr Kerr Cross, on furlough at the time of the General Assembly of 1890, spoke both of the nine schools, with 3000 scholars, run by Dr Laws at Bandawe, and also of the ravages caused by the Arabs at the north end of the Lake.[62] Later that summer, when Dr Elmslie was at home he reported that Dr Laws did not tell one tenth of his own work, and Dr Smith wrote to Laws saying 'Think not of your own self-obliteration but of the Church's right and duty on your behalf.'[63]

Dr and Mrs Laws, and their daughter Amelia, had not been at risk in the Arab struggle as they had in the Atonga/Angoni rivalry of a few years earlier. Throughout, however, Laws had been head of the Mission with overall responsibility for outlying stations, and must have been under considerable strain. In March 1890 he became seriously ill at Njuyu in Ngoniland, and was greatly relieved when Dr Elmslie responded to his cry for help by making a forced march and reaching Njuyu only a day and a half after receiving Laws' letter.[64]

Six days later Elmslie wrote that Laws was still very ill, and was exhausted by the effort of writing a short letter.[65] The seriousness of his illness may be judged from a letter written by Dr Smith in June to both Laws and Elmslie in which he says, 'We thank God for the... restoration of Dr Laws from the gates of death.'[66] When he had another severe attack of fever the following year, J.C.White (later Lord Overtoun), convener of the Committee, sent a telegram saying 'Return home now.'[67]

Laws was busy up to the last with Mission affairs. On September 13th he baptized 10 men and two women at Bandawe, the first Atonga women to be baptized, on the 20th of the month he gave communion to 58 Africans and six Europeans, and on the 27th he performed another baptism.[68]

Laws finally sailed from Bandawe with Mrs Laws and Amy, now a little girl of five, in October 1891. Even this did not mean that he had left the duties of the Mission behind. When they reached Cape Maclear he examined many candidates for baptism, and this resulted in 15 adults and 18 children being baptized on 11th November, and 32 people taking communion.[69] He had with him some young Africans whom he intended to leave at Lovedale to receive training whle he was in Britain.[70] One was his house servant, Charles Domingo; one was an Atonga teacher, Yuraiah Chirwa.[71] We shall hear more of both of them presently. From Lovedale he proceeded to the Cape visiting many DRC churches as he went, conferring with DRC leaders and discussing affairs in Nyasaland with Cecil Rhodes.[72]

Dr Smith had written to say that if Laws were to be in London on a Sunday, the young men of Highbury Congregational Church, who had contributed over the years to the support of William Koyi, George Williams and Charles Stuart would very much like a visit from him.[73] It was the kind of call to which Laws would be likely to respond even if it delayed his arrival in Scotland by a few days. Eventually he reached Edinburgh in March 1892, the beginning of only his second furlough in 17 years.

PART III

13 BIRTH AND EARLY YEARS OF THE INSTITUTION

HON. DD - WORLD PRESBYTERIAN ALLIANCE & LAWS' STRATEGY - VISITS MARY SLESSOR; RETURNS TO CENTRAL AFRICA - LETTERS TO AMELIA - AIMS OF INSTITUTION; SEARCH FOR A SITE; KONDOWE CHOSEN - MOVE FROM BANDAWE -LAWS' VISION & NEGOTIATIONS - DRC TAKE OVER LIVLEZI & CAPE MACLEAR - BUILDING FUND - SCHOOL & APPRENTICE WORK - JAS.HENDERSON IN CHARGE OF EDUCATION, W.THOMSON OF PRINTING, M.MOFFAT OF AGRICULTURE - DEMAND FOR PLACES - JUBILEE - MISS LIZZIE STEWART - EVANGELISM, WORK & TRAINING - TRAINING IN TEACHING & THEOLOGY - GIRLS' EDUCATION - DEVELOPMENT - MISSION COUNCIL TO SANCTION ALL BUILDING - DONALD FRASER SEES KONDOWE

The Laws family arrived home in the spring of 1892, and took up residence at 56 Craiglea Drive, Edinburgh, where Mrs Gray now lived.[1] She would be glad to see her grand-daughter for the first time. Dr Laws addressed the Synod of the United Presbyterian Church in early May,[2] and the General Assembly of the Free Church later that same month.[3] He went to Aberdeen not only to see his father and step-mother, but also to receive an honorary DD from his old University at the early age of 41. In later life he wrote that he valued his MA and his MD which he 'wrought hard for and exercised self-denial to go through the classes and the work required to obtain such'. His honorary DD he regarded as one 'not wrought for and undeserved'.[4]

Later that summer, as a representative of the Free Church at the fifth General Council of the World Presbyterian Alliance, held at Toronto, Laws addressed the Council on the principles underlying the Livingstonia Mission. He emphasised the fact that the missionaries' job was a temporary one intended to train up a native staff and develop a native church:

We should work towards a Central African Presbyterian Church, which would include Blantyre and the Dutch.[5]

While across the Atlantic, Laws went to see various industrial institutions both in the United States and in Canada. He paid particular attention to the use of water power in the generating of electricity.[6]

At the Free Church General Assembly of 1892 he had reminded his hearers how the Livingstonia Mission had begun 17 years earlier and that it now had 7000 pupils in its 32 schools. All members of its staff had suffered from fever and in the past year four had died. He appealed for more workers and for more financial support, and went on to reveal to his hearers his vision of a Central Institution where native teachers and pastors could be trained:

If Africa is to be won for Christ - and there is no 'if' about it for it will be - then the way to do it is by the Africans themselves.[7]

(This statement was greeted by applause.)

The United Presbyterian Church also was impressed by the importance of a Central Training Institution in the mission field, and asked the Livingstonia Committee to set Laws free for six months in 1893 to visit their station at Old Calabar and advise on developing one.[8] The Free Church Assembly agreed, and on 5th July Laws sailed from Liverpool along with the Revd W.Risk Thomson, formerly of Jamaica, who was to be Superintendent of the Institution   at Calabar.[9]

In Nigeria Laws responded to a call for medical help from Mary Slessor, which involved him in a lengthy journey by canoe and on foot. Miss Slessor tottered out to meet him and was promptly ordered back to bed. He also found himself giving medical advice to his slightly younger cousin, Alexander Cruickshank. Cruickshank was far from well and Laws ordered him home on medical grounds.[10]

In 17 weeks Laws and Thomson visited all the principal stations of the Calabar Mission. By mid-January, 1894, a 26 page report was in the hands of the UP Board of Mission.[11] Its proposals were along the lines subsequently followed at Livingstonia, and the painstaking detail with which they are set forth is typical of Laws.

Before the 1894 General Assembly met Laws had set out again for Central Africa. Mrs Laws accompanied her husband and it must have been with a heavy heart that they left Amelia, not quite eight years old, in the care of one of her aunts. Laws would certainly have rejected any suggestion that a sacrifice was involved, but there is no doubt that separation from their children was part of the price paid by missionaries at this time, and for many years afterwards, until the fast air travel of today revolutionised the situation.

Much of the cost was paid by the children themselves who had little choice in the matter. In May 1894, about the time that Dr and Mrs Laws were setting out again for Africa Dr Smith included in an official letter the words 'The Lord Himself be with you and dear Mrs Laws, and keep your Amy when you are far away.' He wrote again about Amy towards the end of the year saying that he had paid to Miss Gray, one of the sisters of Mrs Laws, the sum of £5.16.8d as the allowance due to Amelia, as the child of a missionary, Class 1, for the seven months from 1st June to the end of December. This is equivalent to £10 per year and Dr Smith mentioned that when Amy became 10 the allowance would increase to £15 per annum.[12] We may note in passing that the children of artisans who had to be left at home by their parents in similar circumstances, did not receive such an allowance, as poor Peter McCallum discovered when he ventured to enquire about it.[13]

Both Robert and Margaret Laws write with deep affection to their daughter usually addressing her as 'My dear Amy' and saying that they must no longer address her as 'Dear little Amy' now that she is growing fast. Her father often writes about what is going on in the Mission, first at Bandawe, and then, soon after, at Kondowe, but he also tries to write about things which might be of interest to a child, telling about the death of Mr Murray's dog, Beauty, which she would have known, or about a puppy which James Henderson brought to Kondowe from Bandawe and which was busy 'tugging away at Mr Murray's trowsers.' Laws had evidently brought a parrot home to Amy from Calabar and, although it had disappointed them by never learning to speak, he commiserated with her when the severe climate of Scotland proved too much for it and it died of the cold. Lions also found a place in his letters which include a somewhat horrific account of the injuries sustained by a man who was attacked by one nearby.

Amy's replies have not survived but it is clear that she wrote about her school work and about doing things in the home. When Mr Henderson travelled out to join the Mission in 1895 Amy sent a parcel with him for her parents. It contained a blotter and a penwiper with his initials on it for her father, and a tray cloth and tea-cosy cover, which she had sewn herself, for her mother. Both parents were warm in their expressions of appreciation.[14]

In the 'Quarterly Paper' which came out in the March before he left Laws had set down his aim in trying to set up a Training Institution. To free the European missionary for preaching, supervision and outstation work, it was necessary, he said, 'to train native agents as artisans, teachers, evangelists and pastors' to assist the missionary. On grounds of economy and efficiency alone, it was essential to use native agents in the work of evangelism.[15]

Although Laws was not present, the Assembly of 1894 upheld the resolution of the Livingstonia Committee to build a Missionary Training Institution; Dr Laws, on his return to Africa, was to explore anew the higher uplands to the north-west of Lake Nyasa to find a suitable site.[16] The part played by the anopheles mosquito in carrying the malaria parasite was not understood until the work of Ronald Ross in 1898, and Laws and his colleagues, in choosing a site on high ground, thought that high ground was in itself a safeguard for the preservation of good health.

The geographical feature which most affected the choice of site was the Lake itself. With the Shire and Zambezi rivers connecting it to the coast, the Lake was the easiest highway along which to travel. Roads there were none, beyond the beaten earth tracks in and around the Mission stations, and, as Dr William Watson has pointed out, the revolution in transport that was to be brought about by the invention of the internal combustion engine was only just beginning.[17] Gottlieb Daimler had put an engine using liquid fuel into a car in 1886, and Rudolph Diesel had made an engine that ran on diesel in 1894, but at the time Laws was searching for a site, steam power was still in the ascendant, and the Lake itself was the obvious highway for travel.

Laws was welcomed back to Bandawe by an enthusiastic crowd on 8th August 1894[18] and called a Mission Council to meet at Ekwendeni on the last day of the month. At the Council it was agreed that Dr Elmslie should accompany Dr Laws on his search for a site; that Dr Steele should take charge at Ekwendeni, and that Mr McAlpine should act as Treasurer.[19]

Laws was certainly conscious that he was making history and resumed the practice of keeping a diary of daily events as he had done for long periods in the earliest days of the Mission, prior to his first furlough. We learn from his diary that he had difficulty in obtaining carriers at Bandawe 'as 5000 men are away at work in the Shire

Highlands and on the River.' Those who were left were anxious to get on with work in their fields before the rains.[20]

At last Laws left Bandawe on Monday 17th September and reached Ekwendeni on the Wednesday evening. Dr Elmslie and Laws then set out from Ekwendeni the following morning, accompanied by Yuraiah Chirwa and a party of carriers.[21] The going must have been rough and they were treading ground probably only once before covered by a European. Livingstone had not come as far north in his Zambezi expedition in 1863, and Dr James Stewart and Laws himself had done most of their early exploration of the north end from the *Ilala*. Only Mr James Stewart had explored this district while on his travels in 1879. They had worship each morning in Chinyanja, each evening in Chingoni, and on Sunday 23rd held services in both tongues.[22]

Laws comments that whereas in 1879 James Stewart had found the Rukuru valley well inhabited, now it had become depopulated as a result of raids by the Angoni. The Poka people had also suffered, being forced to seek refuge in inaccessible places, making their homes in semi-burrows, or on narrow ledges above waterfalls, where their children played in situations of considerable danger, to avoid attack by hostile tribes. Laws wrote:

> After crossing the Rumpi we climbed to the top of Mt Waller and thence had as good a view of the country lying to the north of the Rumpi as we had formerly had of the country to the south of it... Mt Waller rises abrubtly out of the Lake in a succession of terraces, till its flat top is at an elevation of 2,400 feet above the Lake or 4,100 feet above sea level.

Several escarpments stretch west from the Lake, on the north side of Mt Waller, and at the top of the third of these is

> a sort of plateau with trees covering a part of it. This plateau, which is about 4,000 feet above sea level is called Kondowi.[23]

Much arduous climbing was involved in reaching the plateau there, which ultimately became the chosen site. Today a cairn of stones marks the spot where Laws, Elmslie and Yuraiah Chirwa spent the first night on the plateau.

While making a brief exploration further north than Kondowe, Laws and Elmslie narrowly escaped injury from lions. While they were asleep in their tent near what is now called 'Lion Point', a hungry lion clawed through the canvas of the tent at the side occupied by Laws and its claws were within inches of his face. He

roused Elmslie with a shout, and Yuraiah, supported by both
Atonga and Angoni carriers, drove off the lion with blazing brands.[24]

From Karonga, they went to visit Dr Kerr Cross at nearby
Ngerenge, and made enquiries about the country along the Stevenson
Road and to the south of it on the Nyasa-Tanganyika plateau.[25] They
decided, however, that Kondowe was the place to choose for the
projected Institution. The fact that the Lake, although close by as the
crow flies, was some 2400 feet below with a most precipitous ascent
from the lake shore to the plateau does not seem to have been seen
by Laws as a deterrent.

Satisfied with the site Laws and Elmslie set off again for the
south leaving Yuraiah Chirwa and several others 'to collect grass and
bring in building material and to erect one or two houses in the native
way'.[26]

On 26th October Laws wrote to Dr Smith from Bandawe
reporting the return of himself and Elmslie in good health and saying
'Behind Mt. Waller we have found a place where we propose to place
our observing station and I hope to go north again by the first
steamer.'[27]

On 6th November Dr Laws, this time accompanied by Mrs
Laws, Mr William Murray the carpenter, and a number of Atonga
helpers, sailed from Bandawe taking with them a considerable
quantity of goods for Kondowe. After a visit to Mr Swann, the
Magistrate at Deep Bay, slightly further north than the landing point
for Kondowe[28] they disembarked with their goods at Florence Bay,
which had been visited by E.D.Young and Dr Laws in their first
exploration of the Lake on the *Ilala* in 1875.[29] By the evening of 10th
November Laws and his party were back on the plateau and found
that Yuraiah had a house of reeds and grass ready to provide them
with temporary accommodation.[30]

As Mr Malcolm Moffat was expected to join them soon work
was begun on a five roomed house. Labour was hard to obtain as so
many of the local people were at work in their fields, but four church
members from Bandawe, who were among the Africans in the party,
provided the nucleus of a reliable work force and the core of a
Christian congregation.[31]

Laws began an exchange of letters with Alfred Sharpe, HM Acting
Commissioner and Consul General, seeking a title to the land at
Kondowe. Writing to Laws Sharpe says:

> I am glad to hear that you have found what you consider a suitable locality... near Mt. Waller... The land north of the Rukuru is now in the hands of the British South Africa Co. and I am quite sure Mr Rhodes will do everything possible to assist...

At the same time he asks Laws if he can send him a printer or printers, and offers to pay them whatever wages Laws thought would be proper, in addition to giving them some extra comforts such as house, sugar, tea etc.[32] Already those trained by the Livingstonia Mission were being sought after as reliable workers.

Laws' reply to Sharpe shows clearly how he saw the plateau and its potential. He regards the inclusion of the Rumpi within the territory to be granted to the mission as essential since he plans to place a turbine on it with a dynamo attached to generate electric power not only for lighting at the station but to provide power for the workshop. He does not think that there is gold in the area but there might be some coal and iron and he would like the BSA Co. to reserve the mineral rights to themselves and allow the Mission to work them and pay appropriate royalties. He is most anxious to ensure that the company does not allow any third party to work the minerals in the area. As regards arable land he estimates that not more than 1/5th or 1/6th of the whole area is cultivable. Defending his request for such a very large area, Laws writes:

> Were it for my own benefit or that of a company at home, I might have scruples in seeking what I have done, but, as it is for the benefit of the native, the advancement of the country and thus increasing the value of the other property of the BSA Co. as well as helping the work of the Government of British Central Africa, I trust my proposals may not seem extravagant.[33]

To Sharpe Laws mentions that between the plateau and the Lake there is a sheer descent of about 3/4ths of a mile, and when he writes to Dr Smith in the rainy season of the following year he speaks of the difficulty of getting native labour as many of the Africans object to carrying loads up the hill. He adds that Salisbury Crags (a rocky hill in Edinburgh) would be a fair sample of part of the road up from the Lake and that the height of Kondowe above sea level is about the same as Ben Nevis. This illustrates the task involved with cases weighing nearly half a ton.[34] Even today it is a considerable climb using motor transport and the skilfully engineered 'Longmuir Road' with its 22 hairpin bends. One can only marvel at the stamina of those who, having used the Lake for ease of travel as far as Florence Bay, had now to make an ascent of 2400 feet, from the level of the Lake to the plateau, with hardly a track to ease the climb. Ladies were assisted up by having a length of calico put round their waists, with the ends held by people at a higher level, to give them some security and to reduce the amount of effort required.[35]

The physical problem of the climb never daunted Robert Laws, who very soon had the printing press transferred from Bandawe.[36] The task of getting it up from Lake to plateau would fall on the shoulders of the patient Africans, perhaps by this time no longer astonished by any enterprise which the white man might conceive or set in train. One hopes that the payment to them of three yards of calico per fortnight instead of two was considered by them to be satisfactory recompense for such arduous work.[37]

Until the engineering of the road some ten years later reduced the time from the lake-shore to the Mission station, new arrivals were cheered on disembarking from the steamer by a picnic tea sent down by Mrs Laws to welcome them and to give them strength for the last and most strenuous part of their journey.

Although what was at first established on the plateau was known as an 'Observing Station', any small doubts that Laws may have had that he had found the right spot for the Institution of which he dreamed quickly vanished and he began to erect buildings[38] which were of necessity of a temporary nature whilst the decision of the BSA Co. was awaited.

H.H.Johnston, who was British High Commissioner now that Nyasaland was a British Protectorate, was generally sympathetic towards the Mission and had a high opinion of Laws himself, but he was not convinced that such a large tract of land as Laws was seeking was really necessary.[39] It was agreed that it lay with the BSA Co. to give or withold the land, although they did not own it in any way that would have been accepted in the United Kingdom. Cecil Rhodes himself did not come much into the foreground and it was with his agent Major Forbes that Laws had to deal. Their correspondence shows Major Forbes to have been well disposed towards the project put forward by Laws but he told him that he could not assign to the Mission so large an area as 80 square miles, with 20 miles of frontage on the Lake, without seeing the ground for himself.[40] It must have come as a considerable surprise to him when Laws wrote back to say that the amount of land he was asking for was not 80 square miles but between 140 and 150 square miles![41]

In this letter written to Major Forbes towards the end of August 1895 Laws gave an account of what the Mission had done in the past twenty years and what it hoped to do in the future. There were now, he wrote, some 7000 to 8000 scholars in its schools; Africans who, when the Mission arrived, could be got to work for only half a day* were now prepared to enter upon a work contract of five years; and some 1400 Africans were now employed as outdoor workers by the African Lakes Company, and as many as 4000 by the Government - all this apart from the fact that the Gospel had been proclaimed to many thousands. The change in conditions in Central Africa and in the general conduct of many of its inhabitants had been achieved at a cost in money terms of some £90,000 and with the loss of 13 lives.**

Laws asks who else has spent £90,000, over the years, given £10,000 for the work of the Institution and is engaged in making an annual expenditure for the benefit of the Africans of between £6000 and £7000?[42] Laws appeals not only to past achievement but looks 50 years ahead to the time when he sees the Institution housing 1000 pupils and workers and therefore requiring to grow its own food so far as possible, as well as needing an ample water supply.

This letter was written ten months after Laws first decided on the plateau at Kondowe as a suitable site, and it is not surprising that we find him ending his letter to Major Forbes with this paragraph:

> From your letter I take it that you have no objection....and *unless I hear from you to the contrary ,I shall consider myself at liberty to proceed with work here, and also a receiving station on the Lake shore.* (Laws' emphasis)[43]

Not until three years later was Laws able to write home saying that he had got a provisional title for the land at Kondowe from Mr

---

* Dr Fergus Macpherson rightly points out that the Africans had their own work patterns, which at certain seasons (such as seedtime and harvest) brought them under considerable pressure, and that their own work was disrupted when they were coerced into working for foreigners. The assumption made by some Europeans that Africans were simply 'lazy' was unwarranted.

** This is an underestimate, for it includes only European male members of staff. Two of the Africans from Lovedale, Shadrach Ngunana and William Koyi, and two wives of missionaries, Mrs Kerr Cross and Mrs Henry, also died on Mission service within this period (see Donald Fraser, *Livingstonia* pp 86-7)

Codrington (who had replaced Major Forbes as agent for the BSA Co.).[44] He did not obtain as much as he had sought, but in securing for the Mission some 50,000 acres, he had done extremely well. He was now free to proceed with the erection of more permanent buildings, though the work of the Institution was already in process.

The name 'Livingstonia', originally used of the station at Cape Maclear and then more generally of the whole Mission and its work, was sometimes used at this time to denote the station on the plateau at Kondowe, but Laws' colleagues pled that the name 'Livingstonia' should be used, as in the past, to denote the whole Mission, and that the new station should be known as 'The Livingstonia Institution, Kondowe'.[45] This was an understandable request and reflected the sense of pride felt by all who served the Livingstonia Mission. Nowadays, however, when we speak of 'Livingstonia', we mean the station on the plateau. Other stations such as Ekwendeni are known by their own name, and in some places the African name has replaced the name given by the Europeans. Loudon, for example, is now known as Embangweni.

With the move to Kondowe the centre of the Mission had moved northwards and the work done in the area nearest to the south end of the Lake was transferred to the Dutch Reformed Church who had been working closely with the Free Church of Scotland since the Revd A.C. Murray came out in the 1880s. The DRC had their centre at Mvera and it was now proposed that they should take over responsibility also for the Livlezi Valley area and for the station at Cape Maclear (the original site of the Livingstonia Mission). There was a temporary hitch in making this transfer, because the DRC agents were doubtful whether or not they could take on this extra responsibility, but their hesitation was finally overcome and in the Report presented to the Free Church General Assembly of 1895, the DRC are stated to have become responsible not only for Mvera but also for Livlezi and Cape Maclear.[46]

Kondowe was roughly in the centre of the area now served by the Livingstonia Mission. To the south of it were the three stations of Ekwendeni, Njuyu and Hora among the Angoni, and further south among the Atonga, was Bandawe, with outstations stretching both north and south along the Lakeshore.[47]

To the north, on the Lake shore, was Ngerenge with an outstation at Karonga, although the latter was soon to become the more important of the two. Further away still, to the north-west, a centre was opened at Mwenzo on the Stevenson Road, in August 1894, not far from the ALC's depot at Fife.[48]

A special building fund had been set up, separate from the Livingstonia General Fund, to pay for the establishment of the Institution and the carrying on of its work, and the sum of £25,000 was aimed at. In the first instance at least the appeal seems to have been addressed to those who were already supporters of the Livingstonia Mission, and it is not entirely surprising that it was hard to attract the additional money required. Gradually the appeal was addressed to a wider public and an endeavour was made to establish a collector in each congregation of the Free Church, with Presbytery representatives to coordinate the work. Until now the Livingstonia Committee had made its appeal every five years but annual appeals were now introduced and gradually contributions came in although Dr Smith frequently urged upon Laws the need for strict economy.[49]

Laws' vision was of a training institution which would serve the whole Mission. Young men, and to a lesser extent young women, of promise would come from all the stations to train as telegraphists, foresters, carpenters, printers, builders, teachers, evangelists and ministers. When training was complete much of the work which had been done by missionaries would be undertaken by the Africans themselves. This was not only desirable in itself but would also enable the Mission to make the best use of its limited resources in manpower.

Six ingredients would seem to be required in order to establish an Educational Institution of the kind envisaged: land, buildings, pupils, teachers, water and food, and Laws proceeded steadily to acquire each ingredient. He had set his heart on a large quantity of land, to secure a sufficient base for future expansion and to safeguard the sources of the water supply, and he obtained an ample sufficiency for his purpose.

Some building had been embarked upon at the very start, albeit of a temporary kind. As early as January 1895 the five roomed wattle and daub house intended to accommodate Dr and Mrs Laws, Mr William Murray, the carpenter, and Mr Malcolm Moffat, agriculturist, who had just joined the Livingstonia staff from South Africa, was well on the way to completion when it was hit by a tornado which levelled it almost completely to the ground. As a result Dr and Mrs Laws lived for quite a time in what had been planned as the kitchen and servant's room, which were separate from the house proper, and a small house was occupied by Messrs Murray and Moffat.[50]

In the course of the first year a workshop was built, with a wooden frame and reed walls, enclosing a saw-pit; a store with a corrugated iron roof; and six wattle and daub houses for native workers from a distance, some of them from Bandawe, some from Angoniland. It was claimed that the men's health improved in these houses since they were better than the booths they had made for themselves. There was also a workshop with a turning lathe and five work benches, at which doors and windows were made.[51] Of the Africans present at Kondowe in its early days the majority were men from Bandawe or Angoniland who were there to help with the work of construction. Even so, an adult school for workers was held each day in the evening and at the midday recess. The African population in the immediate vicinity was small but an Elementary School was begun with 22 boys and 6 girls in attendance, and among the older age group, two lads from Bandawe were given an apprentice's course in telegraphy.[52] As we have already seen telegraphists were asked for by Commissioner Sharpe in November 1894, and a start was made with supplying government and business establishments with the trained labour of individuals who could be relied upon.[53]

During 1895 the teaching staff was augmented by the arrival of the Revd James Henderson, an ordained man who had attended Moray House Teacher Training Centre, Edinburgh, for more than a year, and had also taken part of a medical course. He was placed in charge of the educational work at Kondowe.[54] Mr Thomson the printer returned from furlough about this time with his wife whom he had recently married. Mr Moffat was in charge of the Agricultural Department and had a garden prepared and experiments made with a variety of seeds. Cattle and sheep were found to thrive, but goats did not do so well. Four young men were being trained in agriculture at this time.[55]

By the following year the number under instruction had greatly increased, with 127 boys on the Roll of the Institution of whom 117 were boarders. They came from a hundred mile spread and from a wide variety of places and tribes, and included 42 Atonga from Bandawe, 23 boys from Angoniland and 13 from Karonga. It was reckoned that all the peoples on the west side of the Lake were represented. Owing to the shortage of accommodation only one out of three of those who sought admission could be accepted. James Henderson tells us that at the close of the session in April 1896, 21 boys from distant villages had pled for admission and that he had been compelled to select only five of them. Fees were charged and were often paid in flour or grain.[56]

A curious glimpse of the extent to which the missionary of those days was cut off from events at home is given us in a letter which Laws wrote to Amy on 22nd June, 1896. He asks her in what ways she has been celebrating the Queen's Diamond Jubilee in Edinburgh, and goes on to speak of the feast with which it has been marked at Kondowe. As a good patriot, he was aware of the approach of this special anniversary in Queen Victora's reign, but in the absence of radio, television or up to date newspapers, he had got the year wrong (although the day and the month were right), and was celebrating it a year too soon![57]

Miss Lizzie Stewart, the first woman appointed to the staff apart from the unfortunate Miss Waterston, had travelled out with Dr and Mrs Laws when they returned from furlough in 1894. After being stationed for a time at Bandawe, and then at Ekwendeni, Miss Stewart was moved to Kondowe where she was engaged in the instruction of girls at the Institution.[58]

On Sundays, what was called 'aggressive Christian work' was undertaken by African Christians who travelled to villages from two to eight miles distant as the crow flies. To facilitate this a Preachers' Class was held each Friday afternoon attended by all male church members. Out of this group volunteers undertook the village work on the Sunday following.[59]

Instruction was by no means confined to academic subjects and we find that on Monday evenings boys were taught how to mend clothes, and some training was given in the carpenter's shop.[60]

On the industrial training side eight sawyers were employed at this time in the carpentry department, where there were nine apprentices. Laws had originally looked to the Rumpi as a source of the Centre's water supply but in fact it was to the Manchewe, with its tributary the Kazichi, and its 150 foot water fall that he turned for his power source. The Manchewe was used also by the agricultural department which diverted a branch of it to irrigate a large field between the spur of the Nyamkowa Mount and the river itself. Experiments were made with a variety of crops including maize, beans, wheat and European potatoes. Fresh vegetables were grown in the kitchen garden and a terrace was prepared for fruit trees. There were four good apprentices in this department.[61]

A new cylinder printing machine had been obtained and to get it up to the plateau:

> Mr Murray constructed three wooden sledges, on which the heavy castings were, one at a time, securely fastened, and about 50 men to each dragged them up the cliffs by the native paths which had to be improved here and there by temporarily filling up the gullies crossed.[62]

The FMC's Report that year informed the Assembly that on the plateau at Kondowe there were now 12 Europeans, including the wives of missionaries, and eight native teachers. In the other stations of the Mission, North Angoniland had now four Europeans, Bandawe had six, Karonga one, and Mwenzo four. In addition there were 146 native Christian teachers and students. In the Boys School there were now 305 pupils, drawn from all the stations of the Mission, both in the Scottish and in the Dutch section. There was also what was called a 'Normal Department,' by which was meant a teachers' training department, and a theological department taught by Dr Laws and Mr Henderson. There had been four students studying theology but two of them withdrew from this course on the completion of their teacher training, leaving two continuing with the ministerial course.[63]

Miss Margaret McCallum and Miss Maria Jackson joined the staff in 1897. Both were trained nurses and they were in charge of the 52 girls who were now boarding at Kondowe. 23 of these girls came from Angoniland, five from Karonga, nine from Bandawe, and the remainder from the Henga villages round about. School fees had brought in £6.12.6d in the past year, quite a large sum in comparison with the earnings of the Africans at that time.[64]

Both Maria Jackson and Margaret McCallum speak of their pleasure in working with the girls and comment on their truthfulness. Miss McCallum finds them 'honest, clean and kind' and declares that they will be 'wise and helpful wives and mothers.' 'In English', she writes, 'the girls are very far behind.' This was partly due to their own feeling that they were not as clever as the boys, a feeling which made them reluctant to ask or answer questions in class. This was an attitude which their teachers tried hard to break down, being quite sure that the girls suffered from no innate lack of ability.[65]

Lord Overtoun informed the General Assembly of 1899 that the title deeds to the land had now been obtained, but what Mr Codrington of the BSA Company had agreed to when he visited Kondowe in August 1898 was still referred to as a 'provisional title',[66] although it was now close on four years since Laws, Elmslie and Yuraiah Chirwa had spent their first night on the plateau.

The School Report of 1899 showed 173 boys and 45 girls on the roll. Co-education had been introduced and competition was felt likely to prove a useful stimulus to both sexes, especially the girls.[67]

The school Session ran from June to September, and the daily regime was strenuous. It began with reveille at 5.30am and continued until Lights Out at 9pm, with a two hour break at midday. The evening was free, once the washing up after the evening meal at 5pm had been completed, until Prayers at 8.30pm.[68] A good deal of practical work was included in the programme and every endeavour was made to avoid giving the impression that those who could read and write should consider themselves to be above doing the practical jobs that had to be done. Laws himself, although conscious of his position as Principal of the Institution, was never one to look down on manual labour.

Mr Walter Henderson was now obtaining good quality stone from the quarry and in August of 1899 he made an addition to Dr Laws' house which measured 37 feet in length by 4 feet by 12 feet. He also went to work on Mr McGregor's house with help from 16 boys who were on vacation at the time.[69]

Meantime Duff MacGregor, who was himself a joiner, had begun preparations for the erection of a turbine, building a dam across the Manchewe, and making a cutting along the hillside for a water flume, and a mill house, the latter built of brick and roofed with corrugated iron. The turbine and machinery had arrived in August and all departments of work lent a hand in bringing the loads up the hill.[70]

Progress had been made in making the station self-supporting, and Mr Moffat was able to report that they were now growing all the food for the boarding department, except for *ufa*, flour ground from maize or other cereals, which was brought from Bandawe, and some rice which was obtained from Kota-Kota.

As for livestock there were 60 young calves and 300 head of cattle, and trek oxen were being found valuable in the hauling of loads. Surprisingly there were no agricultural apprentices at this time, but help was given by a number of yearly workers who liked to be free to move on after a year to higher wages elsewhere. A number of Mlanje cedars were planted, and avenues of cedars are a pleasing feature of the Livingstonia Mission Station today.[71]

Laws received great support and helpful advice from Thomas Binnie of the Home Committee in matters connected with building, and from James Cowan of Beeslack, near Penicuik, who advised Laws on paper and on printing material.[72]

There are signs that Dr Laws' colleagues in the field sometimes felt that the Institution was unduly favoured at the expense of other stations. This can be seen in the passing by Mission Council of a resolution in November - after Laws had gone on furlough - laying it down that new buildings on the plateau should be sanctioned by the Council in the same way as buildings at the other stations.[73]

One of the best glimpses of what was going on at Kondowe in the early years is given to us by the Revd Donald Fraser who writes of his first visit:

Almost all through the last day's march we could see in front of us the high plateau on which Livingstonia is built. But what a multitude of hills and ravines had first to be crossed! ....When, however, you have reached the plateau your courage is amply rewarded, for the situation is magnificent... Of course I did not expect to find Lovedale here for Livingstonia is not yet three years old, while Lovedale is more than fifty. Yet the progress that has been made is quite remarkable. The buildings are still only temporary. The great carpenter's shop and the printer's are built of reeds; the blacksmith's yard is in the shade of a spreading tree; and the missionaries' houses would, most of them, be rejected by the poorest labourer at home... Work is going on with a great swing. Hundreds of natives may be seen bringing the land under cultivation, hoeing roads on the trackless wastes, drawing logs from the mountains or making bricks for the houses. Everywhere there is the sound of song for the African works best when he sings... In the printing shop the cylinder machine was rolling off primers for Mwenzo, in the carpenter's shop boys were hard at work making furniture for the schools... The schools had the deepest interest for me, for there the boys and girls who are to be our teachers and evangelists are being trained. I found Miss Stewart teaching in a stuffy corridor and Mr Henderson among the distractions of plastering... Already Dr Laws and Mr Henderson have visions of a theological class for the training of a native ministry. Towards that great day, when we shall be able to ordain our first minister, we look forward with an eager faith. But the feature that struck me most was the pains that are taken to produce sincere and ripe character. Everyone has to take his turn at manual labour. The ordained missionary will sometimes be seen on the brick-field, and the native teacher sweeping the roads. There is certainly no lack of religious services. Every day and all day Christ is presented to the people. But I look upon the work of Mr Moffat and Mr Murray among the Angoni labourers as one of the most valuable evangelistic agencies of our people. It is something to see Angoni working alongside of Apoka, the people whom they had driven into mountain fastnesses not many years ago... more important is the fact that they hear the message of Christ. Hundreds of them go to Livingstonia every year for a period. Then they scatter to their own villages, to tell about all that they have seen and heard...[74]

14 THE OTHER STATIONS IN THE 1890S

CHURCH AT BANDAWE, 1901 - SCHOOL ATTENDANCE - HOSPITAL
NEEDED - GIRLS' CLASSES IN ANGONILAND - UMCA AT KOTA-KOTA -
CHAUNCY MAPLES DROWNED - DONALD FRASER AT EKWENDENI -
CHRISTIAN INFLUENCE IN CHOICE OF CHIEF - FRASER'S SACRAMENTAL
SEASON - PROGRESS AT MWENZO & KARONGA - GEORGE STEELE'S DEATH
- CLASSIFICATION OF MISSIONARIES - WOMEN DISADVANTAGED - STAFF
MARRIAGES - HENDERSON'S OPINION OF LAWS - GROWTH IN CHURCH AND
SCHOOL - STEPS TOWARDS AN AFRICAN CHURCH - NORTH LIVINGSTONIA
PRESBYTERY - AFRICAN HYMN WRITERS

The 1890s were also a period of marked advance in the other stations
as well. The FMC Report to the GA of 1895 listed the stations from
Mwenzo on the Stevenson Road in the north to Cape Maclear in the
south. It named 22 expatriate missionaries. Five missionary wives
were mentioned, but eight or nine were in the field at this time.
Albert Namalambe was listed as serving at Cape Maclear.[1]

With Livlezi transferred to the DRC, Bandawe was now the
most southerly station of the Livingstonia Mission, Cape Maclear
continuing as a substation. The Revd A.G.MacAlpine was in charge
at Bandawe and in his report for 1894 mentioned that one of the
Africans who was keenest in spreading the Gospel was a blind man,
Bartimeyu Tisipange, who was in the habit of going with a sighted
boy to read God's word to the people of a neighbouring village. He
had been taught braille by George Aitken.[2]

Of Bandawe itself Mr MacAlpine reported that there were
now 101 communicants, that classes for catechumens were in full
swing, and that native preachers were under instruction. He added
that there was now a great need for a proper church.[3] When Dr Laws
had been at Marenga's in June 1883 it had been agreed that all would
help to build a school which would be used for worship on Sundays.[4]
This building was no longer adequate for Sunday worship.

Accordingly we find Mr MacAlpine and two of the elders
from Bandawe, Stephans Potiphar and Benjamin Chizima, petitioning

the Mission Council in May 1896 for help to build a church which would accommodate over 1200 worshippers. The cost was estimated at £700 of which £44 had already been subscribed. Members and catechumens promised to give half a month's pay, worth some £25, plus two months work on the building, worth about £100, so that a total of £169 was being raised locally and it was expected that this total would reach as much as £200. In passing on the request to the Home Committee the Mission Council commended the members at Bandawe for their 'marked liberality'[5] - as indeed it was when the low rate of pay they enjoyed is taken into account.

In 1897 African elders were conducting services along a considerable stretch of the Lake shore north and south of Bandawe, and inland a school was being run at Mzenga, behind Chinteche, within 6 hours march of Dr Elmslie's parish. At Bandawe itself Sunday congregations usually numbered some 950 at Morning Service with about 500-700 attending the Service at midday. Far larger numbers were present on special occasions and a new and bigger church was certainly needed.[6] The Free Church General Assembly of that year heard that quite a sum of money had been raised locally and that 120,000 bricks had been made for the expected new building.[7] In 1898, in preparation for the building of a new church, 400 had offered free labour.[8] The new church was opened in May 1901, still without doors or windows, but 2000 were present at the opening ceremony presided over by Dr Dewar as Moderator of Presbytery. Two months later Dr Laws conducted the first Communion Service there with 340 sharing the Lord's Supper. The church, described as 'roomy and airy', was estimated to have received 1824 months labour on the part of 1324 people - equivalent to a donation of over £181.[9] The local Africans had given most freely both in labour and in money for the building of their church.

School attendance at Bandawe had averaged 1038 throughout the year of 1894, 36 of the pupils being boarders. Over 8,000 medical cases had been dealt with by George Prentice, and it was felt that a hospital was needed. W.D.Macgregor was in charge of what was called 'industrial work', which included both carpentry and brick-making. Printing was temporarily under the Revd R.D.McMinn, Mr Thomson being on furlough. There were at this time one journeyman and six apprentice printers. On the agricultural side three acres of ground had been cleared and a variety of seeds and trees planted.[10]

At Cape Maclear 224 pupils were receiving education but there were only Albert Namalambe and six other helpers for this large number.[11] In Angoniland the pioneering work done by William Koyi and George Williams, followed by the labours of Dr Walter Elmslie, Dr George Steele and Mr Charles Stuart, began increasingly to bear fruit. What were known as 'Girls' Industrial Classes' had an enrolment of 44 at Ekwendeni, and 25 at Hora. At Njuyu there was a Bible Class for both men and women, and early in 1895 a house was ready for the arrival of A.C.Scott, the teacher, and a reed and mud school had been prepared. There were also seven sub-stations as well as the three main Centres mentioned.[12]

The new Centre at Kondowe was staffed at this time by Dr and Mrs Laws, with Malcolm Moffat the agriculturist and William Murray the joiner, as colleagues.[13] At Ngerenge, Dr Kerr Cross was engaged in medical work and in evangelism, education, industrial work and women's work. The Revd Alexander Dewar and his wife were now established at Mwenzo, having moved from Livlezi when the DRC took charge there.[14]

The Livingstonia Mission had not yet established a station at Kota-Kota, some 70 miles south of Bandawe, although the matter had been spoken of, and it came as a disappointment to members of the Mission when the Anglicans, from UMCA on Likoma Island, acquired ground there with a view to starting mission work. Robert Laws wrote home that the important thing was that the Gospel should be preached rather than which body undertook to do so, but he also wrote in plain terms to Archdeacon Chauncey Maples reminding him of a discussion they had had together some time previously. Laws had understood the outcome of this to be that the Anglicans would confine their work to the vast extent of land lying to the east side of Lake Nyasa. This would avoid introducing into an African situation the divisions in church life which were familiar enough at home but which had no relevance for the Africans. The Anglicans argued that as the Free Church of Scotland had not in fact begun work at Kota-Kota they themselves were quite free to do so.[15]

There was considerable personal goodwill towards Laws and his colleagues; in appreciation of all the help that the Free Church Mission had given to members of UMCA who had been ill, and nursed back to health at Livingstonia, a letter of thanks and a cheque for 50 guineas had been sent by UMCA in 1891 to support the work of the Scottish Mission.[16] The Anglicans now offered to withdraw from Kota-Kota if the Livingstonia Mission would buy the ground they had acquired and also undertake to send a missionary there to begin work right away. Laws readily accepted the first condition, but had to say on the second, that he could give no immediate guarantee.[17]

Sadly, Chauncey Maples, who had been consecrated Bishop of Likoma in London in June 1895, was drowned with one of his companions in a storm on the Lake in September of the same year.[18] When Bishop Hine took over, the discussion about Kota-Kota was resumed, and in the end UMCA established work there under the Revd A.F.Sim, so that there was now an Anglican enclave in an otherwise Presbyterian area.[19]

In Angoniland the Mission team had been strengthened by the appointment in 1896 of the Revd Donald Fraser, with his excellent record of service to the Student Christian Volunteer Movement behind him. Fraser arrived at Livingstonia early in 1897 and was posted to Ekwendeni.[20] When Dr Elmslie came home on furlough he told the Assembly of 1898 that

the largest and fiercest of the warrior tribes in British Central Africa has become peacable and industrious without the firing of a single shot or even the visit of an agent or officer of the Government administration.

Although the first Angoni baptisms had taken place as recently as 1890, there were now 172 adult church members among the Angoni with 600 candidates for baptism.[21]

The influence of Christian ideas was clearly seen when a new paramount chief, in succession to the late M'mbelwa, was being chosen. It had been the custom after such an appointment was made for a party of warriors to be sent out 'to wash their spears in blood'. On this occasion, although chief Mperembe had wanted to be paramount chief himself he did in fact actively further the appointment of Mbalekelwa, the eldest son of M'mbelwa, and asked Mawalera Tembo, the first Angoni Christian, to stay throughout the ceremony so that they might do all things in proper order. The choice of paramount chief was accordingly made in the context of Christian worship. Mawalera Tembo urged the new chief to rule his people by the word of God and for ever to sheath the sword of his fathers.

Ng'onomo, who was chief in the Mzimba area, tried to raise the war spirit but Mawalera and other Christians opposed this and,

when Donald Fraser and Charles Stuart went to visit the chiefs,
Mperembe was friendly and promised that no *impis* would be sent
out, and the young Mbalekelwa showed himself well disposed
towards the missionaries and their plea. It was in keeping with his
whole attitude to the Mission that Mbalekelwa asked for schools to
be established in the villages and indicated that he himself intended
to be a pupil.[22]

In May of 1898, Mr Fraser (who had grown up in Lochgilphead,
where his father was Free Church minister) promoted among the
Angoni a Communion Season after the old Highland fashion. He
called the people together for a week of services, five days being spent
together 'humbling themselves before God'. A large grass screen
marked off an area sufficient for 2000 to 3000 people with a raised
platform in the centre. On the Saturday 195 adults were to be
received into the Church and 89 children. On the Sunday a huge
crowd of some 4000 people watched the celebration of Holy
Communion, which was served to the communicants present by
three ministers and seven elders. Fraser concludes his account with
the words:

Some faces that had been heavy and dull with the memory of
sin caught the radiance of the joy of the Lord.[23]

Writing home to Dr Smith by the same mail Dr Laws referred to 'Mr
Fraser's remarkable sacramental season' and added, 'Surely the Lord
hath done great things for us whereof we are glad.'[24]

By 1899 four European staff were located at Mwenzo and one
at Karonga, and a group of 13 boys, mostly from Wemba country
further west, had been freed from slavery by the administration and
placed in the care of the Mission at Mwenzo.[25] At Karonga it took Dr
Laws two days to interview applicants for the catechumens' class,
and to examine candidates for baptism. On this occasion 11 adults
and nine children were baptized and 43 people took Communion.
When the first 'church collection' was taken it brought in 6s 2d, plus
a quantity of beads and other things. One man, whose wage was
known to be 3s per month cast in one shilling as his offering. Eleven
schools were now in being with an average total attendance of over
1000, and a school of brick and lime had been erected, the people
giving their labour free, and making 174,000 bricks for it in the
course of a year.[26]

Although missionaries' wives were not regarded as 'staff' it is
fair to mention that at this time Mrs Laws, Mrs Elmslie, Mrs Kerr

Cross the second, Mrs McCallum, Mrs George Aitken, Mrs MacAlpine, Mrs Dewar, Mrs Thomson, and probably also Mrs William Murray, were all making a valuable contribution to the work. Miss Lizzie Stewart's appointment was mentioned in the last chapter. The women and girls at Bandawe, delighted to have her with them, were most disappointed when she was moved to Ekwendeni after only a month.[27] It is sad to record that Miss Stewart and the Revd George Steele having become engaged to be married in February of 1895, Mr Steele died within a few months of the engagement.[28]

As we have seen Miss Margaret McCallum and Miss Maria Jackson, who were nurses, followed Miss Stewart to the field in 1897. Miss M.J.Fleming, also a nurse, joined the staff in 1900. The contracts of employment under which women were sent out were as stringent as those of male artisans. New regulations for the Livingstonia Mission had been passed by the GA of 1894, and had laid down four Classes of Missionary:

1 Ordained Men and Doctors.

2 Graduates in Arts and Science, and Certificated Teachers.

3 Artisans and non-certificated Teachers.

4 Women missionaries, 'to assist in evangelistic, industrial and educational work among women and girls.'

Women were paid much less even than the artisans and it was laid down that should a woman missionary marry that would be regarded as the equivalent of resignation. She would therefore become liable to pay her own passage home.[29]

Of the six ladies appointed as salaried members of staff between 1894 and 1901, one was invalided home and the other five all married members of Mission staff. They would lose their entitlement to passage home as single missionaries, but would become eligible for it as the wives of serving missionaries![30]

The attitude of Dr Laws towards marriage among members of staff was ambivalent. On the one hand we find him writing to Dr Smith in 1898, 'Another turn up. Mr Moffat and Miss Jackson have got engaged.' The following year, however, while on furlough, he wrote to Dr Smith from Aberdeen about the need to make new placements of staff because of marriages which were about to take place and added:

...better our young men marry mission agents... than those who care nothing for the cause.[31]

Sixteen men were appointed between 1894 and the end of the century.[32] Of those men the Revd James Henderson MA went out in 1895 and remained in charge of the educational work at the Institution until his appointment as Principal of Lovedale in 1906.[33] The letters he sent home to his fiancée, Margaret Davidson of Watten, Caithness, during his first tour of duty give an interesting picture of the Mission and of Dr and Mrs Laws. Shortly after his arrival Henderson wrote in these terms:

> My respect and admiration for Dr Laws as a missionary worker and man grow every day. Such fears as I once entertained about not getting on with him seem utterly groundless.[34]

Two months later his regard for Laws has not diminished although he has become aware of certain limitations in his make up, and writes:

> For the Doctor I have the highest respect and admiration. His skill and practical knowledge are extraordinary, and his good sense remarkable. He is in my opinion in most respects the ideal of what a missionary should be, and his kindness to me has been great indeed and his consideration. At times I seem to see in him a smallness in petty things and on certain lines a restriction of outlook which I attribute to his early surroundings and training, but these points in which I may be entirely mistaken are overwhelmed into insignificance by his outstanding merits.[35]

This seems a fair judgment on the Doctor.

James Henderson did not think quite so favourably of Mrs Laws, although he again tries to be fair in his estimate:

> With Mrs Laws I did not get on at first at all well, indeed I know I have often been nothing short of rude to her but now things go quite smoothly and possibly had I known then what I know now my attitude towards her would probably have been somewhat different. During the early years of her stay in the country she had, I believe, some very trying experiences which have so acted upon her that her feelings have become blunted, indeed to such a degree that one wondered sometimes if she had any at all.[36]

He goes on to speak of Mrs Laws' good qualities:

> If it were only the trouble she is taking just now in catering for us all she would be deserving of much gratitude at our hands.[37]

He speaks also of the help which Mrs Laws gave to Yuraiah when he had difficulty in providing a sufficient 'bride price' for the wife of his choice. When first one cow and then two cows proved insufficient Mrs Laws gave Yuraiah a gaudy shawl to add to his gift to the bride's father and this seems to have turned the scales in favour of the suitor.[38]

In Laws himself academic gifts and practical ability were blended in a remarkable way, but the strictness of his upbringing, and perhaps the fact that he was an only child, had made him a man of few words. He did not find it easy to communicate, and, while respected and admired, he lacked the 'charisma' that characterised Fraser.

The many-sidedness of Laws is well illustrated by a telegram he sent to the General Assembly on what he knew would be 'Foreign Mission Day' in 1899 when Dr Stewart of Lovedale, the instigator of the Livingstonia Mission, was occupying the Moderatorial Chair. The Trans-Africa Telegraph line had reached the area of Florence Bay and Laws took the opportunity of marking the occasion by sending home this message:

To FREE, EDINBURGH. From Florence Bay. 24/5/1899. 309 adults, 148 children baptised, Ekwendeni. Send 400 iron sheets, 8 feet 6 inches. LAWS.[39]

The spiritual results of the work in Angoniland, and the practical needs of the station at Kondowe, were of equal concern to Robert Laws. He was as skilled in meeting the one type of need as the other.

The number of pupils at local village schools and the number of church members continued to increase at the various Centres. This was outstandingly the situation in Angoniland where 17 new schools were opened in 1899, attended by all ages; the demand for books increased from 1000 to 4000; a contingent of Zulu Testaments from the NBSS sold out in two months; church membership doubled; and there were no fewer than 1645 candidates for baptism with a similar number seeking admission to the catechumens' class. The examination of each candidate for membership by a European member of staff was seen as a safeguard against any superficial type of Christianity which might have attended a popular movement. At the same time the native church in Angoniland was aware of its missionary responsibilities and had launched a mission to the Sengas who inhabited the country to the west.[40]

In November 1899 the Mission Council agreed that the time had come for organising a truly African Church, with Kirk Sessions,

Presbytery and Synod. Two Presbyteries were envisaged, North and South Livingstonia, the latter comprising the area now looked after by the DRC. An approach was made to Blantyre, in the hope that if a Presbytery were established in that area also, the three Presbyteries might form part of a single Synod.[41]

The first meeting of the North Livingstonia Presbytery was held at Kondowe on 15th November. Dr Elmslie, the senior ordained man present, was elected Moderator, and the Revd A.G.MacAlpine, who had been with the Mission since 1893, was appointed Presbytery Clerk. Charles Stuart, Yakobi Msusa, and Noa Chiporoporo are recorded as being present as elders, and the Revd A.C.Murray of Mvera was associated with the Presbytery. It was agreed that there should be two meetings per year, the next one to be on the second Wednesday of May at Bandawe as the seat of the oldest congregation in the Presbytery. Records were to be submitted and reports given by congregations, and the expenses of Africans attending Presbytery were to be apportioned out among congregations. The Presbytery Minute concludes: 'To the native Christians present the Moderator explained the proceedings enacted before them'.[42]

At present the Presbytery was overloaded with missionaries but even so the latter understood that they were setting in train a process which would lead in time to an independent African Church.

We may note here that an important feature in promoting a genuine 'African Church' - as distinct from a 'Western Church', or a 'Scottish Church'- was the encouragement given by some of the missionaries, notably by the Revd Donald Fraser, to Africans to produce their own hymns and not simply be content with translations of Scottish Hymns and Metrical Psalms.[43]

Dr Fergus Macpherson has drawn attention to this and to the considerable number of hymns written by Malawians in their own tongue, and sung at gatherings which Donald Fraser used to have at Loudon, gatherings which Dr Macpherson says might be called *Eisteddfods*. The quality of these songs and hymns varied considerably but among them were many hymns of good quality, in an African idiom, which presently took the place of, or were added to, those introduced by the missionaries which were usually translations of European hymns. Dr Macpherson names five men deserving of special mention - the Revd Hezekiah Tweya, the Revd Jonathan Chirwa, the Revd Charles Chinula, the Revd Peter Z.Thole, and

Mawalera Tembo - who between them produced 63 hymns which found their way into the Hymnbook *Suma za Ukristu*, which was enlarged and revised some 30 years ago.

These hymns are expressed in terms of African thought and make use of African tunes, Mawalera Tembo courageously taking tunes sung by Angoni warriors and attaching Christian words to them.[44] Africans are natural singers and others besides the author will have been aware, while worshipping in Malawi, of the contrast between the liveliness and joyfulness of the African singing of such hymns as these, compared with their somewhat joyless and almost painfully slow rendering of some of our Scottish Hymns and Psalms - a mode of singing presumably learned from the early missionaries.

15 THIRD FURLOUGH AND SEMI-JUBILEE

CONCERN FOR LAWS' HEALTH - FURLOUGH, & DEMANDS FOR LAWS -
'INVEST IN THE NBSS' - ECUMENICAL CONF. IN USA - FLOUR MILL FOR
LIVINGSTONIA - EDUCATION AT KONDOWE - LAWS AT LIVINGSTONIA
COMMITTEE - LORD OVERTOUN - LAWS STUDIES ELECTRICITY -
ALEX.CHALMERS - SEMI-JUBILEE IN SCOTLAND & LIVINGSTONIA - UNION
OF FREE & UP CHURCHES - UF GA CONGRATULATES THE LAWS - NEW
RECRUITS - PETER MCCALLUM RESIGNS

In August 1898 Miss Margaret McCallum referred in a letter home
to the prevalence of fever in all the Mission stations and mentioned
that Dr Laws himself 'had a bad time in the spring... for a week we
were gravely anxious.'[1] It was no doubt concern for Laws' health that
led the Committee to send him a message via Dr Elmslie in May 1899
expressing their desire that he should take his furlough when the
time came. He agreed to leave for home in August, and on the
Saturday prior to their departure Dr and Mrs Laws were entertained
by the Institution's staff who realised that the Mission's semi-jubilee
was approaching. The following day Laws conducted both the
English and the vernacular services, and Wednesday 23rd being
declared a school holiday, a large crowd accompanied Dr and Mrs
Laws down the steep descent to Florence Bay to see them off on the
first stage of their journey home.[2]

    The Laws' Edinburgh address on this furlough was 70
Thirlestane Road. Mrs Gray had died but Margaret's sister now
resided there.[3] Laws was still greatly sought after as a speaker, and
required no fewer than 5 quires of notepaper (120 folded sheets) to
acknowledge the invitations to speak which he received![4]

    Some engagements he would be eager to fulfil - including
attendance at the Annual Meeting of the NBSS in the spring of 1900.
With his pawky sense of humour Laws observed at this meeting that
just as the price of pig iron had been to investors an indicator of
fluctuations in the price of other commodities, so the circulation of

the Scriptures was an index to the progress of civilisation. He spoke of the changes in Central Africa during the past 25 years from the time when no alphabet or school existed, to the present when there were 30,000 prospective readers of the Bible, and some even prepared to spend the equivalent of three months wages to acquire a New Testament or a Bible.

He teased his audience, many of whom would be business men, by appealing alike to their philanthropy and their business sense:

> If you want good investments in these hard times, put your money in the Bible Society. Where the Bible goes commerce is bound to follow; where the Bible changes the hearts and makes heathen savages into honest men you will find markets for your goods... the most reliable index of commercial progress is not the price of pig iron, but the circulation of the Bible.[5]

The first Ecumenical Conference on Foreign Missions in America was held in the Carnegie Hall, New York from 21st April to 2nd May 1900, and the delegates, who numbered 2800, including 700 missionaries, were welcomed by President McKinlay.[6] Dr and Mrs Laws and the Revd Fairley Daly, convener of FMC were present. Preaching in the Central Presbyterian Church, 57th Street, Mr Daly made special reference to 'the work of the Free Church of Scotland in Livingstonia during the last 25 years'[7] and Laws himself addressed the Conference on the educational aspects of the Livingstonia Mission.[8] Laws also took the opportunity to visit a Negro College in Virginia, and to see the mills at St Paul and Minneapolis, Wisconsin. At Wisconsin he acquired a flour mill for £100, the bill paid by a friend in New York.[9] The mill was later installed in the 'Homestead' at Livingstonia and gave many years of service.

At Livingstonia at this time Charles Stuart was in charge of the Institution school while the Revd James Henderson was on furlough, with Miss Lizzie Stewart and Miss Maria Jackson looking after the girl boarders who came from five or six different areas. The 30 children in the Kindergarten, aged three or four, would come from the immediate vicinity of the Institution, but those who were older were sent from all the other stations of the Mission.[10] At this time there were 10 white and eight African teachers at the Institution itself. Five of the senior pupils were studying theology, and one feels a certain sympathy with them on discovering that in Church

History the period they had to cover was 'from the 13th century to the Reformation!'[11]

At home the Livingstonia Mission Committee met in Glasgow some half a dozen times during the 18 months that Laws was on furlough and he attended regularly. At the first of these meetings - on 9th November 1899 - Laws was welcomed home, along with Peter McCallum and William Murray.[12] At this meeting the Committee expressed its support for Lord Overtoun and its sympathy with him in what are referred to as 'the trials he had passed through since last meeting.'[13]

This is a reference to the severe criticisms publicly made by Keir Hardie of the appalling conditions under which those employed at Lord Overtoun's chemical works at Shawfield had to work, and of the very low wages they received. It was stated that the men had no proper meal breaks but had to eat as they worked with their hands soiled with the chemicals, and should any employee take Sunday off to attend Church or Chapel he was compelled to lose Monday's wages also.[14]

The facts presented by Keir Hardie can hardly be refuted. Iain McLean states that Overtoun's friends were chagrined because he took no steps to rebut the allegations, but we should mark it down to his credit that he had the grace immediately to shorten the hours worked at Shawfield and that he abolished Sunday work, although grim working conditions prevailed at Shawfield till the end, and their legacy continues to affect the people of Rutherglen to this day.[15]

Overtoun is an enigma for he seems to have been a man of genuine personal piety and yet was too much a man of his time to think in other terms than he did of those who were his employees. There is equally no doubt as to the very considerable financial support which Overtoun gave to the Livingstonia Mission. He took responsibility for the salaries of the Revd Dr Elmslie, and the Revd Dr Prentice, and also of Dr Boxer and the Revd D.R.Mackenzie, a total contribution, per annum, of over £1200.[16] In addition to this, when Laws brought forward his proposal for introducing running water into the mission station at Kondowe at a cost of £4000, Overtoun undertook to meet this also.[17]

It is known that Laws undertook some study of electricity during this furlough. Three hard-backed notebooks survive marked 'Heriot Watt College', dealing with 'Practical Electricity', 'Electrical Engineering' and 'Physics'. The two last mentioned both carry the name 'Robert Laws', although there are only a few exercises in each.[18] No record exists of Laws being a matriculated student at Heriot Watt, but he may well have 'sat in' on classes there.[19]

What is certain is that he received helpful advice from Professor Baily of the Chair of Physics and Electrical Engineering, and it was he who selected the electrical system presently to be installed at Livingstonia.[20] A Heriot Watt student, who heard Laws speak from the pulpit, volunteered for service with the Mission and was appointed as technical instructor. This was Alexander S.Chalmers, who had attended the Heriot Watt in sessions 1895/96, in 1897/98 and in 1900/01.[21] Laws sailed for Africa in June, and Chalmers was sent to Zurich in August 1901 to see the machinery packed, before sailing himself from Hamburg.[22]

The semi-jubilee of the Mission fell on 12th October 1900. In Scotland, an article written by Laws entitled *Twenty Five Years* was featured on the front news page of The Record, and ran to 3½ double columned pages, with six illustrations and a sketch map.[23] He emphasised that the Institution at Kondowe was not to be seen 'as a rival but as the helping servant and complement of the other stations.' There was a need to train pastors and teachers, and to prepare people for 'the new environment in which the advance of European civilisation places them.'

This may flatter 'European civilisation', but the central regions of Africa were bound to be brought into contact with the rest of the world sooner or later and it was certainly for the long term good of what was to become the state of Malawi that the missionaries, limited though their outlook might be in many ways, had brought the Good News of the Christian faith to that area before the advent of those who came to exploit its undeveloped resources and to make money for themselves.

At Livingstonia the anniversary was celebrated by the holding of a 'Semi-Jubilee Conference' attended by 37 Europeans drawn from 7 different Missionary Societies - Free Church of Scotland, Established Church of Scotland, Dutch Reformed Church, Zambezi Industrial Mission, Moravian, Tanganyikan and Berlin Missions. A representative of 'Mandala', i.e. ALC, was also present. Alexander Hetherwick of Blantyre preached and dispensed Communion, and cablegrams were sent to Dr Laws and Dr James Stewart on 12th October.[24]

No doubt Laws would attend the Union Assembly which met in Edinburgh on 31st October to unite the Free Church and the UP Church into one body to be known as the United Free Church. He himself had for quarter of a century embodied in himself the principle of such a union, although he had always felt that loyalty to his own UP Church obliged him to remain a minister within it until such time as the Union so many desired should come about. The General Assembly of 1901 expressed thanks for the work of the Livingstonia Mission and their congratulations were extended especially to Dr and Mrs Laws, on the occasion of the Mission attaining its semi-jubilee. The Laws were about to sail at the end of their furlough and were accompanied on the journey by Miss Agnes Lambert, teacher, who later married the Revd Duncan R.Mackenzie and by Miss Winifred Knight who was said to have looked upon Laws' visit to Auchterarder in June 1990 'as a red letter day in her life'. She went out in an honorary capacity.[25]

Also in the party was F.W.Hardie, a young surveyor aged 20. For Hardie this was the start of six years of valuable work 'in connection with the water works, the Longmuir Road, and the surveying required for the supply of water required for the turbines.' During his service Mr Hardie also prepared maps asked for by the Livingstonia Committee, and drew up plans for four churches, besides smaller buildings in the Mission.[26] No fewer than 13 new members of staff were recruited in 1900 and 1901, considerably above the average annual intake.[27]

It is sad to record the loss to the staff at this time of Peter McCallum, the carpenter from Rothesay, who had given three terms of service, beginning in 1881.[28] He gave his wife's health as the reason for his resignation[29] but there were certainly other factors.

When the 1894 regulations were passed by the GA, home allowance was to be provided for the children of doctors and ministers on the staff who had to leave their sons or daughters in Scotland. McCallum later enquired if the allowance could be claimed by artisans.[30] This was not provided for and Dr Smith was unwilling even to discuss the matter with him.[31]

By the time of his third furlough McCallum wanted an assurance that he would be used not simply as a carpenter but would have more opportunity to engage in evangelistic work, or perhaps even be head of a station. The Committee, however, reaffirmed that his appointment was as a carpenter and insisted that any other arrangements were entirely in the hands of the Mission Council.[32] When McCallum finally sent in his resignation, the Committee, at which Laws was present, recorded rather briefly 'their appreciation of the services of Mr Peter McCallum during his terms with the Mission.'[33] He had in fact served for 19 years, and a more generous tribute might have been expected.

The journey back took Dr and Mrs Laws less than two months from London - a marked contrast to the five months taken by the original expedition - and Laws reached Livingstonia on 6th August 1901.[34]

16　EDUCATION AND INDUSTRIAL TRAINING

The Longmuir Road - telegraph line & PO - silver wedding -
electricity switched on - a glance back to start of Institution
- 302 pupils from 13 tribes - rebel girls - courses & regulations;
fallout rate - Senatus established - exam questions; high marks

Back at Livingstonia Laws threw himself into the work of the
Mission with his usual energy. He now had a surveyor and an
electrical engineer to bring their special skills to bear, and further
attention was now given to the road up from the Lake which called
for serious improvement. The previous year the Revd James
Henderson had got a group of boarders, who lived too far away to
return home during one particular vacation, to work on the road and
improve the track,[1] but with the advent of Mr Hardie a real
endeavour was made to make the road broad enough and firm
enough to be used by carts. Hardie aimed at a road 15-20 feet broad
with gradients of 1 in 20. By 1905 the 12 miles of what had come to
be known as the Longmuir Road, after an Aberdeen lady who had
made a bequest for the purpose, was completed.[2] The road is now
known locally as *Gorodi*, possibly the Malawian pronunciation of
the name Gauld (James Gauld the builder, who served at Livingstonia
from 1900 to 1905). The road ascends and descends by 22 hairpin
bends while rising over 2,000 feet within three miles. To travel on
it today, even by car, is quite an experience!

The telegraph line, which up to now had terminated at
Florence Bay, now had a loop running up to the plateau,[3] and it was
not long until a Post Office was set up at Livingstonia. The PO
Building with its clock tower remains, although it is not now the
Post Office, and while telegraph wires can no longer be seen, the
cutting through the trees along the route they followed is still clearly
visible from the plateau.

By 1904 the five miles of steel pipes to carry the water from
the hills had not only been shipped out, and laboriously hauled up

from the lake, but laid in position from the source of the water supply in the hills down and up the slopes of the intervening valleys to the buildings on the plateau. On 20th January of that year a telegram was sent to Lord Overtoun: 'Water turned on. All send you grateful thanks.'[4] W.P.Livingstone tells us that when Mr Hardie checked the measurements which Dr Laws had previously made for the water supply (used to calculate the quantities of material needed), the Doctor's measurements were found to be accurate, and so further delay and additional expense were avoided.[5]

On 28th August 1904 the Mission staff, European and African, celebrated the Silver Wedding of Robert and Margaret Laws. An address was read in the native tongue by Yuraiah Chirwa on behalf of the Africans, and was signed by Yuraiah on behalf of the Church at Livingstonia, by Charles Domingo for the school, and by Ephraim Ziwake on behalf of the apprentices and journeymen.[6]

In the evening a special dinner was held at which an Illuminated Address was presented by Mr Thomson and a reply made by Dr Laws. The Revd J.S.Moffat CMG, son of Robert Moffat of Kuruman, and father of Malcolm Moffat (with the Mission for the past 10 years) was present as a guest and the blue flag with the white dove, which had flown from the masthead of the *Ilala* in 1875 was on display.[7]

Meantime work on the turbines at the Manchewe falls and on the necessary dynamos had been proceeding. On 12th October 1905, the 30th anniversary of the Mission, a holiday was arranged to mark the switching on of the electricity. Most of the Europeans walked the two to three miles from the station to the Manchewe Falls, breakfasted within sight of them, and saw the dynamo set running; Dr Elmslie was called on to 'switch on' in the motor room of the new workshop. In the evening Europeans and Africans gathered in the school/church, the oil lamps were put out, and little James Innes, son of Dr Frank Innes, who was just over a year old[8] and was seated on his mother's knee, was encouraged to put his finger on the button and all the electric lamps glowed. There were cheers of surprise and wonder all round. Sadly, the unexpected death of Winifred Knight, who had married Dr Ernest Boxer in 1903,[9] threw a gloom over the proceedings.

The provision of electricity meant that keen pupils would no longer have to stand outside the windows of the rooms which were lit by oil lamps to obtain sufficient light to study after sunset.[10]

To understand how educational work at the Institution developed, we need to go back a little and look at what was done in school and training Centre in the first three years. In July 1895 the Revd James Henderson, with teacher training behind him, took over the school classes which had been carried on by Mrs Laws since the station opened at the end of the previous year. There were five pupils in the upper school; classes were held in a reed shed and practically no teaching material was available. At the same time an elementary school was conducted in the vernacular by Charles Domingo for the children of Mission workers who came from nearby villages.[11]

In December 1895 Dr Laws admitted one pupil from Blantyre, 19 new pupils from Bandawe, of whom three were teachers hoping to train for the ministry, and 10 from Angoniland. Further additions in the next few months from Bandawe, Hora and nearby, brought the total of Upper School boys up to 46 at the end of the first year.[12]

When school reopened in June there was what was described as 'an invasion of applicants', and this despite lack of accommodation. Many came from districts where no missionary work had yet been done, and it was found impossible to refuse them. The roll rose to 106 of whom 96 were boarders. Six pupils were in the 'Normal' Class to do teacher training, and in the evening they became pupil teachers in the night school: here Mrs Laws conducted classes for English reading.[13] When the second school Session closed in April 1897, 119 pupils had been examined from standard VI down.[14]

School restarted in June with the addition to the roll of one pupil from Mvera, three from Cape Maclear, and eight from Mwenzo well on the way to Lake Tanganyika in the north. In August a continuation school was begun for teachers from the Mission stations, and 41 attended the five week course. 16 passed the entrance exam for the Acting Teacher Probationers Certificate. Three students, Yuraiah Chatonda Chirwa, Charles Domingo and Samuel Kauti, received Teacher Probationer Certificates, the first named scoring 89% in Scripture Knowledge. None of the three scored nearly so well in the Theory and Practice of Teaching![15]

By the end of the calendar year 1897, 302 pupils were under instruction in 4 groups:

Theological Students, Normal & Upper School	19
Lower School	158
Evening School	72
Ruatizi Village (2 miles away)	53

This was an increase of 24 on the previous year, and those under instruction came from 13 different tribes - *Henga, Tonga, Ngoni, Poka, Namwanga, Nyanja, Tumbuka, Konde, Wanda, Kondanga, Senga, Siska, and Gunda. When the end of the session came in May 1898, 112 were examined according to what was called 'the new code'. The difficulty of subjects presented in English was noted, as well as the fact that in the middle and normal school classes were too large.[16]

Occasionally there were outbreaks of near rebellion among the pupils. For example in July 1897 the Angoni girls protested about the cold in the early morning, and objected to taking a bath even at mid-day because of the cold. Five of them were called in to see Dr Laws, and it was agreed that the girls could start the day half an hour later in the cold weather.[17]

The following month a junior girl from Bandawe, Lizzie Njaa, received flour from home and asked one of the married women to cook porridge for herself and several others who accordingly left their breakfast maize untouched. The report of this incident records in rather hurt tones that 'four of our baptized girls were leaders in the deception.' When challenged the girls expressed their regret, and Lizzie herself was not expelled 'because she was young and had been influenced by the seniors.'[18]

Apart altogether from 'Classroom teaching' there was considerable emphasis on the apprenticeship courses, and these covered carpentry, building, printing and bookbinding, and at a later date, clerking, blacksmithing and engineering, storekeeping and tailoring.[19] The full apprentice course was one of five years, and one can see the hand of Laws in insisting on so long and thorough a training. The aim was admirable, but not everyone, be his skin black or white, has the staying power or the commitment of a Robert Laws, and it is not surprising to find that a great many abandoned their apprenticeship before their time was out. Five years was a long time to be away from one's own village - with a visit home perhaps only in the long vacation - while at Blantyre apprentices became journeymen after only three years![20]

*Note: the people of many African tribes are properly denoted by an A-prefix (Ahenga etc), and - for the Bantu group of peoples - the language by a Ki- or Chi- prefix. But the issue is complicated, and practice not uniform.

The working day was from 6am to 5pm (6am to noon on Saturdays) with 1 hour allowed for breakfast and 2 hours for the midday meal. For the first six months apprentices were considered to be 'on trial' and no pay was given, although they were entitled to board and lodging and were provided with a blanket for use at night and a garment for day time. It was estimated that the food provided for an apprentice cost the Mission, on average, 4s per month.[21]

After the first six months apprentices received 3s per month and this gradually increased until, in their final year, they were receiving 6s per month, plus board and lodging, with small extra payments of 6d, 1s, or 1/6d, for those who had passed Standards III, IV, or V respectively at school. To secure better educated lads as apprentice printers a further extra 6d was given to those in this category who had passed Standards IV or V. A bonus of £3 was given to the who satisfactorily completed their 5 year apprenticeship. The Table shows the situation between 1894 and 1914.

Subject	No. of Apprentices enrolled	No. who completed the course (with or without bonus)
AGRICULTURE	49	28
BUILDING	107	41
BLACKSMITHING and ENGINEERING	14	8
CARPENTRY	154	80
BOOKBINDING & PRINTING	27	10
TAILORS (1908-1913 only)	5	4
CLERKS AND STOREMEN	1	1
	---	---
TOTAL	357	172

It is clear from this that there was a high fall-out rate. One or two died, a few were dismissed, but many simply went home after shorter or longer periods.[24] In the 20 year period prior to the First World War only 48 per cent completed a full course. Many of those who left early had nevertheless received a considerable amount of training and would be able to make use of their skills either in their own villages, or in the employment of the Colonial Government or of planters. Men trained at Livingstonia were soon sought after because they had a reputation for honesty and reliability as well as for good workmanship.

It was not only from the stations of the Livingstonia Mission that young people came seeking training at the Institution. It was used also by the LMS, who worked in the area of Lake Tanganyika, and by the Garengaze Mission much further to the west; in 1906 the Revd D.R.Mackenzie reported that 12 young men travelled 200 miles in the hope of gaining admission and only three could be accepted.[25]

A Senatus to be in charge of the Livingstonia Missionary Institution was brought into being on 9th August 1901, and on this occasion Dr Laws stated that it had been his custom fron the start to consult with his colleagues on the work.[26] There is no reason to doubt that Laws sincerely believed this to be true, but many of his colleagues must have been a little surprised, for it would seem that Laws was inclined to take most decisions of any importance himself, and then perhaps ask his colleagues if they agreed, with their agreement virtually assumed. Certainly the Revd James Henderson wrote to Dr Smith in March 1901 asking that a Senatus should be formed since he felt that control of the Institution had passed out of the hands of the Mission Council, on which he had a voice, and that he did not now know where he stood. In particular he was protesting because he had heard that at home Laws was making certain arrangements which were contrary to what had been arranged before Laws left on furlough. Wrote Henderson:

> I cannot protest against it except to Dr Laws himself, who will, as in all or nearly all previous cases, agree with what I say entirely but follow quite another course.

Henderson felt very disheartened by the working conditions at that time.[27] With the arrival of the Revd Duncan Mackenzie in 1901 there were three ordained men at Kondowe, when the Senatus was formed. Dr Laws, Principal of the Institution, was the executive member; industrial and artisan staff were to be in his hands.[28] At this time, although there were several women on the staff of the Institution, there was no one but the ministers on the Senatus.

The subject matter in school was somewhat biased towards Scotland, with pupils of Standard V being asked, for example, to explain the right of James VI of Scotland to the throne of England, or to describe the shortest sea route from Glasgow to Inverness telling the Capes and Lochs on the way![29] Some attempt to come nearer to the pupils' experience was shown in questions to Standard IV such as 'A man gets 3d a day. How much will he earn in the month of September?' - to be done mentally - or in the written question, 'I give my Capitao (or foreman) £30 to pay 15 men a fortnight's wages at 19s per week. What change should he return to me?'[30]

The theological students, who were at the top end of the training ladder, found themselves asked in Systematic Theology to 'Distinguish Trinity from Triunity', and to discuss the statement, 'God does not by predestination destroy that freedom in me which is essential to moral growth.'[31]

The Africans are patient people, and not only submitted to learning things quite remote from their own situation but, in many cases, passed their examinations with extraordinarily high marks. For example, in the Normal Department in April 1905 there were 24 in Standard VII and marks ranged from 61% up to 69%, while the 30 pupils in Standard V scored between 63% and 69%. Among those studying theology, Jonathan Chirwa came first among the six taking that course, with 92%, while the lowest mark of any was 57%. In the medical course, Yoram Mayanji scored 70% in what was called osteology, and 90% in chemistry, while Isaac Mkuzo gained 85% and 62% respectively in the same two subjects.[32]

The missionaries certainly had no monopoly of brain power, and Robert Laws' faith in the ability of the Africans to respond to higher education was fully justified.

17 THE AFRICAN CHURCH EVANGELISES

INCREASING AFRICAN INITIATIVE - WESTWARD EXPANSION - CHITAMBO
OPENED - MOFFAT FAMILY - ANGONI ENTER PROTECTORATE - SALARIES
OF CERTIFICATED TEACHERS - SCHOOL FEES - AFRICAN THEOLOGICAL
STUDENTS - LICENSING AS PROBATIONERS

Progress in Livingstonia was not, however, to be measured solely in terms of improvements in plumbing, lighting and power, nor yet in terms of the education being provided by the European for the African.

The seeds of the Gospel had taken root and now Africans themselves were taking an increasing share in educational and evangelistic work. In some ways the later 1890s and the first years of the 20th century may be seen as the time when the Livingstonia Mission reached its high water mark. Considered in another way, these years may be seen as the watershed when the initiative in evangelisation began to pass from the European to the African, albeit with a long way to go before the transition was complete.

The influence of the Institution as a centre of higher education was on the increase; and the indigenous church was taking an increasing part in communicating the Gospel to those who had hitherto been beyond the influence of the Mission.[1]

outh - Work had been going on at Kasungu, five days journey westwards from Bandawe, among the Chewa people, since 1900, and Dr Prentice had given valuable service there. With the help of 10 Bandawe Christians pioneering work was undertaken west of Kasungu, and in eight centres Atonga and Achewa worked together.[2]

One indication of progress was the number of Bibles being sold. In Angoniland the figure had risen from about 20 to 4000 in seven years.[3] The natives of Angoniland had also awakened to their responsibilities for 'the tribes beyond': 37 teachers undertook two months extension work in the Marambo[4] - the area of the plain which

lies to the west of the hills bordering the Lake. The Institution also
sent teachers, during vacation at the Institution, first of all to villages
seven days march away and then to places 14 days away. In some
villages people of all ages helped by giving their labour free to build
a church which would be used also as a school.[5] This outreach was
not a new development for as early as 1896, we hear of 'aggressive
Christian work' by native Christians in villages from two to eight
miles away as the crow flies,[6] a group from the Institution going out
during school vacation to bring the Gospel to the Poka people and
others.

A few years later there was missionary work among the Senga
also. 20 schools among them were led by Angoni Christians, and the
church at Bandawe sent 22 men to evangelise the Senga. They were
away five months, opened 13 schools and brought back 12 Senga to
the Mission Boarding school at Bandawe, all paid for by the native
church.[7]

The offer by the Administrator for NE Rhodesia of a tract of
land, which included Chitambo's village of Ilala where Livingstone
died, led to plans to establish a new station at Chitambo some 250
miles west of Lake Nyasa and more than 200 miles from Kasungu.[8]

In July 1906 Malcolm Moffat and his wife (Maria Jackson) and
family arrived at Chitambo from Mwenzo, almost 300 miles away,
and three weeks later they were joined by Alex Chalmers, the civil
and electrical engineer from Livingstonia.[9] The following year, on
returning from South Africa Mr and Mrs Moffat and their children
travelled via the Cape to Cairo railway as far as Broken Hill, and then
marched eastwards on foot, accompanied by 70 carriers; it was a two
week journey through country hitherto untouched by missionary
influence.[10] Their children at the time must have been under 5 years
of age. Dr Alex Brown arrived about the same time by the Nyasa
route, and commented on the magnificence of the country which
resembled Kondowe. The people of this area were Awisa, and were
described by Dr Brown as 'shy, poor and ignorant', and 'in need of
the Gospel'.[11] In July of the same year Laws sought volunteers at
Kondowe to go to Chitambo and sufficient responded to meet the
need.[12]

An event of considerable significance was the annexation of the
Angoni into the British Protectorate in 1904. Up to this time the
Angoni had been left under the rule of their own chiefs provided

peace was maintained and war parties no longer sent out. With the passing of some of the more dominant among the Angoni chiefs there was some danger of a breakdown in the system. On 2nd September, 1904, Sir Alfred Sharpe met with the chiefs and headmen of the Angoni, and carefully explained what would be involved if they agreed to come under the rule of the Protectorate. It was largely due to the Mission that the Angoni were willing to meet government representatives in this way and that the officials of the Protectorate were willing to discuss a settlement with the Angoni without imposing it by force.

A Government official was to be appointed to be in charge of affairs assisted by the paramount chief, and half a dozen other chiefs in council. No old cases were to be heard by the Council but a new book would be begun that day, and the police force would be made up of Angoni with a Zulu from the south, the nephew of a great Angoni chief, as head policeman.[13]

Dr Elmslie wrote of the occasion with enthusiasm, and emphasised the complete absence of military display. He wrote:

> It was the mission that took the spear from the warrior's hand and put into it the hoe, the trowel and the carpenter's chisel, and induced yearly thousands of able-bodied Angoni to go to the coffee and cotton fields at Blantyre, and to the mines and farms in Rhodesia where they labour contentedly and profitably for a given term, and return to their homes unscathed physically or morally.[14]

Towards the end Elmslie is letting his enthusiasm run away with him, for where migrant labour was involved there were both pros and cons to be considered, but his main point was a valid one.

It was through school as much as church that Christian knowledge spread. Many Africans had now been trained at the Institution and had returned to their villages as certificated teachers. Those with 1st Class Certificates received 19s per month; those with 2nd Class Certificates 17s per month; and those with 3rd Class Certificates 4s per month.[15]

The salaries were paid for only the eight months of the school year. They were small by European standards but nevertheless put the school master, who would still grow much of his food in his own garden, in a favourable position over against his neighbours. Parents were expected to pay school fees. These did not exceed 2d per quarter but this has to be seen against the average wage of 1d a day.[16] In Malawi today fees are still charged for pupils attending both primary and secondary schools.

Statistics are not everything but the fact that the General Assembly of 1904 could be told that the Mission now had seven main Centres and 220 outstations, with 323 schools, 718 teachers, and 18,000 scholars does give some indication of how the influence of the Mission had spread over the land.[17] At the Institution several Africans had now taken the Theological course as well as the Arts course, and by November 1900 two students had passed their exit examinations. Sadly, one of them, Yakobi Msusa Muwamba, of Bandawe, who had gained a teacher's diploma as well as passing in theology with credit, died shortly afterwards. The Presbytery recorded its deep sorrow and its appreciation of his 'sterling character, wisdom and zeal.'[18]

Charles Domingo passed with an overall average of 65% and with 85% in New Testament.[19] Domingo was the first African assistant teacher at the Institution, a post he held for two years. On May 13th 1903 he passed his trials for Licence as a Preacher of the Gospel and became the first African Licentiate. He was appointed by the Presbytery to assist Donald Fraser at Hora.[20]

On the same day the Presbytery learned that Yesaya Zerenji Mwasi and Hezekiah Marova Tweya had passed their exit exams - with average marks of 88% and 73% respectively. Yesaya was appointed to work at Bandawe, and Hezekiah at Njuyu, but neither was licensed until three years had passed, Yesaya in May 1906 and Hezekiah in September of that year.[21]

It took a long time for Laws and his fellow missionaries to give to the Africans in practice what they readily conceded in words to be their due. There seems to be no excuse for a delay of two and a half to three years between a divinity student passing his exit exam and his licensing; and while it is desirable that any young minister, whether European or African, should undertake a probationary period under a more experienced minister before seeking ordination, it is with dismay that we find that although Hezekiah Tweya and Yesaya Mwasi passed their finals in May 1903, and were licensed in 1906, they were not ordained until 18th May 1914. The process was only slightly speeded up for Jonathan Chirwa, who was ordained on the same date as the other two, having passed his exams in 1910 and been licensed in 1911.[22]

18 MISSIONARY MODERATOR

INSTITUTION WELL ESTABLISHED - MIGRANT LABOUR - CLASSES & SOCIETIES
- LAWS' NOMINATION AS MODERATOR - MEETS AMY AT NAPLES - DEATH
OF LORD OVERTOUN - INSTALLATION AS MODERATOR - VALUE OF
WOMEN MISSIONARIES - SWISS HOLIDAY - MODERATORIAL PROGRAMME -
ALBERT NAMALAMBE'S DEATH - VALEDICTORY AT NEW COLLEGE -
NBSS & NT IN FIVE LAKESIDE LANGUAGES - WHY AFRICA HAD NOT
BEEN 'OPENED UP' SOONER - 'THE OTHER SHEEP' - SERVANTHOOD -
ETHIOPIANISM - KAMWANA - CLASSES ON TROPICAL DISEASES - BLANTYRE
BY TRAIN

The fame of the Institution, which Laws had begun to set up on
returning from his second furlough in 1894, was now drawing
students from a wide area. By 1906, in the whole area of the Mission
33,000 children were being taught by 1000 teachers.[1] and at the
Institution itself there were apprentices in Agriculture, Building,
Carpentry, Blacksmithing and Printing.[2]

One result of all this was that many of those trained now left
home every year to obtain work in Johannesburg or Salisbury, or in
other labour markets of the Zambezi, or at the new mining centres
of Broken Hill and Kamboye, away to the west. This migrant force
created its own problems, with men away from their wives and
families for long periods, but they did bring home a larger cash
income, and the Gospel spread among people who had not heard it
before. Those who had become Christians were in the habit of
coming together for Sunday worship, thereby bearing witness to
their faith.

In the area of the Institution alone there were nearly 1000
baptisms in 1905, and 3000 were now members of the Church.[3]

Outside the classroom a Literary Society had been formed in
1898, and discussed such subjects as whether betrothal payments
should be reduced or abolished, and whether the people of Central
Africa were progressing, standing still, or retrograding when the
Gospel came to them.[4] A Debating Society followed in 1901, to meet

on Saturday evenings, intended to give practice in public speaking, and a branch of the Christian Endeavour was started two years later with 80 members on the roll, each one promising to undertake some piece of work for God every week.[5]

At home, in November 1907, the name of Robert Laws was proposed as Moderator of the UF Church General Assembly of 1908. Laws seems to have been genuinely surprised by the nomination but after a few days reflection he cabled his reply: 'Obediently accept nomination.'[6]

The news of Laws' nomination brought forth many tributes both at home and abroad. The Presbytery of North Livingstonia referred to the choice of one 'who has spent his life in the service of a race other than that to which the church belongs' and went on to say that the honour was 'in harmony with the warm regard and high appreciation in which he is held by his colleagues and native fellow Christians in the Church in Nyasaland.'[7] The Livingstonia News which came out in February 1908, formerly known as The Aurora, referred to 'Dr Laws' extraordinary habit of taking infinite pains in the smallest as well as the greatest details of life and duty.'[8]

Dr and Mrs Laws were given a send off by their colleagues and some hundreds of Africans as they set sail down Lake Nyasa on the *Queen Victoria* on 31st January, 1908. They were making their way to Scotland via Rome, and expected to reach Naples on 25th March.[9] They were welcomed by Mrs Laws' brother Dr Gordon Gray and by their daughter Amy of whom we have heard very little in the intervening years. She was now a young woman of 21, 'with a fluent command of French, German and Italian.'[10]

It was while he was at Rome that Laws heard the news of the death of Lord Overtoun - a serious blow to the Livingstonia Mission. The Committee at home at once instructed Dr Elmslie to reduce expenditure by £500 per annum, to help to compensate for the loss of Overtoun's annual donation of £1000.[11]

When the Assembly opened on 18th May the retiring Moderator, Dr McCrie of Ayr, nominated Laws in a stirring speech in which he spoke of him as one who had been dedicated from infancy by his parents to the cause of foreign missions.[12] On taking the chair Laws referred to his election as Moderator as a tribute to all missionaries, and went on to speak of the death of Lord Overtoun, as an occurrence which brought bereavement 'not only to his own home but to the whole Church and its mission field throughout the world'.[13]

Laws' opening address was a long one, of which The Scotsman politely said, 'Throughout a somewhat lengthened address which occupied an hour and a half the new Moderator commanded the attention and interest of his large audience.'[14] Bouquets were handed up to Mrs Laws and Amelia in the Moderator's gallery.[15]

The FM Report that year spoke of the Institution at Kondowe and drew attention to the fact that 'all lines of activity converged on the Church.'[16] In the words of the late Lord Overtoun the Mission was engaged in the work of 'moulding a nation and founding a Church',[17] and when all allowance is made for a distinctly pro-British point of view this is not an unfair statement of what was going on.

In Scotland 'Assembly-time' was not all meetings and speeches. In accordance with custom the Moderator entertained to breakfast in the Music Hall, George Street, all who were Commissioners to the General Assembly, with ministers and elders from different Synods being invited in turn on six different mornings, and on the Saturday evening the Moderator held an 'at Home' in New College.[18] Laws did not forget to invite to his reception Mrs Smith, his old Edinburgh landlady.[19]

At a public meeting, arranged by the Women's FMC on the Friday of Assembly week Laws spoke of the days when people looked askance at Medical Missionary work and when lady medical missionaries were undreamt of. The work of women among women, Laws said, was very important for the formation of Christian homes.[20] Clearly he had widened his outlook in the 29 years since Miss Jane Waterston's unhappy experience.

With the Assembly over Laws holidayed in Switzerland not only to let him recover from past activities but also to enable him to build up his strength for the strenuous months that lay ahead. From the Livingstonia Reports we know that Laws himself visited over 80 gatherings in 1908 (and this must have been done mainly in the last 4 months of the year), and 65 in 1909, while Mrs Laws carried out 43 speaking engagements in 1908 and 45 in 1909.[21]

One formal engagement he undertook was the laying of the Memorial stone at St Colm's, the women's missionary College in Inverleith Terrace, Edinburgh on 17th October,1908. He expressed the wish that a similar training Centre could be provided for men before they set out for the mission field.[22] That wish has been fulfilled for St Colm's is no longer a college for women only. The wall plaque on the stone includes a representation not only of the Burning Bush, the symbol of the Free Church of Scotland, (as of the old Established Church), but also of the Dove, symbol of the UP Church - the symbol which Laws had flown from the masthead of the *Ilala* in 1875.

It was about this time that word reached Scotland of the death of Albert Namalambe, who was the first Central African to become a Christian as the result of the work of the Livingstonia Mission. The Livingstonia News said of Albert that he was a man of considerable mental power but more outstanding were the qualities of his heart. Humble, eager to do right, ever willing to serve whenever and wherever called upon, he became a deeply loved messenger of the Master to many. In spite of tempting offers to enter Government service, Albert had held by his first choice of being a preacher and teacher to his own people.[23]

In March 1909 Laws delivered what was called a 'Valedictory' to the Divinity Students of New College, the UF Church College on the Mound. It was rich in counsel, not without humour and contained a number of memorable phrases. He urged his hearers to 'preach Christ crucified' and reminded them that a simple Gospel suited the needy heart of man. 'Preach that ye do know', he cried, 'and keep your doubts to yourself. Any fool can state his doubts.' He stressed the importance of pastoral visiting. Old and young alike were to be cared for, and a short prayer said with any who were sick.

Ministers and congregations alike, Laws said, had a responsibility for the slums, the drunk and the outcast as well as for 'the heathen world.' 'A lazy minister', declared Laws, in a sentence which must have roused any whose attention was flagging, 'is the glory of hell.'[24]

At the Annual Meeting of the NBSS in April 1909 Laws surveyed 34 years of work. In 1875 there was no written language around the Lake but now the complete New Testament was available in five tongues and portions of it in other languages.

'The throb of the Livingstonia Mission Press when printing the word of God in a new tongue', Laws said, 'made the sweetest music he ever heard.' He went on to draw attention to the contributions made by the Africans themselves to the work of the Bible Society.[25]

The previous year, at his installation as Moderator, Laws had asked the question why, in the providence of God, Africa had remained so long unknown to the nations of the west. The answer he gave was that God 'could not entrust the knowledge of Africa to Christendom. The evils of the slave trade would have been greatly multiplied had Africa been opened up 150 years sooner. God could only allow the Church into Africa when its conscience was awakened to the evils of slavery'.[26]

Now, in May 1909, at the end of his year as Moderator he took as the text for his closing address the words of St John 10 v.16, 'Other sheep I have which are not of this fold: them also I must bring, and there shall be one fold and one shepherd.' He emphasised the importance of seeking to bring all God's peoples into the fellowship of the Church. Christ's vision, he declared, was wider than that of his disciples and he saw in the despised Gentile the other sheep for whom, as well as for the Jew, he was soon to die. Our Lord's vision took in not only the limited world of his own day: 'The world with its multitudinous nations, known to the 20th century, as well as peoples yet unborn, all, all, are within the ken of our blessed Lord'.

He added that Christ had introduced into the world a new idea that was to act as a ferment in it, namely the idea that 'whosoever will be chiefest will be **servant** of all'. This idea was now at work in nations each of which up till then had been 'ring-fenced among its own possessions.'[27]

At the same time Laws declared that there could be peace only when the nations became one family, and that while arms could prevent war they could not build peace. The fact that slavery had been abolished raised the hope that the Christian conscience would be similarly awakened to the horrors of war. 'The inflowing of Christ's Spirit, and the outflowing of His love would yet sweep away all barriers', and pave the way for bringing every individual of mankind into the one flock of Christ.[28]

At the Annual Livingstonia Meeting of 1909 both Dr and Mrs Laws were among the speakers, as were Dr Frank Innes who had been on the staff since 1899, and Dr Alex Brown, who had been one of the pioneers at Chitambo. Laws spoke on this occasion about what was then called 'The Ethiopian movement', meaning the tendency among some Africans to break away and form an all native African church separately from Europeans. The movement had been experienced in the Bandawe area but no one had been drawn away from the church there, and Laws thought that the movement had spent its force.[29] This proved too optimistic a view, but it was true that Ethiopianism had little effect on the Church of Central Africa at that time.

About this time, however, a young man called Kamwana, who had been educated at Bandawe and Livingstonia, and had later become acquainted with Joseph Booth, formerly of the Zambezi Industrial Mission, began to proclaim that Christ would return to reign on the throne of David in 1914, when, in his view, all earthly governments would end. Kamwana protested about what he saw as obstacles put in the way of those seeking baptism at the Scottish Missions, pointing out that Jesus and the apostles had no catechumens' class but baptized all who were prepared to profess their faith. This young man baptized thousands by immersion without prior examination. The Government recognised him as a disturbing element and arrested him with a view to holding him at Port Herald till the year 1914 had come and gone.[30]

Laws' thoughts were constantly on the Mission and its needs, and W.P.Livingstone tells us that about this time he put down as his wish in Dr Ballantyne's 'Missionaries Wish Book' - 'The Regions Beyond - I'll try'. Underneath are written the words 'Margaret Laws - I'll help'.[31] In the autumn of 1909 Laws attended medical classes at Edinburgh University, including some on tropical diseases and the nutrition of infants. According to W.P.Livingstone these occupied his day from 9am to 6pm with sometimes an evening class as well. He also recruited Miss E.B.Cole, assistant matron at the Western Infirmary, Glasgow, for service at the new hospital at Livingstonia.[32]

At the end of their furlough the Laws left Edinburgh in December 1909. On this journey back to Livingstonia Dr and Mrs Laws arrived at Blantyre for the first time by train, using the railway which was being laid down at that time. Transport up the Lake was still by boat and on arrival at Bandawe Dr Laws conducted a Communion Service for no fewer than 1643 Africans.[33] A few days later they reached Livingstonia. It was May 1910 and they had been absent for just over two years and three months.[34]

PART IV

19 FINANCE AND THE LIVINGSTONIA TITLE DEEDS

EDUCATIONAL GRANT, & HOW TO DIVIDE IT - STAFF RETRENCHMENT - IN
LAWS' ABSENCE, MISSION COUNCIL RECOMMENDS CHANGES -
LIVINGSTONIA COMMITTEE COMES INTO FMC - LIVINGSTONIA &
BLANTYRE TO FORM ONE SYNOD; 'CCAP' - MATTERS OF CHURCH
DISCIPLINE - CENTRAL FUNDING; ORDINATION OF AFRICANS - DAVID
GORDON MEMORIAL HOSPITAL - TITLE TO KONDOWE - TRANSLATIONS
- LAWS IN TANGANYIKA - MR INWOOD - LAWS TO BE ON LEGISLATIVE
COUNCIL

Before leaving for Scotland in 1908, Laws had attended a Conference
at Blantyre to which the Acting Governor had invited eight mission
bodies to decide how a grant by the Treasury of £1000 for educational
purposes should be allocated. Alexander Hetherwick, Robert Laws,
and A.C.Murray of the DRC were all present along with
representatives of the White Fathers, the Zambezi Industrial Mission,
the Nyasa Industrial Mission, the South African General Mission
and the Seventh Day Adventists. Such a grant was less than the joint
deputation which met Lord Elgin had hoped for, but the offer of a
grant at all marked a new recognition by the British Government of
the important educational work done by the missions.[1]

Later in the year, when the Livingstonia Mission Council was
considering how to divide up their share of the grant (£275) within
their own Mission, it was proposed that nine tenths should go
towards Primary Education and one tenth towards Technical
Education, the home grant being reduced in proportion.[2] It seems a
pity that government money was used not to expand and improve
educational provision but to reduce the contribution from Scotland,
but the Livingstonia Committee was deeply concerned about its
finances at this time.

In September 1908, at a meeting at which Laws was present,
the Committee resolved to reduce its expenditure by £700 by

dispensing with a mason and a carpenter, and delaying the appointment of a printer.[3] The mason was Walter J.Henderson, who had been serving the Mission since 1896, and had been responsible for opening up the Livingstonia quarry.[4] The carpenter was William Murray, whose appointment dated from 1888! The insensitivity of the Committee - and Laws was a consenting party - is all the more strange since the same meeting agreed to aim at raising at least £2500 as a memorial to Lord Overtoun, the memorial to take the form of a portrait of Overtoun for the Assembly building, and a Memorial Hall at the Overtoun Institution.[5]

Laws himself also suggested that John McGregor, who had served the Mission as a joiner since 1899, should not be reappointed, but that David Adamson, who began his service in 1901, should take his place. The main reason for this suggestion was, it appeared, that one third of Adamson's salary was met by friends of his, and consequently, in his case a lesser financial outlay was required from Mission funds.[6]

These proposals to dispense with long-serving members of staff were strongly opposed by the Mission Council. Dr Elmslie cabled baldly: 'Murray remains Loudon protest superseding McGregor'.[7]

With funds scarce the Livingstonia Committee adhered to its decision about Murray, but decided that, as McGregor's term would not be up until 1911, they would postpone a final decision about him until later. In September 1909 the Mission Council reaffirmed its opposition to the decision to discharge Mr Murray after 21 years of service and pled strongly for reconsideration. The Council emphasised his faithfulness and his 'intimate knowledge of native life and thought.'[8]

In the event Mr McGregor continued to serve the Mission for many years, but William Murray resigned in 1910, and when he offered the following year to return to Livingstonia his offer was refused. Instead the Committee recommended that Muray be given an honorarium of £100 from the Bain Memorial Fund 'in consideration of his long and faithful services.' Murray wrote to thank the Committee for the £100, but he was clearly deeply hurt by the treatment he had received. He joined the Free Church, was ordained and appointed to serve in South Africa.[9] Henderson was not reappointed after leave in 1907-08 and later served in the New Hebrides.[10]

While Laws was in Scotland the Mission Council advocated a number of radical changes in the Institution. It recommended that the middle school at Kondowe should be closed and the boarding schools at each station used instead; that the infant department should be separated from the Institution and be run as a village school with a good staff; and that the continuation school should cease to be run centrally because numbers had grown too large.

For the future, the Institution should consist of a Normal School for teacher training, and a College for training evangelists and candidates for the ministry, and medical assistants. The courses in what might be called the 'Faculty of Arts' were considered out of touch with need and should be dropped. The minute ran as follows:

> In sending home these resolutions the Council are conscious that some of them touch on departments of work with which Dr Laws has been particularly identified. They feel considerable delicacy in discussing and recommending changes in these matters while he is still on furlough, but as the need for reorganisation and economy is pressing they have been compelled to review the situation at once and make their recommendations.[11]

Reading between the lines we can sense that members of Mission Council did not like to oppose Dr Laws when he was himself present, and yet wanted to make their views known to the Home Committee. It is noticeable that although the Minutes of the Mission Council meeting of 9th September were in the hands of the Livingstonia Committee at its meeting on 16th December, these radical proposals were simply not taken up or discussed - showing just how strongly the personal views of Robert Laws affected decisions about the work on the plateau.

At home the hitherto independent Livingstonia Committee was incorporated within the Foreign Mission Committee of the United Free Church. The latter was to appoint to what would now be the Livingstonia Mission Committee of the FMC, 16 representatives of the FMC and 16 drawn from subscribers to the Livingstonia Mission. The Committee would administer the affairs of the Mission, but would submit its minutes for the approval of the FMC, and would not undertake any new work without such approval. It made sense to bring the Livingstonia Mission within the overall control of the FMC, but some drop in revenue was anticipated as the link between subscribers and Mission would no longer be so direct. On the other hand the Livingstonia Mission would now be eligible for some share in legacies and grants to mission work in general.[12]

At the other end of the axis, in Central Africa, a union was also being pursued, this time between the Livingstonia Mission and the Blantyre Mission. Progress towards the union was made easier because of the long-standing friendship between those two giants of missionary enterprise, Alexander Hetherwick of Blantyre and Robert Laws of Livingstonia.

At a Conference held at Mvera in 1910 it was agreed that to unite Blantyre and Livingstonia in one Synod, with a Synod meeting held every three years, would make for the extension of the Kingdom of God. Some, like Dr Donald Fraser wanted the new church to be called simply the CCA (the Church of Central Africa), but most, including Dr Elmslie and Dr Hetherwick, carried the day with CCAP - Church of Central Africa Presbyterian. At least the word 'Presbyterian' was in a subordinate place, the type of church government being a secondary matter compared with the existence of the Christian Church itself in Central Africa. Those in Africa were more aware of the importance of this than those at home, many of whom favoured 'Presbyterian Church of Central Africa'. When Livingstonia Presbytery met in September it gave thanks to God that at last they were seeing the day when African pastors were being raised up to shepherd African congregations.[13]

In preparation for the union a joint committee, with Laws as Convener, had been set up to prepare a common 'Statement of Faith'. Seven European ministers, one European elder, and 28 African elders were present at a meeting of North Livingstonia Presbytery in October 1912 when Dr Laws presented the findings in seven paragraphs. It was agreed to send down the Statement for Kirk Sessions to consider.[14]

There were some matters of discipline in which different views were held by the two uniting bodies. For example, the drinking of beer by church members was a disciplinary offence in the Livingstonia Mission area, but it was not so at Blantyre, where the Church of Scotland Mission took a broader view in line with that of the Established Church in Scotland. The question was referred to a group of African elders and it was agreed that 'each Presbytery should recognise the discipline of the other.' For example, the Presbytery of Livingstonia decided on the principle of abstinence, and expected people coming from elsewhere to adhere to this if seeking membership within its bounds.[15]

Robert Laws was not only involved in drawing up the 'Statement of Faith' but with his practical approach argued for the establishment of a Central Fund to enable an independent African Church to provide stipends for its ministers and evangelists. He insisted that before any congregation should be allowed to call a minister of its own it should have in hand at least enough to provide for the first year's stipend. In addition self-supporting congregations should be asked to contribute at least 10 per cent of their total income to the Central Fund in order to help provide stipends for the ministers of less well off congregations. The stipend for African ministers was to be £2 per month, inclusive of ministerial income from all sources; licentiates were to receive £1.15s; and evangelists £1 per month.[16]

The following year, in August 1913, the Presbytery of Livingstonia adhered to the name CCAP, in spite of the Home Committee favouring Presbyterian Church of Central Africa, and accepted the proposed 'Statement of Faith'. As to the Central Fund, nine Kirk Sessions were in favour but the Kirk Session of Loudon, while approving in principle did not think that the time had yet come for such an arrangement.[17]

The question of the ordination of licentiates was bound to arise, and Laws, with his usual caution, moved that even when a local congregation had called a minister, the Presbytery might review such an appointment later and even transfer the minister to another congregation needing a pastor. At this August Presbytery meeting, the Loudon Kirk Session requested the ordination of Jonathan Chirwa. Dr Laws concurred, and proposed that to make the occasion as impressive as possible the three men who were at that time licentiates should be ordained together. Presbytery agreed that the ordinations should take place at Bandawe, the oldest of the congregations within the Mission, but fixed a date 10 months ahead.[18]

At long last, on 18th May 1914, the first three African ministers were ordained. Hezekiah Tweya was of Atonga origin but had grown up within the social structure of the Angoni; Yesaya Mwasi was an Atonga; and Jonathan Chirwa was an Angoni of Tumbuka origin. Angoni - Atonga - Tumbuka - 25 years earlier they had been raiding and fighting each other. Now the power of the

Gospel had overcome their enmity and united them within the family of the Christian Church.

Both European and African members of the Presbytery were well aware how important a step was being taken in ordaining these men. A Deputy from the Home Church, the Revd J.H.Morrison was present. Dr Laws put the prescribed questions to the ordinands, and when they had signed the formula,

x y

> Descended from the pulpit and by prayer and the laying on of hands, in which the members of the Presbtery joined, did solemnly ordain them to the work of the Holy Ministry, and did admit them to pastoral work within the bounds.

When the Right Hand of Fellowship had been given, the Revd A.G.MacAlpine addressed the ordinands, and the Revd Dr Elmslie the congregation. It was all very Scottish and Presbyterian, but at the same time it was another step towards what was to become the CCAP - the Church of Central Africa Presbyterian.[19] The inauguration of the Synod of the CCAP, however, was delayed by the outbreak of war in Europe in 1914.

Meantime, on the plateau at Kondowe the foundation stone of the David Gordon Memorial Hospital had been laid on 11th February 1910. Two sisters, Miss Isabel and Miss Jane Gordon of Montrose, had offered the sum of £5000 in October 1902, in memory of their brother the Revd David Gordon who had died in July that year. Their desire was that the building should be of a 'substantial' nature and not of a temporary character, and they envisaged £2000 being spent in the erection of the building with the remaining £3000 invested to provide for its maintenance. Should future enlargement be desired this could be paid for out of the balance of capital, but such a decision would obviously mean that a smaller annual income would be forthcoming.

The views of the Mission Council as to a suitable site were to be sought but the final decision was to rest with Dr Laws.[20] He decided to make an exhaustive study of hospital construction and equipment, and wrote to India and elsewhere for information.[21]

Three and a half years later the Home Committee learned that Laws had put forward plans for a much larger hospital than the resources allowed[22] and smaller scale plans were prepared by Dr Mackintosh, foremost authority in Scotland on hospital construction, and Mr Burnett, architect of the Western Infirmary, Glasgow, who suggested a central administrative building with two wards, each of eight beds, on each side of it, but capable of enlargement.[23]

The plans commended themselves to the Committee who cabled to Laws to call a meeting of Mission Council to consider them before he himself came home on furlough. Some modifications, suggested by the Council, were accepted and in June the revised plans were finally approved, and permission was given to spend £3000 of capital on the assurance of the architects that this was necessary.[24]

The Hospital was finally opened on August 16th 1911 by H.E. the Governor Sir William Manning, and Lady Manning.[25] The key for the door was offered to Lady Manning on a tray and when she had turned the key she was given a bouquet by the small daughter of Yuraiah Chirwa.[26] It was nine years since the original gift was made, and one can understand if the Misses Gordon were puzzled by the length of time taken by Dr Laws to use their gift. Much later, when the worth of the hospital had come to be widely recognised, we find Laws writing at considerable length:

> We have tried to make the Hospital the worthy memorial of your brother you and your dear sister wanted it to become and it is recognised throughout the Nyasaland Protectorate as being the model hospital and even far beyond it.[27]

There was at first some apprehension on the part of the Africans about making use of this large and strange building,[28] but confidence grew and in the year 1914, 6843 outpatients were seen. There were 114 inpatients, and some 59 surgical operations were carried out that year.[29] Miss Cole had come out from the Western Infirmary, Glasgow, to be the hospital's first matron.[30]

One serious problem which continued to recur over a period of years was the question of the titles to the land at Kondowe, and the amount of land which the Mission might regard as its own. Naturally, Laws was anxious to push ahead with his plans for the Institution, and with 302 pupils under instruction at the end of 1897[31] some accommodation of a temporary nature must clearly have been provided.

Assembly Reports in the years that follow express no doubts about the validity of the titles and the FM Report to the Assembly of 1909 mentions that the Livingstonia estate has accepted from the BSA Co. an amount of land 146 square miles in extent.[32] It must have come as a shock to Laws to learn, when he was on his way back to Africa, in 1910, that the BSA Co. now wanted a new survey carried out by their own representative, and wished to insert a clause in the lease that should the land ever cease to belong to the Mission it should revert to the Company.[33] From Rome Laws sent a strongly worded objection.[34]

Negotiations followed throughout 1910 and into the following year, the representatives of the Home Committee emphasising to the Directors of the BSA Co. how much had been achieved in the development of this part of Central Africa and the cost of that achievement. The statement was signed by Thomas Binnie, who had succeeded Lord Overtoun as Chairman of the Livingstonia Committee.

Laws felt that the amount of land now being offered by the BSA Co. was much too small and that the Mission must not let slip 'a trust which to me is sacred as the birthright of the children of the land for their education in the years to come as well as now.' All profits should be for the work of the Mission, and he ended his Memo thus:

> A gift handed over with the condition that the whole or any part thereof can be taken back at any time may be expected among children in a nursery, but is hardly compatible with the dignity of the BSA Company.[35]

The argument continued throughout 1911, with the Home Committee, the BSA Co., the Mission Council, and Dr Laws all exchanging letters and memos, and with a deputation from the Committee meeting representatives of the Company in London. In July the BSA Co. offered 50,000 acres, twice their previous offer but still only about half of what the Mission had claimed. The Committee at home awaited a response from Laws and must have been relieved when, in October, a telegram arrived 'FREE, EDINBURGH, ACCEPT.'[36]

Finally, an exchange of letters between the Revd Fairley Daly and the Secretary of the BSA Co. in July 1912 brought the long saga to a close 18 years after Dr Laws, accompanied by Dr Elmslie and Yuraiah Chirwa had spent their first night on the plateau at Kondowe.[37]

No doubt Laws had displayed some stubborness in holding out for so large a tract of land - 50,000 acres equals approximately 78 square miles, which is between one third and one half the size of the Island of Arran in the Firth of Clyde - but equally there can be no doubt of the unselfishness of his motives, or of his genuine conviction that the Africans of his own day and of the future deserved the best possible terms that could be negotiated. And the following year we find the BSA Co. promising £75 for 5 years to the Overtoun Institution to train young men for service in Rhodesia![38]

The work of translation continued in these years. The publication of Mr McAlpine's translation of the New Testament Epistles from 1 Corinthians to 2 Thessalonians, and of 1 and 2 Samuel into Chitonga by the NBSS was agreed in the autumn of 1909, to be followed some months later by reprints of Matthew, Mark and John in Chitonga.[39]

A thousand copies of a Namwanga translation of the General Epistles by Dr Chisholm of Mwenzo was produced to sell at 2d per copy.[40] 10,000 Nyanja New Testaments and 5000 combined Gospels, described as being 'of all the scriptures in the region the most fruitful' had been published in 1906, and since then a further 10,000 NTs and a further 10,000 combined Gospels had proved insufficient to meet the need. A further printing was now required.[41]

The issue of a Tumbuka New Testament was approved in 1912 as were 1000 copies of the Gospels in Chiwisa at the request of the Revd Malcolm Moffat of Chitambo. They were printed at the Institution, and arrived at Chitambo in time for the centenary of Livingstone's birth in March 1913.[42] Meantime R.D.McMinn had finished translating Jude and Revelation into Chitonga, and submitted it to the NBSS by June 1912.[43]

The Africans, in spite of the low level of their earnings, were prepared not only to pay for their scriptures, but to contribute to the funds of the Bible Societies. In March 1907 for example, the congregation at Livingstonia sent a donation of £10 for the NBSS, and in October 1913 the sum of £70.11s.4d was forwarded to the BFBS from sales of scriptures in Angoniland.[44]

Dr Laws had earlier made translations into Chinyanja, and Chitonga. Now, he was busy with the overall supervision of a very large area, and other gifted men were translating the Scriptures for different tribes.

It was proposed at the Mission Council in April 1905 that Dr Laws should be asked to set apart at least one month of each year to visit the outstations of the Mission, with expenses paid, in order 'to advise and help missionaries at the outstations and solidify the unity and policy of the Mission.'[45] The idea was sound and one likely to appeal to Robert Laws. He did in fact visit Mwenzo in May of that year, and being given leave of absence by the Livingstonia Committee, he paid a visit to Tanganyika at the request of the Directors of the LMS to deal with some trouble which had arisen in their field there. This tour lasted 3 months and, in company with Dr Chisholm, Laws covered a distance of 1500 miles. He was impressed by the peaceful condition of the country compared with ten years earlier, and attributed this to the British Central African Administration and the BSA Co.[46]

It is doubtful, however, whether a man even of Laws energy and capacity for work could have undertaken so taxing a task as to visit all the stations of the Livingstonia Mission as often as once a year. At this time the Mission had seven main stations and 360 out-stations, the main Centres being those at Kondowe, Ekwendeni, Loudon, Bandawe, Kasungu, Karonga and Mwenzo.[47] The new station planned at Chitambo, in Awisa country, was well established by now[48] and two further stations, at Tamanda and Chinsali (Lubwa), both in Northern Rhodesia, were opened in 1913.[49] The whole area covered in some sort by these 10 stations and their outstations was enormous - extending over some 90,000 square miles. There were of course vast sweeps of territory untouched by the Christian church, but figures given to the General Assembly of 1915 would suggest a Christian Community of over 38,000 souls, which must have included the families of communicants, and those who were in hearers' and catechumens' classes, in a total population estimated at 304,000.[50]

Laws himself concentrated increasingly on the work at the Institution and some of his colleagues felt that too large a proportion of Mission funds was used at Kondowe. At the same time Laws was the acknowledged head of the whole Livingstonia Mission, and well deserved the tribute paid to him by the Revd Mr Inwood of Brighton, a notable supporter of the Keswick Convention, who had visited the Livingstonia area in 1910. Addressing the General Assembly of the UF Church the following year, Mr Inwood said:

I venture to believe that Dr Laws never thinks a thought by day or dreams a dream by night which is not related to the redemption of Africa.[51]

And no one could have questioned the wisdom of his appointment in 1912 as a member of the Legislative Council of Nyasaland, nor felt that the honour should have gone to anyone else. The offer was made to Laws by the Governor, Sir William Manning, and the Home Committee recommended his acceptance of the position.[52]

MAP 3.

OUR WORK IN CENTRAL AFRICA

Scale of English Miles

THURSO
MWENZO
Doctor with wife
and nurse

PETERHEAD
KARONGA
Minister and wife

TOBERMORY
CHINSALE
Minister and wife

MONTROSE
LIVINGSTONIA
D'Laws, a doctor & a nurse 2 Teachers
3 Technical Instructors agriculturalist

EDINBURGH
EKWENDENI
Doctor, a nurse and
a lady worker

BERWICK ON TWEED
BANDAWE
A Minister and a doctor

CARLISLE
LOUDON
Minister and a lady worker

SLIGO
CHITAMBO
Minister and a teacher

YORK
KASUNGU
Doctor a wife and a nurse

BRADFORD
TAMANDA
A Teacher and wife

Map illustrating in a striking way the wide area in which our missions are
working, and the relative positions of the stations, with the staff at each.
By Rev. T. Cullen Young

20 THE 1914 WAR AND ITS EFFECTS

DIFFERENT VIEWS ABOUT 'JOINING UP' - 'LOYALTY' EXPECTED OF AFRICANS
- EXTENT OF 'LIVINGSTONIA' - TYPES OF WAR SERVICE - LUBWA
DEVELOPMENT - AFRICANS IN THE WAR - EFFECT ON SCHOOLS AND
AGRICULTURE - BLOODSHED AVERTED IN ANGONILAND - POOR
CONDITIONS - CHILEMBWE RISING, COMMISSION OF ENQUIRY,
H.H.JOHNSTON'S PROTEST - DAMAGE TO 'CHRISTIAN IMAGE',
EDUCATION - THE LAWS' LONG SERVICE - 'FLU EPIDEMIC - SLOW
RESUMPTION OF TEACHING - MORE AFRICAN MINISTERS - HELP FOR
GERMAN MISSIONS - MRS LAWS ILL - FURLOUGH - RESISTANCE TO
AFRICANS SEEKING INFLUENCE ON MISSION COUNCIL

When war broke out in Europe on 4th August 1914, Robert Laws was 63 years of age. From the furlough in the course of which he had occupied the Moderator's chair, Laws had returned to Livingstonia with his wife in April 1910 and he had no further furlough until 1921, giving him 11 years of unbroken service.

One might suppose that this was due to the impossibility of travelling home from Central Africa in the middle of a major war but the Revd Donald Fraser, at home when war broke out, was able to sail for Africa in June 1915, and Dr Walter Elmslie travelled home from Africa in November 1916.[1]

The first observable effects of the war on the Mission occurred in September 1914 when Mr John Howie, the agriculturist, responded to an appeal from the Officer Commanding British troops at Karonga for Despatch Riders with their own cycles. The same day the Senatus of the Overtoun Institution discussed the war situation and Dr Frank Innes, and Mr Peter Kirkwood, who had been in charge of the school work at the Institute since the Revd James Henderson went to Lovedale in 1906, took the view that Mission staff should not at present accept positions involving active participation in the war. Dr Laws, Alex Chalmers, the engineer, and John McGregor, the carpenter, disagreed.[2]

Laws himself was strongly patriotic. When George V was crowned King on 20th June 1911, two bullocks were killed to provide a feast for the Africans, and at an earlier date Queen Victoria's Diamond Jubilee had been marked both by worship and by feasting on the part of Europeans and Africans alike.[3]

When war with Germany came, Laws and his fellow missionaries saw it as a fight for freedom, and took it for granted that the Africans in the Protectorate would be, as they phrased it, 'loyal to Britain.' The possibility that Africans might wish to stand aloof from what was essentially a quarrel between European nations was not one which even occurred to the missionaries, and when active campaigning began against German forces in what was then German East Africa, north of Nyasaland, a war which had started in Europe was brought very close to the people of Central Africa. Missionaries, Mission stations and Mission converts were willy-nilly caught up in it, and a large percentage of the population - men, women and children - were affected by it to a greater or lesser extent.

By 1918 all European men of military age on the Mission staff - over 20 in all - had given war service of some kind either in Africa or in Europe.[4] Dr Laws himself, although he never left Nyasaland, is mentioned in the *Fasti* of the UF Church as having given 'War Service in Livingstonia, hospital work, engineering and printing work for the army.'[5] This was correct, for Livingstonia was not very far from the border with German East Africa, and the Mission at Kondowe not only produced grain and fruits for the troops stationed at Karonga, but provided a hospital in which the wounded could convalesce, undertook printing on behalf of the army and in 1916, entered into a contract for the production and supply of 230 saddles for ox transport.[6]

In 1914 the Livingstonia Mission had a staff of 30, not counting 16 wives who were not regarded as 'Staff' but who certainly made a very big contribution to the work of the Mission.[7] The missionaries were spread over a wide area. A sketch map, prepared by Cullen Young CA, which appeared in the Record for October 1914, showed Scotland and the northern part of England and Ireland with the Livingstonia Mission stations superimposed, and enabled the reader at home to gain some impression of the huge area that was now denoted by the general term 'Livingstonia', and to realise how far separated from each other many of the missionaries were although all were part of the Livingstonia Mission.[8]

Those stationed at Mwenzo in the far north, almost on the border of German East Africa, and at Karonga, on the northern part of the Lake shore, could hardly have avoided involvement in the war. Both places were occupied as army bases, and the Mission buildings became hospitals.[9] At Mwenzo Dr James Chisholm decided that it would be prudent to move some 30 to 40 miles to the south, and a hospital was set up which was kept busy catering for the needs of African and European alike. When the missionaries withdrew from Mwenzo an African, John Banda, insisted on remaining to complete the roofing of the half-built church whose ~~mud~~-dried bricks might otherwise have suffered damage when the rains came. John Banda did not suffer personally but reported the looting of the Mandala store and the loss of a quantity of goods as a result of enemy action.[10]

sun-dried {margin annotation}

At Karonga a confused struggle took place between German and British forces in the first week of September, 1914, and the Mission Hospital was taken over as a military hospital.[11]

Mrs Charles Stuart, who, as Margaret McCallum, had joined the mission in 1897 and married Charles Stuart four years later, arrived at Karonga in November 1915 to join the Nyasaland Field Force as a nursing Sister. Her husband, the longest serving missionary after Laws and Elmslie, was himself engaged in war service in East Africa. When Langenburg was captured from the Germans Charles Stuart was sent there in June 1916 to be in charge of transport.[12]

Both Dr Frank Innes and Mr Peter Kirkwood changed their views as the war went on. The former was on service from 1917-1919, while Mr Kirkwood, who went home on furlough in 1915, began service with the YMCA in France the following year. In October 1918 he was returning to Africa to resume his educational work at Livingstonia when the Japanese ship on which he was travelling was torpedoed off the south west of Ireland. Only eleven passengers survived and Peter Kirkwood was not among them.[13]

At far away Chitambo the Revd Malcolm Moffat had been in charge since the station was opened. He and his wife seem to have remained at Chitambo throughout the period of the war, Mrs Moffat not returning to the UK till 1919 and her husband not till the following year.[14]

In 1913 the Revd R.D.McMinn, who had joined the Mission in 1893 and been ordained in 1906, was sent to Chinsali, Northern Rhodesia, and sited his station at Lubwa. He was the first European missionary to be there on a permanent basis but evangelistic and educational work had been pioneered over a wide area by David Julizya Kaunda (father of Kenneth Kaunda, the first President of Zambia), one of the 18 students from the Overtoun Institution who travelled west with James Henderson on an evangelistic campaign in 1904. By 1913 there were already 45 centres of evangelism and schools staffed by 100 teachers. Pupils numbered 2517, of whom 996 were girls. These things were the fruits of David Kaunda's work, and it is unfortunate that in later years Dr Laws made no mention of him in his *Reminiscences of Livingstonia*, and that from the start Mr McMinn referred to David Kaunda as his 'native assistant'.[15]

Since Lubwa lay fully 100 miles south-west of Mwenzo, and Chitambo a further 180 miles as the crow flies, these stations might seem too remote to be affected by the war, but in fact, the able bodied males around Chinsali had to apply themselves to the production of food stuffs, or to serve as carriers, or join the Kings African Rifles, while Chitambo lay on the main line of communication to German East Africa from Rhodesia and South Africa and many of its people were carrying war loads to the northern border.[16]

From Bandawe the Revd W.Y.Turner reported that 1915 had been 'a year of unbroken quiet'; but added:

A good many Tonga are fighting in the forces defending Nyasaland. A large number are acting as carriers and labourers so that many villages are almost without men but there has been immunity from the harassment to which the brethren have been subjected at other stations.[17]

Turner's furlough would have been due, on the completion of five years, in 1917 but it was not till December of the following year, when the war was over, that he left Bandawe.[18]

The report to the 1916 General Assembly stated that at Livingstonia 'the work connected with supplying the troops at Karonga had largely occupied the time of the whole staff, but that the ordinary district work had been carried on as far as possible.' It was mentioned that the demand for carriers had affected the outschools. Not only had many African school-masters joined the services but the work of teacher training had suffered from the absence of European staff.[19]

The Revd W.P.Young, who had been appointed in 1910, was on leave from war service at the time of the 1916 General Assembly and spoke at it with deep concern about the effect that war between European nations would be likely to have on the Africans, to whom for so long the missionaries had proclaimed the virtues of peace.

Twenty years earlier, he said, the Africans had stopped raiding and had been at peace ever since. Now, the white men were making war and were calling on the Africans to help.[20]

At Kondowe itself, both John McGregor and John Howie were on war service. Alex Chalmers the engineer who had been with the Mission since 1901, and taken a major part in installing electric power and light in 1905, had returned from furlough in 1913.[21]

Ekwendeni was said to be only indirectly affected by the war but even there, in the second half of 1915, a large number of men were called on to act as carriers, roadmakers and so on, and a year later it was reported that 'many, including 40 teachers, went to road-making, and transport', and some schools were closed.[22]

North of Livingstonia, Karonga was again threatened by enemy attack and work interrupted from July to November 1915. The following year schools in that area were closed as most teachers volunteered for war service as guides, interpreters or recruiting sergeants.[23]

Those missionaries who were either ministers, or doctors, or both were in the fortunate position of being able, at least to some extent, to continue with the work for which they had been trained, although it is clear that they were also used in various positions of responsibility for which they were considered qualified simply by virtue of being Europeans. They might, for example, find themselves acting as interpreters, or put in charge of transport units, or supervising roadmaking. Because they had some knowledge of one, or more than one, African language they would be able to reassure Africans who found themselves in situations which were frequently strange, often bewildering, and occasionally quite menacing. As the war continued the Africans of Nyasaland were even more affected by it than the Europeans, and were certainly expected by the authorities to join up in defence of the northern frontier. In September 1914 130 Angoni armed with spears were recruited in the Mzimba district 'for special service as scouts and skirmishers', but this experiment was unsuccessful and was abandoned within a month.[24]

Many of the chiefs encouraged their tribesmen to enlist with the KAR for fear of losing their land should the Germans win. This was the main thrust of recruitment among the Africans in the first year of the war, and to encourage service in East Africa recruits were offered 'an extraordinary £1.1.4d per month' as Askaris.[25] By the end of the war there were almost 19,000 serving in the KAR.[26] Of those who offered to serve as Askaris some 35% were rejected before the end of their training[27] and many of them became *tenga-tengas* or carriers. Such men were in great demand and the fighting troops could hardly advance without them. The Rhodesia Native Regiment, the Naval Department, the Roads and Telegraph lines, and the P.O.W. camps at Blantyre and Zomba were among units which cried out for labour. In addition buildings had to be put up and wood for fuel, required by vessels on the Lake had to be cut down and made ready at appropriate points around the shore.[28]

The missionaries urged upon their flocks that it was a Christian duty to serve, and that to evade service was to act against good Christian principles.[29] None of the Mission staff took up the pacifist position, and war service would seem to have been given priority over Mission service in the thinking of the majority. In German East Africa, by contrast, Gemuseus, the Moravian missionary, wrote to Laws in 1914 deploring 'this dreadful war' and seeking a local truce, but the Scottish missionaries saw it as a struggle between good and evil and gave it their unquestioning support.[30]

The tribal chiefs were caught between the demands of the Government and traditional loyalties, and in the words of Alexander Hetherwick of the Blantyre mission, 'from all parts of Nyasaland men were recruited - pressed rather - into service.'[31] Sometimes night raids were carried out and men were forcibly enlisted. Dr Turner, writing to Laws in 1917, said 'no matter what the need is this is not a pleasant happening.'[32] Almost 30% of adult males from all parts of Nyasaland were recruited for service as labourers, in addition to the 3% who served as Askaris in the KAR.[33] The effect on village life and village agriculture can be imagined. Old men, women and boys had to do most of the tilling, sowing and reaping.

In September 1915 the Revd Donald Fraser learned that the chief Chimtunga had ignored a call for labour and for food for the troops at Karonga. Not only so but the chief, who had had too much to drink, had given a rude answer to the official messenger. As a result troops had been sent for from Zomba to come to Loudon to enforce the government requirements. The chief sought Dr Fraser's protection and was advised by him to surrender himself to save bloodshed. A Christian Convention, attended by people from a wide area, was being held at the time and Dr Fraser sent those present home to tell their women folk to assemble as much food as possible, and to ask teachers in the villages to volunteer for service themselves and to encourage others to do likewise. In the end, twice the quota of men and food required was forthcoming, and the quartering of soldiers in the area was avoided. Laws wrote to Fraser, 'I am glad that you managed to save bloodshed which might easily have taken place.'[34]

Bloodshed had certainly been avoided but there was no way in which the Africans of Nyasaland at that time could avoid being pressed into service, either as Askaris or as carriers. The missionaries considered such service a fair return for the abolition of slavery and the benefits of civilisation brought by the white man, but it is doubtful if things were seen in this light by the Africans themselves.

Mrs Margaret Stuart tells of an episode at Karonga in April 1916 when the Africans who were working as *machila* carriers for the hospital came to her for chits to exempt them from *tenga-tenga* work. She gave them all pencilled notes saying that they were employed in No 1 Hospital but, although she signed the notes, they were apparently not formal enough and the men were conscripted until Miss Pallot, who held a senior position, got them back again from an apologetic officer. This enabled the work of bringing firewood for the hospital, drawing water or getting baths for the patients to be resumed. The quality of the men's work thereafter was exemplary as they were determined to avoid having to carry boxes through floods and undertake the kind of tasks which were the usual lot of the *tenga-tengas*.[35]

At Kondowe, when 60 Africans were asked for in March 1916 to transport convalescents from Florence Bay up to the plateau it was agreed to offer the services of 45 men who had been working with Mr Chalmers on the road, and 15 who were employed at the hospital, but two months later, when the authorities at Karonga conscripted two Mission workers, Laws insisted that unless they were restored to the Mission it would no longer be possible to continue with the transport and other work being undertaken for the war effort.[36]

The response was a telegram saying that the Government would be content with one person. The Senatus decided that in that case the 'one' would require to be the Revd A.Macdonald if shop work was not to stop, the conscription of a minister clearly having less serious consequences on the work being done for the war effort than that of someone with more practical skills! Macdonald's call up, however, had serious consequences, nevertheless, as it forced the Senatus to decide that pupils on their way to Livingstonia must be met and turned back, and that District schools must be closed.[37]

Many Africans accepted war service because they had come to trust the missionaries and recognised their integrity and the honesty of their intentions. But there were times when they were pressed into service in ways that left them little choice.

The carriers were poorly paid, and inadequately provided with protection against cold and wet, and many tried to escape and return to their homes. Those who survived the war were kept waiting until 1920 for the bounty promised them, and when it was eventually awarded the War Office refused to pay more than half what had been promised by the Colonial Office.[38] The resentment felt by those forced to be *tenga-tengas* was deep-seated and lasting, and Dr William Petrie, who served as an M.O. in Nyasaland during the Second World War, speaks of the reluctance of the Atonga even then to give service as *tenga-tengas* because of what they had heard from fathers and uncles about conditions of service in the earlier war.[39]

Mention should be made in passing of the 1915 'Chilembwe Rising'. In some ways it was a purely local affair, but it brought to the surface deeply held feelings of resentment on the part of the Africans of which Europeans were generally unaware. As well as feeling it unfair that they should be expected to fight in a 'white man's war', the Africans were aggrieved that, whereas previously they had free access to land which was properly theirs, they now found themselves reduced to the status of tenants on European estates, and expected to pay at least some part of their rent in the form of labour.[40]

One of those deeply concerned about the injustice suffered by Africans was the Revd John Chilembwe, founder of the Provident Industrial Mission at Chiradzulu in the Shire Highlands, a few miles from the Magomero Estate of Alexander Livingstone Bruce. No schools were allowed on this estate and the manager, William Jervis Livingstone, was particularly harsh in his treatment of the Africans.[41] When the 1914 war broke out Chilembwe, who had studied for three years in the USA and been ordained there,[42] wrote to the Nyasaland Times, declaring the loyalty of Africans to the Government, and their readiness to support it, but expressing disappointment that in times of peace the needs of Africans seemed to be forgotten. He hoped that some day justice might prevail.[43]

Early in 1915 the Government became alarmed about Chilembwe's attitude and resolved to deport him.[44] Some hint of this reached Chilembwe and led him to take certain steps which had already been in his mind but which had not been fully thought out. A party of Africans forced entry into W.J.Livingstone's house, on 23rd January, and killed Livingstone himself. His head was cut off and next day displayed in church on the end of a pole.[45] This piece of savagery was strangely at variance with other aspects of the attack, for Mrs Livingstone and her children, although taken into custody, were treated with consideration and released the following day. No looting took place at the Livingstone home.[46] A raid was also made on the ALC store at Mandala to obtain arms, but only five rifles and 605 rounds of ammunition were taken leaving a much larger stock behind.[47]

The Government acted swiftly and on February 3rd John Chilembwe was shot while trying to reach the Portuguese border. Some of his colleagues suffered the same fate while others were brought to trial and hanged. By 14th February all was over.[48]

At Livingstonia, in the north of the country, the rising made hardly a ripple, and some Ngoni soldiers were among those who helped to suppress it. When the Legislative Council met on 15th March the Governor expressed some suspicion of Mission teaching.[49] This led Dr Laws, a member of the Council, to ask if the Government intended to set up a committee of Enquiry into the Rising, a request which Dr Hetherwick had already made through the Chamber of Commerce. Laws also expressed the view that not less but more and better education for the African was what was needed.[50]

Hetherwick's reply to the complaint that Africans showed disrespect to Europeans has been often quoted:

> The smallest drummer boy in the British Army if he salutes Lord Kitchener receives a salute in return. There will be no difficulty if the European makes acknowledgment; it indicates that two gentlemen have met and not only one.[51]

A Commission was duly set up but the only churchman among its five members was a High Anglican with little sympathy with the Scottish Missions, and the latter were angered by the suggestion at the Enquiry that their Missions were more likely than Roman Catholic or Anglican Missions to allow 'undesirable political propaganda by native teachers.'[52] Their anger is understandable since Central African education had been in their hands for the past 40 years and out of the £11,000 spent annually on education at this time only £1000 came by way of Government Grant, the greater part of the rest being provided by the Scottish Missions.[53]

When the findings of the Commission of Enquiry were published in January 1916[54] the contribution of the Missions to Central Africa in general and to Education in particular had been largely ignored, and when no discussion of the report was permitted at the Legislative Council Robert Laws protested very strongly.[55]

At home there was considerable support for the missionary view and it was at this time that Sir Harry H.Johnston, who had been the first Commissioner in 1891 (and was not always sympathetic towards Missions), wrote an article entitled 'The Bitter Cry of the Educated African', in which he protested against any endeavour to reduce the African to 'helotry.'[56]

Those Africans who had become Christians, and were in the habit of reading their Bibles, as a great many of them were, were familiar with the claim of the New Testament that 'In Christ there is neither Jew nor Greek' and understood quite well that, since Christ had died for all and not just for those of any one race, Africans and Europeans alike deserved to be treated with justice and dignity. They could not help noticing that where Africans were concerned this was not always done, and those in the service of the Colonial Government, generally speaking, were insensitive.

The Rising brought some improvement in educational arrangements and in social relations, but not in the matter of land tenure which continued to be a source of friction. Hetherwick's view was that so far as land tenure was concerned 'the whole matter was speedily forgotten'.[57] One positive result of the Rising is mentioned by Professor John McCracken who claims that it convinced Robert Laws of the need to increase African responsibilities still further since 'religious secession more commonly resulted from a denial of African authority than it did from granting that authority too soon.'[58]

Perhaps the most serious effect of the war as a whole was the realisation by the Africans that the white man, who had so often spoken of the iniquity of one tribe going to war against another, was now plainly seen engaging in war himself. Apart from the damage to what might be called 'the Christian image', the progress of African education was greatly slowed down, and in some places brought to a standstill by the war. In the Livingstonia Mission alone the 907 schools which were open in 1914 had fallen to 702 by 1918; the number of teachers from 1674 to 1189, and the number of pupils from 58,656 to 39,868. Students engaged in higher education fell from 157 to 25 in the same period.[59]

When we turn from education to church affairs, however, a brighter picture emerges. The number of African office-bearers i.e. elders and catechists, actually increased during the war years, in spite of, or more probably because of, the smaller number of missionaries on the ground, and in spite of the number of Africans on war service. 441 office-bearers in 1914 had increased to 505 by 1918 (and to 595 by 1919), the number of communicants had risen from 9,513 to 11,395, and the number of baptized adherents from 9,529 to 14,252.[60]

Altogether, the African Church would seem to have been affected by the war much less than the educational system, and this is a tribute both to the way in which the missionaries had sown the seed of the Gospel over the previous 40 years and to the response of the Africans to that Gospel. If there were any among the members of the African church in 1914 who would have been called, in another culture, 'rice Christians', clearly they could not have been many in number.

At home, the general policy of the UFC General Assembly during the war years was to maintain what was essential but to avoid any new commitments.[61] The Assembly of 1917 was told that Mission hospitals and other buildings had been used as medical bases, and that schools had been interrupted as 'most teachers had volunteered for service'.[62]

A more cheerful note was struck by Donald Fraser's report from Loudon which included the words: 'We close the year [1916] full of good cheer with the sense of the good hand of God upon us.'[63]

Very few references to Dr Laws in person appear in Assembly Reports throughout the war until we come to 1918 when we find this sentence:

> It is disquieting to realise that after his long years of brilliant and patient service, Dr Laws has been for many months alone at his post, the sole missionary of the Overtoun Institution at Livingstonia.[64]

Mrs Laws had been with her husband throughout, and until 1916 several of the men of the staff were still at Kondowe. Alex Chalmers and his wife (he had married Miss Trotter, the teacher, in 1909) remained until early in 1918, when they moved to Lovedale. Nurse Patrick had returned to Livingstonia after furlough in 1915, and Nurse Cole the following year.[65]

It was hoped that with the ending of the campaign in German East Africa in 1917 the staffing situation would improve with the release from service of missionaries who had been attached to General Northey's column, but it was not until 1920 that numbers began to build up again in an appreciable way.[66]

The 1919 FM Report claimed that 'No part of our mission field has paid the price of war so heavily as Livingstonia'. It mentioned that missionaries on war service were still being retained and that many able-bodied teachers (by which is meant African teachers) from the Lake shore were also being kept in the forces.[67] The influenza epidemic which took such a toll of life in Europe also affected Africa very badly.[68]

Astonishingly, apprehension was expressed in the church in Scotland about the increase of wealth which had come into the hands of the Africans as a result of the war, but the effect of inflation in pushing up prices and reducing the value of money seems to have been totally overlooked![69]

It was Donald Fraser who once more, in 1919, found cause for gratitude. He wrote, 'In spite of many contending forces, such as war, plague, influenza, food scarcity, high prices, tragedies of sin, this year has been the best we have ever had.' He meant that school attainments had been higher and progress greater; and that church membership at Loudon had now risen above 3000, with contributions up by 370% in four years. All church work was now paid for by the people themselves and more than half the money spent on education came from the local people. There were other signs of life in the church and 60 deaconesses had been elected at Loudon to do women's work and to act as female elders.[70]

Much of the teaching work at the Institution was still in abeyance, and even in 1921 a letter from Dr Laws said that it had still not been possible to resume all courses at the Institution. Courses for pastors and evangelists had been discontinued for some years and the church was suffering as a result.[71] At the same time the suspension of teacher training at Kondowe aggravated the situation in the schools for it meant that no newly trained teachers were available to replace those who had become casualties in the war.

The Presbytery of Livingstonia had come into being as early as 1899 and we have seen that the long delayed ordination of African ministers had taken place in the month of May prior to the outbreak of war. But real independence from Mission control was still some way off, as can be seen from the tension which arose at Bandawe between the Revd W.Y.Turner and his colleague the Revd Yesaya Mwasi. The matter was referred to Presbytery in February 1915, and Mr Mwasi eventually had to give way under pressure from the Presbytery.[72]

But progress there was and later that same year, at its August meeting, Presbytery heard that the Revd Hezekiah Tweya at Ekwendeni, the Revd Jonatham Chirwa at Loudon and the Revd Yesaya Mwasi, who was caring for two districts at Bandawe, had all proved satisfactory, and were accordingly continued in their existing posts.[73]

It was at this Presbytery also that Edward Boti Manda, Yafet Mkhandawire, Andrew Mkochi, and Daniel Nhlane were licensed as preachers of the Gospel. Sadly Daniel Nhlane died in July 1917, but Andrew Nkochi was ordained on 4th November of that year, and the other two on 21st July 1918.[74] The continuance of the church, as an African church, was assured.

In the autumn of 1916 a call came from the Sanga congregation to the Revd Yesaya Mwasi and the Presbytery agreed to proceed with the call.[75] It was reported also at this Presbytery that the Christians of the Moravian Mission in German East Africa were 'shepherdless' and it was decided to ask the Government to allow African agents to go to their assistance.[76] In July of 1917 Dr Laws reported that it was not yet possible to send help but by November of that year it was stated at Presbytery that, although Europeans could not themselves enter the former German Colony, Africans were now to be permitted to do so. Accordingly it was agreed to send Yoram Mphande and a number of helpers, with the congregations at Bandawe and Livingstonia contributing towards the financial cost.[77] The Presbytery also resolved that the Revd Hezekiah Tweya should be sent to Karonga for three months to help there.[78]

The congregation of Loudon had been divided into nine in October 1916, and it was there that the Revd Andrew Mkochi was ordained the following year.[79]

The Revd Yesaya Mwasi was elected Moderator of the Presbytery in July 1918; a few days later he shared with Dr Laws in the ordination of Boti Manda and Yafet Mkhandawiri.[80] When the Presbytery met in July 1919 the Revd Hezekiah Tweya was chosen as Moderator,[81] and in February 1920 Mr P.R.Mwamlima was licensed at Ekwendeni as a preacher of the Gospel, and ordained at

Karonga on 1st August of the following year.[82] The African Church was now well established, but even at that time European ministers outnumbered African ministers by 13 to six.[83]

A proposal that women should be eligible for the eldership found favour with the Presbytery in 1921, but as union with Blantyre was imminent it was decided to consult Blantyre Presbytery before taking a final decision.[84]

A Committee appointed at this time to consider what further study should be done by ministers certainly showed no desire to lower standards in order to encourage recruitment for it recommended that subjects for further study should include Greek, Latin, and Hebrew; that Church History should include the study of the Church in the Middle Ages; and that in Systematic Theology attention should be given to eschatology, resurrection and a consideration of the state of souls after death.[85]

In the General Assembly reports of 1920 the Roll of Missionaries under the heading 'Livingstonia and New Langenburg', the latter in what had previously been German East Africa, includes 31 names in all. Of these, 23 (including six women) had been on the strength of the Livingstonia Mission prior to the outbreak of war, and eight had been appointed since 1914. Of the total, 15 were ordained men.[86]

With such a large number of those who had previously been on the staff returning to service in Africa it can be seen that the four years of war had taken remarkably little toll of the Livingstonia missionaries. Mr Peter Kirkwood, the educationist, alone had lost his life.

Robert Laws at Kondowe, W.Y.Turner at Bandawe, and Malcolm Moffat at Chitambo, with Miss Howie Brown and Miss Mima Maxwell also serving in some part of the Livingstonia field, remained with the Mission throughout the whole period of the war. Alex Chalmers, with his wife, was at Kondowe until January 1918. Mrs Laws and Mrs Moffat remained in the field with their husbands throughout.[87]

With the end of the war in 1918 those whose furlough had been so long delayed were able to have a spell at home, but Dr and Mrs Laws were the last to take furlough. When it came to April 1921 Laws wrote to Ashcroft who was then Secretary of the FMC referring to the fact that the Committee wished them to take their furlough as soon as possible. He agreed adding that it was now

imperative because of Mrs Laws' health, and her need for expert
medical advice.[88] By the third week in May Dr and Mrs Laws were
on their way home. They expected to leave Chinde on the SS
Norman on June 10th and to reach Southampton on June 27th. Laws
wrote to Ashcroft at that time that 'Mrs Laws was much the same',[89]
but in fact she was gravely ill. The ship's surgeon said that he had
never seen a braver woman.[90] The sad truth is that the 'expert medical
advice' had been too long delayed and it must have been a great relief
to both Dr and Mrs Laws to find Amy and Miss Gray, Mrs Laws'
sister, at Southampton to meet them.[91]

Back at Livingstonia one problem was raised at the Mission Council
a few weeks after Laws had left - raised then perhaps precisely because
Laws had left and would not be present at the Council.

A feeling had clearly been growing among the Africans that
the time had come when they should have some say in the decisions
of the Mission Council, the body which, under the FMC in far off
Scotland, took the decisions about the work of the Mission throughout
the whole area of Livingstonia.

The Mission Council of July 1921 had before it a letter and
memo from Yesaya Chibambo asking that African Mission workers
should have some representation on the Council. The request seems
to have come as a shock and a surprise to the members of the Council,
who sound almost hurt at the suggestion that the Africans have been
in any way unfairly treated. The Council expressed its appreciation
of all that was done by Africans but pointed out that not all
Europeans were on the Council and that with 3/4ths of the finances
of the Mission coming from Scotland those appointed by the Church
in Scotland must carry the responsibility for taking the decisions.

Mr Chibambo's memo to the Council was a full, frank but
respectful presentation of the feelings of the African Mission workers.
In government service provision was made for retirement pensions
but it was not so in the Mission, and when an African employee,
engaged in Mission service died, his dependants were not cared for.
'A native is not regarded as a co-worker', the complaint ran, 'he is
commonly called "boy" by the missionary without any distinction
and he is "slightly esteemed".' Neither was a native allowed to report
on his own work.'[92]

The Council's reply ran to four quarto pages. It is highly
defensive, and shows a lack of sensitivity. It denies that native

teachers and others are not considered to be co-workers or that they are lightly esteemed. It was decided to send Mr Chibambo's letter to all stations so that what was in the mind of the Africans might be considered by the missionaries and their leading African assistants, with a view to full and fair consideration being given to the matter at a future meeting.[93]

In fact no African ever sat on the Mission Council, and more than 30 years later, the Revd James Dougall, who was then General Secretary of the FMC in Scotland, said to the Revd Neil Bernard that as independence was clearly coming to Malawi it was essential that the church there should begin to carry more responsibility. Mr Bernard was therefore asked to set up 'Joint Councils', with both Africans and Europeans as members. At first the Joint Council reported to the FMC but gradually took increasing responsibility and presently this responsibility passed to the Synod. By this time the Mission Council had ceased to have a role and the African church had at last the opportunity of dealing with its own affairs.[94]

This however lay in the future and we must now return to the events of 1921.

21 SADNESS ON FURLOUGH: TOWARDS AN INDEPENDENT CHURCH

DEATH OF MRS LAWS - UFC GA TRIBUTE TO LAWS - JOINING OF FMC & WFMC - RETURN TO AFRICA - 13 MAIN STATIONS - BURNETT & CASEBY'S WORK IN FORESTRY & AGRICULTURE - FORMER GERMAN MISSIONS - KASUNGU & TAMANDA TRANSFERRED TO DRC - STATIONS IN NORTHERN RHODESIA - PATRICK MWAMLIMA AT KARONGA - BANDAWE CONGREGATION DIVIDED - THIPURA - GROWING AFRICAN CONTRIBUTION IN ANGONILAND - CMG FOR LAWS - SYNOD OF CCAP (AHEAD OF SCOTTISH CHURCH REUNION & MALAWIAN INDEPENDENCE) - DRC PRESBYTERY JOINS CCAP

On taking up residence in Edinburgh Laws' first concern must surely have been to obtain for his wife the medical care and attention she so greatly required. Unfortunately nothing could be done for what was described as 'serious internal trouble', and within three months, on 17th September, Margaret Laws died.[1] Margaret and Robert had been friends for over half a century, and had enjoyed 42 years of marriage in which they had given themselves untiringly to the service of the Livingstonia Mission, and to the people of what is now the northern part of Malawi.

In the November issue of The Record Margaret Fairley Daly described Mrs Laws as a heroine: 'The Dona', she wrote, 'never intruded herself on the notice of the public.' She was, however a trained and born teacher, and from early days showed her aptitude for inspiring and informing the minds of those who came under her sway.[2]

The writer claimed that she was very successful in the training of her house-boys, but in Livingstonia she left behind her a reputation for strictness, and was known as *Nyakalaunjuchi* - which means 'as stingily as a bee' - among the local Africans.[3]

There was no doubt at all about her courage and in the early days at Bandawe, when Amelia was a baby, and the Angoni were threatening attack, Laws returned on one occasion to find her with the baby in her arms crooning the words of 'The Lord's my shepherd.' Later, as Moderator's wife, she displayed quiet dignity and courtesy and when on deputation did much to inform the women of the church about life and conditions in Nyasaland. Having returned to Livingstonia with Laws in 1910 Margaret laboured with him all through the years of the 1914 war, and although often urged to take furlough, she remained throughout with her husband.[4]

Laws himself told Professor D.S.Cairns: 'I owe more than I can tell to Mrs Laws. We have come through perilous times together. Many a time she and I never knew what the morn would bring.'[5] News of her death quickly reached Livingstonia and when the Senatus of the Livingstonia Institution met on 26th September they passed a minute expressing their appreciation of Mrs Laws:

> It can be said that her courage and hopefulness even in the darkest days were a stimulus to all in the Mission, and despite growing infirmity and latterly physical pain she was actively engaged in helping backward students in the Institute up to within a few days of her departure for Scotland.

Her kindness and hospitality were mentioned and sympathy was expressed to Dr Laws and his daughter, and to the Misses Gray.[6] At a later date the Mission Council made reference to Mrs Laws' translation of Christian hymns as a special factor in the devotional life of the African church.[7]

Back in Scotland Laws had been welcomed by all who knew him, and by a great number who did not know him personally to whom he had become a living legend. 'That's Laws of Livingstonia', they would say as the slightly stooped figure with the white beard was seen in the streets of Edinburgh, or in the vicinity of the Assembly Hall on the Mound. In May 1922 the UFC General Assembly rose to their feet by a common impulse and cheered for two minutes in tribute to the 'Grand Old Man' of the Livingstonia Mission. At the Foreign Mission Evening Sederunt Laws spoke of the day, 47 years earlier the previous week, when he had set sail for Central Africa, and rehearsed some of the changes which had been brought about there.

Where no schools had been there were now 768 with over 40,000 pupils. The 42 African congregations had about 15,000 Church members with six ordained African ministers. At the training Institution courses were run for teachers, evangelists, pastors, and hospital assistants, and the temporary buildings were needing to be replaced by a permanent College. The whole Bible had been translated into Chinyanja, the New Testament into three other languages, and some of the Gospels into at least eight other tongues.

'The work was great', said Laws ,'but God was greater.' The Gospel had spread in Africa largely by African agency, and Laws instanced the work of Noah from Bandawe who had taken the news of Christ to the Marambo, the plain country to the west on either side of the Loangwa river, knowing that sleeping sickness was rife there and that because of Government health regulations he would not be able to return to his home district. In the end Noah and a colleague had died of the sleeping sickness, bearing faithful witness to the Gospel.[8]

The Report of the FMC that year, in referring to Nyasaland, said that the Missionaries, with Government help, had 'turned a cockpit of bloody warring tribes into a land of peaceful trading people.'[9] While it was right to acknowledge Government help, to no one person were the changes which had come about due more than to Robert Laws. He and his many devoted companions had testified by the quality of their lives as well as by their words to the love Christ has shown for us and commanded us to show to our fellows.

At this Assembly Laws moved that the FMC and the Women's FMC should be amalgamated. He felt that one Committee was desirable and recognised the necessity of having women serving on it. The matter was remitted to a special Committee which included all members of both FMC and WFMC, together with 12 additional members. Not until 1925 did it finally recommend an amalgamation, and then for three years only in the first instance.[10] Men and women seem to have been surprised, if agreeably so, to find that they could work together harmoniously on the same Committee, and there is no doubt that the amalgamation was a step which had to be taken sooner or later.

It was probably because he felt Margaret's loss so keenly that Robert Laws on this occasion spent less than 14 months in the United Kingdom, in spite of his recently completed tour of duty having been an unusually long one. In his grief he sought solace in taking up again the work to which he was so devoted in the country and among the people he loved so much.

He left Scotland in August 1922, to return to Livingstonia on what was to prove his last tour of duty. Several others were going to

Livingstonia at the same time, including the veteran Charles Stuart, who had been with the Mission since 1889, and his wife Margaret, and Alex Caseby, a young man going out for the first time. Caseby had seen War Service in France and was going to Livingstonia as an agriculturist. He and Laws shared a cabin and developed a strong bond of friendship.

There were those who thought that Laws was without humour but that is certainly not so. Humour he had but it was dry and pawky and the hasty observer might be unaware of it. Alex Caseby tells us that at a service of worship held on the ship the officiant offered prayer for a variety of people including, as he put it, 'our brother who is in the eventide of life.' At the end, Laws, aged 71, looked round with a twinkle in his eye and solemnly enquired who the minister could have meant? 'For my part', he said, 'I'm only in the afternoon of life.'[11] When the party reached the northern part of what is now Malawi,

> The welcome to Dr Laws was one of love and affection, large gatherings singing hymns of praise... [At Florence Bay] thousands of people were on the shore - cheering, singing, dancing - a marvellous tribute to a great man. All the way up the 3000 feet of hillside to the Livingstonia plateau, were masses of happy delightful Africans.[12]

The Livingstonia Mission to which Laws returned was at this time at its greatest extent, for in the north, the former German missions in what was now the British Protectorate of Tanganyika had been taken under the wing of the Scottish missions, the responsibility being shared by the Established Church of Scotland and the UF Church missions.[13] At the southern extremity of the Livingstonia area were Kasungu and Tamanda, later to be transferred to the DRC, but at this time still part of the Livingstonia Mission.

Laws had claimed at the Foreign Mission evening sederunt of the Assembly in 1922 that Nyasaland was 1.25 times the size of Scotland, and said that, taking into account the work in Northern Rhodesia, the total area of the Mission added up to 291,000 square miles.[14] It was a huge area, and even a Robert Laws could not effectively control all the stations within it. He was, however, the acknowledged leader, and his seniority, both in years and in length of service, made it difficult for any other on the Mission Council to differ from him.

Of the 13 main stations at this time some had had no resident European missionary for five years.[15] Gradually staff numbers, diminished by the years of war, were being made up. At the same time greater responsibility was now being carried by the African Christians themselves.

On the staff at the Overtoun Institution there were at this time 13 men and five women missionaries; also at Kondowe 12 men doing what was called 'district work', unconnected with the Institution.[16] The Institution was training teachers from all three areas of the mission, and in the middle school at Livingstonia girls were being taught separately from the boys, as it was now felt that this gave the girls a better chance. In mixed classes they tended to allow the boys to overshadow them because women had always been accustomed to play a subordinate role.[17]

A picture of everyday life at Kondowe is given by Alex Caseby who tells us that Dr Laws was wont to say, 'Stay in bed after sunrise and you are tired all day.' Accordingly every morning before 6am all workers assembled for a simple act of worship. Then work was given out for the day. Caseby himelf had 100 workers under him and describes them as 'men and women of character and honesty', and with 'a fine sense of humour'. Each department had its own staff with first class African clerks.[18]

Mr Caseby's own training was in agriculture, horticulture and forestry, but all missionaries were specialists in their own field and at the same time were partners in bringing the Good News to the people of Central Africa. 'Our job,' he says, 'was not so much to preach but to witness by our daily living, our skill and patience, and our love for a really charming race.'[19] After describing the many buildings of the station Caseby adds:

> The Plateau has wide tree lined roads, pockets of flowering shrubs, and fir trees. Being 4000 feet up the air was pleasant by day, chilly at night. The quarters for married tradesmen, and key African leaders, were selective and well designed and the quarters for the Boarders were up to date and clean. The marvel of Livingstonia was the water supply. Each house had running water... drawn from a mountain side, miles away.

He goes on to mention the number and variety of wild animals which prowled around, including lions, leopards and hyenas, but adds that the three main hazards were mosquitoes, carrying malaria, ticks, which caused fever, and jiggers, which pierced the skin and caused infection. Quinine tablets were taken every day by all white people.[20]

Mr Caseby was at first assistant to Mr Archie Burnett and they had assigned to them 52,000 acres for development. In a period of seven months they held conferences with a dozen chiefs of an area extending about 50 miles north and south along the lakeshore and about 50 miles inland to the west, won their confidence and plotted areas of priority. 20 nursery beds were made and 500,000 seeds, of trees, shrubs and coffee, were planted. On March 19th, David Livingstone's birthday, a special tree planting ceremony was arranged. When Caseby called at Dr Laws' office that day the latter examined his Log Book and maps very carefully. The only comment he made to the new young missionary was to say in one crisp sentence, 'You are settling in well.'[21]

Of the mission stations in what had been German East Africa nine had been run by the Berlin Mission with 15 agents in the field and nine by the Moravians with 20 agents.[22] As we have seen the Livingstonia Mission sent African helpers to support their Christian brethren there while the continuance of the war prevented British missionaries from entering that area themselves.[23] Once the war was over the Revd D.R.Mackenzie, who had resigned from the Mission during the war, offered himself for service again and in 1919 was appointed to New Langenburg. Presently four missionaries from Scotland were serving in Tanganyika, some of the cost being borne by the Moravians.[24] George Nyasuru, who had been trained at the Overtoun Institution, also did excellent work as an evangelist in this area.[25]

The Scottish missionaries were warmly welcomed by the African Christians. When Mr Mackenzie came to address the General Assembly of 1925 he jocularly claimed that the 35 German missionaries previously in the field had been replaced by one man, namely himself! (In fact the Hallidays, the Faulds, and the Browns all shared with him in the work.) Mr Mackenzie reported 3000 baptisms in five years, the setting up of 100 schools and the establishment of a training centre to maintain the supply of teachers.[26] There was certainly a thirst for education and one African said to Dr George Prentice, 'If you will give us the schools of Livingstonia we will run to them.'[27]

The first African to be ordained in this area was Yoram Mphande who came originally from Bandawe. He had served in the former German mission area from 1917 to 1920, and had then trained for the ministry. He was ordained at Kyimibila on 13th December 1924.[28]

At the southern end of the huge area covered by the term 'Livingstonia' were the stations of Kasungu, opened in 1897 as a centre among the Chewas (served for many years by Dr George Prentice) and Tamanda, opened in 1913 by J.M.Riddell Henderson. Mr Henderson returned to Tamanda after the war and was ordained in 1920.[29] One African of the Chewa tribe, and one from the Wisas, were in training for the ministry at this time,[30] and in August 1922 a girls' Boarding School was opened at Kasungu with 22 on the roll. The girls were reported to be 'very keen'.[31] At Tamanda six African catechists were hard at work, and in several villages new school buildings were put up by the locals in spite of warnings from the missionaries that no teachers were available to staff them.[32]

With so very extensive an area of responsibility there was a growing feeling that the DRC mission, which operated in the Chichewa language area and had its HQ at Mvera, should be asked to take over Kasungu and Tamanda. The local congregations do not seem to have wanted the transfer and at first the DRC Mission Council was hesitant. Eventually, however, the Mission Council, with the approval of their Mission Board in South Africa, agreed.[33] The UF FMC was anxious to use the money saved on missionary salaries at these stations to provide additional help in Tanganyika, and when the Revd Frank Ashcroft, secretary of the FMC, toured the Livingstonia Mission in 1923 he emphasised in his report that this would give satisfaction to the Dutch who would feel that they were sharing, indirectly, in helping the Moravian and Berlin missions. The transfer was approved by the General Assembly of 1924.[34]

To the west of the main area of the Livingstonia mission, in what had become Northern Rhodesia (now Zambia) were three far flung stations. At Chitambo, Malcolm and Maria Moffat had served faithfully throughout the war years and neither had home leave until the war was over.[35] Dr Hubert Livingstone Wilson and his sister Ruth had both begun service at Chitambo in 1914 but had later offered themselves for war service. Dr Wilson returned to Chitambo in 1919.[36] Eight Africans were set apart as evangelists in 1921.[37] The need to strengthen the women's work was recognised; it was hoped that women missionaries from Scotland would be forthcoming.[38]

At Chinsali (Lubwa) further north, eight villages were asking for teachers,[39] and there was a similar eagerness for education at Mwenzo in the far north almost on the border of Tanganyika. In January 1923 a 'Women's School' was held there and the following month a small boarding establishment was opened for girls with 13 pupils on the roll.[40]

The readiness of the Kirk Session of Mwenzo to look outwards is seen in the concern it expressed about the large area lying roughly in the triangle between Mwenzo, Chinsali and Karonga. In that triangle there were a great many villages untouched by the Mission although there was a keen desire for education among the villagers.[41]

Karonga had been without a European missionary since 1915. The church itself had been burned in the course of 1921 but the local members made a brave endeavour to raise the money for a new building[42] and the Revd Patrick Mwamlima provided them with the services of an ordained minister.

The other 'Lake-side station' was Bandawe, where the year 1922 was regarded as 'a year of advance' with the restarting of classes and schools after the return of Dr Turner in 1921. The eight congregations in the area all increased in number, and tribute was paid at the 1923 GA to the faithful service as an elder of Gideon Mbali.[43] In the 1920s a new station came into being some four miles further north, at Thipura, on what was regarded as a better and healthier site. Now that the congregation at Bandawe had been divided into eight, smaller buildings were adequate for local needs and these were erected by the congregation at their own expense and entirely without European supervision.* When this was reported to the GA of 1926 the people of Bandawe were described as 'good attenders, good listeners, and good speakers'.[44] The Revd Yoram Mphande, now returned from Tanganyika, was giving excellent service as an itinerant pastor,[45] and, thanks largely to the work of the Revd A.G.MacAlpine, the Atonga now had the New Testament in their own tongue.[46]

Of the missionaries in Angoniland, Dr Elmslie was on furlough until November 1919, but Donald Fraser, as we saw, returned from his furlough in the middle of 1915.[47] Charles Stuart and his wife, after their war service, were sometimes at Ekwendeni and sometimes at

---

*The present church at Thipura was built by the Revd Jack Martin, in memory of his wife Mamie; it was opened in 1931

Loudon. Loudon, being a well establised station, came through the war years well.[48] At Ekwendeni, 28 girl boarders came from all five of the congregations in the area, namely Ekwendeni, Loudon, Henga, Emcisweni, and Usisya. Practical domestic work was included in their syllabus. Seven of these girls became communicants, nine others enrolled in the catechumens' class, and three became Bible women.[49]

In this area also the Africans themselves were making an increasingly important contribution. The Revd Andrew Mkochi, ordained in 1917,[50] was vigorously campaigning throughout the country, administering the sacrament in many congregations, and Charles Chinula, who was training for the ministry, was successfully running a teachers' training school.[51]

In 1923 a notable event in Angoniland was the induction of the Revd Hezekiah M. Tweya to be pastor of the Henga congregation. It was nine years since Hezekiah and his two fellow Africans had been ordained, but they had continued to work as assistants to European ministers. Henga was the first congregation 'to assume the responsibility of calling a minister and satisfying the requirements of the central Fund' - in other words of guaranteeing a stipend for their own minister and at the same time making a contribution to the Central Stipend Fund.[52]

Writing an account of this occasion in The Record Dr Elmslie remarks, 'It cannot be said that we have been too hasty.' This is a masterly understatement for Hezekiah Tweya had passed his exit exam from the training college - with an average mark of over 74% - in 1903, had been licensed as a preacher in 1906, and the people of Usisya, to whom he had already commended himself by his work, asked for him as their pastor in 1910. Dr Laws said on that occasion that it was 'not as yet in the power of the Presbytery to allocate him to any particular sphere.'[53]

After ordination in 1914 Hezekiah Tweya worked as a probationer at Ekwendeni, and in 1917 he was posted to Karonga in the absence of any European minister there. In 1919 he became Moderator of the Presbytery of North Livingstonia.[54] Now at last, in 1923, the conditions laid down by Presbytery on the advice of the missionaries - namely, that adequate arrangements for payment of stipend should be ensured - were satisfied; accordingly, he went as minister to the Henga congregation with his maintenance provided for. He had waited all of 20 years since completing his training in divinity, even though Dr Elmslie could describe Hezekiah as 'a soul winner and specially beloved by the poor and helpless.'[55]

The ordination of Andrew Mkochi had been followed in 1918 by that of Edward Boti Manda and Yafet Mponda Mkandawire,[56] so that when Patrick Mwamlima was ordained at Karonga in 1921 the number of ordained Africans in the CCAP reached a total of seven.[57]

Another memorable event of 1923 was the award of the CMG to Robert Laws. As the Record said at the time 'No honour was more worthily earned'[58] and the Mission Council, minuting its congratulations, said of Dr Laws: 'His service to the cause of Christ, to Christian civilisation and to the British Empire merited recognition.'[59] In October, Mr Rankine, the acting Governor of Nyasaland, having learned that Laws was unlikely to travel to Zomba from Livingstonia wrote to say that his wife and he planned to visit Livingstonia and that he would present the award to Laws in person.[60]

The official party arrived at Florence Bay on the *Gwendolen* on 27th November and Mr Caseby arranged transport for them by bush-car up the zig-zag 11 miles of road to the plateau 2,400 feet above. When they neared the mission station an archway with the word WELCOME spanned the roadway. Over tea at Dr Laws' house Mr and Mrs Rankine met 15 members of the Livingstonia staff and 7 of the missionaries' wives.[61]

The following day at an open air ceremony the presentation of the insignia of the CMG was made, and a snapshot of the time shows Dr Laws in his Moderatorial robes with a solar topee on his head. Mr MacAlpine held up an umbrella to provide shade.[62]

In his despatch Mr Rankine spoke of Livingstonia as a township at which work among Africans was taking place 'on exceedingly sound and practical lines' which should prove of inestimable value to Nyasaland. The Acting Governor made an extensive and thorough inspection of the plateau and saw all that was going on from the turbines which powered the electricity system and the two mile long aqueduct which brought the station its water supply to the David Gordon Memorial Hospital where Africans were being trained to be medical assistants or nurses. He commented on the magnificent view from the European Hospital, and reflected on the fact that less than 50 years previously Atonga and Angoni had been fighting and raiding each other. He wrote:

> I came away deeply impressed... and convinced that Dr Laws
> is giving effect to his avowed policy, *viz.* to train up in Central
> Africa a Bible reading and a Bible loving people, intelligent and
> sensible in their outlook and skilled with their hands.[63]

The possibility of uniting the UFC Mission Presbytery of North
Livingstonia with the Established Church Mission Presbytery of
Blantyre and perhaps also with the Presbytery of the DRC, thereby
forming one African Church in Central Africa, had been envisaged
as early as the 1890s, and when Livingstonia Presbytery was brought
into being on 15th November 1899 it was given the name 'North
Livingstonia Presbytery' in the hope that the DRC mission would
soon form in its own area the 'South Livingstonia Presbytery.' The
vision was there but the working out of it was long delayed.
Discussions between representatives of the two Scottish missions
took place over a period of years in the 1900s, and at a Conference
at Mvera in 1910 they expressed the hope that they would soon be
united in one Synod.[64]

The Livingstonia Mission Council had agreed to this in
August 1910,[65] and the General Assemblies of the two churches at
home had accepted the proposals in May 1914. The outbreak of war
in Europe in August of that year put an end to further progress for
the time being and it was not finally until 1924 that the CCAP came
into being.[66]

The historic moment occurred on 17th September 1924 when
the Presbytery of Livingstonia, which was in session at Livingstonia,
adjourned to the Church for a joint meeting with the Presbytery of
Blantyre. Dr Hetherwick was in the chair when the resolution to
unite was formally put and carried. The first act of the Synod after
it came into being was to elect Dr Laws as its Moderator. Livingstonia
brought into the Synod 25 ministers and the same number of elders.
Of the ministers 18 were European and seven were African, while
there were 23 African elders and two European elders.[67] Blantyre
brought in 9 ministers, of whom 6 were African, and 9 elders all of
whom were African. This gave a total of 34 ministers and 34 elders,
made up of 23 Europeans and 45 Africans.[68]

A telegram from Laws on 20th September 1924 to the UF
Church authorities at home carried the message 'Livingstonia and
Blantyre Presbyteries happily united Sept. 17th in Synod of CCAP'[69]
Copies of the printed minutes of the first meeting of the Synod, and

the full nominal roll followed later.[70] This was a notable landmark for Malawian Christians in the progression from mission status to independent church. Although the Synod might still be dominated by the missionaries nevertheless a significant step forward had been taken, and it can be seen that in terms of voting power the Africans outnumbered the Europeans.

In uniting in this way the Mission bodies were five years ahead of their parent churches in Scotland, and in terms of African independence the CCAP was well on its way to autonomy 40 years before the nation of Malawi came into being as an independent state.

It had been hoped that the DRC would also join the Synod. This did not prove possible in 1924 but two years later, after the second meeting of the Synod, which was held in Blantyre, Laws was able to write home to Ashcroft on 20th October 1926, 'Since then [7th October] we had our meeting of Synod, and the Presbytery of Nkhoma of the DRC has now joined the Synod.'[71]

Plans by the Livingstonia missionaries to mark this occasion by holding an 'Agape', or 'love-feast', when all present at the Synod would sit down to a meal together (as well as sharing Communion in church) had to be abandoned because the members of the DRC would not eat with the Africans. Shared Communion was acceptable to the Dutch but not a shared meal. Patrick Mwamlima was led to say to Dr Laws, more in sorrow than in anger, 'We have been chased away.'[72]

Sad though this episode is, it was a cause of satisfaction that the three Presbyterian bodies which had been engaged in missionary work in Malawi had come together into one church, for the difficulties at one time had seemed considerable. Prejudice would lessen in time, and I have myself enjoyed a meal in Malawi, in the home of a lady who belonged to the DRC, in the company of both Africans and Europeans.

22 EDUCATIONAL CONCERN AND JUBILEE CELEBRATION

EDUCATION - ASHCROFT'S TOUR & REACTIONS - ORMSBY-GORE REPORT
- PHELPS STOKES COMMISSION - NYASALAND DISADVANTAGED -
MISSIONARY CONTRIBUTION - J.W.C.DOUGALL'S DIARY - CRITICISM OF
LAWS - WORK AT LOUDON - NEED FOR AFRICAN AGRICULTURAL ADVISERS
- SENATUS URGES REVIEW OF TRAINING POLICY - STONE HOUSE -
FORESTRY & AGRICULTURE - JUBILEE 'RECORD' - ABERDEEN'S GIFT -
ELMSLIE IN RETIREMENT - AFRICAN ORDINATIONS - GOVERNOR LAYS
FOUNDATION STONE

In the early 1920s no fewer than three investigations were carried out in Central Africa by individuals or bodies concerned in one way or another with the well-being of the Africans and in particular with the education being provided for them.

The Revd Frank Ashcroft, secretary of the FMC, set out in February 1923 on an extended tour of the Livingstonia Mission stations. His interest was in all the work that was being done but a large part of his report was concerned with education. According to Dr Laws Ashcroft was the first representative from Scotland to visit all the stations of the extended Mission.[1]

Of Livingstonia itself Ashcroft says, 'The founder's faith and courage have justified themselves', but of its future he writes:

Whether it becomes the great industrial centre of which Dr Laws dreams is doubtful. It seems to me to depend upon increased traffic facilities to the outside world, which should include a railway to the coast through Tanganyika Territory, but it is obviously already a great educational centre whose well-trained students are eagerly sought for everywhere.[2]

Ashcroft was critical of the educational system of the Mission. He pointed out that its 700 village schools had been started as evangelical agencies to teach converts or potential converts to read the Bible, but claimed that now 'a more thorough, though simple, education was required.' He proposed fewer village schools to facilitate more frequent visitation by supervisors, and better pay for teachers with the introduction of a school session of 9 months instead of the present 6 months.[3] (Teachers were paid only for the months during which the schools were operating.*)

Ashcroft's report produced varying reactions. Dr Hubert Wilson of Chitambo, wrote to Ashcroft pointing out that Africans would be most unwilling to send children of Primary School age to a central school owing to the danger of attack by lions, and that consequently each valley still needed its own bush school.[4]

Donald Fraser was also highly critical.[5] Dr Elmslie took a more sympathetic view ,and declared that he was glad that Ashcroft had 'given a clear verdict on the educational question.'[6] Charles Stuart, without giving the report blanket endorsement, was less critical than Donald Fraser and wrote, 'The report is a document that causes thought and will no doubt cause a good deal of discussion at our next Council meeting. I hope most of your recommendations will be acted on.'[7]

Education was also one of the main subjects considered by the Committee sent out to East Africa by the Labour Government of 1924 under the chairmanship of the Hon. W.Ormsby-Gore MP. This Committee was unable to visit Northern Nyasaland, North East Rhodesia, or Tanganyika, but was well aware of the educational work done by the Missions who deserved, their report said, 'unstinted recognition for their efforts as pioneers in economic development and in civilising'. In Nyasaland 'very exceptional work had been done by Christian missions.' While reluctant to criticise, the report said that 'some mission schools need much more European supervision.' The Record commented that this was not true of the UFCS, the C of S or the DRC, 'whose teachers are, on the whole, trained and competent for the simple duties required of them.' The value of the Ormsby-Gore report, said the Record, was its insistence on the need for increased transport facilities, and for better communication with the sea.[8]

The third body concerned with African education at this time was the Phelps Stokes Commission. There were two such Commissions made possible by the will of Miss Caroline Phelps

---

* In the late 1930s, Walter Yesaiah Chibambo, son of the Revd Yesaiah Chibambo, after teacher training at Livingstonia was paid for only 8 months each year, until after the Second World War when the Government began to pay teachers for 10 months of the year. (Interview at Ekwendeni on 15th May 1985)

Stokes which established a fund to further 'The Education of negroes both in Africa and in the USA'. The first Commission had dealt with the educational needs of West Africans. The second, with Dr Thomas Jesse Jones as chairman, and as secretary a young Scot, the Revd J.W.C.Dougall, many years later to become General Secretary of the C of S FMC, turned its attention to East and Central Africa.[9]

This commission referred to the 'unusually effective type of missionary education' [in Nyasaland] but pointed out that the development of Nyasaland's potential wealth awaited an adequate system of transportation within the country and a reasonable outlet to the sea. Nyasaland natives, the report said, trained in handcraft, sanitation, and hygiene, and dependable in character were welcomed by Governments and commercial bodies in Tanganyika, Belgian Congo, Rhodesia and Portuguese East Africa. 'Other colonies they are serving but their own people they cannot serve', ran the report.[10]
In spite of having six times the population of Gambia or Zanzibar and in spite of having an area of fertile land 10 times that of Gambia and 40 times that of Zanzibar, Nyasaland was below these countries both in exports and expenditure. Land was plentiful but market facilities were lacking - hence the need for better international transport and more direct outlet to the sea so that there might be a greater incentive to improve agriculture.[11]

At the same time opportunities for employment were few in Nyasaland but plentiful elsewhere, with the result that a big proportion of men left home to work in mines or plantations or seek work in the towns as labourers or artisans, clerks or house servants. Mission trained men could be found in all the East African colonies south of Kenya, and held responsibile hospital, clerical or mechanical positions.[12]

In financial terms, out of a total of £50,817 allocated by the Government to Education, Agriculture and Health, only £3000 went to education, which worked out at ½d per head of population. In Tanganyika the figure was the same, compared with an expenditure per head of 1d in Uganda, 11d in the Gold Coast and 5s 6d in Mauritius.[13]

The Phelps Stokes Commission reported that the 11 main missionary societies working in Nyasaland at that time had 2,521 schools and training centres and 126,900 pupils. This represented roughly half the estimated number of children of school age.[14] When Laws had addressed the UFC GA of 1922 he had given the number of schools in the Livingstonia Mission as 768 with 40,723 pupils,[15] and the Commission plainly recognised how much had been accomplished by the Mission. In the space of 50 years, and almost without government help, it had brought to the peoples of Central Africa 'health, habits of industry, freedom from fear, and faith in a God of love'.[16]

The Commission considered that the supervision of schools was not as regular or as extensive as it should be, but recognised that the mission authorities, while aware of this, were limited in their efforts to bring about an improvement by shortage of staff and funds.[17] It also stated that although the pioneering efforts of the larger missions had been of great value, too great an emphasis had been placed on literary subjects to the neglect of health, agriculture and native crafts.[18]

The Revd J.W.C.Dougall, Secretary of the Commission, kept a personal diary, and his comments give us the views of one visitor coming with fresh eyes to look at the mission work in Nyasaland.[19] Of Alexander Hetherwick of Blantyre, Dougall says that he had been 41 years in Nyasaland, had white hair and was 'very brisk.'[20] When he reached Livingstonia some four days later we look in vain for any similar comments on Dr Laws. Jim Dougall had just had his 28th birthday and Robert Laws was within a week of his 73rd. Was there a lack of empathy between the two men?

Alex Caseby, the agriculturist, whose fiancée Miss McFarlane had been allowed to travel north with the Commission from Blantyre and so made the journey from Scotland in what was then a record time of 28 days, met the party at Florence Bay.[21] They were given tea in a house on the beach before being carried up to the plateau, the ladies in *machilas* and the men in bush-cars. W.P.Young came down part of the way to meet the party and Jim Dougall and he plunged at once into a discussion on the work of the Mission. 'W.P.' writes Dougall, 'feels that the Institution is not serving the native so much as the European planters.' Apprentices were learning about electric saws but had none in their own villages. Brickwork was being taught but this would be of use only in the building of latrines.[22]

Later in the week visits were paid to some of the school classes and a contrasting picture is given by Dougall. In one class Mr Cullen [Young] taught a rare lesson in arithmetic, carefully using illustrations from things in the boys' own experience, to explain the mystery of division into fractions. Later they heard Dr Laws taking Standard VI in Hygiene, and Dougall records 'He has little chance of making them understand for he uses English rapidly and they learn by heart.'[23]

The proportion of girls to boys at school - roughly one girl to four boys (in contrast to South Africa where girls at school outnumbered boys by six to four) - was considered much too small, and the strength and weakness of Livingstonia was well summed up by Jim Dougall when he wrote, 'The defect of this Institution is that every department hangs on the one man. When he goes there is no correlation.' The headmaster, for example, had no say in the work of the technical department, nor in the dormitories.[24]

In dealing with the mission work at Loudon the Commission relied heavily upon the reports of Donald Fraser. He reckoned that in the Loudon area 11% of the population were attending school with pupils varying in age from five to 30. The village teachers might not themselves have gone beyond Standard 7, but they were men of sterling character and able to relate the schools to village life. The Mission paid the teachers - 14s to £2 per month for those trained at the Institution - but the school itself was provided by the village.[25]

Fraser considered that an Agricultural Native Demonstrator should be appointed for each area to give lessons on caring for stock, from poultry to cattle, and on the growing of crops in order to increase the wealth, comfort and capacity of the people.[26] He and Laws might differ in the emphasis which each put on village schools, and higher schools, but both were deeply concerned for the well-being of the African. Laws held strongly that the African should receive as high a level of education as he was capable of receiving. He would have agreed with his old acquaintance, H.H.Johnston, the former Governor of Nyasaland, who had written in 1916, 'The white man would like to thrust him [the African] back into helotry and into exclusively manual work'.[27]

Laws picked up the word 'helotry' in 1927 when he presented a paper on 'The Co-ordination of Technical and Literary Education' to the Education Conference at Zomba, declaring that to discard or even lessen the literary training would block the advancement of native leaders and reduce the Africans to a class of 'helots'.[28]

As Laws made clear each class, from Primary 1 upwards, spent some part of each day doing practical tasks around the Mission,[29] but even so, some of the subjects taught at the Institution were out of touch with African needs. For example, the ability to make doors and window frames could be useful in a village, the ability to make inlaid table tops less so. It is good to notice that at Loudon:

> Care has been taken to preserve and stimulate Native music. Nearly all the Hymns in use are set to native tunes. Prizes are given for the best compositions and a considerable body of very characteristic Native school songs and hymn tunes are now in use.[30]

Donald Fraser put in a plea for agricultural advisers but it is strange that there had not been more attempt at Livingstonia to impart such skills to a greater extent than seems to have been the case. In Chapter 16 we looked at the apprentice situation prior to the 1914 War. If we consider now the 33 years between 1894 and Laws' retiral in 1927, we find that in that period 53 enrolled as agricultural apprentices (none of them between 1902 and 1910, and none in the war years 1914 to 1918). Of the 53 only 31 completed the full five year course and received a Certificate. 12 had left or died, six had been dismissed and the other four are unaccounted for. Perhaps we ought not to press these figures too far but they would seem to show that only a meagre 31 certificated agriculturalists emerged from Overtoun Institution over a period of 33 years.[31]

This compares with an enrolment in the Building Department of 171 in the same period, of whom 95 received a Certificate at the end of their five years; and with an enrolment in the carpentry department of 259, of whom 166 received certificates at the end of their course. 35 apprentice carpenters died or left during the 33 years and 25 were dismissed. The others are unaccounted for.[32]

Certainly a five year period spent away from home, except for annual leave, was a long time for an African to be absent from his own village. It is true also that Dr Laws was one whose own standards were absolutely of the highest in every way, perhaps too high for more ordinary mortals than himself. Some at least of those dismissed were the victims of this extraordinarily high standard. A story is told of a youth who had taken some bananas for himself and hidden them under his oxter. Dr Laws who was investigating their disappearance ordered all the boys present to raise their arms above their heads whereupon the bananas fell to the ground. Laws pointed at the guilty party and said 'Away with you, we can't have thieves here.' The boy is reported to have gone mad and died.[33] Even if the story is apocryphal it illustrates both the high standards set by Laws and also the enormous awe in which he was held.

It is true that many of those who left Livingstonia without Certificates - thereby forfeiting the bonus of £3 to which they would have been entitled[34] - may nevertheless have learned sufficient about carpentry to do a satisfactory job of work in their home villages or possibly to find employment with Europeans.

Many members of the Mission staff were very uneasy about the policy of training so many Africans in skills that might not be appropriate to the African situation, and as early as 1908, when Laws came home to Scotland to be Moderator, the Senatus of the Overtoun Institution sent home to the Livingstonia Committee a long statement of eight foolscap pages urging the need for a revision of the Industrial Training Policy. The statement was sent by Dr Elmslie in the name of himself, W.Y.Turner, D.R.Mackenzie and Alex.Chalmers, the electrical engineer.[35]

This is an example of what happened on more than one occasion when points of disagreement with Dr Laws were expressed in his absence. He had left on 31st January and the minute of the Senatus was passed on 2nd May. Clearly Laws' colleagues despaired of getting their views through to the Home Committee so long as Laws was the channel of communication, and in a position to filter out expressions of opinion with which he disagreed.

There was criticism also of the Stone House which Laws was building for himself. 'Stones take time to be hewn', the statement ran, and at that time a European builder was needed for that, 'but as that is not yet a matter dealt with by Board and Senatus, no further remarks need be made.' That is a coded way of saying that Dr Laws had taken all the decisions! The statement added that no future building would be other than 'plain', and such as could be erected without European staff.

When the Home Committee finally dealt with what is called 'this important Memo' we find that the main thrust of the Memo from the Senatus has been played down and the claim that a different approach was now called for has been largely ignored.[36]

In one way this reveals the Committee's complete faith in Robert Laws; in another it shows how much the policies pursued at the Institution were in the hands of one man. Had that one man been one who found it easier to consult his colleagues and carry them with him it seems likely that the memo of 1908 would not have been written. Looking back after the lapse of years we can see that there was real truth in the feeling that some at least of the training was not close enough to African needs, and that the development of transport systems in Nyasaland was not going to benefit Livingstonia as much as Blantyre.

In agriculture, even the arrival of Alex Caseby as agriculturist in 1922 does not seem to have led to a greater willingness on the part of the Africans to commit themselves to this type of apprenticeship, and only four apprentices were enrolled between 1919 and 1927.[37]

Mr Caseby undertook a vast amount of afforestation - 80,000 trees were planted in 1924 - which would be of great importance in the long term in conserving the soil and increasing the amount of rain retained in it. He tells us himself of a wide variety of fruit successfully grown but there is no evidence that the Africans began to cultivate many of these crops themselves.[38]

Cattle rearing was impossible in the western part of the Livingstonia area because of tsetse fly but at Livingstonia itself in 1922 Mr Caseby speaks of 100 cart oxen, trained or in training, for field work, and of more than 300 beef cattle, goats, pigs, and sheep.[39]

He also records that in 1924 Dr Laws told him that the Director of Agriculture wished to create small holdings for Africans in upland areas for the growing of mountain wheat, rice etc. and asked him to make a survey with this in mind. As a result he produced a survey of 540 holdings, varying in size from two to 10 acres, and intended to be operational by 1926.[40]

The policy now seems to have been to approach agricultural improvement through regular meetings with the chiefs who were given 'instruction in simple means of increasing crops' and were expected to pass on this knowledge. At the same time, in Standard VI at school, 'Lessons on soils, manures, cultivation and rotation of crops, fruit culture, pruning, budding, general care of crops and a few lessons in forestry were given.'[41]

On 12th October, 1925 the Jubilee of the Mission was celebrated with enthusiasm both in Central Africa and in Scotland. At home the UFC Record, edited by W.P.Livingstone whose 'Laws of Livingstonia' had sold well in 1921 and subsequent years, brought out a 'Special Livingstonia Jubilee Number'. Dr Laws and Dr Hetherwick appeared together on the front cover, in a photograph taken by Mrs Margaret Stuart of Ekwendeni, and of the 80 pages of this enlarged issue of The Record 20 were devoted to the Livingstonia Mission.[42]

Laws claimed that in the first nine years of the Mission's work 40 per cent of its members died. It is true that the five graves at Cape Maclear speak eloquently of the cost of service in Central Africa at that time but in fact the records show that of the 39 mission agents, European and African, who served between 1875 and 1885 the number who died was eight, although it is true that a further seven were invalided home. The point which Laws was seeking to make, however, was that, compared with the early days, no deaths due to African disease occurred between 1906 and 1924.[43]

From the beginning, Laws says, the aim had always been to produce a church that was 'self-supporting, self-governing and self-propagating', and he instances the fact that, at a time when there were only nine communicants, eight of them, at Bandawe, helped the ninth to be a preacher of the Gospel at Cape Maclear. Later, several Bandawe leaders risked the danger of sleeping sickness to take the Gospel to the people who lived well to the west of them, and many died in so doing. In addition some of those trained in the industrial department at Livingstonia became unpaid missionaries of the African church by carrying with them to the places to which they went to work: 'God's word in their pockets and his love in their hearts.' As an example Laws cited a printer who had gone to work at Elisabethville, and there gathered together a small congregation for worship and opened a night school for those who wanted to learn to read.[44]

In Dr Laws home town of Aberdeen a presentation to mark the Jubilee was made. The aim was to raise £1000, and by 12th October £630 had been received from over 60 donors, £100 of it coming from Laws' old college friend, slightly his senior, James Shepherd who had served for so long in Rajputana. Miss Amelia Laws was in Aberdeen to receive the gift on behalf of her father.[45]

In Livingstonia also there was celebration. Sadly one who was not present to share in the occasion was Dr Walter Elmslie who had resigned the previous year on account of his wife's health. He had given outstanding service for 40 years, and more than once had stood in for Dr Laws at the Institution. He had been with Laws and Yuraiah Chirwa on the historic day in 1894 when they spent their first night on the plateau at Kondowe. His main work however had been at Ekwendeni and he had played a big part in bringing 'The Wild

Ngoni' into the British Empire 'with peace in their heart'. At Ekwendeni he is still remembered as one who spoke Chitumbuka well, in contrast to Laws who is said to have been reluctant to learn Chitumbuka and to have spoken Chinyanja with a bad accent.[46] In the Church at Ekwendeni Elmslie is fittingly commemorated with a tablet inscribed in Chingoni 'Blessed are the peace-makers for they shall be called the children of God' (Matthew 5 v9), and '1884-1924'.

Laws and Elmslie may not always have seen eye to eye but they respected each other and had shared many hardships together. On one occasion, when Laws was very ill, Elmslie had come down and carried him off to the hills in a *machila*. The journey lasted for four days, Laws' condition was very poor but he survived, and never doubted that he owed his recovery to the skill and unwearying care of Walter Elmslie.[47]

The Presbytery of North Livingstonia met on 11th October and ordained three more Africans, the Revd Peter Zimema Thole, the Revd Samuel S.Chibumbo, and the Revd Charles Chidonga Chinula, to the Christian ministry, which means that by the date of the Jubilee the number of African pastors in the Presbytery had risen to 11. A twelfth African was added to their number with the ordination of Zekariah Ziwa the following year.[48]

On October 12th 1925 the Governor of Nyasaland and his party, together with representatives of commercial and planting interests, and over 100 Africans, were present at the Jubilee Celebrations, and joined in singing the 100th Psalm, sung 50 years previously when the *Ilala* first sailed on to the waters of what became Lake Malawi.[49]

Sir Charles Bowring, the Governor, laid a memorial stone, which was also the Foundation stone of the Educational Building of the Institution, and presented Laws with an illuminated address from the public bodies in Nyasaland.[50] Presentations were also made from the Mission staff, and from Africans throughout the district. Laws must have wished that Margaret, who had shared so many years of hardship and toil with him, could have been present on this notable occasion. He had had many helpers, well over 100 of them, but since 1877 he it was who had been the leader *par excellence* of the Livingstonia Mission. His vision, his courage, his concern for the well being of the Africans, together with his indomitable spirit had ensured the steady progress that had been made throughout the past half century.

But even Robert Laws could not escape from the infirmities that come with increase of years, and not even he could surmount the financial stringency that was one factor at least in preventing the fulfilment of his plans to develop what he would have liked to see become the University of Malawi at Livingstonia.

23 DISAPPOINTMENT AND NEW HOPE

LAWS' VISION OF 'UNIVERSITY OF LIVINGSTONIA' - W.P.YOUNG AS HIS
SUCCESSOR - PROS & CONS OF KONDOWE SITE - WANING OF LAWS'
INFLUENCE - DIFFERENT AIMS - MISSIONS CRITICAL OF USE OF GRANT -
CONFLICT OVER PLACES ON ADVISORY BOARD - HETHERWICK'S INFLUENCE

With Commissions discharged and Jubilee celebrations at an end,
Laws returned to his vision of erecting at Livingstonia a two storey
building, surmounted by a crown on the model of his old College,
King's, at Aberdeen. His plea was that they were not building for the
present but for the future, and were envisaging what would become
the Overtoun College of the University of Livingstonia. Some might
regard it as a mere dream but, said Laws, 'Not a few of my laughed
at dreams are realities today.'[1]

Not all Laws' colleagues thought it wise to develop a university
so far from the main centres of population, and saw the whole idea
as a heavy drain on the resources of the Mission as a whole.
W.P.Young the educationist, whom the Mission Council, meeting
just prior to the Jubilee celebrations, had recommended to the Home
Committee as Laws' successor,[2] was totally opposed to such an
expensive scheme being started on the high plateau at Kondowe.[3]

In the early days of the Mission a large percentage of financial
support had come from a relatively small number of business men
in the west of Scotland. Most of these men had died and the
Livingstonia Mission, now part of the wider Foreign Mission work
of the church, had to depend on receiving its share along with the
many other fields of missionary activity.

There was considerable discussion over a period of some years
about the plans for the new building, and as late as December 1926
Laws sent Ashcroft nine foolscap pages of typescript, with an
accompanying Memo of two pages, pleading for permission to
proceed with the two-storeyed building which had been agreed on
while he was at home. Laws quoted, in support of his plan, a letter
from Sir Charles Bowring, the Governor, written unasked a year

earlier, in which he said, 'Livingstonia appeals to me enormously as a training centre because of site, comparative isolation and... easy accessibility.'[4]

Laws pled with the Committee to secure Christian education for the future and not to throw away the harvest of past years.[5] There is no doubting Laws' sincerity, but with it mingled something of the obstinacy of an old man holding on to a vision of past years. It was not to be. Laws was permitted to proceed only to the extent of the £4740 already in hand.[6] Plans to surmount the building with a crown like that at King's, Aberdeen (which Laws hoped an appeal to Aberdeen graduates would pay for) were shelved.

Looking back we can see that the FMC, charged with the whole overseas work of the UF Church, took the only responsible decision that was open to them, although it was by no means obvious that this was the way the decision had to go. If Malawi is considered on its own and transport from one area of it to another is thought of as road transport, ignoring the importance of the Lake for communication before the construction of metalled roads, then the plateau at Kondowe was too far from the main centres of population. If, however, we note that Livingstonia was readily accessible to the people of what is now Zambia and to those in the western part of what is now Tanzania, the idea is not so absurd.[7] Sir Herbert Stanley, Governor of Northern Rhodesia, as well as the Governor of Nyasaland, was favourably disposed to the idea of a centre of higher learning at Kondowe, to be attended by Africans from Nyasaland, Northern Rhodesia and Tanganyika.[8]

In 1925 the Moravian and Berlin Missionary Societies took over their former missions in East Africa and sent a letter to their 'Brothers in Christ' paying tribute to the work done by the Revd D.R.Mackenzie and his colleagues in the years just past. In May 1926 the Berlin Missionary Society sent their congratulations to Dr Laws on attaining his 75th Birthday.[9]

At the Second General Synod of the CCAP held at Blantyre in October 1926 - the occasion on which the DRC Presbytery joined the Synod - Dr Laws, as Moderator, preached at the opening. He read the whole of Acts Ch 23, dealing with Paul's defence before Agrippa, and then took verses 22 and 23 as his text:

Having therefore obtained help of God, I continue unto this day, witnessing both to small and great, saying none other

things than those which the prophets and Moses did say should
come; that Christ should suffer, and that he should be the first
that should rise from the dead, and should shew light unto the
people, and to the Gentiles.

He emphasised the importance of witness bearing by the individual
Christian and by the corporate life of the Church. 'The life of the
individual Christian', he said, 'is the sermon that tells. It is preached
minute by minute, hour by hour, and day by day.'

He then took up again the question he had raised in his address
to the GA when he was installed as Moderator 18 years before, the
question why, in the providence of God, Africa had been sealed up
for so many centuries? The answer to which he felt driven was that
had Africa been known sooner, 'the shambles that would have
resulted would have been even worse, before the Christian conscience
was aroused to see how far short Christians come of the law of love.'
They were all called to think carefully about the problems facing
them and to find the answer via the love of Christ, rising, through
obedience to Him, to greater heights of holiness, service and love.[10]

In the affairs of the CCAP the influence of Laws was beginning
to wane. Two pieces of business in the Presbytery of Livingstonia
illustrate this. In 1918 the Revd Jonathan Chirwa, who had been
guilty of adultery, made confession of his fault and resigned his status
as a minister. For several years after that, proposals that Mr Chirwa,
being penitent, should be reinstated as a minister, were moved
annually, and for one reason or another, were defeated. Finally,
when the Presbytery met in 1924, the Revd Andrew Mkochi moved,
and the Revd Donald Fraser seconded, a motion to restore Mr
Chirwa to full status. Dr Laws moved that the motion be amended
by adding the words 'not now', but Mr Mkochi's motion was carried
by 36 votes to two and Mr Chirwa was 'reponed' to the ministry.[11]

Laws also came out on the losing side three years later on the
question of the appointment of a treasurer for the Central Fund. The
Revd Yesaiah Mwasi moved that an African be appointed with a
European assistant. Laws proposed that the treasurer should be a
European and the assistant an African. After considerable discussion
Mr Mwasi's motion carried by a large majority.[12]

It was also agreed at this Presbytery to ordain Yona Mvula at
Livingstonia on 16th September - the 13th African to be ordained in
Dr Laws' time, although Laws himself had left Livingstonia before
the ordination took place.

One of the most important meetings attended by Laws very near the end of his time in Central Africa was a Conference on African Education, called by the Governor Sir Charles Bowring, which met in Zomba from 17th to 20th May 1927. The Conference was attended by representatives of 11 mission bodies as well as by representatives of the Nyasaland Chamber of Agriculture and Commerce, and of the Nyasaland Planters' Association. The Governor spoke of the occasion as a landmark on the eve of the Government assuming control of educational policy. He paid tribute to the amount of educational work done by the missions compared with which the government's contribution up to date had been insignificant. He pled for better relations between all mission bodies, and hoped they could agree on what constituted indispensable teaching ncessary for religious instruction. Apart from that the Government must say what was to be taught. So far as the grant was concerned it had begun in 1908 at £1000, been raised to £2000 in 1920 and for 1926-27 stood at £4,000, which it was hoped to increase to nearer £10,000 for the year 1927-28.[13]

Mr R.F.Gaunt, an alumnus of Queen's College, Oxford, and with 11 years of experience in Nigeria and Kenya behind him, had been appointed Director of Education. He stated that the aim of education should be the production of 'good, contented and loyal African citizens', and that it should aim at the formation of character. Religious instruction should have a place in all types of schools. Agriculture should be extended to the village schools, and there should be teaching on health and hygiene. The standard of teaching must be raised by extending the training of teachers and by regular inspection of schools. Too literary an emphasis should be avoided, although he accepted that village schools were agencies for teaching religion and the catechism.[14]

When Dr Laws was called on to speak on 'The Coordination of Technical and Literary Training in the Education of Africans' he expressed the aim of education rather differently from Mr Gaunt. Education, said Laws, was intended 'to fit the individual to make the most of his life for the service of God, for his own good, and for the good of his fellowmen.'[15]

The reason missionaries had not done more to improve agriculture and other technical training was that the African had first to see the need for it, and that technical education was costly and required Government help. Agriculture was the last thing the

African had seen he could improve in, partly due to his innate conservatism, and partly to the difficulty of marketing agricultural products should he produce more than was required for his immediate needs. In the absence of a good transport system the furthest an African could carry goods for sale was the distance they could be carried on his back along with sufficient food for the journey to the place of sale and return. What was needed, Laws concluded, was not to lower the literary side but to add the technical.[16]

In the discussion that followed Major I.C.Sanderson, representing the Nyasaland Chamber of Commerce and Agriculture, expressed his disappointment at Laws' presentation of educational aims. 'The planters,' he said, 'disagreed with missions devoting special attention to engineering, carpentry and technical trades ... Nyasaland was an agricultural country and... the natives should be taught the dignity of work on the land.'[17]

We see here the clash between those who wished to have Africans trained simply to the level at which they could be useful as employees to Europeans and the ideal of Laws, even if he failed to achieve its fulfilment in the way he had envisaged, that the African should be offered the best education which he was capable of receiving.

Donald Fraser was not present but later submitted a Memo to Mr Gaunt. He was not happy about making the aim of education the production of 'contented and loyal Africans.' Sometimes education must rouse 'discontent with poor conditions'! They must not just aim at Africans who would be 'no trouble to the Government.'[18]

At the Conference itself Laws was openly critical of the suggested financial provisions. He declared, 'You are recognising the work of the missions in the past, but now you are going to use the missions as a saving of Government money.'[19]

Donald Fraser was critical also, and in a long letter to Mr Gaunt, written on 25th May, pointed out that although the proposal to raise the Government grant to £9,300 was welcome, the suggestion that £4700 of this should be spent on European Administrators of education, and £600 on the education of white children in Nyasaland left only £4,000 for the direct stimulation of Africans.[20] This was felt by the missionaries to be far too small a sum. There was also dissatisfaction about the offer of only three places on the Advisory Board to the Federated Missions (ie mission bodies other than the UMCA and the Roman Catholics) with one place going to UMCA and one to each of the two R.C. Missions. This made six missionaries in all, together with four officials and three appointees other than the officials. Laws prepared a long Memo, dated 6th June, in which he claimed that the proposals represented 'not co-operation but confiscation' of mission work, pointing out that in 1926 Protestant Missions had spent £45,000 on education in Nyasaland, the R.C.s had spent £10,000, whereas the Government had not given more than £2000. Even the £4,000 proposed for African education in 1928 was only 7% of the total. He realised that to oppose the whole education act would lead to an end of cooperation between Government and Church, and therefore sought to have the grant enlarged.[21]

Dr Hetherwick was also greatly exercised about the size of the grant and the smallness of representation on the Board. He saw the Director of Education at Zomba on 27th June and was asked by the Governor to call the following day. He pled for four places on the Educational Advisory Board, instead of the proposed three and he said that without this they would not cooperate. The two had what would nowadays be called 'a frank discussion' and parted in disagreement but on terms of personal goodwill.[22]

In July, Hetherwick sent a cablegram to the C of S FMC claiming that with a Government grant of £10,000, of which half was to go on the salaries of officials, and with the R.C.s spending £10,000, UMCA £10,000 and the Federated Missions £35,000 per annum, the last named group should have four representatives on the Board in proportion to their expenditure and the work they were doing. As the Governor refused to agree Hetherwick asked for strong representations to be made to the Colonial Office.[23]

By early August the matter was resolved, and a telegram was received by the Church of Scotland from Hetherwick saying 'Difference with Government satisfactorily settled. Governor acceded Federated Missions. Please inform Ashcroft and others.'[24]

The question of representation on the Board was settled but the proportion of the grant to be spent on African schools compared with the amount allocated for the salaries of administrators continued to cause dissatisfaction.[25] In spite of this, the fact that the Government was now undertaking responsibilty for education in Nyasaland and was endeavouring to take the mission bodies, which had been carrying for so long the burden of education, along with it, was a step to be welcomed and a sign of hope for the future.

24 THE END OF A LONG CHAPTER

SENATUS, MISSION COUNCIL & PRESBYTERY - APPRECIATION OF LAWS
- LAWS TAKEN ILL - BAPTISM OF WHITE BABY BY AFRICAN - LAWS RETURN
HOME - MERCHISTON CRESCENT - VISIT TO BOSTON - HOLIDAYS IN
EUROPE - VISITS JOHN MOIR -*REMINISCENCES* PUBLISHED - RC MISSIONS
- IN EALING WITH AMY - HIS DEATH AND BURIAL - PULPIT & NEWSPAPER
TRIBUTES - YURIAH CHIRWA SUMS UP

Back at Livingstonia Dr Laws attended successively, in the month of
July, meetings of the Senatus of the Overtoun Institution, of the
Mission Council and of the Presbytery of North Livingstonia. He
was in fact attending each of them for the last time.

He chaired the Senatus on 4th July. Since 1924 all members of
staff had been allowed to be present, but decisions remained with
those who were actually members of it, which meant in practice the
ministers and doctors. Not until 1928, a year after Laws retired, were
all members of staff recognised as full members of the Senatus.[1]

When the Senate next met, on 4th October, Dr Laws was well
on the way to Scotland, and a long minute paid tribute to his work
in establishing the Overtoun Institution. Reference was made to the
introduction of water, light and power and to the development of
industrial training; but there was tacit criticism of the accommodation
provided for the trainees concealed in the sentence:

> The development of the Institution has been so rapid as to
> outrun the available accommodation. The dormitories and
> dwellings of pupils and apprentices are inadequate... The
> educational buildings are out of date and the church calls for
> new accommodation.

There was recognition of the part played by the many men and
women colleagues who had assisted Dr Laws with the development
of the Institution, including the late Mrs Laws, 'to whose steady help
and encouragement the Institution owed so much.' W.P. Young was
in the chair and the minute was unanimously approved by the nine
missionaries present.[2]

The Mission Council met in July six days after the Senatus with 25 present, and their tribute to Dr Laws was largely reproduced in the Record in the month of November.[3]

When the Presbytery of Livingstonia met later the same month a committee of three African ministers and elders was appointed to prepare an appropriate minute.[4] It ran to eight pages, plus a message to the FM Committee in Scotland, and when all allowance has been made for the enthusiastic language to be expected in a eulogy, and for the natural courtesy of Africans and their delight in oratory, it remains a moving tribute. The minute runs:

> All spiritual, mental and physical uplifting or prosperity in Central Africa are in the main due to Dr Laws. That his missionary career has wrought far reaching and wonderful conquest is verified by tangible facts in the whole area of the Livingstonia Mission... Among other things Dr Laws in his Farewell Address on July 17th 1927 to his colleagues and native representatives of all congregations of the Livingstonia Mission said 'Be in Peace, I am going away but I trust you to cultivate peace among yourselves.' And we in reply say to him, 'Go in peace; cease from anxieties regarding the work that you are leaving behind you and of which you have been the honoured instrument. Your God will take care of it. He is with the work as well as with the instrument.' Dr Laws may go away but Dr Laws' Mulungu remains in the work in Central Africa.

Laws' many-sided work was referred to, schoolwork, manual labour and religious services. His love for black men was genuine, the minute continued, and mention was made of an incident at the Overtoun Institution when an Atonga girl had died and Laws was seen with tears running down his cheeks. His 'humility, meekness, patience, and compassion' were singled out for mention, as was the example he set for the African as a man of labour:

> Now in divine services, now in medical work, he has served as a servant of Christ as well as a servant of Africa. We do not remember a single day which was spent by him in idleness.[5]

Along with the minute a message to the Home Committee was despatched expressing the gratitude of the people of Africa for the work which Dr Laws had wrought in Nyasaland, a wonderful work which had surpassed the expectations of his countrymen:

> The signs of Dr Laws as an apostle of Christ are we ordained ministers, evangelists, elders, teachers, deacons, and churches...

Your prayers have been answered and realised beyond your
hope. You cast your bread upon the waters. Now you find it
after 52 years of Dr Laws'labour.[6]

Not long after this Laws left Livingstonia for Zomba to see the
Governor and the Director of Education. This proved to be his
farewell to the community he had brought into being at Kondowe
and nurtured for the past 33 years. He had wished to remain in charge
until 12th October and the FMC had agreed to this. Unfortunately,
he found neither of the men he sought at Zomba. He then set out for
Blantyre but took ill on the way there. He had to spend some weeks
at Dr Hetherwick's house, and was in bed for three of them. To be
laid up in this way was to him a trial to be borne with patience, but
he wrote with appreciation, and in the most humble way, of those
who cared for him: 'Everybody is most kind... why I cannot
understand'.[7]

Arrangements were made for him to sail from Beira on 10th
September and he left Blantyre on the 8th.[8]

One of the first things he had done 52 years earlier had been
to lift an African child in his arms and ask a blessing with the words,
'God bless this child and make her a blessing to others.' Now, as Laws
was leaving, Alex Caseby and his wife had reached Blantyre on their
way back from furlough, and with them was their daughter Margaret,
born on 25th May. Laws took her up in his arms and repeated the
same blessing saying, 'First a black child and now a white child,
Amen.' Caseby adds:

As I said goodbye to my much loved chief I saw this man of
courage, endurance, patience and unquestioning faith in a new
light - great tenderness - tears streaming down his face. The
great crowd of Africans and Whites were in tears too. It was a
moving experience.[9]

The Casebys were shocked to see Dr Laws looking so ill, but
W.P.Young reports that the 'invalid' stepped briskly enough across
the platform at Blantyre Railway Station with the aid of a stout stick,
and was shown to the private saloon set apart for his comfort by the
railway manager:

Then from the window he holds *levée*. One after another steps
forward to shake hands and wish him a comfortable journey -
it is one of those moments too fraught with meaning and
emotion for words to have any adequacy at all... The time for
farewells is mercifully brief. The guard, one of his own

Livingstonia pupils, blows the whistle and the train moves slowly out... the white head at the window remains for a moment giving a long, close look, and then is gone.[10]

Meantime a notable event had taken place on Sunday 21st August, while Laws was ill at Blantyre - the baptism at Ekwendeni of the first white baby in the Livingstonia Mission area to be baptized by an African minister. Margaret Elizabeth, daughter of Jack and Mamie Martin, who had served both at Bandawe and Ekwendeni, was the baby, and the Revd Hezekiah Tweya of the CCAP was the minister. There were four baptisms that day, three African babies, Miriam, Rosa Lira, and Violet being baptized at the same time. In his sermon Hezekiah took his text from 1 Corinthians ch.1 and spoke eloquently of the progression they had seen over the years from white ministers baptizing white babies, to white ministers baptizing black babies, and then on to black ministers baptizing black babies and now to a black minister baptizing a white baby. 'Now they had seen a new thing', he declared, 'the white people standing along with the black people and making the same covenant before God.' There was one God for black and white and one baptism for both.[11]

Considering that 13 years had passed since Africans were first ordained as ministers, missionaries with young children had not been in a hurry to involve their African colleagues in this way, but it was good that the step had at last been taken and it clearly gave Hezekiah Tweya much satisfaction. Although Laws was not present the event arose out of the work he had begun so many years before.

W.P.Young, Laws' successor as head of the Livingstonia Institution, had not always been in agreement with him on matters of policy but he recognised his greatness and ends his account of his departure from Malawi with the words:

He has proved to us who inherit that Faith works - that there is nothing God cannot do in and with a man who wholly and sincerely surrenders himself. But he gives all the glory to God.[12]

It had been arranged that Dr Turner would accompany Laws on the first part of his journey and that Mr James Smith would travel with him all the way.[13]

Laws might be voyaging towards home but his thoughts turned often to Africa, and from HMMV *Carnarven Castle* he wrote on 12th October: 'To the Native Ministers, Office Bearers, Teachers, Church Members, and Adherents of the Livingstonia Mission -

Greeting.' After expressing his regret that he had been unable to visit all the stations of the Mission, as the Council had asked him to do, to say farewell before leaving Africa, Laws drew attention to the fact that he was writing on the 52nd anniversary of the day on which he first sailed on Lake Malawi. He spoke of Christ as the only Saviour and exhorted his readers to prove that their faith was real by trying to become like Christ through obeying his commandments and doing his will. This meant serving God and serving their fellow men.

The Holy Spirit will help them to live in Christ's way, he writes, and points out that their 'daily life will tell people more what Christ is like than words alone can ever do.' After reminding them of the need to tell other tribes how God has made his love known through Christ, he goes on to insist that in their homes Christ is to rule, and points out that it is as people see them loving and serving, and helping the sick and the suffering, that they will be led to recognise that the reason they act in this way is because the love of Christ constrains them.

He stresses the importance of daily Bible reading and daily family worship, and asks particularly that those to whom he is writing should help the European missionaries as far as they could. If the latter had been the means of leading them to Christ it would cheer them greatly to be told of this. 'By your uniting with them in the work of Christ', he says, 'you will strengthen them and yourselves and promote the Glory of God.' Laws concludes with Paul's words to the Colossians:

> We do not cease to pray for you, and to desire that ye might be filled with the knowledge of his will in all wisdom and spiritual understanding; That ye might walk worthy of the Lord unto all pleasing, being fruitful in every good work, and increasing in the knowledge of God; strengthened with all might, according to his glorious power, unto all patience and longsuffering with joyfulness', and signs himself 'Your loving missionary and friend, Robert Laws.'[14]

The November issue of the Record was by way of being a welcome home, with a Front Cover Photograph of Dr Laws and Archdeacon Johnson of UMCA who between them had given 103 years to Central Africa, and had been friends for many years. The Record also included, almost in full, the lengthy tribute paid to Laws by the Mission Council at the last meeting he had attended.[15] The Overtoun Institution had grown under Laws to be:

a great centre of education in almost every department of progress in which Africa needs instruction. In the preparation of men for preaching the evangel, for healing the sick, for teaching the young, for guiding the industrial development of the people, the Overtoun Institution (along with the Henderson Institute) [at Blantyre] form educational centres of which any British Colony could justly be proud.

Many men and women had shared in this task but it was Laws who had guided the movement from the beginning:

To him has been granted the felicity, in the grace of God, of seeing a whole race rising from age-long darkness and taking its place in history with credit and success.

There followed an affectionate reference to Mrs Laws:

She was a pioneer of work among the women of the land; her hymns nourished for a generation the spiritual life of the people; her hospitality was such as became her husband's position in the country; and Dr Laws' friends are not unaware of how frequently her high courage was his own strength and stay in many a difficult position.[16]

In Nyasaland itself the quarterly Livingstonia News also carried its tribute in an article entitled EPOCH. It drew attention to the changes that had come about in the land in the course of a single life time with the war dance giving way to the Sacrament of the Lord's Supper as the chief gathering of the tribes, and with so many, previously familiar only with the hoe, acquiring the ability to be engineers, carpenters, brick-builders, compositors or telegraphists.[17]

Dr Laws got home on 25th October and took up house at 69 Merchiston Crescent, Edinburgh, where his daughter Amy already had a flat. For the next two years Laws occupied it on his own, after which Amelia returned to Edinburgh and they shared that address until Laws' death in 1934.[18]

The Record of December 1927 reported that he was gradually recovering his health, but even by March of 1928 we find him telling F.W.Hardie, who had been a surveyor at Livingstonia from 1901 till 1907, that his strength was slow in returning.[19]

By the autumn of 1928 he was clearly much more himself again for he undertook a heavy week of engagements in Aberdeen, preaching on Sunday 23rd September in East and Belmont Church in the morning and in the North UF Church in the evening. The following Sunday he was in John Knox UF in the morning and in Carden Place in the evening. In between these two Sundays he addressed an evening meeting in his own old church, St Nicholas Lane.[20] On Wednesday 26th he was made a Freeman of Aberdeen, an honour conferred on Laws along with Admiral Jellicoe, and Sir Thomas Jaffrey, LL.D. of Edgehill, Milltimber. At the Freedom Ceremony it was said of Laws:

> No pioneer - missionary or explorer - is better known than 'Laws of Livingstonia', his half-century of civilising and Christianising work in Nyasaland reading like a veritable romance.[21]

The lunch given in the Town and County Hall for the new burgesses after the Freedom Ceremony had a 7 course Menu,[22] and one wonders how a man of 77, used for so many years to a simple diet, managed to cope with the rich fare provided! However this may be, it seems likely that Laws valued the gift of the Freedom of his native city above the many other honours which came to to him.

A letter to Dr Tilsley of Luanza the following year shows Laws' attitude to worldy honours. He writes,

> You will see that I have struck out 'Right Rev.' before my name. I do not like even 'Rev.' Some years ago 'Right Rev.' was, and still is, for the Moderator of our Church during his year of office, and though I never used it, I felt there might be as much self-conceit shewn by continually objecting to my friends using it as by letting it stand when I could not help it.[23]

He continued to plead for the erection of a major building at Livingstonia,[24] and not until 1931 did he finally write to W.P.Young saying that those who had subscribed money to build a crown similar to that at King's College, Aberdeen had agreed that their contributions should be transferred to the the the 'Overtoun Memorial Church Building Fund.'[25]

He was far from inactive. An article by Laws on 'Native Education In Nyasaland' appeared in the Journal of the African Society in which, among other things, he expressed the view that South Africa was heading for civil war.[26] That warning was given in 1929.

In the autumn of that year he addressed the meeting in Boston, Massachusetts, of the 13th General Council of the Presbyterian Alliance of Reformed Churches. It may have been on this occasion that he delivered a paper on 'Missions in Africa', in which, after giving a very comprehensive survey of African Missions he said,

'The Church, to which her Lord committed, as the object of her existence, the evangelisation of the world has not awakened to her responsibility and is but trifling with her commission.'[27]

If the charge was true it was certainly not the fault of Robert Laws.

In December 1931, he was at Bon Accord Church, Aberdeen at a BB Parade, and the press photograph shows Dr Hetherwick and Dr Laws flanking Dr Graham of Kalimpong who was taking the salute at the March Past.[28]

The following year he renewed his passport and from this document we learn that with increase of years he had lost 1½ inches in height, being now only 5ft. 7½ inches tall compared with five years earlier. His travels this time took him to mainland Europe. He disembarked at Boulogne in June and we may guess that he was going to spend a holiday with his brother-in-law Dr Gordon Gray who often left Rome in the summer to take the services at Pontresina.[29]

Laws was not always on the move, and sometimes he would walk only the short distance from Merchiston Crescent to 15 Polwarth Grove, to visit his old friend, John Moir of the African Lakes Company, in retirement like himself and living in the same part of Edinburgh.[30]

When in Edinburgh Laws worshipped in Bristo Church, where, with his long scarf worn on top of his overcoat, he was a familiar figure to the children of the congregation. One who was a child at the time recalls how eagerly she and her friends in the Sunday School listened to the story of the ship that was sent out in sections ready to be erected at the mouth of the Zambezi and then taken to pieces later for transportation past the cataracts.[31]

Dr Laws wrote his *Reminiscences* during his retirement, and these were published in January 1934. A Foreword by Lord Lugard, said that the outstanding characteristic of the Livingstonia Mission as he had seen it 46 years earlier had been its eminently practical nature. 'Dr Laws was not only a skilled surgeon and physician but a "handyman" with a turn for mechanics.'[32]

Even allowing for the tricks that memory plays on us all Laws' book is a clear account of the establishment of the Livingstonia Mission, first at Cape Maclear, then at Bandawe, and finally on the high plateau at Kondowe. He gives us a picture of the superstitions which prevailed in Africa in the early days of the Mission and of the difficulties involved in reducing a strange language to writing. His account of the growth of the African Church combines a realisation from the start that Africa must be evangelised by the Africans with a strong reluctance to hand over real responsibility to Africans even after many years of training. He writes of the educational work done at the Institution but without awareness of the criticism that it was too Europeanised in its orientation. A chapter is devoted to the other stations of the Mission, and another is entitled 'Other Missions'. Two chapters deal with the Fauna and the Flora of the country and the final chapter is entitled 'Farewell to Africa.'

After speaking of the Moravian and Berlin Missions in what was formerly German East Africa, Laws went on to mention the DRC, UMCA, CMS and LMS, and to refer briefly to the Seventh Day Adventists and the Watch Tower Movement. Curiously there is no mention of Roman Catholic Missions. This may be partly due to the fact that they were hardly present in Nyasaland during the first half of Laws' time there. The Montford Marist Fathers began work there in 1901, and the White Fathers, after some months of work in 1889-90, did not make their real start until 1902 - although the Roman Catholic Church has grown rapidly, especially since 1950, and its membership is approaching that of the CCAP.[33]

During the 1914 War, the Nursing Sisters of La Sagesse, who had come to Malawi early in the century, gave service near Karonga, at Mwaya at the extreme north of the Lake, and at Old Langenburg on the north east coast, areas where General Northey's troops were operating, and there were many sick and wounded to care for.[34]

Margaret Stuart (wife of Charles Stuart of Ekwendeni) had some contact with the White Fathers in 1915, during her nursing service, and tells also of riding out to have tea with the Marist Fathers when she 'took them some bananas and mulberries'. She found them living in a 'long reed thatched erection', with a table 'made of reeds laced together.'[35]

Inter-church relations were by no means cordial earlier this century. We caught a glimpse in the last chapter of Laws' (and Hetherwick's) unhappiness at the suggestion that the two RC missionary bodies should each be represented on the Educational Advisory Committee in 1927, while the 'Federated Missions' were being offered only three places on it altogether, and in July 1927, W.P.Young wrote from the UK that although the number and quality of Federated Mission Schools probably made a good case for greater representation, there was some rivalry between Protestants and RCs. He added:

> Both Dr Laws and Dr Hetherwick have a strong complex on the subject and will be prepared to fight anything that they think will give undue preference to RCs.[36]

In this Laws was a man of his time.

Lord Lugard in his foreword to *Reminiscences* drew attention to one item of which there is little mention in the book itself, and that is the very real danger encountered by Laws and his companions:

> Of the physical courage with which Dr Laws and his colleagues went among these hostile people, of the deadly malaria for which at that time prophylactic precautions were unknown, there is little mention in these reminiscences, though page after page records the death of a comrade, till one exclaimed 'Have you nothing but graves to show me?'[37]

There are indications that *Reminiscences* did not sell as well as W.P.Livingstone's *Laws of Livingstonia* published 13 years earlier and in part at least this was due to a change in the climate of interest among the general public. Africa had ceased to be quite so mysterious as in the early years of the Mission; a good many people now had some knowledge of it, and at least a general understanding of what had been done in Central Africa by the Scottish Missions. Laws himself had been the central figure of W.P.Livingstone's book and was clearly a man of great stature who faced problems, difficulties, and dangers with determination and courage, and saw in his own life time an astonishing transformation in the African scene. But Laws did not have the gift of 'communication' in the same way as a man like Donald Fraser, and his natural reserve perhaps prevented him from presenting himself in the heroic light which was possible, and legitimate, by a third party. At all events the publishers, Oliver & Boyd, wrote to Miss Laws three years after her father's death, not only to enclose a postal order for some royalties due but also to acknowledge £100 which Miss Laws had sent to them 'towards the loss on the book.'[38] To send such money was hardly a legal obligation but it shows a sense of honour on the part of Miss Laws which was characteristic also of her father.

In the summer of 1934 Robert Laws had travelled to London to spend some time with Amy in her house at Ealing where she had a small garden. He took ill while visiting the British Museum and after two days at Amy's was admitted to a nursing home. An operation was recommended although the success of it was not guaranteed. The following day he was no better and was in fact suffering from peritonitis. When the situation was put to him he at once agreed to an operation. He surprised the staff in the operating theatre by offering prayer for all concerned before the operation as he had been accustomed to do before undertaking operations in Central Africa. He regained consciousness after the operation but his condition was very weak and on 6th August, 1934, he died at the age of 83.[39]

Two days later a short service was held in the mortuary chapel in Kings Road, Chelsea, and was conducted by the Revd Archibald Fleming, of St Columba's, Pont Street. Referring to Dr Laws as 'a staunch old fashioned evangelical Presbyterian', he said that he found it 'remarkable that one of the warmest tributes to his memory appears in the most advanced of High Church Anglican papers.'[40]

But it was not only church papers which took note of the death of Robert Laws. The London Times devoted most of a column to an obituary and declared that 'the Protectorate [of Nyasaland] owed more to him than to any other man', while the Manchester Guardian of the same date spoke of his 'unfailing tenacity of purpose, unwearying industry, rare courage and stern loyalty to his duty as a Christian disciple and pastor.'[41]

In Scotland the Glasgow Bulletin said: 'In private life Laws was known as a man with a great sense of humour, blunt of speech and transparently sincere', and The Scotsman spoke warmly of the influence on Robert Laws of his father whom it described as 'one of the saintliest of men.'[42]

On the day of the funeral service in Aberdeen the flag on the Town Hall flew at half mast. The service in St Nicholas Church, Union Grove, was conducted by the Revd Dr Walter Elmslie, and by the Revd Alexander Hetherwick, now retired from Blantyre. 'To the African,' Hetherwick said, 'Laws was the head, and they recognised his power, while every missionary in Africa looked up to him and honoured him. They all loved him. He was their Archbishop. Laws' monument,' he continued, 'was in the lives of thousands who were Christians in Central Africa.' After the Benediction the Hallelujah chorus was played as the coffin was being carried out of church.[43]

The interment took place in the family grave in St Machar's churchyard where the Service was conducted by the Revd Henry Arnott, minister of Bristo Church, Edinburgh. Although it was a dull day, the sun came out as the coffin was lowered into the grave, as if joining in the last farewell.[44]

On Sunday August 12th the death of Robert Laws was in the minds of many ministers in Scotland. In Bristo, which had supported him for so long through the Laing bequest, and which he had joined when he took up house in Edinburgh on his retiral, the Revd D.R.Mackenzie, for so many years his colleague, said that Laws had such an ascendancy over the wild tribes of Central Africa that the chiefs would ask before taking any kind of action 'What will Robarti say?'[45]

In the old parish church of St Cuthbert's, at Edinburgh's west end, the Revd Norman Maclean took as his text the words of 2nd Samuel 3 v38: 'And the king said unto his servants, "Know ye not there is a prince and a great man fallen this day in Israel?"' and went on to say that over a territory as big as Britain Laws had 'turned war into peace, cruelty into mercy, and the cries of the perishing races into songs of thanksgiving.'[46]

In the Glasgow Evening Citizen, 'Churchman' also paid tribute to the influence of Laws' father - 'venerable in appearance, gracious in manner, he went about doing good in his own quiet way. Few men had such a remarkable gift of prayer.' Of Laws himself, the article said that while he had no special gifts as a speaker - there were no frills or thrills about his speaking but facts told in a bare unadorned way - yet his personality never failed to impress. Masterful, and even autocratic, he may have been, but, said the writer, 'Nothing impressed me more about Dr Laws than his humility. He was a great man who was unconscious of his greatness.'[47]

Periodicals with very diverse views were at one in paying tribute to Robert Laws. The Life of Faith quoted Lord Lugard's reference to Laws as 'that most practical and ideal missionary'; while the BMJ hailed him as 'a great doctor... immensely patient, and prepared to await results'.[48]

A representative of the UMCA spoke of the debt that their society owed to Laws for his services to Archdeacon Johnson, and referred to the 'tact, sympathy and understanding between the two men'. The writer noted that Laws had died on 6th August - the Feast of the Transfiguration.[49]

W.P.Livingstone, Editor of Life and Work, the monthly magazine of the united Church of Scotland, and author of Laws of Livingstonia which had sold so well when it was published in 1921, had spent several weeks with Laws in Africa while preparing his book, and got to know him well. He mentioned that Laws had no small talk, even at table, but that he did have abundant reserves of inner strength. To some he appeared blunt and forbidding but really he was tender and sympathetic. Livingstone described his personal life as 'spartan in its simplicity' and added that to the Africans he was 'kind, just, and infinitely patient' and yet 'ruled with authority'. They loved and revered him.

W.P.Livingstone saw the houses for Africans at Kondowe as 'utilitarian Scottish buildings... so grim... not in harmony with African character and environment.' Nevertheless he called Laws unique among missionary pioneers, administrators, and statesmen. In variety of attainments, in capacity for all forms of work, in indomitable faith and patience, and with magnificent practical achievements, no one has surpassed him. He was a super-missionary. Laws was all the time unconscious of the heroism of his life, but was one who had learned that 'God guides, helps and sustains his servants, and never forsakes them, and in moments of trial and crisis He gives them a sense of His presence and blessing.' No doubt, Livingstone added, it was this awareness of God's presence that characterized the life of Laws, which led Yuraiah Chirwa to say, 'Anyone can preach... but the Sing'anga, he has the something else without which preaching is vain.'[50]

25 THE STATURE OF THE MAN

TRANSFORMATION IN A LIFETIME - SOURCE OF LAWS' STRENGTH - 150
COLLEAGUES - VERSATILE, AUTOCRATIC - NO COLOUR BAR - THIRST FOR
KNOWLEDGE - INFLUENCE ON G.M.KERR - MARGARET'S SUPPORT -
SEPARATION FROM AMY - MUSIC AND ART IN HIS LIFE - A CRITIQUE OF LAWS
- SURE OF REALITY OF GOD'S LOVE - HIS CONTRIBUTION TO MAKING OF
MALAWI - LIFE PRESIDENT BANDA'S TRIBUTE - A GREAT SERVANT OF
AFRICA

What then are we to say, almost 60 years after his death, of this man
who so devotedly served God and his fellows throughout his life and
gave 52 years of that life to the people of Central Africa, and in
particular to those of them who lived in the northern part of what
is now Malawi?

It is given to few people to see such a complete transformation
in the lives and manners of those among whom they labour. For
many Laws sowed the seed of the Gospel message, and not only
sowed but tended the seed and saw it reach fruition and harvest.
David Livingstone had been the pioneer, the one who blazed the
trail. Catching the imagination of the western English speaking
world, Livingstone inspired others to follow, and to establish the
Christian Church in places from which he himself had moved on to
further unknown regions. The work to which Robert Laws was
called was quite different, and how well suited to it he was.

A man of granite was needed to face the hardships of the early
years and press on undeterred by fear or fever, by the dangers of
storm and flood, by exposure to the attacks of wild animals, or by
all the discomforts of life in Central Africa at that time. Nor was he
put off either by the suspicion of those who could not be expected
to understand, until it was demonstrated to them, that he came
among them in love, nor yet by the hostility and greed of those who
saw only too well that the acceptance of his message of love must
slowly and surely lead to the ending of their own nefarious ways of
making a living. 'Laws the indomitable' was a phrase that came to be

used of him and not without good reason. The hardships and dangers he had to face would have overcome many a lesser man.

He himself was well aware of the source of his strength and when he looked back on his life and work in Central Africa he gave to God the glory. Certainly Laws had many colleagues, almost 150 of them over the years, but from early days his was the vision, the courage, the drive and the determination that pressed on unswervingly. He was rewarded by seeing the slave trade suppressed with the help of British arms, and by witnessing the growth of an indigenous African Church, slowly at first and then with gathering momentum as Africans of diverse tribes and languages were prepared for Christian baptism and began to sit round the Lord's Table, drawing their strength from communion with God and then going out in their turn to pass on to others the good news they had themselves received.

One of the most astonishing things about Robert Laws was the range of his gifts. He had trained in three University faculties, Arts, Medicine and Divinity, and well deserved the honorary DD which came to him from his own University when he was only 40, and the LLD which the University of Cape Town awarded him after 50 years service in Central Africa. But he was far from being a cloistered academic. There is a folding bookcase, which doubled as bookcase and trunk for the carriage of the books, made so skillfully for him by his father when Laws left Aberdeen to pursue his studies elsewhere: that bookcase now houses books on missiology in the Divinity Library, King's College, Aberdeen; and it was no doubt from his father that Robert inherited the skill of the carpenter and the cabinet maker. A photograph frame, beautifully made and neatly jointed, firmly held together without the use of any nails, stands in the author's study, and is said by Mr Caseby, who kindly gifted it, to have been made by Laws in his years as an apprentice cabinet maker.

No one with high academic qualifications was ever less disposed to think lightly of manual skills than Robert Laws. In the early days at Cape Maclear he laboured at the felling of trees and the building of a house along with the others in the original party, working even on the Sabbath in order to have the building complete before the rains came. Years later, when news came of his nomination as Moderator of the UFC General Assembly, he was preparing a load of bricks for transport to the UMCA Mission on Likoma Island.[1]

There were times when his own satisfaction in good craftmanship led him too far, and he placed too great an emphasis on training people to make such things as inlaid tables or trays when articles of more general utility and less artistry would have been closer to African needs. If, however, there was any tendency for those who had learned literary skills to think themselves above manual labour, it was not from the example of Robert Laws that they derived any such idea.

Laws was not obviously characterised by what nowadays would be called 'charisma', and yet his sterling qualities were there for the discerning eye to see. People knew where they were with him; he was all the time predictable and reliable; he did not say one thing and mean another. He set a high standard for himself and expected a high standard from others. He was a man of few words, and not given to much praise when a task had been well done. A hand clap on the shoulder might indicate approval - or a silent turning away his disapproval.[2]

He has been accused of being autocratic in his dealings with his missionary colleagues, and paternalistic towards the Africans he sought to serve. These charges can hardly be denied and yet his attitudes are not difficult to understand. After the first few years of the Mission, Laws was not only senior in age to his European colleagues but, increasingly as time went on, had behind him a much longer experience of Central Africa than any of them. Even Walter Elmslie, nearest to Laws in years and length of service, began his service nine years later than Laws, and retired three years before him.

Laws was not however a good communicator - the result in part of his early years when his step-mother expected him as a child to be seen but not heard - and at times he was inclined to take decisions without consulting his colleagues or even letting them know what was going on in his mind.

There is no trace in Laws of any kind of colour discrimination. It was all one to him whether a person's skin was black, brown or white, but he was a child of his age in his thinking about the relationship of 'master' and 'men'. He had been an apprentice himself and worked under a 'master' but he had graduated from that in more ways than one and had been virtually in charge of the Livingstonia Mission since Dr Stewart left to return to Lovedale in January 1878. The Livingstonia Committee at home clearly minuted in March 1879 that 'Dr Laws be considered the official head of the Mission' (unless Dr Stewart were present).[3] Laws had therefore reason for assuming that in Mission affairs he was in the position of 'master', and regarded all Mission staff, whether European or African, as there to serve under his direction.

His construction of 'The Stone House' at Livingstonia - unique in Malawi being built of dressed stone from a nearby quarry,[4] and on a grander scale than any of the other houses - was in line with such thinking, and it does not seem to have struck him that there was any impropriety about it. The Committee at home did its best to dissuade him, without actually forbidding him to build it. In December 1904 J.Fairley Daly more than once drew Laws' attention to the feeling of the Home Committee 'against building [the Homestead and the Stone House] in a large expensive style' for to do so would set a standard for the other buildings which it would not be possible to keep up. Speaking in another letter of the need for economy, Daly suggested to Laws as tactfully as possible that the Stone House would be the first thing to occur to him as requiring reconsideration.[5] But Laws did not reconsider and proceeded to build it with hewn ashlar work on three sides, between 24 and 27 inches thick. He included in it a massively built strong room with a studded iron door. The strong room was to have been the stair well to the upper floor where the bedrooms were to have been, but the upper storey was never built. In Laws' absence Dr Elmslie had the roof put on to the building while it was still only one storey high, and as a result the large dining room and Laws' own study had to be used as bedrooms by his successors.[6]

Laws was certainly looking to the future, and was convinced that he was engaged in a mighty enterprise that would affect the whole future of Central Africa. A missionary who went out to Livingstonia in the year in which Laws died, remembers hearing that Laws had declared how important it was to provide higher education for the African who was going to rule his own country in the future.[7]

Laws may have thought of himself as 'Master' of the Mission, but at the same time, no consideration of status ever stood in the way of him giving freely and unhesitatingly of his time and medical skill to any who were in need, no matter who they were, what their position or colour, or whether they were near at hand or far away. From W.P.Young we learn the origin of Yuraiah Chirwa's lifelong devotion to Laws. In the early days an African had been gravely ill and it was not expected at that time that a European would turn out in the middle of the night to give succour to an African. Laws did and Yuraiah never forgot it.[8]

Not only was Laws a doctor and a preacher, a brick-maker and a carpenter. He was also responsible for having more than one African language reduced to writing, and produced school Primers in both Chinyanja and Chitonga, as well as a grammar and dictionary in Chinyanja. He also translated the New Testament into Chinyanja and St Mark's Gospel into Chitonga. Under him the Livingstonia Mission was responsible for publishing, either at Lovedale, at home through the NBSS, or later on through the printing press at Bandawe or Kondowe, translations of the Gospels into at least eight African languages.

Some skill in navigation was his also for he was in charge of the *Ilala* from the time E.D.Young left until the arrival of Captain Benzie, and no doubt at other times as well. When the headquarters of the Mission moved to Kondowe, he displayed some knowledge of civil engineering, having water brought several miles to flow through taps at the Mission station, and harnessing its energy to provide electric power as early as 1905. Francis Hardie served the Livingstonia Mission as surveyor from 1901 until 1907, and Alex Chalmers as a civil and electrical engineer from 1901 till 1918, but one may be sure that Laws took a keen interest in the work that was being done, whether road building or the construction of the turbines for the electricity system, and that he would be able to discuss the technical problems and difficulties involved in a knowledgeable way.

Laws was always on the search for new knowledge for himself which might enable him the better to fulfil his role in Africa, whether it was the study of electrical engineering and physics on his furlough in 1899-90, or of child care and infant feeding before he returned to Africa in 1909.[9]

Those who were divinity students in the years of Laws' retirement remember him as a man who was short of middle height, and as one who was not outstanding as a public speaker. What did impress people was, not his fluency in the use of words, but the absolute sincerity with which he spoke and his deep devotion to the cause of Christ, and to the needs of the African.

Just as Laws himself had been influenced as a youth by hearing Mr Fairbrother of the LMS[10], so he in turn influenced others. We know, for example, that it was through Laws that the call to missionary service came to G.M.Kerr, who served the Methodist Church for many years at Nizamabad. On his second furlough, in 1890, Laws dropped in to the YMCA in Aberdeen which he had himself frequented as a youth, and a group of young men asked him about his work in Africa. Among them was G.M.Kerr, aged 16 at the time, and Kerr tells us himself how greatly that hour's talk was responsible for his offering himself as a missionary.[11]

Of the domestic side of Laws' life much less is known, partly because his letters seldom contain references to personal matters, and partly because he had so little 'private life', being almost completely absorbed in his work. For over 40 years Margaret Gray gave him loyal support, and herself made a valuable contribution on the educational side of missionary work and in the translating of a number of hymns, as well as a catechism, into Chinyanja.

It is a sad fact about missionary work in those days that children born in the mission field generally came home with their parents when they reached the age of eight or thereabouts and were not expected to accompany them when they returned to the field .

Amelia Laws confided to a friend in later life that she did not think her father had always been fair to her mother through his absorption in his work, but she also denied any kind of rift between herself and her parents as a result of many years of separation. In a recorded message sent to the members of the Church in Malawi at the Centenary of the Livingstonia Mission she said that although she was brought up by an aunt while at school in Edinburgh and was later under the care of her uncle, the Revd Dr J.Gordon Gray, in Rome, she was in constant touch with her parents in Central Africa and knew what was taking place there. She said of her parents, 'The fragrance of their contact remains a precious memory to me.'[12] And yet she was not entirely happy about her upbringing and not long before her death, at a ripe old age, it was still a source of concern to her that her parents had left her to such an extent in the care of others, however well disposed and kindly they were.[13]

We hear little of music in the life of Robert Laws - certainly nothing is told of him that is at all comparable to Albert Schweitzer's organ playing in West Africa - but we do learn from Mrs A.E.Mackenzie, who with her husband the Revd D.R.Mackenzie spent many years at Bandawe and Karonga, that music meant a lot to Robert Laws.

Mrs Mackenzie tells us that she first met Laws before going out to Livingstonia in 1900. She had dreaded the interview but he soon put her at her ease.

'Do you know how to live with a hedgehog?' he asked. When she answered that she had some experience of this, he then asked if she could scrub a floor. When she said that she was willing to learn Dr Laws told her that she was not going to live in a mud hut and eat off enamel dishes, denying herself in every way. 'God does not want your grave,' he said, 'He wants your work and your best work.'

The next enquiry as to whether or not she was musical and fond of beautiful pictures and of reading, led on to the advice to take with her some musical instruments, pictures, and books. He also advised her to take good table appointments, for that helped one to keep a good appetite.

Laws himself, Mrs Mackenzie wrote, was fond of classical music, and would often ask what the voluntary was when she played for a service. Once, when the Mackenzies had given him a book of sacred pictures, he said that they were among the few who realised his love for music and art.[14] It is good to know that there were these gentler interests hidden within Laws' rugged exterior.

A further glimpse of Laws' pastoral care for his staff is given by Mrs Alex Chalmers who, as Miss E.B.Trotter, began as a teacher at Livingstonia in 1904, and continued to live at Kondowe from the time of her marriage to Alex Chalmers, the electrical and mechanical engineer, in 1909, until 1918 when Mr and Mrs Chalmers and their family moved to Lovedale. She found Laws a caring and understanding pastor, and her daughter, Mrs Helen Neil of Edinburgh, states her mother had the very highest regard for Robert Laws.[15]

Looking back as an elderly lady in 1952 Mrs Chalmers recalls that one day Dr Laws met her as she was returning home and said,

I came to see you today because I think you are doing too much now. You are over-taxing your strength. Take things easier for a bit. A dead missionary is no use to God here, but he can use a living one very much. The best work you and Miss Fiddes can do here just now is the way you live together before these girls. Now go quietly for a bit. Good-bye.

Mrs Chalmers adds, 'He left me with his usual smile which was a blessing.'[16]

Mrs Chalmers tells us also that when her engagement to Alex Chalmers was announced she received a note from Mrs Laws saying,

'Come to breakfast tomorrow and tell us all about it.' After the Laws
had expressed their warm congratulations, the Doctor said, 'But
what am I to tell the Committee? They say that my ladies always get
married and they don't like it. In your case I can only say, "Send me
one like you, for I know that although love came to you, your heart
was always in the Master's work."' She could hardly utter a 'Thank
you, Doctor' but tells us that she cherished these words ever since.[17]

Laws was not one who readily showed his feelings or his faith,
but at the centenary of his birth, in 1951, a retired lady missionary
recalled having passed the Stone House early one Easter morning,
and seen Laws standing in his garden. He raised his hat as she passed,
and greeted her with the words, 'The Lord is risen!'[18]

A 'saint' in the conventional stereotype of a man without faults
Robert Laws certainly was not. A saint, however, has been defined
as 'one in whom there is a high degree of cooperation with God', and
if we accept this definition then Laws was certainly a saint. He tried
from his earliest years to do what God required of him, and he went
on doing it through thick and thin, with the utmost determination,
and with an unswerving loyalty to the Lord Jesus Christ. As a result,
the life of many hundreds of people of Central Africa was transformed.
Superstition and ignorance were replaced by understanding and
knowledge; fear of evil spirits by trust in a God who cares. The truth
of the centrality of love in the universe was not merely proclaimed
in words but was demonstrated in the lives of Laws and his
colleagues, and even their shortcomings could not wholly obscure it.

That some tribal customs were destroyed and some facets of
African culture misunderstood and undervalued by the missionaries
cannot be denied. Sooner or later Africa, so long the unknown
continent, had to come into a relationship with Europe, and some
adjustment of *mores* there had to be. Some customs could not survive
the coming of the Christian way of life. For example, the practice of
burying a chief's wives in the grave with him, or the custom of
establishing guilt or innocence by the administration of *mwavi*, had
sooner or later to be superseded. No religious or ethical system of
today could possibly defend them.

On the other hand there were times when the concern of the
missionaries for 'right conduct' blinded them to the true nature of
certain aspects of African life and led them to see evil where none was
intended. Tribal dancing, for example, was condemned by the

missionaries, because they feared it would lead to dissolute behaviour, but much depends on the conventions observed in a particular society. For example, when Life President Hastings Banda came to the UK in the late 1930s to improve his medical qualifications he was shocked to find men and women engaged in ballroom dancing![19]

Polygamy was another African custom, understandably condemned by Laws and his colleagues, but not understood by them in its setting in African society as they found it.

The Christian ideal for marriage is clearly the union of one man with one woman, committing themselves to each other for life, and in the context of such commitment providing a secure setting for the upbringing of children. Polygamy, however, should be understood before it is condemned. Certainly it is open to abuse, and rich old men could provide themselves with several young girls who had no say in the matter and were little better than concubines. But, at its best, polygamy had its place under the social conditions of the time, when tribal warfare was rife and the number of women considerably exceeded the number of men, and the whole idea of an unmarried woman living alone was unthought of - who would protect her? who maintain her? what job whereby she might earn her own living was available for her? In such a society polygamy provides the necessary means whereby all women are under some man's care and protection, are provided for, and are given the opportunity of motherhood. Where polygamy prevails each wife is provided with her own hut, one of a little cluster grouped round that of her husband, where she brings up her children. That there can be jealousy between wives is clear enough but good family relations all round are not necessarily poorer than they are in a monogamous society.

Again, where a paramount chief is ruling over a loose confederation of tribes, it is of vital importance that he takes a wife from each tribe. Otherwise the tribe, or tribes, from which he has not taken a wife will be offended, strife is likely, and the confederation may even break up.[20] Even apart from the special situation of such a chief, it was not unknown for a man's first wife to complain if he delayed too long in taking a second or third wife. An African wife, certainly in a village situation, had a great deal of hard work to do, water to carry, perhaps for a long distance, maize to pound and so on, and she knew that the load would be lightened when shared between two or three.

Mission teaching on monogamy was right but the missionaries were sometimes in too big a hurry to introduce it, and often showed themselves insensitive to human feelings by too rigid an insistence on it where tribal marriages were already in existence. It was this difficulty, as we saw in Chapter 12, that led one of the Tembo brothers to refuse the Christian baptism he desired, because he had a concern for all his wives and felt he ought to go on caring for all of them and not simply for the first of them.

The problem was not open to any perfect solution in the short term. That had to await the development of society along Christian, and, to some extent at least, along Western lines, with a greater general emancipation of women, and greater opportunties for unmarried women to find employment on their own.

Laws was limited by the ideas of his own time and by a certain lack of flexibility when it came to the application of rules and the importance of maintaining the highest possible standards of behaviour. For the Africans he had a genuine love and a deep concern and yet he did not readily understand ways of thought which were different from those of Europeans. Donald Fraser who published *Winning A Primitive People* in 1914, and D.R.Mackenzie, whose book *The Spirit Ridden Konde* came out in 1925 tried to record the thoughts and customs of some of the African tribes they knew, but it was T.Cullen Young, who joined the Livingstonia Mission in 1904, who really began to enter into the African mind. He wrote extensively for periodicals from 1909 onwards but his *African Ways and Wisdom* was not published until 1937, and his *Contemporary Ancestors* until 1940. *Our African Way of Life*, by T.C.Young in collaboration with Dr Hastings Banda, did not come out until 1946.[21] In these books Cullen Young was coming much closer than Laws ever did to a true understanding of African values and ways of thought.

What Laws had was a firm grasp of the reality of the love of God, as Christ had made it known to the world, and this he strove with deep sincerity and considerable success to convey to the African both in words and by the quality of his own life. How a missionary who has grown up in any particular culture can convey the core of the Christian message to those of another culture without imposing, directly or indirectly, features of his own culture which are not of the essence of the Christian faith, is an unavoidable problem, but it was not one of which 19th century missionaries were aware. Rightly they knew that they had something to give but neither they - nor we

- can be wholly free from the assumptions of the environment in which we have grown up. The Revd A.G.MacAlpine, who gave many years of faithful service to the Mission, made a remarkable admission many years later when he said to the Revd Fergus Macpherson, as the latter set out for Livingstonia after the Second World War, that one thing which he and his colleagues had forgotten when they went out to Central Africa was that God was there before them.[22]

We have already noted that the siting of the Overtoun Institution at Kondowe was not without good reason at the end of the 19th century. The Lake provided the main channel of communication, and for a time it did look as if Livingstonia might have served as a suitable educational centre for Africans from what is now Zambia, and from what is now Tanzania, as well as for Africans from Malawi.

A more serious criticism is that a great deal of the education provided in the early days was much too 'Scotland centred', with African pupils being asked to learn, for example, details about Scottish geography or history as mentioned in Chapter 16.[23] The education offered also seemed to many to be too literary. Laws of course would have contested this, and pointed out that all the way up the school each class was expected to carry out manual work of one kind or another. Apart from this he consistently argued that it was essential to provide the opportunity for Africans to develop the full extent of their potential and not simply to give them sufficient training to enable them to grow cabbages or cook for Europeans.[24]

To recognise that Robert Laws was a man with shortcomings like the rest of us need not blind us to the astonishing nature of his achievements nor make us unaware of his stature, second only to that of David Livingstone, among those who have gone out from the United Kingdom as missionaries to Central Africa. He came in 1875 to a huge region without a single Christian, and to leave it 52 years later with a Christian community of over 30,000,* with more than 19,000 communicants, together with a whole network of schools attended by many thousands - that was an achievement![25] More than

---

*In his long letter to Ashcroft on 23/12/1926, pleading the case for further expansion at Livingstonia, Laws speaks of 880 schools and 51,117 pupils. In his *Reminiscences*, he gives the figures for 1932 as 655 schools and 26,078 pupils. In both sources the number of communicants is given as exceeding 20,000.

that, in the making of Malawi as a nation, the education provided in the northern part of the country by the Livingstonia Mission enabled those from the north to play an outstanding part - out of proportion to their numbers - both as government ministers and as civil servants, when Malawi gained her independence in 1964.[26] Many of them, and perhaps their fathers also, had been educated at Livingstonia. There they had not only studied a wide range of subjects in the classroom, and undertaken a good deal of manual labour during their time at the Institution, but, more important still for the responsibilities they were now to undertake, they had received a character training which was widely recognised in Central and East Africa as producing people of reliability and honesty who were well fitted for high position.

Laws had done his work well, and the work of Robert Laws at Livingstonia, together with that of his slightly younger contemporary Alexander Hetherwick at Blantyre, was recognised by Life President Banda when he was visited by the Moderator of the General Assembly of the Church of Scotland, the Right Revd John R.Gray, in 1977, and by the Right Revd W.J.G.McDonald, who visited him as Moderator in 1989. To both Moderators the President spoke memorable words. He said, 'Had there been no Church of Scotland there would have been no Malawi.'[27]

Scotland has sent many of her sons and daughters as missionaries to Malawi, but none has given greater or more single-minded service than Robert Laws of Aberdeen, whom the people of Malawi still think of as 'Laws of Livingstonia'.

APPENDIX 1

AFRICANS ORDAINED AS CCAP MINISTERS BY 1927
(with ordination dates)

Revd Jonathan P.Chirwa	18th May 1914
Revd Yesaya Zerenji Mwasi	
Revd Hezekiah Marova Tweya	
Revd Andrew Mkochi	4th November 1917
Revd Edward Boti Manda	21st July 1918
Revd Yafet Mponda Mkandawire	
Revd Patrick R.Mwamlima	1st August 1921
Revd Yoram Mphande	13th December 1924
Revd Peter Z.Thole	11th October 1925
Revd Samuel S.Chibumbo	
Revd Charles Chidonga Chinula	
Revd Zekariah Ziwa	25th December 1926
Revd Yona Mvula	16th September 1927

(Based on Malawi National Archives, LI 1/3/21; LI 1/3/24 -
Minutes of Presbytery of Livingstonia at relevant dates)

APPENDIX 2

LIVINGSTONIA MISSIONARIES
(from 1875 to 1927)

Year of Appt.	Name	Occupation
1875	Revd Robert Laws CMG MA MD DD LLD FRGS (and Mrs Laws)	
	Mr E.D.Young RN (Leader of Original Expedition)	Master, the *Ilala*
	Revd William Black MB CM	
	Mr G.Johnston	Carpenter
	Mr J McFadyen	Engineer
	Mr A Simpson	Engineer
	Mr A.Riddel	Agriculturist
	Mr W.Baker	Seaman
	Mr T Crooks	Seaman
	Mr J.Gunn	Agriculturist
1876	Revd James Stewart MD DD (returned to Lovedale 1878)	
	Mr R.S.Ross	Engineer
	Mr A.C.Miller	Weaver
1877	Mr William Koyi)	Africans
	Mr Shadrach Ngunana)	from
	Mr Mapas Ntintili)	Lovedale
	Mr Isaac Wauchope)	
1878	Mr James Stewart CE FRGS	
	Mr George Benzie	Master, the *Ilala*
	Mr Robert Reid	Carpenter
	Mr J.Paterson	Engineer
	Mr William Reid	Seaman
	Miss Jane E.Waterston MD LLD	
1880	Mr James Sutherland	Agriculturist
	Mr George Fairly	Master, the *Ilala*
	Mr William Harkness	Engineer, the *Ilala*

1881	Mr R.Gowans	Master, the *Ilala*
	Mr J.Smith	Teacher
	Mr Peter McCallum (& Mrs)	Carpenter
	Revd R.Hannington, MB CM	
	Mr Donald Munro	Builder
1882	Mr George Williams (African from Lovedale)	
1883	Revd J.Alexander Bain MA	
	Mr William Scott MB CM (& Mrs)	
1884	Mr W.McEwan CE	
	Revd Walter A.Elmslie MB CM (& Mrs)	
1885	Revd D.Kerr Cross MB CM (& Mrs)	
	Mr George Rollo	Teacher
1886	Mr Hugh MacIntosh	Carpenter
	Mr M McIntyre	Teacher
	Mr J.B.McCurrie	Teacher
	Mr R.Gossip	Bookkeeper
1887	Revd George Henry MA MB CM (& Mrs)	
	Revd Charles Stuart (& Mrs)	
1888	Mr William Murray (& Mrs)	Carpenter
1889	Mr William Thomson (& Mrs)	Printer
1890	Revd George Steel MB CM	
	Mr James Aitken	Teacher
	Mr George Aitken (& Mrs)	
	Revd D.Fotheringham MB CM	
1891	Mr Govan Robertson	Teacher
	Mr A.C.Scott	Teacher
	Mr Donald MacGregor	Agriculturist
	Mr W.Morrison	Joiner
1892	Mr W.Duff MacGregor (& Mrs)	Joiner
	Mr Roderick Macdonald	Joiner
1893	Revd A.G.MacAlpine (& Mrs)	
	Revd R.D McMinn (& Mrs)	

Revd Alexander Dewar (& Mrs)

1894	Miss L.A.Stewart	Teacher
	(married A.D.McMinn, 1901)	
	Revd Malcolm Moffat (& Mrs)	
	Mr Hugh Steven	Joiner
	Revd Geo.Prentice LRCP & SEd DTM (& Mrs)	

| 1895 | Revd James Henderson MA (& Mrs) | |

1896	Mr Walter J.Henderson (& Mrs)	Builder
	Revd Donald Fraser (Moderator,	
	UFC 1922) (& Mrs Fraser)	
	Revd J.C.Ramsay LRCP & SEd	
	Mr J.M.Riddell-Henderson (& Mrs)	

1897	Miss Margaret McCallum	Nurse
	(married Rev C.Stuart 1901)	
	Mr A.W.Roby-Fletcher BSc MB CM	
	Miss Maria Jackson (married	Nurse
	Revd Malcolm Moffat 1900)	

| 1898 | Mr Robert Scott MB CM | |

| 1899 | Mr John McGregor (& Mrs) | Joiner |
| | Revd Frank Innes MA MB ChB DTM (& Mrs) | |

1900	Miss M.J.Fleming	Nurse
	Revd J.A.Chisholm LRCP & SEd DTM (& Mrs)	
	Mr William Sutherland	Builder
	Mr James Gauld, Jnr.	Builder
	Miss J.Martin (honorary)	
	Mr Ernest A.Boxer LRCP & SEd (& Mrs)	

1901	Miss Winifred A.Knight	Nurse
	(married Dr Boxer 1903)	
	Revd Duncan R.Mackenzie (& Mrs)	
	Miss Agnes Lambert (married	Teacher
	Revd D.Mackenzie 1904)	
	Mr Alex.S.Chalmers AMInst CE & AMI	
	MechE (& Mrs)	
	Mr James D.Meldrum	Joiner
	Mr David Adamson (& Mrs)	Carpenter
	Mr Francis W.Hardie	Surveyor

1903	Miss Jessie Fiddes LLA (married T.Cullen Young 1908)	Teacher
1904	Rev T.Cullen Young, CA (& Mrs)	
	Miss E.B.Trotter (married Mr A.S.Chalmers 1909)	Teacher
1905	Mr Alex Brown MB ChB (Abdn)	
	Miss M.P.Ballantyne	Nurse
1906	Mr Berkeley H.Robertson MA BSc MB ChB	
	Mr John S.Howie	Agriculturist
	Mr Peter S.Kirkwood MA (& Mrs)	Teacher
	Miss Agnes T.S Lawson (honorary)	Teacher
	Rev Wm.Y.Turner MA MB ChB DTM (& Mrs)	
1907	Miss C.M.Irvine	Teacher
	Miss Mary H.Y.Henderson	Nurse
	Miss A.Howie Brown	Teacher
1909	Miss E.B.Cole	Nurse
1910	Revd W.P.Young MA (became Principal of Overtoun Institution, Livingstonia, 1927)	
1911	Miss J.S.Hart (honorary)	Teacher
1913	Miss R.M.Livingstone Wilson (married Revd A.Macdonald 1920)	Nurse
	Mr Hubert Livingstone Wilson MB CM (Camb) DTM	
	Miss M.Maxwell	Teacher
	Revd Alexander Macdonald MA (& Mrs)	
	Revd T.T.Alexander MA (& Mrs)	
1914	Miss M.M.Patrick	Nurse
1917	Miss M.Gilchrist	Teacher
1919	Mr Thomas Gordon (& Mrs)	Joiner
	Miss C.M.Petrie (married Revd D.Maxwell Robertson 1928)	Teacher
	Miss M.F.Grant	Teacher
	Miss Anne Ferguson	Nurse
	Mr A.A.Burnett (& Mrs)	Agriculturist
	Revd M.H.Faulds MA (& Mrs)	

250

1920	Mr S.B.Straiton (& Mrs)	Lay Agent
	Mr William Johnston (& Mrs, 1931)	Carpenter
	Mr J.A.Davidson (& Mrs)	Printer
1921	Revd D.D.M.Brown (& Mrs)	
	Mr John Brown (& Mrs)	Engineer
	Revd J.R.Martin MA (& Mrs)	
	Revd Alex Halliday (& Mrs)	
	Miss Bessie Muir	Bookkeeper
	Miss M.B.Christie	Nurse
	Miss Helen Patrick	Nurse
1922	Mr Alex Caseby (& Mrs)	Agriculturist
	Mr James Smith	Lay Agent
	Miss Isobel Reid	Nurse
	Miss Grace R.Allison	Teacher
	Miss C.Masterton	Nurse
1923	Mr William C.Smith (& Mrs)	Builder
	Dr John Todd (& Mrs)	
	Revd James Youngson MA (& Mrs)	
	Miss Ivy M. Murray MA	
	Miss Ruth Service	Nurse
	Miss G.Genner (honorary)	
	Miss Ishbel Macdonald	
1924	Mr James A.Brown (& Mrs)	Accountant
	Mr Charles Barclay (& Mrs)	Carpenter
	Dr A.G.Badenoch	
1925	Revd D.Maxwell Robertson (& Mrs)	
	Revd W.C.Galbraith MA BSc	
	Miss M.R.Coutts	Nurse
	Miss M.L.M.Muir (honorary)	Nurse
	Mrs Treu	Nurse
1926	Dr Geo.B.Burnett (& Mrs, 1930)	

Those appointed between 1875 and 1914 are taken from the list in Donald Fraser's *Livingstonia* pp.86-88. Those appointed between 1914 and Dr Laws' retiral in 1927 are based on NLS, Acc.7548,D.72 - *Central Africa, Livingstonia missionaries*. One or two missionaries married again after the death of their first wives.

PRIMARY SOURCES

NLS   NATIONAL LIBRARY OF SCOTLAND, Edinburgh
  Minutes of Livingstonia Sub-committee, FMC of Free (later United
  Free) Church; Letters from/to their Secretaries
    Cape Maclear, Bandawe and Kaningina Journals;
    United Presbyterian Church Records;
    Papers formerly in the Shepperson Collection.

EUL   EDINBURGH UNI. LIBRARY SPECIAL COLLECTIONS
    Laws' Collection, Gen.561,562,563;
    Diaries of Robert Laws, for certain years from 1875, & other papers about
  origin & dev't of the Livingstonia Mission;
    Newspaper cuttings, including tributes on Laws' death;
    Photographs, other papers.

MNA   MALAWI NATIONAL ARCHIVES, Zomba
    Minutes of Livingstonia Mission Council;
    Minutes of Senatus of Liv'nia Training Institution
    Minutes of Presb. of N.Livingstonia of CCAP;
    Correspondence and other records of the Mission, including exam
  papers and results;
    Record of Apprenticeships; Contracts of Employment;
    Some Volumes of Aurora, and Livingstonia News;
    Notes by Laws for sermons and addresses.

AUL   ABERDEEN UNIVERSITY LIBRARY
    Laws' Collection, MS 3290, incl. letters from Margaret Gray, 1872-74
    Caseby Collection, MS 3289;
    Archives - Students Register, Medical Grad'n Schedule;
    Record of Arts Classes 1868-1872;   AUL Calendar 1870-1871;
    R.Laws, *Woman's Work in Heathen Lands* (Parlane, Paisley 1886).

SRO   SCOTTISH RECORD OFFICE
    Minutes of UP Presbytery of Aberdeen 1867-1878;
    Minutes of Glasgow Presb. of UP Church 1871-1875;
    UP Synod Records 1875.

AGR   ARCHIVES, Grampian Region
    Crimond School Log 1873-1874.

ABR   ARCHIVES, Borders Region
    Galashiels School Board Minutes 1873-1880.

NBSS NATIONAL BIBLE SOCIETY OF SCOTLAND, Edinburgh
    Minutes 1855-1891;   Anniversary Meetings 1863-1912;
    Quarterly Records 1878-1911;   Min. of Eastern Committee 1893-99.

SOAS SCHOOL OF ORIENTAL & AFRICAN STUDIES, Lon. Uni.
    Diary of Revd James Dougall, while Sec. of Phelps-Stokes Commission;
    Papers relating to education in Nyasaland in the 1920s.

MLS MITCHELL LIBRARY, Glasgow
    History of Glasgow City Mission (1920), Annual Reports 1874 & 1875.

    Document apprenticing William Laws to John Milne, Cart and Plough
Wright 1810, in possession of Langstane Kirk, Aberdeen;
    Census Returns for Aberdeen 1851, 1861, 1871;
    Central African Journal of A.C.Scott (1891-1896), published in Facsimile
by CLAIM);
    Letters from Robert and Margaret Laws to Amelia (1894-1899), in
possession of Mrs Margaret Hansford (née Caseby), Aberdeen;
    Copies of Old Letters from Nyasaland: 1889 Rev C.Stuart; 1915 Diary
of Margaret Stuart (1915-1916) in possession of Dr W.O.Petrie, Edinburgh;
    Letters from Jack and Mamie Martin of Bandawe, & Letter of Farewell
from Dr Laws to all African staff in 1927, in possession of Mrs M.E.Sinclair
(née Martin), Stirling;
    Proceedings of GA of Free Church, and from 1901 of UF Church;
    Minutes of UP Church FM Board 1876 & 1878;
    Free Church Record (later the United Free Church Record);
    Life and Work - the Record of the Church of Scotland;
    Robert Laws, *Reminiscences of Livingstonia* (Edinburgh 1934);
    Nyasaland Times December 1952 to June 1953, incl. *Memories of
Nyasaland* by Mrs E.B.Chalmers;
    Letter dated August 1984, from Miss Seonaid Mackenzie, member of
Bristo congregation as a child.

Interviews with:
    Mr Alex Caseby (app. Livingstonia 1921) & Mrs Caseby (Glenrothes,
December 1983);
    Mr & Mrs Colin McFadyen, son of J.McFadyen, engineer of the
original party (Crieff, February 1986);
    Miss Agnes Hardie, daughter of Francis W.Hardie, surveyor at
Livingstonia 1901-1907 (Colinton, March 1986);
    Miss Helen M.Taylor MBE, Livingstonia staff 1933-1964 (Oct 1990)
    Revd Neil Bernard (Oct 1990);
    Dr Fergus Macpherson (June 1991).

BIBLIOGRAPHY

Aberdeen University Students' Register, Vol 1, Fac. of Arts, 1868-72

A.E.M.Anderson-Morshead, *History of UMCA* (London, 6th ed.1955)

African Papers No.1 (ed.Jas.Stewart)

Ballantyne & Shepherd (ed.), *Forerunners of Modern Malawi* (Lovedale 1968)

Sheila M.Brock, unpublished paper, *Dr Jane E.Waterston* drawing upon the Stewart Papers at Harare and The University of Cape Town

Sheila M.Brock, *A Broad Strong Life, Dr Jane Waterston* (in *The Enterprising Scot*, ed. Jenni Calder, HMSO Edinburgh 1986)

George H.Campbell, *Lonely Warrior* (CLAIM 1975)

Frank Debenham, *Nyasaland, the Land of the Lake* (London 1955)

Henry Dummond, *Tropical Africa* (London 1889)

East Central Africa - Livingstonia: The Mission to Lake Nyassa (Free Church, Edinburgh, 2nd ed. 1876)

W.A.Elmslie, *Among the Wild Ngoni* (Edinburgh, 1899; London 1970)

William Ewing, *Annals of the Free Church of Scotland, 1843-1900* (Edinburgh 1914)

Agnes R.Fraser, *Donald Fraser, of Livingstonia* (London 1934)

Donald Fraser, *African Idylls* (London 1923)

Donald Fraser, *Autobiography of an African* (London 1925)

Donald Fraser, *Livingstonia, the Story of our Mission* (Edinburgh 1915)

Donald Fraser, *The Future of Africa* (Edinburgh 1911)

Donald Fraser, *The New Africa* (Edinburgh House Press 1927)

Donald Fraser, *Winning a Primitive People* (London 1914)

Sir Bartle Frère, *Eastern Africa as a Field for Missionary Labour* (London 1874)

Peter G.Forster, *T.Cullen Young, Missionary and Anthropologist* (Hull Univ.Press 1989)

L.Monteith Fotheringham, *Adventures in Nyassaland* (London 1891)

Michael Gelfand, *Lakeside Pioneers* (Oxford 1964)

Keir Hardie, *Speeches and Writings (from 1885-1915)* ed.Emrys Hughes (Forward Print. & Pub.Co., Glasgow)

John D.Hargreaves, *Aberdeenshire to Africa* (AUP 1981)

Alexander Hetherwick, *The Romance of Blantyre* (London 1932)

James W.Jack, *Daybreak in Livingstonia* (London 1901) with Intro. by R.Laws

W.P.Johnson, *My African Reminiscences* (London 1924)

H.H.Johnston, Sir, *British Central Africa* (London 1897)

H.H.Johnston, Sir, *The Story of My Life* (London 1923)

P.Landreth, *The U.P. Divinity Hall* (Edinburgh 1876)

M. & E.King, *The Story of Medicine and Disease in Malawi* (Blantyre 1992)

John A.Lamb, *Fasti of U.F.Church of Scotland 1900-1929* (Edinburgh 1956)

Robert Laws, *Reminiscences of Livingstonia* (London 1934)

Robert Laws, *Women's Work at Livingstonia* (Paisley 1886)

Robert Laws, *Nyanja School Primers, Grammars and Hymn Books*

W.P.Livingstone, *Laws of Livingstonia* (London 1921)

254

W.P.Livingstone, *A Prince of Missionaries; Alexander Hetherwick* (London 1931)

F.D.Lugard, (Captain), *The Rise of our East African Empire* (Edinburgh & London 1893)

F.D.Lugard, (now Sir), *The Dual Mandate in British Tropical Africa* (Edinburgh & London 1922)

K.John McCracken, *Politics and Christianity in Malawi, 1875-1940* (CUP 1977)

K.John McCracken, *Livingstonia as an Industrial Mission, 1875-1900* in *Religion in Africa* (Edinburgh 1964)

K.John McCracken, *African Politics in Twentieth Century Malawi* in Ranger T.O (ed.), *Aspects of Central African History* (London 1968)

K.John McCracken, *Religion and Politics in Northern Ngoniland 1881-1904* in Pachai, *Early History of Malawi* (London 1972)

K.John McCracken, *Livingstone and the Aftermath: The Origins & Development of the Livingstonia Mission* in *Livingstone, Man of Africa* (ed. Pachai, London, 1973)

Duff MacDonald, *Africana or The Heart of Heathen Africa* (London & Edinburgh 1882)

D.R.Mackenzie, *The Spirit Ridden Konde* (London 1925)

Ian McLean, *Keir Hardie* (Allen Lane 1975)

Hugh Macmillan, *Origins of the A.L.C. 1878-1908* (PhD Thesis, Edinburgh 1970)

Fergus Macpherson, *The British Annexation of Northern Zambezia, 1884-1924: Anatomy of a Conquest* (Ed.Univ. PhD Thesis 1976)

Fergus Macpherson, *Kenneth Kaunda of Zambia - The Times and The Man* (OUP 1974)

Fergus Macpherson, *Appropriation of the Gospel as shown in Christian Songs of Malawi* (Seminar Paper at Centre for Study of Christianity in Non-Western World, New College, Edinburgh, 11/6/1991)

Fred.L.M.Moir, *After Livingstone, An African Trade Romance* (London, 1923)

Jane F.Moir, *A Lady's Letters from Central Africa* (Glasgow, 1891)

J.M.Morrison, *Forty Years in Darkest Africa* (Edinburgh 1917)

Roland Oliver, *The Missionary Factor in East Africa* (London 1952, 2nd ed. 1965)

Roland Oliver, *Sir Harry Johnston and the Scramble for Africa* (London 1957)

Bridglal Pachai (ed.), *The Early History of Malawi* (London 1972)

Bridglal Pachai, *Malawi, the History of a Nation* (London 1973)

Bridglal Pachai (ed.), *Livingstone, Man of Africa, Memorial Essays 1873-1973* (London, 1973)

Melvin E.Page, *Malawians in the Great War and After, 1914-1925* (submitted to Michigan State University as PhD Thesis 1977)

Records of Arts Classes, Aberdeen 1868-72, ed.P.J.Anderson (Aberdeen 1892)

Robinson & Gallagher, with Alice Denny, *Africa and the Victorians* (London 1961)

W.J.W.Roome, *A Great Emancipation* (London 1926)

Andrew C.Ross, *The Foundations of the Blantyre Mission* in *Nyasaland, Religion in Africa*, (Edinburgh, 1964)

Andrew C.Ross, *Scottish Missionary Concern, 1874-1914; a golden era?* in Scottish Historical Review L1.151, 1971

George Shepperson (ed.) and Thomas Price,*Independent African; John*Chilembwe and the origins, setting and significance of the*Nyasaland native rising of 1915* (Edinburgh 1958; paperback 1989)

James Stewart, *Livingstonia: its Origin* (Edinburgh 1894)

Joseph Thomson, *To the Central African Lakes and Back* (1878-1880) (London, 1881 & 1968)

Horace Waller, *The Title Deeds to Nyassaland* (London 1887)

James Wells, *Stewart of Lovedale* (London 1908)

E.D.Young, *The Search for Livingstone* (London 1868)

E.D.Young, *Mission to Nyassa, a Journal of Adventures* (London 1877)

T.Cullen Young, *African Ways and Wisdom* (London 1937)

T.C.Young and Hastings Kamuzu Banda (ed.),*Our African Way of Life* (London 1964)

T.C.Young, *Contemporary Ancestors* (London 1940)

(A bibliography of the works of T.C.Young, published as books or articles between 1909 and 1970, is given in Peter G.Forster, op.cit.)

Periodicals

Aberdeen University Calendars, 1868-74

Journal of Social Science, Vol.2, 1973 (Univ. of Malawi)

Journal of Social Science, Vol.10, 1983 (Univ. of Malawi)

The Society of Malawi Journal, Vol.38. No.1 1985; Vol.39, No 2, 1986

A Portrait of Malawi (Published on the occasion of MALAWI's Independence, 1964)

Scottish Geographical Magazine, 1934

Papers by the Author

Contracts of Employment and the Influence of Class in the First 30 Years of the Livingstonia Mission, SCHS Records vol. xxiii, part 1, 1987-88

Robert Laws as Preacher, Bulletin of Scottish Institute of Missionary Studies, New Series nos. 3-4, 1985-87

The Effect of the 1914-18 War on the Livingstonia Mission, Bulletin of Scottish Institute of Missionary Studies, New Series nos. 4-5, 1988-89 ed. A.F.Walls

REFERENCES

Chapter 1

1 FCGA Reports 26/5/1874; and Dr Duff's statement to Commission of FCGA 1875
2 Old Machar Register of Marriages 11/6/1846; Census Returns, 1851, District of Old Machar
3 Article of Appr'ship 8/6/1810 - to be seen at the Langstane Kirk, Aberdeen
4 Laws' Tombstone, St Machar's Churchyard, Aberdeen
5 AUL Spec.Coll.MS 3290/3; notes by Miss A.N.Laws on her father
6 Census Returns 1861, 1871 - District of St Nicholas, Aberdeen
7 Notes by Miss A.N.Laws, as above
8 W.P.Livingstone, *Laws of Liv'ia* pp.13-15; D.P.Thomson, *Miss Janet Melville*
9 WPL *op.cit.* p.15
10 *Ibid.* p.15 11 *Ibid.* p.18 12 *Ibid.* p.19
13 Census Returns, 1851; 1861; 1871
14 WPL *op.cit.* p.19
15 Aberdeen Uni. Calendar 1868-1870
16 NLS 7648, 7649, 7650, UPC FM Records, Letters, Hamilton McGill to R.Laws, 2/10/1868; 5/8/1869; 9/9/1869; 13/11/1869; 3/12/1869
17 WPL *op.cit.* p.20
18 AUC 1868-1870   19 *Ibid.* 1870-1871
20 Records of Arts Classes, Aberdeen, 1868-1872, ed. P.J.Anderson (Ab. 1892)
21 Census Returns, 1871 - Dist. of Old Machar, Aberdeen
22 NLS 7870, Alex. Duff to Mr Macdonald, Treasurer Free Church, 20/5/1875
23 AUC 1868-1872
24 Ab. Univ. Students' Register Vol 1, Fac. of Arts, 1868-1872
25 AUC 1873-1874
26 AUL Spec. Coll. MS 3290/2; Medical Report Sheet, No.216
27 WPL *op.cit.* p.24
28 SRO CH3/2/14, Mins. of UP Pres. of Aberdeen, 4/6/1872
29 *Ibid.* 9/7/1872
30 P.Landreth, *The U.P.Divinity Hall* (Edinburgh 1876) p.288
31 *Ibid.* p.288; AUL Spec.Coll. MS 3290/1, Mgt.Gray to R.Laws, 13/9/1873
32 SRO CH3/2/14, Mins. of U.P.Pres. of Aberdeen, 8/10/1872

Chapter 2

1 WPL *op.cit.* p.27
2 EUL Laws' Collection, Gen.561/1
3 AUL Spec.Coll. MS 3290,/1, M. Gray to R.Laws, 3/9/1873
4 *Ibid.* 16/8/1872   5 *Ibid.* 23/9/1872
6 *Ibid.* 24/8/1872
7 SRO CH3/2/14, Mins. of U.P.Pres. of Aberdeen, 3/6/1873; 15/7/1873
8 Grampian Reg. Archives, Crimond Sch. Board Mins, 23/8/1873, 28/8/1874; and Crimond Sch. Log Book: AUL Spec.Coll. MS 3290/1, M.Gray to R.Laws, 7/8/1873
9 *Short Hist.of Glasgow City Mission*, Mitchell Library, Glasgow; Annual Report, 1875, p.11
10 Glasgow City Mission Annual Report, 1874, p.7,8
11 WPL *op.cit.* p.28
12 Gl.City Miss.Ann.Report 1874 p.7
13 *Ibid.* p.8
14 *Ibid.* 1875 pp.11,12
15 WPL *op.cit.* p.32
16 Census Returns 1871
17 AUL Spec.Coll.MS 3290/1, M Gray to R.Laws, Oct.1873; Census Returns, 1871, 184 District 2
18 AUL Spec.Coll.MS 3290/1, M.Gray to R.Laws, 20/10/1873
19 *Ibid.* Nov.1873   20 *Ibid.* Oct.1873
21 *Ibid.* 19/2/1874
22 *Ibid.* 20/10/1873; 10/1/1874
23 *Ibid.* 10/1/1874; and others
24 *Ibid.* 7/1/1874
25 *Ibid.* M.Laws 27/5/1874
26 SRO CH3 146/58
27 Africa Papers No.1 (ed.Jas.Stewart) Liv'nia, by Dr Duff, p.26
28 WPL *op.cit.* p.8
29 *Eastern Central Africa, Livingstonia* (Free Church, Edinburgh 1876) p.45
30 NLS 7912, and 7913, Mins.of Liv. Sub-Committee, 3/11/1874
31 *East Cent. Africa*, as above, pp.45,46-48
32 *Ibid.* p.44
33 Drummond & Bulloch, *The Church in Late Victorian Scotland* (Edinburgh 1978) p.98

34 AUL Spec.Coll.MS 3290/1, M.Gray to R.Laws, 24/6/1874

35 *Ibid.* 17/6/1874; and 13/7/1874

36 Grampian Reg.Archives, Crimond Sch.Board Mins. 28/8/1874

37 Border Reg.Archives, Mins.of Galashiels Sch.Board, 15/9/1874

38 *Ibid.* 29/9/1874   39 *Ibid.* 5/10/1874

40 *Ibid.* 17/12/1874

41 University of Aberdeen Graduate Schedules (Medical) 1871-1875

42 NLS 7654/573, H.P.MacGill to R.Laws, 3/10/1874

43 AUL Spec.Coll.MS 3290/1, M.Gray to R.Laws, 19/10/1874

44 *Ibid.* 3290/2, Laws from Glasgow, 17/1/1875

45 *Ibid.* 3/2/1875

46 NLS 7654, UPC FMC Mins. 10/2/1875

47 *Ibid.* 23/2/1875

48 NLS 7654, UPC FMC Mins. 23/2/1875

49 SRO CH3/146/58, Glasgow Pres. of UPC, Mins. 8/6/1875

50 SRO CH3/2/14 Aberdeen Presbytery of UPC, Mins. 23/3/1875

51 *Ibid.*   52 *Ibid.* 23/3/1875; 13/4/1875

53 EUL Laws Coll. Gen. 562/3 (for fuller treatment of the *Homily* see author's paper on *Robt.Laws as Preacher* in Bulletin of Scottish Missionary Studies, New Series, No.1-4, 1985-87 p.43)

54 SRO CH3/2/14, Ab.Pres.of UPC Mins. 13/4/1875

55 *Ibid.* 26/4/1875   56 *Ibid.*

57 AUL, Daily Free Press 27/4/1875

58 NLS 7655/209, Laws'letter of Aug.1875 from Zambezi mouth

59 AUC 1873-74

60 AUL Spec.Coll.MS 3290/2, Laws from Aberdeen, 7/5/1875

61 WPL *op.cit.* p.45

62 SRO CH3/985/5, Synod of UPC, Mins. 13/5/1875

63 AUL Spec.Coll. MS 3290 Laws/2, Laws from London, 14/5/1875

Chapter 3

1 *East Central Africa, Livingstonia* (Free Church, Edinburgh 1876) pp.13,14,44; WPL *op.cit.* p.42

2 E.D.Young, *The Search for Livingstone* (London, 1868) p.138ff; Jas. Wells *Stewart of Lovedale,* (3rd ed., London 1909) p.124

3 *East Central Africa* p.9; NLS 7870, Mrs Eliz Young to Mr Mitchell, 31/7/1875; 5/8/1875

4 *East Central Africa* p.9

5 NLS 7876, E.D.Young to Dr Stewart 26/12/1874; NLS 7870, Admiralty to Dr Stewart, 22/12/1874

6 NLS 7870, Mrs Mary Baker to R.Young, FC FMC 5/6/1875

7 NLS 7871, R.Laws snr. to R.Young, 5/5/1876

8 NLS 7870, Colin McFadyen to R.Young, 25/5/1875; NLS 7871, Revd David Imrie to R.Young, April 1876; W.Riddel to R.Young, 31/5/1876

9 WPL, *op.cit.* p.41,42

10 A.E.M.Anderson-Morshead, *History of Universities Mission (1859-1896),* (London 1897) p.9

11 NLS 7871, Mrs Young, from Lydd, to R.Young, FC FMC 1/12/1876; NLS 7872, Mrs Young to R.Young, 29/7/1876

12 See Chap.2

13 NLS 7871, A.Johnston to R.Young, 5/4/1876, & NLS 7872, 6/6/1876; NLS 7872 John McFadyen to R.Young 14/5/1875; NLS 7876, *Letters from Dr Laws* 31/7/1876; 16/12/1878; &NLS 7876/233-247

14 NLS 7748, R.Young to Mrs Baker 3/6/1876; NLS 7749, R.Young to Mr Baker, 9/10/1877; for a fuller discussion of remuneration of Livingstonia Staff, see the author's *Contracts of Employment and the Influence of Class in the First 30 Years of the Livingstonia Mission,* in SCHS Records, Vol.xxiii, part 1, 1987-1988

15 NLS 7876, R.Laws to Dr Mitchell 31/7/1876; Dr Stewart to Dr Duff 4/12/1876, 6/12/1876; NLS 7912, Mins.of Liv. Sub.Com. 13/11/1879

16 AUL Spec.Coll. MS 3290/2, R.Laws from Bedford Hotel, London, 14/5/75

17 Illustrated London News, 12/6/75

18 NLS 7876/11, R.Laws to Dr MacGill, 21/5/1875

19 AUL Spec.Coll. MS 3290/3, Notes by Miss Laws on her father

20 WPL *op.cit.* p.45

21 NLS 7876/11, R.Laws to Dr MacGill 21/5/1875

22 *Ibid.*   23 *Ibid.*

24 NLS 7870/39, Letter by Horace Waller, from Campdenkirk, 24/5/1875

Chapter 4

1 NLS 7871, R.Laws (snr.) to R.Young, FC FMC, 11/2/1876

2 *East Central Africa, Livingstonia* (Free Church, Edinburgh 1876) pp.18,20,22

3 E.D.Young, *Mission to Nyassa* (Lon. 1877), pp.54,77,99-108,193

4 Roland Oliver, *Missionary Factor in East Africa* (London, 2nd ed. 1965), p.15 note 3

5 E.D.Young, *op.cit.* p.148

6 *East Central Africa,* as above, p.28

7 W.P.Johnson, *My African Reminiscences* (London 1924) p.35

8 R.Oliver, *op.cit.* p.16

9 *Ibid.* pp.21,22

10 *East Central Africa,* as above, p.28

11 *Ibid.* p.28   12 *Ibid.* p.12

13 NLS 7907 Laws' Diary from 23rd July -12th Oct.1875; NLS7876, E.D.Young to Murray Mitchell, 24/6/1875

14 *Ibid.*; NLS 7908, Cape Maclear Journal for 1875, Prefatory Note; and WPL *op.cit.* p.47

15 NLS 7876, E.D.Young to Murray Mitchell, 24/6/1875

16 *East Central Africa,* as above, p.32

17 NLS 7870, letter from Yarrows, 29/12/1875

18 NLS 7907, Laws' Diary, 3/8/1875

19 *Ibid.* 23/7/1875

20 *East Central Africa,* as above, pp.25,26

21 NLS 7907, Laws' Diary, 16/8/1875

22 *Ibid.* 25/7/1875   23 *Ibid.* 29/7/1875

24 EUL Laws Coll. Gen.562/1, list of goods

25 NLS 7907, Laws' Diary 7/8/1875; 12/8/1875; *East Cent. Africa,* as above, p.33, E.D.Young to Sec. of FMC, 17/8/1875

26 NLS 7907, Laws' Diary, 12/8/1875

27 *Ibid.* 17/8/1875

28 *Ibid.* 25/8/1875

29 *Ibid.* 31/8/1975

30 *Ibid.* 7/9/1875; 9/9/1875

31 WPL *op.cit.* p.63

32 NLS 7907, Laws' Diary, 5/9/1875; 6/9/1875

33 *Ibid.* 12/8/1875   34 *Ibid.*

35 *Ibid.* 13/9/1875   36 *Ibid.* 18/9/1875

37 *Ibid.* 19/9/1875   38 *Ibid.*

39 *Ibid.* 21/9/1875

40 E.D.Young, *Mission to Nyassa,* p.59

41 *East Central Africa* p.34

42 *Woman's Work in Livingstonia* (Paisley 1886)

43 NLS 7907, Laws' Diary, 22/9/1875, 28/9/1875

44 *Ibid.* 8/10/1875   45 *Ibid.* 11/10/1875

46 *Ibid.*   47 *Ibid.* 12/10/1875   48 *Ibid.*

49 E.D.Young, *op.cit.* p.59

50 *Ibid.* pp.75,76

51 NLS 7907, Laws' Diary, 17/10/1875. (Young & Laws avoided marshes as unhealthy because they believed that "mal-air" arose from them. The link between the mosquito and malaria came later. See Ch.13)

52 *Ibid.* 20/10/1875; 21/10/1875

53 *East Central Africa* p.36

Chapter 5

1 *East Central Africa, Livingstonia* (Free Church, Edinburgh 1876) p.26

2 NLS 7907, Laws' Diary, 1875-1876.

3 NLS 7908, Extracts from Journal of Liv. Mission, 1875; NLS 7909, Scroll Mins., beginning 17/11/1876

4 NLS 7907, Diary, 24/10/1875

5 *Donald Fraser* by Agnes Fraser (London, 1934) p.168

6 NLS 7907, Diary, 14/11/1875

7 NLS 7912, Mins. of Liv. Sub-Com. 19/5/79, 6/6/79, 6/2/80, 9/3/80

8 NLS 7909, Cape Maclear Journal 25/8/78, 14/9/78, 5/10/78, 1/12/78

9 NLS 7907, Diary, 19/11/75, 12/12/75

10 E.D.Young, *Mission to Nyassa* (London 1877) p.111,119

11 *Ibid.* p.114

12 *East Central Africa, Livingstonia* (Free Church, Edinburgh 1876)   13 *Ibid.*

14 NLS 7907, Diary 10/9/75, 11/9/75

15 *Ibid.* 25/11/75, 26/11/75, 3/12/75; and E.D.Young, *op.cit.* pp.104-108

16 NLS 7907, Diary, 10/12/1875
17 *Ibid.*
18 *Ibid.* 11/12/1875
19 *Ibid.* 12/12/1875
20 *Ibid.* 17/12/1875
21 *Ibid.* 25/12/1875, 26/12/1875
22 *Ibid.* 1/1/1876
23 *Ibid.* 14/2/1876
24 *Ibid.* 16/2/1876, 17/2/1876
25 *Ibid.* 19/2/1876, 20/2/1876
26 *Ibid.* 1/3/1876-3/3/1876
27 *Ibid.* 14/3/1876
28 *Ibid.* 22/3/1876; E.D.Young, *op.cit.*
    p.151
29 *Ibid.* 16/4/1876, 23/4/1876, 24/4/
    1876, 1/5/1876
30 *Ibid.* 17/5/1876, 12/6/1876
31 *Ibid.* 19/5/1876, 23/5/1876
32 *Ibid.* 28/5/1876
33 *Ibid.* 29/5/1876
34 *Ibid.* 1/6/1876, 31/5/1876
35 NLS 7909, 18/1/1877
36 *Ibid.* 22/8/1878, 24/8/1878
37 *Ibid.* 26/9/1878
38 W.P.Johnson, *My African Reminis-
    cences*, (London 1924) pp.59-62
39 NLS 7871/135; 7909/80 of 5/5/1877
40 NLS 7907, Diary, 24/1/1876
41 *Ibid.* 14/12/1875; 11/7/1876
42 NLS 7909, 5/3/77, 18/3/77, 21/3/77
43 E.D.Young, *op.cit.* pp.225,227,155
44 *Ibid.* pp.239,189
45 NLS 7915/50, Mins. of FC FMC, 1877
46 NLS 7872, J.Cowan, Beeslack, to
    Robert Young, 16/8/1877
47 *Ibid.* Foreign Office to Secy.Liv.Com.
    31/5/1877, 14/9/1877
48 *Ibid.* Mrs E.Young to Robert Young,
    10/1/1877; NLS 7876, E.D.Young to
    R.Young, 1/8/1877
49 *Livingstone, Man of Africa* (ed.Pachai),
    article by John McCracken, *Livingstone
    & the Aftermath* p.224, quoting
    Jas.Stewart to his wife, 1/6/1877
    (Stewart Papers, ST.1/1/1)
50 E.D.Young, *op.cit.* p.86
51 NLS 7876, Jas.Stewart to Dr Duff,
    from Blantyre, 20/12/1876
52 Jas.Wells, *Stewart of Lovedale*
    pp.137,141
53 NLS 7876/213, Memorial to Dr Duff,
    6/8/1877

54 *Ibid.* A.Riddel to Dr Duff, 6/8/1877
55 NLS 7872, Jas.Stewart to Jas.White,
    from Livingstonia, 28/2/1877
56 Proceedings of RGS Vol.1 1879, p.289ff.
57 EUL Laws Coll.Gen.561/8, Laws'
    Almanac, entry for 7/10/1877
58 W.P.Johnson, *op.cit.* p.124
59 EUL Laws Coll.Gen.561/8, Laws'
    Almanac, entry for 19/10/1877
60 WPL *op.cit.* pp.95,96,104
61 Proceedings RGS Vol.1 1879, p.299
62 *Ibid.* p.300   63 *Ibid.* p.303
64 *Ibid.* p.304
65 Jas.Wells, *op.cit.* p.141
66 NLS 7871/162
67 NLS 7876/97
68 *Ibid.* Dr Black to Dr W.Smith, 3/3/77
69 NLS 7908, Report on 1877, Medical
    Section   70 *Ibid.*   71 *Ibid.*
72 *Ibid.*   73 *Ibid.*   74 *Ibid.*
75 R.Laws, *Reminiscences of Livingstonia*
    (Edinburgh 1934) pp.57,58
76 *Ibid.* p.59

Chapter 6
1 Laws, *Reminiscences* p.55; WPL *op.cit.*
    p.105
2 NLS 7876, Dr Stewart to Dr Duff 20/
    12/1876
3 Jas.Wells, *Stewart of Lovedale* (3rd ed.
    London 1909) p.140
4 NLS 7876/151, Mins. of meeting at
    Blantyre
5 A Ross, *Livingstone and the Aftermath,
    The Origins & Development of the
    Blantyre Mission* in *Livingstone, Man of
    Africa* (London 1973 ed.Pachai) pp.199-
    200
6 Proceedings of RGS Vol.1 1879 p.311
7 *Ibid.* p.313
8 *Ibid.* p.316; EUL Laws' Coll.Gen.561/
    1, Laws' Notebook, 22/9/1878
9 Laws *Reminiscences* pp.74,75; EUL
    Laws' Coll.Gen.561/1, Notebook 25/
    9/1878
10 EUL Laws' Coll.Gen.561/1, Note-
    book 28/9/1878; 29/9/1878
11 *Ibid.* 17/10/1878, and Proceedings,
    RGS Vol.1 1879 p.318
12 *Ibid.* 9/10/1878, as above
13 *Ibid.* 12/10/1878, as above
14 *Ibid.* 28/10/1878, as above

15 Proceedings RGS 1879, Vol.1 p.320; NLS 7909, Cape Maclear Scroll Mins. 4/11/1878

16 NLS 7909, Cape Maclear Scroll Mins. 9/11/1878

17 NLS 7876/233-247, R.Laws to Revd Thomas Main, 16/12/1878

18 NLS 7910, Bandawe Journal, 28/11/1878; 6/12/1878; & Expenditure List on p.35 of the Journal

19 NLS 7910, Kaning'ina Journal, 2/12/1878

20 NLS 7909, Cape Maclear Scroll Mins. 13/12/1878

21 *Ibid.* and NLS 7876, R.Laws to Revd T.Main, 16/12/1878

22 NLS 7876/244, R.Laws, Report for 1878

23 NLS 8021, Livingstonia Central Africa Co. Prospectus, 1878

24 Horace Waller, *Title Deeds of Nyassaland* (Clowes & Sons, London 1887) p.28; a fuller acount in Hugh Macmillan, *Origins of the ALC, 1878-1908*

25 WPL *op.cit.* pp.143-145

26 NLS 7912, Mins. of Liv.Sub-Com. 17/3/1879; 3/9/1879

27 *Ibid.* 17/3/1879

28 *Ibid.* 17/3/1879

29 *Ibid.* 3/9/1879, including letters from Mr Stewart of 18/2/1879; from Dr Stewart of 14/7/1879; from Dr Laws of 8/5/1879, the two latter from Lovedale

30 NLS 7876, R.Laws to Revd T.Main, from Blantyre, 5/1/1879

31 Border Region Archives, Galashiels Sch.Board Mins 2/3/1875

32 NLS 7912, Mins.of Liv.Sub-Com. 9/11/1880

33 Unpublished paper by Dr Sheila Brock, based on the Stewart Papers, *Miss J.E.Waterston*

34 WPL *op.cit.* p.167

35 EUL, Laws' Coll. Gen.562/2; Aberdeen Free Press 22/11/1879

36 NLS 7876, R.Laws to Dr Smith 20/9/1879

37 WPL *op.cit.* p.168

38 EUL, Laws' Coll.Gen. 561/7; Gen. 561/11

Chapter 7

1 NLS 7909, Cape Maclear Scroll Minute Book, 24/8/1878

2 *Ibid.* 6/9/1878; 21/9/1878; 1/10/1878

3 *Ibid.* 16/10/1878; 19/10/1878

4 *Ibid.* 20/11/1878; 21/11/1878

5 WPL *op.cit.* pp.136-138; and NLS 7872, J.Stephen to Dr Smith, 12/3/1881, quoting J.McFadyen

6 NLS 7910, Bandawe Journal, 10/1/1879; 3/2/1879; 24/5/1879; 25/5/1879; 8/6/1879; 29/6/1879; 12/1/1880

7 Col. H. de Watteville *The British Soldier* (Dent, 1954) p.195

8 NLS 7912, Mins.of Liv.Sub-Com. 6/6/1879

9 *Ibid.* 3/9/1879   10 *Ibid.*

11 *Ibid.* 13/11/1879; NLS 7913, Dr Stewart's Memo of 23/9/1879

12 NLS 7912, Mins.of Liv. Sub-Com. 10/12/1879, containing Laws' letter of 20/9/1879

13 *Ibid.* 2/6/1880, containing Laws' letter of 3/2/1880

14 *Ibid.* 2/6/1880, containing Laws' letter of 18/3/1880

15 *Ibid.*

16 John McCracken, *Politics and Christianity in Malawi, 1875-1940* (Cambridge 1977) p.52

17 EUL Laws' Coll.Gen. 562/2 Diary, 11/1/1879

18 NLS 7909, Cape Maclear Scroll Min.Book, 17/1/1879; 6/2/1879

19 *Ibid.* 21/2/1879

20 NLS 7910, Kaning'ina Journal, 17/9/1879

21 Dr Sheila Brock, unpublished Paper on *Miss Jane E. Waterston*

22 WPL *op.cit.* p.45

23 NLS 7750, R.Young to Miss Jane Waterston, 14/2/1879

24 NLS 7913, Mins.of Liv.Sub-Com. 5/12/1878

25 NLS 7876, R.Laws to Thos. Main, 5/1/1879

26 Dr Brock, *op.cit.*, Letter of J.E.W.'s 11/11/1879

27 Dr Brock, *op.cit.*

28 *Ibid.*   29 *Ibid.*

30 EUL Laws Coll. Gen.561/2, Diary, 20/3/1880

31 Dr Brock, *op.cit.*
32 NLS 7751, Letter Book of R.Young, Young to Miss W. 8/6/1881
33 NLS 7913, Mins.of Liv.Sub.Com. 12/7/1894, §22, quoting letter from Dr Laws
34 NLS 7912, 4/4/1881, containing Laws' letter of 15/12/1880
35 *Ibid.* 28/6/1881, containing Lord Granville's letter of 11/5/1881

Note: for Miss Waterston see also *A Broad, Strong Life; Dr Jane Waterston* by Sheila M.Brock, in *The Enterprising Scot* (ed. Jenni Calder) HMSO 1986

Chapter 8
1 NLS 7910, Kaning'ina Journal, Dec.1878-Oct.1879, (part of *Bandawe and Kaning'ina Journal*) 2/12/1878; 19/12/1878; 20/12/1878
2 *Ibid.* 20/12/1878
3 *Ibid.* 1/1/1879
4 *Ibid.* 4/1/1879; 13/2/1879; 17/2/1879; 20/2/1879
5 *Ibid.* 5/1/1879; 19/1/1879; 2/2/1879; 23/2/1879; 9/3/1879; 16/3/1879
6 NLS 7909, Cape Maclear Scroll Min.Book 15/1/1879; 17/1/1879
7 NLS 7910, Bandawe Journal 19/1/79
8 *Ibid.* 20/1/1879; and Kaning'ina Journal 21/1/1879
9 NLS 7910, Kan. Journal 22/1/1879
10 *Lonely Warrior* by Revd Geo. H.Campbell (CLAIM 1975) p.27
11 NLS 7876, Laws to FC FMC Feb.1879
12 Geo.H.Campbell *op.cit.* pp.28,29
13 NLS 7910, Kan.Journal 1/2/1879; 3/2/1879; 7/4/1879; 9/4/1879
14 NLS 7909, Cape Maclear Journal, Mins. 21/2/1879
15 NLS 7910, Kan.Journal 19/1/1879; 5/4/1879
16 *Ibid.* 14/5/1879; 15/5/1879
17 *Ibid.* 7/7/1879; 16/8/1879
18 *Ibid.* 17/9/1879
19 NLS 7910, Bandawe Journal No.2. Note signed by Laws, after entry of 15/10/1879
20 *Ibid.* 16/10/1879; 17/10/1879
21 NLS 7910, Kan.Journal 18/10/1879
22 *Ibid.*

23 NLS 7876, Laws to Dr Smith, 20/9/1879   24 *Ibid.*
25 NLS 7910, Kan.Journal 17/9/1879
26 *Ibid.* 24/8/1879, and R.Laws, *op.cit.* p.130
27 *Ibid.* Bandawe Journal No.2, Dec.1879
28 NLS 7910, 17/2/1879; 18/2/1879; Bandawe Journal No.2, Dec.1879
29 *Ibid.* 9/3/1880
30 EUL Laws' Coll. Gen 561/2, Laws' Diary 26/4/1880
31 University of Malawi Journal of Soc.Science Vol.10 1983, pp.5,6 *Dr Laws* by Violet G.Bonga
32 WPL *op.cit.* pp 113,114
33 Cape Maclear Journal, 24/6/1879
34 EUL Laws' Coll. Gen.561/2, Laws' Diary, 30/1/1881; 17/3/1881
35 *Ibid.* 10/2/1881; 16/2/1881
36 *Ibid.* 27/3/1881
37 NLS 7912, Glasgow Sub.Com.of Liv.Miss. 27/12/1881; FC Record, Feb.1882, quoting extract from Mission Journal

Chapter 9
1 FC Monthly Record, Aug.1880
2 Donald Fraser, *Livingstonia* (Edinburgh 1915) pp.86-88, List of Missionaries
3 EUL Laws' Coll. Gen.561/2, Laws' Diary, 29/3/1881
4 NLS 7911, Bandawe Journal 9/4/81
5 *Ibid.* 10/4/1881
6 *Ibid.* 21/4/1881; 22/4/1881; 24/4/81
7 EUL Laws' Coll. Gen 561/2, Diary, 27/10/1881
8 *Ibid.* 27/10/1881
9 *Ibid.* 29/10/1881
10 EUL Laws' Coll. Gen.561/2, Diary, 30/10/1881
11 *Ibid.* 31/10/1881; 1/11/1881; 2/11/81
12 *Ibid.* 3/11/1881
13 *Ibid.* 22/12/1881, and letter from Dr Hannington, FC Record May 1882
14 EUL Laws' Coll.Gen.561/2, Diary 25/12/1881; FC Record May 1882
15 FCGA Reports, May 1882, Report of FMC p.16; NLS 7912, Liv.Sub-Com. 19/6/1882; FC Record, July 1882
16 EUL Laws' Coll.Gen 561/2, 12/11/81
17 *Ibid.* 18/11/1881; 19/11/1881

18 *Ibid.* 20/11/1881
19 *Ibid.* 6/12/1881
20 EUL Laws' Coll. Gen.561/3, 12/2/1882
21 *Ibid.* 15/2/1882   22 *Ibid.*
23 *Ibid.* 14/3/1882   24 *Ibid.* 15/3/1882
25 *Ibid.* 18/4/1882; 19/4/1882
26 *Ibid.* 26/4/1882   27 *Ibid.* 3/5/1882
28 *Ibid.* 18/6/82; 19/6/82; 21/6/82
29 *Ibid.* 21/6/1882
30 FC Record, Nov 1882
31 Jas.W.Jack, *Daybreak in Livingstonia* (Edinburgh 1901) pp.334,335; Henry Drummond, *Tropical Africa* (London 1889) pp.117,118
32 EUL Laws Coll.Gen.561/3, Diary, 20/7/1882
33 *Ibid.* 17/8/1882
34 W.P.Johnson, *op.cit.* p.67
35 *Ibid.* and EUL Laws' Coll.Gen 561/3, Diary, 1/9/1882, 22/9/1882
36 FC Record March 1882, report from Laws of 28/10/1881
37 EUL Laws' Coll.Gen.561/3, Diary, 5/11/1882, 17/12/1882
38 EUL Laws' Coll.Gen.561/3, Diary 2/1/1883; 29/1/1883; 8/2/1883; NLS 7911, Bandawe Journal, 8/2/1883
39 NLS 7911 Bandawe Journal, 19/2/1883
40 *Ibid.* 20/2/1883
41 *Ibid.* 1/5/1883; 2/5/1883; and EUL Laws' Coll. Gen.561/3, Diary 1/5/1883, 2/5/1883
42 NLS 7911, Bandawe Journal 3/5/1883
43 *Ibid.* 6/5/1883
44 *Ibid.* 4/6/1883; and EUL Laws' Coll. Gen.561/3, Diary 4/6/1883, 30/6/1883
45 EUL Laws' Coll.Gen.561/3, Diary 25/6/1883; 18/7/1883; 31/7/1883
46 *Ibid.* 5/6/1883; and NLS 7911, Bandawe Journal 5/6/1883
47 NLS 7911, Bandawe Journal 5/6/1883

Chapter 10
1 R.Laws, *Reminiscences of Livingstonia* (Edinburgh 1934) Ch.VI p.127
2 *Ibid.* p.127
3 FCGA Reports 1884 p.102
4 R.Laws, *op.cit.* p.129   5 *Ibid.* p.130
6 EUL Laws' Coll. Gen.561/2, Diary 1/2/81; 17/3/81; 18/3/81

7 NBSS Ann. Report 1885 p.44
8 *Ibid.* Quarterly Record, July 1884
9 R.Laws, *op.cit.* p.131
10 EUL Laws, Coll. Gen.561/3, Diary for dates mentioned
11 NLS 7911 Bandawe Journal 11/5/83
12 NBSS 18th Ann. Meeting March 1879
13 *Ibid.*
14 R.Laws, *op.cit.* p.96
15 NBSS Ann. Report 1888, p.39; 1889 p.41; 1890 p.46
16 MNA LI. 1/4/11, Sermons by Dr Laws, Jan to Aug 1883
17 *Ibid.* Sermon for 11/3/83
18 *Ibid.* 21/1/83   19 *Ibid.*
20 *Ibid.* 11/2/83
21 NLS 7912 Mins. of Liv.Sub-Com. 15/2/81
22 Donald Fraser, *Livingstonia* (Edinburgh 1915) pp 86, 87
23 FC Record Oct.1882
24 NLS 7912 Mins. of Liv.Sub-Com. 31/8/82; 10/10/82
25 NLS 7903 G.Johnston to R.Laws 3/11/82; 4/1/83
26 NLS 7912 Mins. of Liv.Sub-Com. 27/3/83
27 NLS 7903 G.Johnston to R.Laws 23/5/83
28 *Ibid.* 28/3/83   29 *Ibid.*
30 WPL. *op.cit.* p.263
31 NLS 7912 Mins. of Liv Sub-Com. 26/6/83
32 NLS 7911 Bandawe Journal 20/9/83
33 Henry Drummond, *Tropical Africa* (London 1889) pp.41ff.
34 See Ch.9, pp.78,80
35 FC Record Feb 1882
36 NLS 7911 Bandawe Journal 22/9/83
37 NLS Acc 9220 i(ii) Donald Munro to R.Laws from Karonga 12/9/83
38 NLS 7911 Bandawe Journal 1/12/83
39 *Ibid.* 2/12/83
40 *Ibid.*   41 *Ibid.* 4/12/83

Chapter 11
1 NLS 7897 G.Smith to R.Laws 30/4/1884
2 NLS 7903 G.Milne to Dr and Mrs Laws, 13/9/1883
3 NLS 7912 Mins. of Liv. Sub-Com. 2/5/1884

4 NLS Acc. 9220 (3) (i) W.F.G.Moir to R.Laws, 5/5/1884

5 *Ibid.* Jas.Thin to R.Laws, 16/4/1884

6 *Ibid.*

7 *Ibid.* 26/3/1884; 16/4/1884

8 *Ibid.* G.Johnston to R.Laws (undated but begins "Welcome home")

9 NLS 9220(3)(ii) Donald Macintosh to R.Laws, 18/11/1884; 22/11/1884

10 NLS 7897 G.Smith to R.Laws, 19/5/1884

11 NLS Acc, 9220(3)(i) W.Martin to R.Laws, 30/7/1884; S.Chisholm to R.Laws, 30/7/1884; and NLS Acc.9220(3)(ii) S.Gemmell to R.Laws 16/12/1884; 20/12 1884; S.Chisholm to R.Laws 24/9/1884

12 FGCA Proceedings 1884, pp.101-104

13 NLS Acc.9220(3)(i) Agenda of NBSS Western Com. for 9/6/1884, in letter from W.J.Slowan, Secy., to Laws

14 *Ibid.* J.Murray Mitchell to R.Laws, 10/6/1884 and W.J.Blaikie to R. Laws 7/7/1884

15 FC Record, October l886

16 NLS 7912 Mins.of Liv.Sub-Com. 24/12/1885

17 NLS Acc.9220(3)(ii) A.Thomson to R.Laws, 19/9/1884; G.Rankin to R.Laws, 18/10/1884

18 NLS Acc.9220(3)(i) G.S.Muir to R.Laws, 4/7/1884

19 FC Record, October 1884

20 NLS 9220(3)(ii) Telegrams from G.Smith to R.Laws and from Dr Moir to R.Laws, 10/12/1884; and from Mrs Laws to R.Laws, 12/10/1884; also FC Record, Jan.1885

21 FC Record, Jan.1885 - Article 9 of *Congress of Berlin*

22 Dr Fergus Macpherson, letter to the author, July 1991

23 NLS Acc.9220(1)(iii) Telegrams exchanged by K.Cross and R.Laws, 16/7/1885; letters from K.Cross to R.Laws, 4/7/1885; 11/7/1885; 18/7/1885; W.A.Elmslie to R.Laws, 7/6/1884; 12/12/1884; and FC Record, June l886

24 *Women's Work in Livingstonia* (Parlane, Paisley, 1886 -available in AUL, and in African Papers l)

25 *Ibid.* pp.9,12

26 *Ibid.* p.14   27 *Ibid.* p.28

28 NLS Acc.9220(3)(v) Miss Rainy to R.Laws, 19/3/1886

29 NLS 7912 Mins.of Liv.Sub-Com. 24/12/1885; 26/1/1886; 24/12/1886

30 FC Record, May 1886

31 *Ibid.*

32 Letters from all those mentioned are in NLS Acc.9220

33 NLS Acc.9220(3)(i) Alex.Gill to R.Laws, 6/6/1884

34 NLS 7902 A.Cruikshank to R.Laws, 1/9/1881

35 NLS Acc.9220(3)(vi) J.Robson to R.Laws, 11th June, (probably of 1885); J.Robson to R.Laws, 9/1/1889

36 NLS Acc.9220(3)(iv) Morrison and Gibb to R.Laws, 2/6/1885

37 FC Record, June, July, 1886

38 *Ibid.* November 1886

39 Verbal communication to the author on 9/2/1986 by Mrs Gardiner of 19 Kings Avenue, Longniddry, who had been a patient , and become a friend, of Dr Amelia Laws, while she was practising in Edinburgh in her later years as an osteopath at 7 Merchiston Crescent

40 NLS 7911, Bandawe Journal, 28/9/86

41 *Ibid.* 29/9/1886, and Laws' letter of 20/10/86 in FC Record, March 1887

42 *Ibid.* 3/10/1886

43 *Ibid.* 4/10/1886; NLS 7898 Mins of FC FMC 11/5/1886 Min.167

44 NLS 7911 Bandawe Journal, 4/10/1886; FC Record, March 1887

45 NLS 7911 Bandawe Journal, 14/10/1886; FC Record, March 1887

46 FC Record, March 1887; NLS 7911 Bandawe Journal, 16/11/1886

47 FC Record, October 1886 and July 1887 [Tributes to Koyi]

48 W.A.Elmslie, *Among the Wild Ngoni*, Chapter ix, (Oliphant, Anderson and Ferrier, Edinburgh 1899; 3rd Edition, London 1970)

49 FC Record, October 1886

50 *Ibid.*; see also article in the Society of Malawi Journal No.2, 1986, pp 15-23, by Jack Thompson. A short booklet on Koyi entitled *Lonely Warrior*, by G.H.Campbell was published by CLAIM in 1975

51 NLS Acc.9220(1)(iv) Elmslie to Laws, 10/5/1886, and NLS 7911, Bandawe Journal, 10/5/1886

52 NLS 7911, Bandawe Journal, 29/3/1887; 30/3/1887; 1/6/1887; 1/10/1887

53 NLS Acc.9220(1)(iv), Elmslie to Cross, 8/2/1886

54 MNA, LI 1/1/2/1, Elmslie to Laws, 18/9/1888

55 NLS 7911 Bandawe Journal, 28/2/86

56 MNA LI 1/1/2/1/11 (i); NLS 7890 Bain to Laws, 18/1/87; NLS 7912 Mins of Liv Sub-Com 12/10/86; 18/4/87

57 SRO CH 3 692/2; Kirk Session Mins of Aberuthven FC 1/12/1887

58 NLS 7912 Mins.of Liv Sub-Com 15/10/1889; 28/11/1889; 28/1/1890 and NLS 7898, Smith to Laws 9/4/1890

59 NLS 7912 Mins.of Liv Sub-Com 18/4/1887

60 NLS 7911 Bandawe Journal 11/1/1887; 12/1/1887; 14/1/1887

61 Ibid. 16/9/1887

62 Ibid. 8/8/1887; 28/8/1887

63 Ibid. 6/10/1887; 21/10/1887

64 Ibid. 18/8/1887   65 Ibid. 13/9/1887

66 Ibid. 17/9/1887   67 Ibid. 25/9/1887

68 Ibid. 26/9/1887   69 Ibid. 4/10/1887

70 Ibid. 22/9/1887, 9/10/1887

71 EUL Laws Coll. Gen.562/3. Letter of Mrs Laws to 'Father and Mother', dated 11/10/1887   72 Ibid.

73 NLS 7911 Bandawe Journal, 1/11/87

74 NLS The Scottish Leader 19/1/1888, p.5, and 27/1/1888, p.7

75 Ibid. 27/1/88 p.7   76 Ibid.

77 NLS 7898 Smith to Laws, 23/11/1887

78 FC Record, Sept 1888, p.267 Bandawe Report for 1887 by Dr Laws

Chapter 12

1 L.Monteith Fotheringham, Adventures in Nyassaland (London 1891) pp.34,41,42

2 Ibid. p.50

3 Jas W.Jack, Daybreak in Livingstonia (Edinburgh & London, 1901) p.272

4 Ibid. p.273

5 NLS The Scottish Leader, 27/1/88, p.7

6 Ibid. and J.W.Jack, op.cit. p.273; NLS 7911 Bandawe Journal, 2/11/1887

7 J.W.Jack, op.cit. p.274

8 Ibid. p.275   9 Ibid. p.276

10 The Scotsman 15/2/1888 p.7 The Arabs on Lake Nyasa

11 NLS 7912 Mins.of Liv.Sub-Com.10/4/1888

12 Ibid. 25/7/1888

13 FC Record, Oct.1888, p.307; J.W.Jack, op.cit. p.276

14 Ibid. Jan.1889; quoting Laws' letter to his father, dated 22/8/1888

15 Ibid. Nov.1888

16 J.W.Jack, op.cit. p.277; FC Record, Oct.1888

17 L.M.Fotheringham, op.cit. p.224

18 Ibid. pp.228-236

19 FC Record April 1889 (Malindu did not become a permanent station of the Liv. Mission, as it proved to be on the German side of the boundary with what became German East Africa)

20 L.M.Fotheringham, op.cit. p.242,243

21 Ibid. and NLS 7912 Mins.of Liv.Sub-Com. 15/10/1889

22 J.W.Jack op.cit. p.280; L.M. Fotheringham op.cit. p.277

23 J.W.Jack op.cit. p.280; L.M. Fotheringham op.cit. p.278

24 H.W.Macmillan, Notes on Origins of the Arab War, in Early History of Malawi, ed. Bridgal Pachai, p.276

25 H.H.Johnston, British Central Africa (London 1897) p.96

26 NLS 7898 G.Smith to R.Laws 13/3/1889, quoting letter from Fred. Moir (the Liv.Sub-Com.agreed to pay £1500 immediately)

27 WPL op.cit. pp.257,258

28 H.H.Johnston, op.cit. p.135

29 Ibid. p.137   30 Ibid. pp.136-143

31 FM Report to GA, 1889 p.49ff

32 Donald Fraser, Livingstonia (Edinburgh 1915), List of missionaries, p.86

33 FM Report, 1889, p.49ff.   34 Ibid.

35 FM Report, 1891, p.55ff., Laws' Report for 1886-1890

36 FM Report, 1889, App.viii

37 FM Report, 1891, p.55ff., Laws' Report for 1886-1890

38 FM Report, 1889

39 Ibid.; MNA LI/1/1/2/1, letter from Elmslie to Laws 18/9/1888; NLS 7912 Min.of Liv.Sub-Com. 10/1/89

40 FM Report, 1889, Livlezi

41 J.W.Jack, *op.cit.* p.182

42 FM Report, 1891, p.55ff.& p.69; NLS 7912 Mins.of Liv.Sub-Com. 12/12/1887; 25/3/1890. Also J.W.Jack, *op.cit.* p.176ff.

43 FM Report, 1894, p.8; 1895, p.85ff.

44 FM Report, 1889, p.49ff.

45 FM Report, 1891, p.55ff, Laws' Report for 1886-1890

46 EUL Laws' Coll. Gen.561/7, at back of notebook, note on Baptisms

47 WPL, *op.cit.* p.249, quoting Elmslie; W.A.Elmslie, *Among the Wild Ngoni* (London 1899) p.285; J.W.Jack, *op.cit.* pp.159,162

48 EUL Laws' Coll. Gen/561/7, as above

49 FC Record, April 1890, Elmslie's letter of 2/10/1889; F.M.Report 1890, p.53ff.

50 *Ibid.*

51 FM Report 1890, p.53ff.

52 NLS 7910, Bandawe & Kaning'ina Journal from 28/11/1878; entry for 12/12/1878: "Riddell making contact with M'mbelwa & other Angoni chiefs"

53 W.A.Elmslie, *op.cit.* p.220

54 FM Report 1892, p.63ff.

55 *Ibid.*; J.W.Jack, *op.cit.* pp.254-257; WPL *op.cit.* pp.254,255

56 FM Report, 1891, p.55ff; FM Report 1894 p.9ff; 1895 p.85ff; J.W.Jack, *op.cit.* p.161

57 FM Report 1891, p.55ff, Laws' Report for 1886-1890; and AUL Spec.Coll. MS 3290/3 Centenary Message from Miss Laws   58 *Ibid.*

59 NBSS Annual Reports, 1890, p.43; and 1893 p.48

60 NBSS Ann.Meeting, 1889,p.41; letter from Laws in Dec.Quarterly, 1889

61 FM Report 1891, p.62, Laws' Report for 1886-1890

62 FC GA FM Sederunt 28/5/1890, p.140

63 NLS 7898, G.Smith to R.Laws 12/8/1890

64 FC Record, July 1890 *The Crisis in East Central Africa*, incl. Laws' letter from Njuyu of 18/3/1890

65 *Ibid.* Elmslie's letter from Bandawe of 24/3/1890

66 NLS 7898, G.Smith to Laws and Elmslie, 17/6/1890

67 FC Record, Oct.1891

68 *Ibid.* March 1892

69 *Ibid.* Feb.1892, quoting Laws' letter from Cape Colony of 3/12/1891

70 *Ibid.* Feb.1892

71 WPL *op.cit.* p.257

72 FC Record Feb.1892; WPL *op.cit.* p.258

73 NLS 7899 G.Smith to R.Laws 31/12/1891

Chapter 13

1 Edinburgh & Leith P.O.Directories, 1891-92; 1892-93

2 UP Church Synod Records. 4/5/1892

3 Proceedings of FC GA 1892 p.133

4 AUL Spec.Coll. MS 3290/2 R.Laws to Dr Tilsley, 25/10/1929

5 WPL *op.cit.* p.260

6 *Ibid.* p.260,261

7 Proceedings of FC GA 1892, p.133

8 UP Church Report to Synod of 1892 on FMs iii Old Calabar

9 *Ibid.*; & Report to UP FM Board 30/1/1894

10 WPL *op.cit.* p.263-265

11 UP FM Board 30/1/1894

12 NLS 7899 G.Smith to R.Laws 23/5/1894; 7/12/1894

13 NLS 7877 Copy of Mission Council Mins. 31/8/1894 - 3/9/1894, Letter from McCallum 3/9/1894

14 Letter Coll., R.& M.Laws to Amy Laws, (between Aug.1894 and March 1899) in care of Mrs Margaret Hansford (née Caseby), Aberdeen

15 Proceedings of FC GA 1894, F.M.Report, viii p.8."Quarterly Report"

16 *Ibid.* p.9

17 Conversation with the late Dr Wm.Watson, Aberdeen, formerly of Livingstonia, in autumn of 1985

18 NLS 7877 R.Laws to G.Smith, 21/8/1894

19 NLS 7877 Mins of Miss.Council of 31/8/1894 - 3/9/1894

20 EUL, Laws' Coll. Gen.561/1 Diary, 24/9/1894

21 *Ibid.* 19/9/1894; 20/9/1894; 21/9/94

22 EUL, Laws' Coll.Gen.561/1 Diary, 23/9/1894

23 NLS 7878 Laws' Report, pp.15-23
24 NLS 7900 G.Smith to R.Laws 17/1/ 1895; Overtoun to R.Laws 26/7/1895; WPL *op.cit.* p.272
25 NLS 7878/19   26 *Ibid.*
27 NLS 7877 R.Laws to G.Smith 26/10/ 1894
28 *Ibid.* 6/11/1894; 3/12/1894
29 See Ch.5, and AUL Spec.Coll. MS 3290/3, "The First Voyage round the Lake" 1875
30 NLS 7877 R.Laws to G.Smith 3/12/94
31 Proceedings of FC GA 1895 FM Report, "Kondowe"
32 NLS 7877 A.Sharpe to R.Laws 30/11/ 1894
33 *Ibid.* R.Laws to A.Sharpe 16/12/1894
34 NLS 7878 R.Laws to G.Smith 11/11/ 1895
35 Proceedings of FC GA 1898, FM Report pp.125ff.
36 NLS 7878 R.Laws to G.Smith 4/10/ 95; W.Thomson to G.Smith 9/11/95
37 WPL *op.cit.* p.276
38 Proceedings, FC GA 1895, FM Report, VIII "Kondowe"
39 NLS 7878 R.Laws to G.Smith 12/8/ 1895, account of meeting with H.H.Johnston on 19/7/1895
40 NLS 7878 P.W.Forbes to R.Laws, 17/ 8/[1895]
41 NLS 7878 R.Laws to P.W.Forbes 24/ 8/1895
42 *Ibid.*   43 *Ibid.*
44 NLS 7881 R.Laws to G.Smith 28/9/98
45 NLS 7882 Mins of Miss.Council 6/11/ 1899, §9
46 NLS 7878 Correspondence between A.C.Murray and R.Laws 5/11/1894, 5/12/1894, 12/8/1895; and Proceedings of GA 1895, FM Report
47 NLS 7880 G.Prentice to G.Smith 6/1/ 1897
48 Proc. of FC GA 1895, FM Report
49 NLS 7900 G.Smith to R.Laws 17/1/ 1895, 24/5/1895, 31/1/1896; J.Fairley, Daly to R.Laws 25/12/1895; T.Binnie to R.Laws 30/1/1896
50 Proceedings of FC GA 1895, FM Report "Kondowe"; and FC GA 1896, F.M.Report V "Livingstonia Institution"

51 Proceedings of FC GA, 1896 FM Report V "Livingstonia Institution"
52 *Ibid.*
53 See above, note 32
54 *Forerunners of Modern Malawi* (ed. Ballantyne & Shepherd, Lovedale 1968) p.vii
55 Proceedings of FC GA 1896, FM Report V "Livingstonia Institution"
56 Proceedings of FC GA 1897, 1 "Livingstonia Institution"
57 R.Laws (from Liv'ia) to Amy, 23rd June 1896 (Hansford Coll. as above)
58 Proceedings of FC GA 1897, 1 "Livingstonia Institution"
59 *Ibid.*   60 *Ibid.*   61 *Ibid.*   62 *Ibid.*
63 *Ibid.* FM Report p.97ff.   64 *Ibid.*
65 NLS 7881 Maria Jackson to G.Smith, 22/8/1898; Mgt.McCallum to G.Smith 29/8/1898
66 NLS 7881 R.Laws to G.Smith, 28/9/ 1898
67 Proceedings of FC GA 1900, FM Report V111 "Liv.Miss.Inst."
68 *Ibid.*
69 *Ibid.* "Building Dept. Mr W. Henderson"
70 *Ibid.* "Workshop. Mr W.D.MacGregor"
71 *Ibid.* "Agriculture. Mr M.Moffat"
72 NLS 7900 T.Binnie to R.Laws 30/1/ 96, 15/9/96 (12 page letter), 6/11/96, 2/8/97, 14/9/97, 13/12/97, 22/7/01: G.Smith to R.Laws 15/9/98 "J.Cowan is shipping the paper"
73 NLS 7882 Miss.Council Mins. 6/11/ 1899, Resolution 33
74 NLS 7900/177 G.Smith to R.Laws, 11/ 11/97, enclosing "A Visit to Livingstonia" by Donald Fraser (copy of article for The Record, Dec. 1897)

Chapter 14
1 FMC Report to GA, 1895 p.85ff.
2 *Ibid.*
3 *Ibid.*
4 NLS 7911 Bandawe Journal, 2/6/1883
5 NLS 7979 Copy of Mission Council Mins. 18/5/1896
6 NLS 7880 G.Prentice to G Smith 6/1/ 1897
7 FMC Report to GA 1897, p.101 ff. III Bandawe

8 NLS 7881 A.G.MacAlpine to G.Smith 25/6/1898
9 FMC Report to GA 1902, p.69ff. Bandawe: FC Record July & Oct.1901
10 FMC Report to GA 1895, p.85ff. I Bandawe
11 *Ibid.* III Cape Maclear
12 *Ibid.* II Ngoniland
13 *Ibid.* & NLS 7878, pp.15-23, Laws' account of the exploration and of the decision to settle at Kondowe
14 FMC Report to GA 1895, pp.85ff. III Ngerenje; and FMC Report to GA 1898, p.127 A.Dewar at Evening Sederunt
15 NLS 7877 R.Laws to G.Smith 17/9/1894: NLS 7878 Chauncy Maples to Laws 20/8/1894; Laws to Maples 3/12/1894; Maples to Laws 27/3/1895, 30/3/1895; Laws to Maples 7/8/1895
16 NLS 7899 G.Smith to R.Laws, 31/12/1891, enclosing extract min. of FC FMC, 22/12/1891, §102
17 NLS 7878 Maples to Laws 30/3/1895; Laws to Maples 7/8/1895
18 *Bishop Maples*, by his sister (Longman's, Green & Co., London 1897)
19 A.E.M.Anderson-Morshead, History of UMCA (London 1897) p.362ff.
20 NLS 7880 D.Fraser to G.Smith 16/1/1897
21 Proceedings of FC GA 1898, Evening Sederunt p.133
22 NLS 7880 D.Fraser to G.Smith, 20/10/1897; W.Elmslie, *Among the Wild Ngoni* pp.296,297
23 NLS 7881 D.Fraser to G.Smith, 16/5/1898
24 *Ibid.* R.Laws to Dr Smith, 16/5/1898
25 Proceedings of FC GA 1899, FM Report p.97ff.   26 *Ibid.*
27 NLS 7877 R.Laws to G.Smith 21/8/1894; A.G.MacAlpine to G.Smith 14/9/1894
28 NLS 7878 Miss Stewart to G.Smith 9/2/1895; G.Steel to G.Smith 19/2/1895; W.Elmslie to G.Smith 1/7/1895
29 Proceedings of FC GA 1894, FM Report App.iii.
30 Miss L.A.Stewart married R.D.McMinn in 1901; Miss M.McCallum m.Charles Stuart in 1901;

Miss M.Jackson m.M.Moffat in 1900; Miss W.Knight m. E.A.Boxer in 1903; Miss A.Lambert m.D.R.Mackenzie in 1904. Miss M.J.Fleming was invalided home. Miss J.Martin, an Honorary appointee, served from 1900 to 1909 (Donald Fraser, *Livingstonia* p.87, Edinburgh 1915)
31 NLS 7881 R.Laws to G.Smith 8/8/1898; NLS 7882 R.Laws to G.Smith 21/11/1899
32 Donald Fraser, *op.cit.* p.86
33 Fasti of UFC
34 Ballantyne & Shepherd, *Forerunners of Modern Malawi - the Early Missionary Adventures of Dr James Henderson (1895 to 1898)* (Lovedale 1968) p.32, letter dated 21/7/1895
35 *Ibid.* p.52, letter dated 22/9/1895
36 *Ibid.*   37 *Ibid.*
38 *Ibid.* p.173, letter dated 23/7/1896
39 NLS 7882 Telegram 24/5/1899
40 Proceedings of FC GA 1900, FM Report, Liv.Mission - Report on N.Angoniland by Donald Fraser
41 NLS 7882 Mins.of Miss.Council 9/11/1899, Resol.43
42 MNA Zomba, LI 1/3/21, and Proceedings of FC GA 1900, p.105, App.1 - Mins. of N.Liv.Presbytery, 15/11/1899, First Meeting
43 Fergus Macpherson, *Appropriation of the Gospel as shown in Christian Songs in Malawi* - paper read at Seminar at Centre for Study of Christianity in the Non-Western World, New College, Edinburgh, 11/6/1991
44 *Ibid.*

Chapter 15

1 NLS 7881 M.McCallum to G.Smith, 29/8/1898
2 FC Record Jan.1900; NLS 7882 Telegram from Florence Bay to "Free, Edinburgh"; Proceedings of FC GA 1900, FMC Report VIII, Liv.Miss.Instit.4
3 Edinburgh & Leith P.O.Directory, 1897-1898; NLS 7882 R.Laws to G.Smith, 21/11/1898
4 Proceedings of FC GA 1901, p.246
5 NBSS Quarterly Record, April 1900

6 FC Record, April 1900; August 1900
7 British Newspaper Library, Colindale; N.Y.Herald 22 April - 1 May 1900; N.Y.Evening Post 21 April - 2 May 1900
8 WPL *op.cit.* p.301
9 *Ibid.*
10 FC GA 1900, FM Report, VIII, Liv.Miss.Instit.
11 *Ibid.*
12 NLS Dep. 298/139a. Mins.of Liv. Miss.Com. 9/11/1899 §4
13 *Ibid.* §5
14 Keir Hardie, *Speeches & Writings* (from 1885-1915) ed.by Emrys Hughes (Forward Printing & Publishing Co.Ltd., Glasgow) ch.19 pp.85ff.
15 Iain McLean, *Keir Hardie* (Allen Lane 1975) p.75; Ewan Ferguson, Scotland on Sunday 20/10/1991, p.4
16 NLS Dep.298/139a. Expenditure & Revenue Estimates for 1901- Sub-Com.Report of meetings held on 27th Feb. and 12th March (1900)
17 NLS Dep.298/139a Mins.of Liv. Miss.Com. 15/3/1900 §19
18 EUL Laws' Collection, Gen.561/17; 561/18; 561/19
19 Letter from Archivist, Heriot Watt, to author, July 1987
20 FC Record, Nov.1901, p.515
21 WPL *op.cit.* p.299; Archivist, Heriot Watt, to author, July 1987
22 FC Record, Sept.1901, p.419
23 *Ibid.* Nov. 1900
24 Proceedings of UFC GA 1901, First Report on FMs to UFC GA p.52 (1) *Liv.Instit.*; Aurora, Dec.1900, pp.61,62
25 Proceedings of UFC GA 1901; UFC Record, May and June 1901
26 NLS Dep.298/142 Extract Min. of UFC Liv.Miss.Com.(Min.60) of 26/9/1907; copy in hands of Hardie's daughter, Miss A.G.N.Hardie, of 27 Redford Loan, Edinburgh
27 Donald Fraser, *Livingstonia*, pp.86-88
28 *Ibid.*
NLS 29 Dep.298/139, Mins.of Liv.Miss.Com. 30/5/1900, §37
30 NLS 7778/432 G.Smith to R.Laws, March 1899
31 NLS 7877 A.G.MacAlpine to G.Smith

14/9/1894, enclosing copy of Mins. of Liv.Miss.Council of 31/8/1894, & 1/9/1894, recording P.McCallum's enquiry about his children's allowance and his contacts with Dr Smith
32 NLS Dep.298/139, Mins.of Liv. Miss.Com. 15/3/1900 §23
33 *Ibid.* 30/5/1900 §37
34 UFC Record, June 1901; Dec.1901

Chapter 16
1 FC Record, Oct.1900
2 UFC GA Proceedings 1906, FM Report; WPL *op.cit.* p.304
3 UFC GA Proc. 1906, FM Report
4 UFC GA Proc. 1904, FM Report
5 WPL *op.cit.* p.305
6 AUL Spec.Coll.MS 3290/2
7 WPL *op.cit.* p.327 (the flag may be seen in the Museum of Malawi at Mzuzu)
8 Liv.Museum, R.Laws to Dr Innes, 25/9/1904 - congratulations to Dr and Mrs Innes on birth of their son
9 UFC Record, March 1906, *Gathering In* by Dr Laws, describing events of 12/10/1905
10 FC Record, Nov.1901, pp.515ff.
11 MNA LI 1/8/8 Educational Reports, 1895-1915 Liv.Miss.Institution, First Year   12 *Ibid.*
13 *Ibid.* Report, 12/6/1896
14 *Ibid.* Report, 27/4/1897
15 *Ibid.* Report, 2nd June, 30th Aug., 1st Oct. 1897
16 *Ibid.* Report 28/12/1897, 27/5/1898
17 MNA LI 1/8/11, Govt.School reports 1897-1903; 2/7/1897
18 *Ibid.* 13/8/1897
19 MNA LI 1/8/13, School Log Book 1894-1942
20 MNA LI 1/3/31, Mins. of Senatus of Liv.Train.Instit. 2/5/1908, Memo on need for review of Industrial Training Policy
21 *Ibid.*, and MNA LI 1/8/13, School Log Book (1894 to 1942) & "Regulations for Apprentices, 1898"
22 *Ibid.*   23 *Ibid.*   24 *Ibid.*
25 UFC GA Proceedings 1906, FM Report p.96
26 MNA LI 1/3/31 Mins. of Senatus of Liv.Miss.Instit. 9/8/1901

27 NLS 7884, J.Henderson to G.Smith, 21/3/1901
28 MNA LI 1/3/31, Mins.of Senatus, 9/8/1901
29 MNA LI 1/4/19, Liv.Miss.Instit., Exam papers 1903
30 *Ibid.*
31 *Ibid.* Exam Papers Oct.1907
32 MNA LI 1/8/9, Exam Results, 1904-21

Chapter 17
1 UFC GA Proceedings, 1905 p.47
2 *Ibid.* FM Report, "Kasungu"
3 UFC GA 1904, Walter Elmslie at FM Evening Sederunt, 26/5/1904
4 *Ibid.* 1905 FM Report, p.86ff.
5 UFC Record, Dec.1904, J.Henderson, *Evangelising the Villages from Livingstonia*
6 FC GA Proceedings 1897, FM Report, "The Livingstonia Institution"
7 UFC GA Proc. 1906, FM Report p.96ff.
8 UFC GA Proc. 1906, FM Report; 1908 FM Report,p.71; WPL *op.cit.* p.321
9 UFC Record, Sept.1906
10 *Ibid.* August and October 1907
11 *Ibid.* Oct.1907   12 *Ibid.* Nov.1907
13 *Ibid.* Jan.1905
14 *Ibid.* Feb 1905; UFC GA Proceedings 1905, FM Report p.86ff.
15 NLS 7883/ps.174-184; Copy of Mins. of Liv.Miss.Council, 2/11/1900, §25
16 UFC Record, Aug.1905, p.364
17 UFC GA Proc. 1904, FM Report
18 MNA LI 1/3/21, Mins.of N.Liv. Presbytery of CCA, 2/11/1900
19 *Ibid.*
20 *Ibid.* Mins.of 13/5/1903, and UFC Record Sept.1903
21 MNA LI 1/3/21, Mins.of N.Liv.Pres.of CCA 13/5/1903; 11/5/1906; 19/9/06
22 *Ibid.* Mins. of 21/8/1913; 18/5/1914; 8/10/1911; for ordinations see chap.19

Chapter 18
1 FMC Report to GA 1906, p.60, Livingstonia Mission
2 MNA LI 1/8/13, School Log Book, 1894-1942
3 FMC Report to GA, 1906 p.60. Liv.Mission

4 NLS Acc. 7548, D 71, p.42
5 MNA LI 1/3/31. Mins.of Senatus of Liv.Miss.Institut. 19/9/1901; UFC Record Sept.1903, p.411
6 NLS Dep.298/142, Mins.of Liv.Miss. Com.19/12/1907 §85
7 MNA LI 1/3/21, Mins.of N.Liv.Pres.of CCA 29/1/1908
8 MNA *The Livingstonia News*, Vol.1 No.1 Feb.1908, "Moderator of UFC GA"
9 UFC Record April 1908, p.152
10 WPL *op.cit.* p.333
11 NLS 7866, J.F.Daly to R.Laws 12/3/1908
12 Scotsman Newspaper,20/5/1908,p.13
13 Scotsman Newspaper,20/5/1908,p.13; Proceedings of UFC GA 1908, p.3
14 Scotsman Newspaper, 20/5/1908, pp.13,14
15 *Ibid.*
16 Proceedings of UFC G.A.1908, FM Report p.97ff.
17 UFC Record, July 1908, p.300
18 *Ibid.* May 1908 p.207; NLS 7866, J.F.Daly to R.Laws, 26/3/1908
19 WPL *op.cit.* p.335
20 UFC Record, July 1908, p.313
21 NLS Dep.298/127 and 128, Liv.Miss. Reports 1904-1909, "Churches Visited"
22 UFC Record Dec.1908, p.555
23 MNA *The Livingstonia News* Vol.1 No.5, Oct.1908
24 MNA LI 1/4/2, Valedictory Address at New College, 24/3/1909
25 NBSS Anniversary Meeting, April 1909, as reported in The Quarterly Record
26 The Scotsman Newspaper,20/5/1908, Report on Opening of UFC GA, 19/5/1908
27 Laws, *Sermon as Moderator*, in Livingstonia Museum; Scotsman Newspaper, 19/5/1909
28 Scotsman Newspaper 19/5/1909, UFC GA, *Retiring Moderator's Sermon*
29 UFC Record July, 1909 p.311
30 *Ibid.* p.321
31 WPL *op.cit.* p.337. The words "The Regions Beyond - I'll try" may be seen on Laws' seal ring at the Langstane Kirk, Aberdeen

32 NLS 7866 J.F.Daly to R.Laws, 9/9/ 1909; EUL Laws Coll.Gen.561/16; WPL *op.cit.* pp.338,339
33 WPL *op.cit.* pp.340
34 MNA LI 1/3/17, Mins. of Liv.Miss Council, 9/5/1910

Chapter 19

1 NLS Dep.298/142, Mins.of Liv.Miss. Com.18/6/08 §60 and App.1; and FMC Report to FC GA 1909
2 *Ibid.* 17/12/1908, containing Miss. Council Mins.of Sept.1908 §119
3 *Ibid.* 17/9/1908 §83 & §88 (Business Sub-Com.)
4 Aurora 1/10/1901
5 NLS Dep.298/142, Mins.of L.M.Com. 17/9/1908, §84
6 *Ibid.* 17/9/1908, §88
7 *Ibid.* 15/2/1909, §4; 17/6/1909, §33
8 *Ibid.* 16/12/1909, §70 (Mins.of Miss. Council, Sept.1909); and App.1 §15
9 NLS Dep.298/143 Mins.of L.M.Com. 20/6/1911, §49; 19/9/1911, §58; NLS Acc.7548/D72, Staff Record Book, p.99
10 NLS 7548/D72 Staff Record Book p.103
11 NLS Dep.298/142 Mins.of L.M.Com. 16/12/1909, App.1 (Mins.of Liv.Miss. Council, 9/9/1909, §38,39,40)
12 *Ibid.* 4/5/1910 §43 and App.; Mins.of 9/6/1910, §51
13 MNA LI 1/3/21, Mins.of N.Liv.Pres.of CCA, 24/9/1910
14 *Ibid.* 17/10/12   15 *Ibid.* 27/9/11
16 *Ibid.* 17/10/12
17 *Ibid.* 20/8/1913; NLS Dep.298/143, Mins.of Liv.Miss.Com.11/11/13, App.
18 MNA LI 1/3/21, Mins.of N.Liv.Pres. 21/8/1913
19 *Ibid.* 18/5/1914
20 NLS Dep.298/141, Mins.of Liv.Miss. Com. 8/10/1902, §56
21 WPL *op.cit.* p.310
22 NLS Dep.298/142, Mins.of Liv.Miss. Com. 1906, §44,§95,§125
23 *Ibid.* Mins.of Liv.Miss.Com. 1907 §45,§69,§101; FMC Report to UFC GA 1908, pp.71ff.
24 *Ibid.* Mins.of Liv.Miss.Com.1907, §101; 1908, §25,§55,§58,§68
25 Glasgow Herald, 23/10/1911, p.13

26 WPL *op.cit.* p.341
27 NLS Acc.9269 R.Laws to Miss Gordon, 24/3/1914
28 WPL *op.cit.* pp.341,342
29 FMC Report to FC GA 1915, p.81ff. "Liv.Mission" - Dr Innes on work at D.G.Memorial Hospital
30 NLS 7548 D 72 Staff Record Book p.150
31 MNA LI 1/8/8 Education Reports, 1895-1915, Report on 28/12/1897
32 FC G.A.1909, FM Report pp.57ff.
33 NLS Dep.298/142, Mins.of Liv.Miss. Com. 15/3/1910, §13
34 *Ibid.* R.Laws from Rome, 12/2/1910
35 *Ibid.* Mins.of Liv.Miss.Com. 20/9/10, §86,App.III
36 NLS Dep.298/143, Mins.of Liv.Miss. Com. 19/9/1911, §65; 17/10/1911,§77
37 *Ibid.* 17/9/1912, §80, and App.II
38 *Ibid.* 14/10/1913, §87
39 NLS Dep.298/142, Mins.of Liv.Miss. Com. 23/9/1909, §47; 15/3/1910, §27
40 *Ibid.* 16/12/1909, enclosing Min.of Miss.Council of Sept.1909, §80
41 *Ibid.* 13/12/1910, §98
42 NLS Dep.298/143, Mins.of Liv.Miss. Com. 20/2/1912, enclosing Min.of Miss.Council of Oct.1911, §37,§35
43 *Ibid.* 18/6/1912, §64
44 NLS Dep.298/142, Mins.of Liv.Miss. Com. 21/3/1907 §19; Dep.298/143, Min.of 14/6/1913, §84 [14/10/1913
45 NLS Acc.7548 D.71, §49-56, Mins.of Miss.Council, April 1905
46 WPL *op.cit.* pp.318,319, quoting Laws writing in "Aurora"
47 UFC GA, 1905, FMC Report p.86
48 *Ibid.* 1908, Proceedings, p.71; FMC Report, p.106
49 *Ibid.* 1914, FMC Report, p.82ff.
50 *Ibid.* 1915, FMC Report, p.81ff.
51 *Ibid.* 1911, FMC Report, p.104
52 *Ibid.* 1913, FMC Report, p.103; NLS 7867, J.F.Daly to R.Laws, 4/9/1912; 17/9/1912

Chapter 20

1 NLS Acc.7548, D 72 Staff Record Book, pp.106 and 104
2 MNA LI 1/3/32 Mins.of Senatus, Liv.Inst. 8/9/1914

3 *Ibid.* 20/6/1911; see also Ch.13 Ref.57

4 NLS Acc.7548 D 72 Staff Record Book

5 J.A.Lamb, *Fasti of U.F.Church, 1900-29*

6 MNA LI 1/3/32, Mins. of Senatus, Liv.Inst., 4/3/1916

7 Donald Fraser, *Livingstonia*, p.86 (FMC 1915) & NLS 7548 D 72, Staff Record Book, p.94ff.

8 UFC Record Oct.1914

9 FMC Report to UFC GA, 1917

10 *Ibid.* 1916; UFC Record Jan.1915, p.9

11 UFC Record Jan.1915, Letter from Miss C.M.Irvine; and Record Feb.1915, "Livingstonia War Zone"

12 NLS Acc.7548 D 72, Staff Record Book, p.107 and Diary of Margaret Stuart (28 Nov.1915 - 12 Oct.1916), in private possession of Dr W.O. Petrie, Edinburgh

13 NLS Acc.7548 D 72, Staff Record Book, pp.119 and 144

14 *Ibid.* p.102

15 Fergus Macpherson, *Kenneth Kaunda of Zambia - the Times and the Man* (OUP 1974) pp.32-37; FMC Report to FC GA 1905, p.86ff. "Livingstonia (Overtoun Institution)"; NLS 7548 D 72, Staff Record Book, p.112

16 FMC Report to UFC GA 1916

17 *Ibid.*

18 NLS Acc.7548 D 72, Staff Record Book, p.145

19 FMC Report to UFC GA 1916

20 FM Sederunt of UFC GA, 25/5/1916

21 NLS Acc.7548 D 72, Staff Record Book, pp.120,140,131

22 FMC Reports to UFC GA, 1916, 1917

23 *Ibid.*

24 Melvin E.Page, *Malawian in the Great War and After, 1914-1925* pp.37,38, referring to letters, Laws to Stuart 23/9/1914; and Laws to McMinn 19/10/1914, in MNA Liv.Mission Papers, Letter Book No.24

25 *Ibid.* pp.38,39,41   26 *Ibid.* p.49

27 *Ibid.* 28 *Ibid.* p.65 29 *Ibid.* p.71

30 John McCracken, *Politics and Christianity in Malawi* (CUP 1977) p.225

31 Melvin E.Page, *op.cit.* p.74

32 *Ibid.* referring to MNA Liv. Miss. Papers, Letter Book No.26, Turner to Laws, 14/3/1917

33 *Ibid.* p.52, Table 1; p.82, Table 2

34 *Ibid.* p.60, Laws to Fraser 27/10/1915, from MNA Liv.Miss.Papers Letter Book No.24; and *Donald Fraser* by Agnes Fraser (London 1934) p.228

35 Diary of Margaret Stuart, *op.cit.* Entries for 15,16,17 April 1916

36 MNA LI 1/3/32, Mins.of Senatus of Liv.Institution 4/3/1916; 9/5/1916

37 *Ibid.* 9/5/1916; 12/5/1916

38 Melvin E.Page, *op.cit.* p.226ff.

39 Dr Wm.O.Petrie, Edinburgh, in conversation with the author, 11/6/1988

40 Geo.Shepperson and Tom Price, *Independent African - John Chilembwe and the Nyasaland Rising of 1915* (Edinburgh 1958, paperback ed.1989) pp.143ff.

41 *Ibid.* pp.178-187

42 *Ibid.* pp.116,127ff.

43 *Ibid.* p.234   44 *Ibid.* p.239

45 *Ibid.* pp.270,285

46 *Ibid.* pp.262,273,285,296

47 *Ibid.* pp.279-281   48 *Ibid.* p.316

49 *Ibid.* p.363

50 *Ibid.* pp.364,366

51 WPL *op.cit.* p.354; Shepperson and Price, *op.cit.* p.369

52 Shepperson and Price, *op.cit.* pp.371,372

53 *Ibid.* p.369   54 *Ibid.* p.370

55 *Ibid.* p.374

56 *Ibid.* p.380; New Statesman, 8/7/1916

57 Shepperson and Price, *op.cit.* pp.395,396

58 John McCracken, *op.cit.* p.245, quoting R.Laws to R.W.Lyell Grant, 2/7/1915, from Hetherwick Papers

59 The figures for each calendar year are taken from UFC GA Reports of the following year

60 *Ibid.*

61 UFC GA Reports, 1915 p.86, FMC Report; 1921, p.108, FMC Report

62 FMC Report to UFC GA 1917, p.42ff.

63 *Ibid.*

64 FMC Report to UFC GA 1918, p.10

65 NLS Acc.7548 D 72, Staff Record Book, pp.131,150,158

66 FMC Report to UFC GA 1920, p.53, Roll of Missionaries

67 FMC Report to UFC GA 1919, p.17

68 Melvin E.Page, *op.cit.* p.203

69 *Ibid.* p.224; FMC Report to UFC GA 1919, p.17ff.

70 FMC Report to UFC GA 1919, p.17ff.
71 *Ibid.* 1921, p.19
72 MNA LI 1/3/21, Mins.of N.Liv.Pres.of CCA 12/2/1915; 13/2/1915; 29/8/1915
73 *Ibid.* 29/8/1915
74 *Ibid.* 29/8/1915; 4/11/1917; 21/7/18
75 *Ibid.* 20/10/1916; 21/10/1916
76 *Ibid.* 21/10/1916
77 *Ibid.* 5/11/1917   78 *Ibid.*
79 *Ibid.* 21/10/1916; 4/11/1917
80 *Ibid.* 16/7/1918; 21/7/1918
81 *Ibid.* 22/7/1919
82 *Ibid.* 21/2/1920; and LI 1/3/24, Mins.of N.Liv.Pres.of CCA 1/8/1921
83 *Ibid.* LI 1/3/21, 20/7/1920
84 *Ibid.* LI 1/3/24, 1/8/1921   85 *Ibid.*
86 FMC Report to UFC GA 1920, p.53, Roll of Missionaries, Table 14
87 NLS Acc.7548 D 72, Staff Record Book
88 NLS 7885, Laws to Ashcroft, 7/4/21
89 *Ibid.* 21/5/1921
90 UFC Record, Nov.1921, p.347, Margaret Fairley Daly, *The Late Mrs Laws*   91 *Ibid.*
92 MNA LI 1/3/17, Liv.Mission Council Mins. July 1921   93 *Ibid.*
94 Revd Neil Bernard, conversation with the author, 31/10/1990

Chapter 21
1 UFC Record, November 1921 p.347ff.
2 *Ibid.*
3 Violet G.Bonga, *Dr Laws, Another Look at His Religious and Educational Leadership*, Journal of Social Science, Univ. of Malawi, Vol.10 1983 p.4
4 UFC Record, Nov.1921 p.347ff., Margaret F. Daly, *The Late Mrs Laws*
5 UFC Record, Dec.1921 p.377ff., Review of *Laws of Livingstonia* by Prof. D.S.Cairns
6 MNA LI 1/3/32, Mins.of Senatus of Liv.Institution 26/9/1921
7 MNA LI 1/3/17, Mins.of Liv.Mission Council, 20/5/1922
8 Proceedings of UFC GA 1922, p.150
9 *Ibid.* p.116
10 *Ibid.* p.124; and Proceedings of FC GA 1925, p.148
11 Revd Alex Caseby, conversation with the author, December 1983
12 AUL Special Collection, MS 3289, Caseby Papers No.2
13 Proceedings of UFC GA 1918, FM Report p.10; 1919, FM Report p.108; 1920, p.30ff., Report from Tanganyika, and p.53 Table 14, Missionaries at Livingstonia and New Langenburg
14 Proceedings of FC GA 1922, p.150, R.Laws' Address on 25/5/1922
15 e.g. Riddell-Henderson, Tamanda, went on furlough in 1916; Geo.Prentice, Kasungu, went on war service in 1917, and then on furlough; D.R.Mackenzie, Karonga, resigned in 1916; R.D.McMinn, Chinsali, went on furlough in 1916. NLS Acc.7548 D 72, Liv.Miss.Staff Record Book pp.114,109,130,112
16 Proceedings of UFC GA 1923, FM Report p.101
17 *Ibid.* Women's Work at Livingstonia
18 AUL Spec.Coll. MS 3289 Caseby papers, No.3
19 *Ibid.*   20 *Ibid.*   21 *Ibid.*
22 Proceedings of UFC GA 1925, p.170
23 See Ch.20
24 Proceedings of UFC GA 1920, FM Report on *Tanganyika Territory*, ibid. 1922, p.40
25 *Ibid.* 1923, Report on Women's Work at Liv. - Tanganyika Report
26 Proceedings of UFC GA 1925, p.170
27 NLS Acc.9269, Typed Memo by Geo.Prentice, *German East Africa* p.8 29/3/1919
28 MNA LI 1/3/21 Mins. of Pres.of Liv. 5/11/17; and LI 1/3/24 *Ibid.* 13/12/24
29 NLS Acc.7548 D 72 p.114
30 Proceedings of UFC GA 1923, FM Report p.102ff., Kasungu
31 *Ibid.* Women's Work at Liv., Kasungu
32 *Ibid.* FM Report p.102ff., Tamanda
33 NLS Acc.9269, F.Ashcroft, *Report on our C.A. Fields*, iii Kasungu and Tamanda; and MNA LI 1/3/24, Mins. of Liv.Pres. 16/9/1924
34 Proceedings of UFC GA 1924, p.104
35 NLS Acc.7548 D 72, p.102
36 *Ibid.* p.155,153
37 Proceedings of UFC GA 1922, FM Report p.38-40, Chitambo

38 *Ibid.* 1923, FM Report p.102ff., Chitambo

39 *Ibid.* 1923, FM Report p.102ff., Lubwa

40 *Ibid.* 1923, FM Report p.102ff., Women's Work at Liv., Mwenzo

41 *Ibid.* 1923, FM Report p.102ff.

42 Proceedings of UFC GA 1922, FM Report, pp.38-40, Karonga

43 *Ibid.* 1923, FM Report p.102ff., Bandawe

44 *Ibid.* 1926, FM Report p.148; *Ibid.* 1927, FM Report pp.15ff.

45 *Ibid.* 1927, FM Report p.15ff.

46 *Ibid.* 1922, FM Report p.38ff., Bandawe

47 NLS Acc.7548 D 72 pp.104,106

48 Proceedings of UFC GA 1922, FM Report p.38ff., Loudon

49 *Ibid.* 1923, FM Report pp.101ff., Women's Work at Liv., Ekwendeni

50 MNA LI 1/3/21, Mins. of Liv.Pres.of CCA 4/11/1917

51 Proceedings of UFC GA 1923, FM Report p.102

52 UFC Record, Feb.1924, p.75; MNA LI 1/3/24, Mins.of Liv.Pres.of CCA 16/4/1923; 24/10/1923

53 *Ibid.* and MNA LI 1/3/21, Mins.of Liv Pres.of CCA 13/5/1903; 19/9/1906; 24/9/1910

54 MNA LI 1/3/21, Mins.of Liv.Pres.of CCA 18/5/14; 5/11/17; 22/7/19

55 UFC Record Feb.1924 p.75

56 MNA LI 1/3/21, Mins.of Liv.Pres.of CCA 4/11/1917; 21/7/1918

57 *Ibid.* LI 1/3/24, Mins.of Liv.Pres.of CCA 1/8/1921

58 UFC Record July 1923, p.267

59 MNA LI 1/3/17, Mins.of Liv.Mission Council August 1923

60 EUL Laws' Coll.Gen.562/3, Rankine to Laws, 9/10/1923; 6/11/1923

61 UFC Record, Mar. 1924, p.103, *Acting Governor of Nyasaland's Despatch*

62 EUL Laws' Coll.Gen 562/7; and NLS 7886, T.Gordon to Ashcroft, 28/12/23

63 UFC Record, March 1924, *Acting Governor's Despatch*

64 NLS Acc.7548 D 71 Printed Reports, Missionary Conference at Mvera 1910, p69; and MNA LI 1/3/21 Mins.of Liv.Pres.of CCA 24/9/1910

65 MNA LI 1/3/17 Mins.of Miss.Council, August 1910

66 NLS 7887/113, Mins.of 1st Meeting of Synod of CCAP 17-22 Sept. 1924, with full Roll, and extract Mins. of GA of UF C.of S. 21/5/1914, and of Est.C.of S. 21/5/1914

67 NLS 7887/113; and MNA LI 1/3/24, Mins.of Liv.Pres.of CCAP 16/9/1924; 17/9/1924

68 NLS 7887/113 #12, Roll of those attending First Synod of CCAP

69 NLS 7887/95 Telegram from Laws 20/9/1924

70 NLS 7887/113 Mins.of First Synod of CCAP

71 NLS 7889/84 Laws to Ashcroft 20/10/1926

72 Dr Fergus Macpherson in conversation with the author, June 1991

Chapter 22

1 NLS Acc.9269 UFC FMC, *Report on our Central African Fields* by F.Ashcroft p.1

2 *Ibid.* Ch.V1   3 *Ibid.* Ch.V11

4 NLS Acc.9269 Hubert Wilson to Ashcroft 13/5/1924

5 NLS 7886 D.Fraser to Ashcroft 26/12/1923

6 *Ibid.* W.Elmslie to Ashcroft 29/1/24

7 *Ibid.* C.Stuart to Ashcroft 5/1/1924

8 UFC Record July 1925 p.291, *The Report on East Africa*

9 NLS S.26a, *Education in East Africa* (Phelps Stokes Commission Report)

10 *Ibid.* Ch.V111 p.193   11 *Ibid.*

12 *Ibid.* Ch.V111 p.196

13 *Ibid.* Ch.V111 p.197; and *Education Policy in Africa, Memo on behalf of Education Com.of Conference of Miss.Socs.*, quoting answer in House of Commons 10/4/1923

14 NLS S26a, *Educ.in E.Africa* Ch.V111 p.200 & 199

15 UFC Record Oct.1925, pp.449,450; and Proceedings of UFC GA 25/5/1922 p.150

16 NLS S26a, *Educ.in E.Africa* p.205

17 *Ibid.*   18 *Ibid.* p.200

19 SOAS London, Box 233 File B, Dr Dougall's Journal 18/2/1924 - 20/6/24

20 *Ibid.* 22/4/1924

21 AUL Spec.Coll. MS 3289 Caseby Papers No.6

22 Dougall's Journal 26/4/1924

23 *Ibid.* 29/4/24

24 *Ibid.* 27/4/24

25 *Ibid.* pp.208-211   26 *Ibid.*

27 New Statesman 8/7/1916 p.321: H.H. Johnston, *The Bitter Cry of the Educated African* (See also Ch.20, Ref.56)

28 SOAS London, Box 1209/A Report of Educ.Confer., Zomba May 1927: R.Laws on *The Coordination of Technical and Literary Training in the Education of Africans* (See Ch.23)

29 Journal of the African Society No.28, 1929: R.Laws, *Native Education in Nyasaland*

30 NLS S26a, *Education in E.Africa* pp.208-211

31 MNA LI 1/8/13, School Log Book 1894-1942

32 *Ibid.*

33 Told to the author at Ekwendeni, May 1985

34 MNA LI 1/8/13, School Log Book 1894 -1942, Regulations for Apprentices, 1898 ; and NLS Dep.298/142 Mins.of Liv.Com. 16/12/1909

35 MNA L1 1/3/31, Mins.of Senatus, 2/5/1908

36 NLS Dep. 298/142, Mins.of Liv.Com. 18/3/1909; as in ref 35, §17 *Senatus Memo of 2nd May 1908*

37 MNA LI 1/8/13 Sch.Log Book 1894-1942

38 UFC Record Oct.1923 p.401, A.Caseby, *The Garden at Livingstonia*

39 Memo in Museum at Livingstonia among papers headded *Livingstonia 1922*

40 AUL Spec.Coll.3289 Caseby Papers No.8

41 MNA Livingstonia News Vol.XII Jan.to March 1925, Overtoun Institution, *Industrial Progress - Agriculture*

42 UFC Record Oct.1925 pp.433-453

43 *Ibid.* pp.449,450: and Donald Fraser, *Livingstonia* (Edinburgh 1915) p.86, List of Missionaries

44 UFC Record, Oct.1925, pp.433-453

45 AUL Spec.Coll. MS 3290/3, *Presentation to Rev.Robt.Laws* on occasion of his Jubilee; UFC Record Oct.1925, *Jubilee Meeting*; and NLS 7888/133 Laws to Ashcroft 9/12/1925

46 Inkosana Jere in conversation with the author, at Ekwendeni, May 1985

47 UFC Record May 1925, *Central African Pioneers - Dr Elmslie, Ngoniland* by The Editor

48 MNA LI 1/3/24, Mins.of Pres of N.Liv. 11/10/1925, 25/12/1926

49 MNA LI 1/3/17, Mins.of Miss.Council 12/10/1925   50 *Ibid.*

(For list of African ministers in the CCAP at the time of the Mission Jubilee see Appendix 1)

Chapter 23

1 MNA Soc.of Malawi Journal, Vol.27 No.2. July 1976, *The University of Livingstonia* by K.J.McCracken: NLS 7889 Læws to Ashcroft 21/4/1926; Laws to A.Balfour 17/4/1926

2 MNA LI 1/3/17 Liv.Miss.Council Mins.8/10/1925

3 W.P.Young to Ashcroft, 25/2/1928 quoted by J.McCracken in *Politics and Christianity in Malawi 1875-1940* (CUP 1977) p.236

4 NLS 7889 Laws to Ashcroft 23/12/1926, quoting Bowring's letter of 22/12/1925   5 *Ibid.*

6 NLS 7889/112; 7889/113

7 NLS 7888/107 Laws to Ashcroft 12/8/1925

8 NLS 7888/115, Laws to Ashcroft 3/10/1925, quoting Sir H.Stanley after visit to Livingstonia

9 UFC Record Jan.1926 p.31, and Aug.1926 p.338

10 MNA LI 1/4/2, Notes for Address at Second Synod of CCAP 1926

11 MNA LI 1/3/21, Mins.of N.Liv.Pres.of CCAP 22/7/1918; 22/7/1919; 20/7/1920 and LI 1/3/24, Mins.of 25/7/1921; 19/7/1922; 11/9/1924; 12/9/1924

12 MNA LI 1/3/24, Mins. of 18/7/1927

13 SOAS London, Box 1209 File A, Printed Report of Native Education Conference, convened by H.E.The Governor, Zomba 17-20 May 1927

14 *Ibid.* Paper on Education by Director

15 *Ibid.* Paper by Dr Laws   16 *Ibid.*
17 *Ibid.* Discussion - Major I.C. Sanderson
18 *Ibid.* Box 1209 File C, Fraser to Gaunt 25/5/1927
19 *Ibid.* Box 1209 File A, p.18
20 *Ibid.* Box 1209 File C, Fraser to Gaunt 25/5/1927
21 *Ibid.* Box 1209 File C, Memo by Laws 6/6/1927
22 *Ibid.* Box 1209 File C, Hetherwick - Interview with Director of Education, 27/6/27; Int. with Governor 28/6/27
23 *Ibid.* Box 1209 File C, Cablegram, Hetherwick to Church of Scotland 9/7/1927
24 *Ibid.* Box 1209 File C, Ashcroft to Miss Gibson, Edinburgh House, quoting telegram, Hetherwick to C.of S. 11/8/1927
25 *Ibid.* Box 1209 File C, Memo on Educ.Ordinance by Donald Fraser 13/12/1927, taken to Africa by J.H.Oldham

Chapter 24
1 MNA Ll 1/3/32, Senatus of Liv.Miss.Inst.Mins. 9/12/1924; 22/12/24; 24/12/28   2 *Ibid.* 4/10/1927
3 *Ibid.* Ll 1/3/18, Liv. Miss.Council Mins. 10/7/1927, Min. 18; UFC Record Nov. 1927 p.467
4 *Ibid.* Ll 1/3/24, Mins.of Pres.of N.Liv. 14/7/1927
5 *Ibid.* 19/7/1927   6 *Ibid.*
7 UFC Record 1927, October p.416; November, p.464   8 *Ibid.* Oct. p.416
9 AUL Spec.Coll. MS 3289, Caseby Papers No.20
10 UFC Record Nov. 1927, p.467 W.P.Young, *Farewell to Africa*
11 Jack Martin to his mother, 22/8/1927, in private coll. of Mrs M.E. Sinclair (née Martin)
12 UFC Record, Nov. 1927, as above
13 *Ibid.* and MNA Ll 1/3/18, Liv.Miss.Council Mins. 8/8/1928
14 Private Coll. of Mrs M.E.Sinclair
15 UFC Record Nov. 1927
16 MNA Ll 1/3/18, Miss.Council Mins. 10/7/1927, Min. 18; and extracts in Record, Nov. 1927 p.467
17 MNA Livingstonia News Vol.xiv, Aug.-Oct.1927
18 NLS Dep.298/135 UFC FMC Min 1514, 15/11/1927; Edinburgh & Leith P.O. Directories 1922-1934
19 UFC Record Dec. 1927 p.533, and AUL Spec. Coll. MS 3290/2 Laws to Hardie, 14/3/1928
20 EUL Laws' Coll.Gen.562/6 (ii), Revd J.K.Thomson to Laws 14/9/1928; Revd S.Band to Laws 17/9/1928
21 AUL Spec.Coll. MS 3290/1 cutting from the Evening Express 26/9/1928 front page, and p.1
22 AUL Spec.Coll. 3290/2
23 AUL Spec.Coll. MS 3290/2, Laws to Tilsley 25/10/1929
24 AUL Spec.Coll. MS 3290/3, Laws to Charles Stuart, n.d.
25 MNA Ll 1/1/10/2 Correspondence 1893-1956, Laws to W.P.Young 5/2/1931; MNA Ll 1/3/32 Mins.of Senatus of Liv.Miss.Inst. 13/4/1931
26 Journal of the African Society, No.28 1929, R.Laws, *A Native Education in Nyasaland*
27 MNA Ll 1/4/2, Address by Dr Laws to 13th Gen. Council of Alliance of Reformed Churches, Boston, Mass. 1929. (This heading is on a sheet of Merchiston Cres. notepaper in the same folder as notes for three Addresses; one, headed *Mission in Africa* seems the likeliest to have been given at Boston, and is the address quoted)
28 AUL Spec.Coll. 3920/1, cutting from the Evening Express 11/12/1931
29 EUL Laws' Coll.Gen. 562/2, Passports
30 MNA Ll 1/1/10/1, Correspondence 1893-1936, J.Moir to Presbytery of N.Liv. 26/1/1936
31 Conversation with the late Miss Seonaid Mackenzie, Edinburgh, in 1984
32 R.Laws, *Reminiscences* (Oliver & Boyd, Edinburgh 1934) Intro.p.xiv
33 M. & E.King, *The Story of Medicine and Disease in Malawi* (Blantyre, Malawi, 1992) pp.146ff.   34 *Ibid.*
35 Chas.& Mgt.Stuart, *Copies of Old Letters from Nyasaland*; 1889, Rev.C Stuart; 1915 Mrs Stuart (in possession of Dr and Mrs W.Petrie of Edinburgh)

36 SOAS Box 1209 File C, W.P.Young from Mortlach 18/7/1927

37 R.Laws, *op.cit.*, Intro.p.xvi

38 AUL Spec.Coll. MS 3290/2, Oliver & Boyd to Dr A.Laws, 12/8/1937

39 EUL Laws' Coll.Gen. 562/6 (i) cutting from Glasgow Evening Citizen 11/8/1934, column by Churchman; Life and Work, Sept. 1934, p.351

40 *Ibid.* The Times Newspaper 8/8/1934; Gen. 562/6 (ii) St Columba's Pont St., Magazine, Sept. 1934, p.154

41 *Ibid.* Gen. 562/6 (1) Times Newspaper, 8/8/34; Manchester Guardian, 8/8/34

42 *Ibid.* The Bulletin, (of Glasgow) 7/8/1934; The Scotsman, 7/8/1934

43 EUL Laws' Coll. Gen. 562/6(i), *Dr Laws Goes to his Rest* - Funeral Oration of Alexander Hetherwick

44 *Ibid.* Press & Journal 10/8/34; & *supra*

45 *Ibid.* The Scotsman 13/8/1934, *Memorial Service in Bristo*

46 *Ibid.* Scotsman, 13/8/1934

47 *Ibid.* Glasgow Evening Citizen, 11/8/1934, column by Churchman

48 *Ibid.* The Life of Faith, 15/8/1934; BMJ 18/8/1934

49 EUL Laws' Coll.Gen. 562/6 (ii) CA - UMCA Sept.1934, p.202

50 Life and Work, Sept 1934, p.351ff.

Chapter 25

1 AUL Spec.Coll. 3290/2 Laws to Tilsley, 25/10/1929

2 Interview with Revd Alex Caseby, December 1983

3 NLS 7912 Mins.of Liv.Sub-Com. 17/3/1879

4 Soc.of Malawi Journal, Vol.38, No.I, 1985, D.Brian Roy, *Historic Buildings in Malawi - the Stone House, Livingstonia.* The house is now divided into a Museum, and a Guest House available for the use of visitors

5 NLS 7865/113, and /140, J.F.Daly to R.Laws, 2/12/1904; and 19/12/1904

6 Conversation with Dr Fergus Macpherson (who himself resided in the Stone House, while Principal of The Institution) 11/6/1991

7 Conversation with Miss Helen Taylor MBE, 30/10/1990

8 Life and Work, October 1934, p.391

9 EUL Laws' Coll.Gen. 561/17; /18; /19 - Heriot Watt Notebooks, 1899-1900; and Gen. 561/16, Notes on Infant Feeding, 1909

10 WPL *op.cit.* p.18

11 Personal notes by G.M.Kerr of Nizamabad, Centre for Study of Christianity in Non-Western World, New College, Edinburgh

12 AUL Spec.Coll. 3290/3, Text of Tape Recording by Miss A.N.Laws, on occasion of Centenary of Liv.Mission

13 Author's conversation with Revd Neil Bernard 25/10/1990

14 Life and Work, Oct.1934, *Dr Laws as I knew him - a Woman's Impression* by Mrs A.E.MacKenzie, late of Livingstonia

15 Conv'n with Mrs Neil, August 1991

16 Nyasaland Times, 4/12/52, p.5, *Memories of Nyasaland* by Mrs E.B.Chalmers

17 *Ibid.* 18/12/1952, p.14

18 Life and Work, April 1951, *Laws the Indomitable*

19 Peter G.Forster, *T.Cullen Young, Missionary and Anthropologist* (Hull University Press 1989) p.150

20 Conversation with Dr Kings Phiri, Chancellor College, Zomba, May 1985

21 For T.C.Young's publications, see P.G.Forster *op.cit.* pp.204-217

22 Author's conversation with Dr Macpherson, June 1991

23 MNA LI 1/4/19, Liv.Instit.Exam Papers 1903, Stand.V Geog & Hist. papers

24 SOAS London, Box 1209 A, *Report on Education Conference, Zomba 1927* - Laws on "Co-ordination of Technical and Literary Training"

25 NLS 7889/103, Laws to Ashcroft, 23/12/1926

26 Conversation with Revd Neil Bernard, 25/10/1990

27 Journal of Friends of Dunblane Cathedral, 1979; and author's conversation with Dr McDonald, June 1990

Index

"The Regions Beyond - I'll try."

(p.162)